言語復興の未来と価値
理論的考察と事例研究

Minority Language Revitalization
Contemporary Approaches

桂木隆夫　ジョン・C・マーハ =編
Edited by Takao Katsuragi and John C. Maher

三元社

言語復興の未来と価値

Minority Language Revitalization - Contemporary Approaches

目次
Contents

はじめに ──────────────────── Preface: the Aesthetic of Networks
桂木 隆夫　*x* ────────────────────── John C. Maher　*xv*

第1部　理論的考察 ────────── Part 1　Theoretical Approaches

◉ ─── 第1章
多文化共生（グローカリゼーション）とマイノリティ（危機）言語復興
桂木 隆夫 (学習院大学)　*002*

- 第1節　はじめに　*002*
- 第2節　ナショナリズム、グローバリゼーション、グローカリゼーション　*007*
  - 第1項　ナショナリズム　*007*／第2項　グローバリゼーション　*008*／第3項　グローカリゼーション　*009*
- 第3節　グローカリゼーションと多文化共生の言語政策枠組み　*012*
- 第4節　おわりに　*014*

Abstract, Chap.1
Glocalization and Minority Language Revitalization
Takao Katsuragi (Gakushuin University)　*017*

◉ ─── 第2章
多様性の承認と高等教育──多言語教育のもう一つの社会的役割
数土 直紀 (学習院大学)　*021*

- 第1節　問題の所在　*021*
- 第2節　データと変数　*024*
  - 第1項　データ　*024*／第2項　分析戦略　*025*／第3項　変数　*026*／第4項　変数の特徴　*027*
- 第3節　分析結果　*029*
- 第4節　考察　*035*

Abstract, Chap.2
Higher Education and Tolerance of Social Diversity:
The Social Role of Multicultural and Multilingual Education
Naoki Sudo (Gakushuin University) *042*

●──第3章
消滅危機言語コミュニティから日本の言語教育政策を観る
──宮古島の経験から
藤田 ラウンド 幸世 (立教大学) *047*

第1節　はじめに　*047*

第2節　ミクロの視点から読み解く　*048*

第1項　宮古島の中学生から投げかけられた問い　*048*／第2項　国の歴史、地域の歴史　*048*／第3項　祖父母世代のことば、「みゃーくふつ（宮古語）」　*049*

第3節　マクロの視点から捉える言語の多様性　*050*

第1項　世界の現用語　*050*／第2項　話しことばとしての言語　*050*／第3項　言語と生物の多様性　*052*／第4項　消滅危機言語とは　*052*

第4節　近代化された「日本語」　*054*

第1項　日本の「標準語」とは　*054*／第2項　「標準語」での教育：アイヌと琉球　*055*／第3項　20世紀の近代化の問い直し　*056*

第5節　言語の多様性に関わる21世紀への課題　*057*

Abstract, Chap.3
Japanese Language Education Policy from the point of view of
an Endangered Language Community: the Miyako Island experience
Sachiyo Fujita-Round (Rikkyo University) *064*

●──第4章
欧州少数言語における文字の重要性、ケルト諸語の事例から
原 聖 (女子美術大学) *069*

第1節　欧州における文字化と文字伝統　*069*

第2節　古代ケルト諸語　*070*

第1項　ケルト諸語と周辺の諸言語　*072*／第2項　ブリテン島とガリア　*072*

第3節　オガム文字　*073*

第1項　オガム文字とルーン文字　*075*

第4節　ブリタニア島からアルモリカ（ブレイス／ブルターニュ）へ　*076*

第5節　書記文化とブレイス語　*077*

第6節　他のケルト諸語の書きことば　*079*

第7節　欧州での「俗語」の書きことばの成立　*080*

第8節　ケルト諸語の少数言語化　*081*

第9節　ケルト諸語の復興　*084*

　　第1項　復興運動の前提としての標準的書きことば　*085*

結びにかえて　*087*

Abstract, Chap.4
The Importance of Written Languages in European Minority Languages :
examples from Celtic Languages
HARA Kiyoshi (Joshibi University of Art and Design)　*089*

⊙──── Chapter 5

Liberating Babel, Notes on Imperialism, Language and Dystopia

John C. Maher (International Christian University)　*093*

1. Introduction　*093*

2. Build Higher　*096*

　　2.1. A Purer Air　*096* / 2.2. Nimrod. Ruler of the High Air　*097*

3. Living Speech, Dead Words　*098*

　　3.1. The Social Soul　*098* / 3.2. A Place of Dead Words　*099* / 3.3. Handing Back the Living Tongues　*100*

4. Emptiness: a Tale of Two Babels　*100*

　　4.1. Kafka and Babel　*101* / 4.2. 'Metropolis' (1927)　*101* / 4.3. 'Blade Runner' (1982)　*102*

5. The Story of Babel　*103*

6. Interpretations　*107*

　　6.1. Storming Heaven　*107* / 6.2. Pentecost: Reversing Babel　*108*

7. Reinterpreting Babel　*110*

　　7.1. The Tragedy of Babel　*110* / 7.2. Reinterpreting Babel: Cultivating Heteregeneity　*110*

第5章　要約
バベルの解放——帝国主義、言語、ディストピアについての覚書
ジョン・C・マーハ (国際基督教大学)（崎山拓郎訳）　*116*

◉────── Chapter 6

Cam's Linguapax Adventure — Helping children learn about languages of the world through an online audio and graphic novel

Dr. Olenka Bilash, Ms. Alanna Wasylkiw (University of Alberta, Canada)　*121*

1. Introduction　*121*
2. The website　*121*

   Site design　*123* / EF　*123* / Literacy　*125* / Motivating and interactive tasks　*126* / Balancing new information with presumed prior knowledge　*126*

3. Website Development　*128*
4. Using the site　*130*
5. Student feedback　*131*
6. Closing comments　*135*
7. Future endeavours　*136*
8. Limitations　*137*

   Appendix A: General feedback　*139* / Appendix B: Revisions　*141*

第6章　要約
Cam's Linguapax Quest を通じたグローバル・ハビトゥスの学習
オレンカ・ビラッシュ＆アランナ・ワシルク (アルバータ大学)（崎山拓郎訳）　*143*

◉────── Chapter 7

Language for Peace: Linguapax in Asia

Jelisava Sethna (Director, Linguapax Asia)　*148*

1. Introduction　*148*
2. The Evolving Philosophy of Linguapax　*150*
3. Linguapax Comes to Asia　*152*

   3.1. Linguapax Asia Symposia　*154* / 3.2. Linguapax Asia Screenings of Documentaries on

Minority and Endangered Languages　*160*

4. Conclusion　*163*

第7章　要約
言語と平和——リンガパックス・アジア
イェリサバ・セスナ（リンガパックス・アジア　ディレクター）（崎山拓郎訳）　*167*

第2部　事例研究 ───────────────── Part 2　Case Studies

◉────第8章
うちなーぐち（おきなわ語）を歴史認識で復興させる試み
──カムリー（ウェールズ）語、カタルーニャ語、ハワイ語復興の源、宗教力に代わる力
比嘉 光龍（ふぃじゃ　ばいろん、歌三線者、うちなーぐち〔おきなわ語〕講師）　*174*

第1節　はじめに　*174*

第1項　うちなーぐち（おきなわ語）復興　*174*／第2項　ハワイ語復興運動からの影響　*175*

第2節　日本の少数言語復興を妨げる「国語」と「方言」という語の弊害　*175*

第1項　「国語」という語の弊害　*175*／第2項　アイヌ人の国語は「アイヌ語」、おきなわ人の国語は「おきなわ語」　*176*／第3項　「方言」という語の弊害　*176*／第4項　日本政府に国連：自由権規約委員会より勧告　*177*

第3節　日本の少数言語　*178*

第1項　日琉語族　*178*／第2項　日琉語族以外の日本の少数言語　*178*

第4節　カムリー（ウェールズ）語、カタルーニャ語、ハワイ語への聖書翻訳　*179*

第1項　カムリー語復興の源流は聖書　*179*／第2項　カタルーニャ語、ハワイ語復興を担う聖書の役割　*179*／第3項　琉球諸語復興には特に関わりのないキリスト教信者　*181*

第5節　琉球諸語を宗教力ではなく歴史認識で復興させる　*182*

第1項　うちなーぐち復興はうちなー地域全体の課題　*182*／第2項　琉球処分では

なく琉球侵略　*182*／第3項　新しい琉球・うちなーの歴史観提唱　*183*／第4項　琉球国の歴史は692年　*184*／第5項　19世紀に欧米と結んだ条約が歴史を覆す　*185*　琉球諸語言語地図（琉球諸語の区分と、区分論）　*187*／琉球・うちなーの歴史簡略表　*194*

Abstract, Chap.8
Attempt to revitalize the Ryukyuan languages by historical awareness,
not by religious awareness
Byron Fija (Okinawan folk musician, Okinawan Lecturer at Okinawa Christian University)　*197*

◉──── 第9章
ネット上のアイヌ・コミュニティにおけるアイヌ語学習

片山 和美 (アイヌ語学習者)　*200*

第1節　アイヌの歴史と現在　*200*

第2節　私の取り組み　*203*

第3節　WiPCE2014　*204*

第4節　最後に　*206*

Abstract, Chap.9
Ainu on the Internet : Learning the Ainu Language in Community
Kazumi Katayama (Ainu Language Learner)　*207*

◉──── Chapter 10
Modernist and ecologist approaches to language and identity — the case of the Ryukyu Islands

Patrick Heinrich (Ca' Foscari University, Venice)　*211*

1. Introduction　*211*

2. Language and Identity in Modernity　*213*

3. Language and identity in the Ryukyus: The modernist position　*217*
   Language and identity before 1945　*217* / Language and identity after 1945　*219*

4. Language and identity in the Ryukyus: The ecological position　*222*

5. Outlook　*227*

第10章　要約
モダニストとエコロジストの言語とアイデンティティへのアプローチ——琉球諸島の事例
パトリック・ハインリヒ（ヴェネツィア大学）（松井真之介訳）　*231*

◉──── Chapter 11

Songs, Language and Culture: Ryukyuan Languages in the Okinawan uta-sanshin tradition

Matt Gillan (International Christian University) *236*

　1. Minority languages and song　*237*

　2. Ryukyuan languages in the classical *uta-sanshin* tradition　*240*

　3. Ryukyuan languages in the performing arts under Japan　*246*

　4. Ryukuan languages and music in the post-WWII broadcast media　*248*

　5. Pronunciation　*255*

　6. Beyond tradition　*258*

第11章　要約
唄、言語、文化——沖縄の「唄三線」伝統における琉球諸語
マット・ギラン（国際基督教大学）（松井真之介訳）　*264*

◉──── Chapter 12

Identification and Practical Situation of Endangered Languages in China

Huang Xing (Chinese Academy of Social Sciences) Bao Lianqun (Oita University) *269*

　1. The Problem of Language Identification　*269*

　2. The Problem of Endangered Language Identification　*270*

　3. Protection Measures for Endangered Languages　*272*

　　Basic linguistic and pedagogical training　*272* / Sustainable development in literacy and local documentation skills　*272* / Supporting and developing national language policy　*273* / Supporting and developing educational policy　*274* / Improving living conditions and respect for the rights of speaker communities　*274*

　4. Case Study of Endangered Languages in China　*275*

　　Mongolians and the Mongolian Language in the Heilongjiang Province　*276* / Manchus and the Manchu language in the Heilongjiang Province *278*

5. Conclusion *281*

第12章　要約
中国における危機言語の認定基準及び使用状況
黄行（中国社会科学院）、包聯群（大分大学）　*283*

◉──── Chapter 13

Endangered Language Speakers Networking: Thailand's Mahidol Model for Language Revitalization and Maintenance

Suwilai Premsrirat (Mahidol University, Thailand) *286*

1. Introduction *286*

2. The Language Situation in Thailand *287*

3. What is being done to slow down the death of languages? *290*

    Language Revival Efforts from Grassroots Communities *290*

4. Mahidol Model for Language Revitalization and Maintenance of Endangered Languages and Cultures *291*

5. Endangered Language Speakers Networking *294*

    Language Revitalization Stakeholder Web *295* / Local Community Participation in Endangered Language Revitalization *296*

6. Case Studies *298*

    Orthography development *299* / School-based language revitalization *299* / Mother Tongue (MT) as a Subject: Chong Language Revitalization Project (CLRP) *300* / Mother Tongue-Based Multilingual Education (MTB MLE): Patani Malay—Thai Bi/multilingual Education in Southern Thailand *301* / Reconsideration of National Language Policy *303* / Current draft of National Language Policy of Thailand *303*

7. Conclusion *304*

第13章　要約
消滅危機言語話者のネットワーク
──言語復興と維持に関するタイの「マヒドン・モデル」について
スウィライ・プレムスリラット（マヒドン大学）（松井真之介訳）　*307*

編著者紹介 / List of contributors *312*

はじめに

桂木 隆夫

　本書『言語復興の未来と価値——理論的考察と事例研究』は、2013年から2014年にかけて実施された学習院大学東洋文化研究所助成研究プロジェクト「日本とアジアにおけるマイノリティ言語（危機言語）復興運動とネットワーク形成」の研究成果、およびこのプロジェクトのいわばメインイベントとして2014年9月13日に開催された国際シンポジウム「危機言語復興ネットワーキング——その意義と今後の可能性」における各研究報告から成っている。そこでまず、本プロジェクトと国際シンポジウムについて簡単に紹介しておきたい。

　研究プロジェクト「日本とアジアにおけるマイノリティ言語（危機言語）復興運動とネットワーク形成」は社会言語学、社会学、公共哲学といった様々な学問分野を背景とする研究者とリングアパックスアジアという国際NGO代表が参加した、学際的でかつ学問実務横断的なプロジェクトとして実施されたユニークなものである。プロジェクトの特徴は、標題から分かるとおり、三つある。一つは、日本とアジア諸国を研究対象としていることであり、二つは、偏狭な国民国家（一つの国民、一つの言語）のイデオロギーに対するアンチテーゼとして、言語の多様性の価値を強調し、そのためのマイノリティ言語（危機言語）復興の重要性を主張する点であり、最後に、マイノリティ言語（危機言語）復興の実践的方法論として「ネットワーキング」を提案していることである。

　そして、こうしたプロジェクトの特徴を最大限アピールする場として開催されたのが、国際シンポジウム「危機言語復興ネットワーキング——その意

義と今後の可能性」である。これはプロジェクトの一環として、先に述べたリングアパックスアジアが主催し学習院大学東洋文化研究所が協賛する形で行われた。シンポジウムは、沖縄セッション、アイヌセッション、中国セッション、タイセッション、マイノリティ問題セッションから成り、さらに、キーノートレクチャーとしてハワイのマイノリティ言語復興ネットワーキングの報告がなされ、その他いくつかのポスターセッションの展示が行われた。参加者は日本とアジアからだけでなく、アメリカ、カナダ、さらにはヨーロッパからの報告者やディスカッサントから成り、各国の経験を生かした多様なネットワーキングの実践的方法論が報告され、論議された。

　本書は、こうした研究プロジェクトと国際シンポジウムの研究成果をまとめたものである。本書の構成上の特徴としてまず述べておきたいのは、本書が、日本人の読者のみならず外国人の読者も想定して、日本語の論文と英語の論文の各章から成り立っていることである。その上で、日本語の論文には英文のAbstractを、英語の論文には日本語の要約をそれぞれ付けることにした。これらのAbstractおよび要約はそれぞれ実質的な内容のものであり、日本人の読者あるいは外国人の読者が各章の内容を理解する上で大いに役に立つと考えている。なお、この方針は研究プロジェクトのメンバーの共通の了解と合意に基づくものである。

　次に、本書の各章の概要については各章それぞれに要約またはAbstractが付されているのでそれに譲るとして、ここでは、本書の構成およびそこにおいて論じられたいくつかの重要なポイントについてごく概略的に述べておきたい。

　本書は、第一部：理論的考察と第二部：事例研究の二部構成からなっている。第一部：理論的考察はマイノリティ言語（危機言語）復興に関する様々な角度からの理論的考察からなっているが、同時にそこには共通する一つのメッセージが存在する。それは、言語の多様性が平和をもたらす、「言語と平和」というメッセージである。これは、絶滅の危機にある言語の保存と再活性化の支援のための国際NGOリングアパックスアジアの活動を紹介したセスナ論文（本書第7章）の*Language for Peace*というタイトルに象徴

的に表されている。もっとも、言語の多様性と平和という考え方に対しては、言語の多様性は社会統合と社会の安定化に反するという固定観念も根強い。この固定観念に対して、数土論文（第2章）は「言語の多様性、より一般的に社会の多様性の容認は社会の一般的信頼を強化する」という仮説をSSP-W2012のデータと構造方程式モデリング（SEM）の分析手法を用いて論証している。また、マーハ論文（第5章）は、「言語の多様性は社会統合に反する」という固定観念の背後にある「単一言語による言語の純粋性と健全な国家」というイデオロギーに対して、聖書「創世記」のバベルの塔の隠喩の再解釈を通じて、「バベルの塔における人類の意志と言語実践の統一を破壊する事で、神は人類に言語と文化の多様な世界を受け入れるよう求めた」と指摘している。

　この「言語の多様性と平和」を推進するための言語政策のあり方について、従来型の「上からの言語政策」ではなく、「下からの言語政策」の重要性がいろいろな形で指摘されている。ビラッシュ＆ワシルク論文（第6章）は、子供たちが、人々の母語を話す力を破壊する邪悪なロップランたちに対して世界の言語の多様性救出に着手するキャムの物語（冒険）にウェブ上で参加することによって、言語の多様性とマイノリティ言語への言語意識を育むことを提案する。藤田論文（第3章）は、下からの言語政策におけるフィールドワークの重要性を指摘し、ローカルな場でのローカルな言語や文化の再評価と共に、ローカルな言語教育、教育現場での「多言語への転換」を提言する。原論文（第4章）は、こうしたローカルな教育現場でのマイノリティ言語教育のための標準的書き言葉を積み上げる必要性を指摘している。また桂木論文（第1章）は、グローカリゼーション（think globally, act locally）という観点から、日本の多文化共生という教育政策が、最近の「寛容な民族性とクール」という文化現象と結びつくことによって、日本のマイノリティ（危機）言語の文化的価値を高める可能性に言及する。

　第二部：事例研究は、ネットワーキングないし「下からの言語政策」に基づくマイノリティ言語（危機言語）復興の可能性および現状について、琉球諸語、アイヌ語、中国のマイノリティ言語、タイのマイノリティ言語を例に

とって論じている。そこから見えてくるのは、マイノリティ言語（危機言語）復興のためのネットワーキング（人々の繋がり方）の多様性である。たとえば、比嘉論文（第8章）は、うちなんちゅう（沖縄人）による琉球国の歴史認識の共有（ネットワーキング）を通じたうちなーぐちの復興を提唱している。「歴史認識をうちなーんちゅう（沖縄人）の視点からきちんと捉えることができれば、うちなーぐちを復興させるのは当たり前だと、うちなーんちゅならば考えるだろう」。ハインリッヒ論文（第10章）は、言語エコロジーという視点から、日本文化の多様性の中の琉球文化の独自性を毎日の実生活において維持する事を通じて、琉球諸語の復興の可能性を説いている。「琉球諸語が生き延びられる方法で言語エコロジーを再興することは、日本と呼ばれる場所に住む多様な人々の幸福に対して重要な貢献をするであろう」。ギラン論文（第11章）は、琉球文化の維持発展と琉球諸語の復興との結びつきについて、「音楽における琉球語使用の最も際立った面は、三線の存在であった」と指摘して、三線の伴奏を通じた琉球諸語の伝統歌謡と伝統演劇の成功を論じている。プレムスリラット論文（第13章）は、タイのマイノリティ言語復興に関する「マヒドン・モデル」と呼ばれるネットワーキングに基づくコミュニティベースの言語再生モデルを論じている。ここでのネットワーキングとは、危機言語コミュニティの活動メンバーを中心として、その周りに、マヒドン大学リソースセンターなどの学術機関やタイ研究財団などの経済基金、地域行政が有機的に連携するというものである。黄＆包論文（第12章）は、中国学会が中国の言語を約130種と認証をしたのに対して、ユネスコなどは約300種を認証しているとして、中国と国際社会における言語身分の認定基準の差異について指摘し、ユネスコの「言語活力」という考え方に注目している。また、片山論文（第9章）は、マイノリティ危機言語としてのアイヌ語の復興の取り組みとして、インターネット上のアイヌコミュニティにおけるアイヌ語学習を紹介している。

　本書の各章全体を通じて、明示的また黙示的に示されている「言語と平和」（言語の多様性が平和をもたらす）というメッセージは、一般の読者に対して必ずしも力強いものと感じられているわけではないかも知れない。また、マ

イノリティ（危機）言語復興の実践的方法論としてのネットワーキングという考え方にしても、まだ端緒に着いたばかりで、十分具体的成果を挙げているとは言えないのが実情である。

　けれども、宗教上や政治上の様々な原理主義が現代世界に深刻な暴力的対立と混沌を生み出している現在、「言語と平和」（言語の多様性が平和をもたらす）というメッセージが生み出す協力とネットワーキングの価値を再認識する必要があるのではないか。特に、多様な文化の習合としての日本文化の寛容性がクールジャパンとして認識されつつある今、むしろ日本においてこそ、「言語と平和」という考え方に基づくマイノリティ言語復興ネットワーキングの可能性が開かれつつあるように思われる。

　本書が成るに当たっては、学習院大学より研究出版助成をいただいた。記して感謝を申し上げる。また、元となった「日本とアジアにおけるマイノリティ（危機言語）復興運動とネットワーク形成」研究プロジェクトのメンバー相互のネットワーキングについても、この場を借りて感謝申し上げたい。また、最後になったが、日本語論文と英語論文が混在し、しかも本論文と要約（Abstract）の並立という極めてユニークな構成を快く受け入れて、出版の労をお取りいただいた三元社の石田俊二社長に心より感謝申し上げて筆を置くこととしたい。

Preface: the Aesthetic of Networks

John C. Maher

> *It would be interesting to know what men are most afraid of. Taking a new step, uttering a new word, is what people fear most.*
> Fyodor Dostoyevsky, Crime and Punishment, Part 1.

A network is a thing of beauty, like an intricate piece of lace, embroidery. A network is dependable like fine metal, like a spider's web. It is a fabric of cords or threads that interlock and weave together.

> *network, n. [f. net n.1 + work n. Cf. Du. netwerk, G. netzwerk, Da. netværk, Sw. nätverk.] Work in which threads, wires, or similar materials, are arranged in the fashion of a net; esp. a light fabric made of netted threads.* The Oxford English Dictionary (2nd Edition).

A network is an aesthetic object. It is 'neat' from the Latin 'nitidus' (elegant). A network is an arrangement, an essence that holds things together. It can cover. It can form a barrier and protection. It is a mesh that involves us, willingly. Networks enmesh us, involve us and mix us up.

Networks fashioned by human hands are meant to resemble the natural order, creation's perfect integration.

> *Thou shalt make vnto it a grate like networke of brasse*, Geneva Bible, Exodus. xxvii. 4, 1560.

In contemporary usage, network reminds us of interconnected computers and how things get moved to and fro through transportation and communication networks. Networks engender a sense of belonging, a kind of loyalty to the thing, to the work in hand. Here I am. A worker. A craftsman. This is mine under my fingers, my hand. The aesthetics of the net-work are different from wider network entities like nation-states. In such networks, essences like 'language' are robbed of their aesthetic quality — the elegance of language *qua* language — in favour of ideology. Language is where loyalty is invented. Language as art is extinguished. When language decays, becomes moribund, it is as if a local form of art, a craft expertise, has disappeared. A network of people, of the past, of thinking is disturbed.

In the dangerous place of language as a national symbol, belonging is forced, like a plant in a hothouse. Language is robbed of the person as persons are robbed of language. In this way, by disruption of the means to reflect and symbolize in some unique manner — what *parole* gives - language loses its redemptive purpose. In this artificial environment, heat and rain, soil and language become an artifice. Belonging is not shared by all but that does not matter to the pulverizing work of nation building. The national language is not a natural art but an artifact — of political design, of the reach for power. The *terroir* is lost, borders erased, from Ezo to Cornwall and Negritos, national languages are set once and for all. For these societies and people who have foraged for their own languages premature obituaries are now written, the pyres are lit and the propaganda drums beat: Ainu is dead, Hawaiian is dead, Cornish is dead, Mok is dead, Manx is dead, Okinawan is dead.

The fatal desire of the nation-state to incorporate and extinguish are subverted by the concept of the network. Languages belong to a network. They do not exist in isolation. The Chomskyan revolution described how the language network is configured. Chomsky's biological theory of language was itself based upon the deep intricacy of the body. It is an overtly Cartesian model that explains the fundamental interconnectedness of language in the wider 'society' of the body. There is only one language in the world — human language and this human language is hard-wired into our human faculty. Like the network of the blood system, just like the perfect symmetry of the eye and the heart. Chomsky's elaboration of interconnections - linguistic, cognitive — has permitted us to see language as part of a complex ecology that can be easily modified, corrected as well as abused. Population decline and shift, the movement of migrants and refugees, the cycle of oppression/suppression are some of the common factors that disturb an apparent equilibrium. Except that society is not — hardly ever - an equilibrium if by that we mean a state of rest or balance between powers and influences. Rather, society is always held in tension, a network yes but always in flux, constantly reformed under the glare of information (Zygmunt Bauman's 'liquid modernity' 1988) subject to the smallest changes in social practice that refer not to tradition but rather to themselves (Anthony Giddens' 'reflexive modernization' 1990).

Language networks started to come apart in post-medieval Europe, in regions and towns, in *sprachbund* communities. The unraveling began prominently with modernity when the ensemble of cultural norms — diverse, geographically spread — were shaped and maneuvered by two massive political forces: the French Revolution, the Treaty of Westphalia. It was in this context of new cultural norms that the centrifugal drift towards common languages first occurred; powerful *lingua franca* that would mediate globalization and the cultural flows that would continue the enterprise of modernity: English, French, Spanish, Dutch, German. Sociolinguistics calls this 'language shift.'

Language shift continues to alter and diminish linguistic diversity in Asia, and other parts of the world. There is general consensus that of the current 6000-7000 spoken languages that exist in the world, at least 50% of them will have become extinct by 2100. How to challenge radical language shift, a process that supplants one thing with another, is not easy to achieve. The papers in this collection attempt to elucidate these developments. The focus on 'network' references the movement away from language *qua* language toward the being of speakers. It is, specifically, a reorientation toward how people networks are established and maintained for the sake of endangered languages, languages in crisis.

How are individuals located and how do they locate themselves within systems of connections? Inevitably, there is a sense of both hopelessness and hope in this familiar narrative. Local connectivity is one thing but being handed the reins of power is another. Networks can flourish in the absence of supportive policies. Compare the situation of a historically discriminated speaker of Breton in a stateless region of northwest France with a small but newly empowered region further south in Europe? Croatian has become, suddenly, the 'national' language of a unitary state and republic (from 1991) and its 'separateness' from Serbo-Croat (*abstand* languages which are mutually intelligible) is essential for national identity. This compares to the subordination of another historic entity — the Breton language in Brittany for which there is little or no hope of autonomy: except through the network of human relations. You might not have a nation but you have people.

The sociolinguist and scholar of Ryukyuan languages, Patrick Heinrich, was instrumental and inspirational in elaborating the Linguapax 2014 symposium's focus on 'network.' The purpose of the gathering was summarized in Heinrich's flagship statement, "Complementary functions between the dominant and the dominating language are not sought, because competition between these languages is simply sidestepped by using the endangered language in all domains, and by making efforts to use or learn the endangered language a necessity for joining the network. Speakers switch and mix languages in order to facilitate language learning of new speakers. New speakers are often not bound by shared place, time, or by ethnicity or nationality." Heinrich follows this with practical questions, "Who are the pioneers putting an endangered language back to use? To whom do they speak the endangered language? Where do they speak the endangered language?" (Summary of Symposium).

Where communities possess the means to access social networks there is the opportunity to climb out of history and into the real and virtual world of connections. The 2014 symposium upon which this collection of papers was based, provides a kind of assessment of the opportunities held out by networks and networking. The symposium aimed to define the concept of network as well as evaluate presence and formation, the values and benefits. Positivity builds minds.

It calls upon resourcefulness and points ways towards the achievement of goals — using the language again. To network is to develop policy and finds ways of implementing it, i.e. 'strategy.' Communicative needs must first be identified, as described by Huang Xing and Bao Lianqun in the context of minority/endangered languages of China (Chapter 12). Communication includes not merely the spoken word but writing. Benedict Anderson's (1991) description of the rise of the nation state in Europe and the role of language in nation building depended crucially, he argued, upon writing. This theme is taken up in Fara Kiyoshi's (Chapter 4) description of the significance of writing in the European minority languages nexus, i.e. the role of the written languages vis-à-vis the larger imagined communities of Europe. Another focus is regional, and the papers presented here derive from various locations which have experienced periodic language shift in large complex (dynastic) entities and later in modern states: the Ainu language learning situation in Tokyo by means of the internet (Katayama, Chapter 11) and how learner groups liaise and interact. The use of online technology and the visual media in language education is also taken up by Olenka Bilash (Chapter 6). Regional models present themselves everywhere and their vision unfolds, in Indonesia, in India, and in E Ola ka 'Ōlelo Hawai'I' a Hawaiian-Medium Model for Language Revitalization.

The refracted lines of identity and loyalty in the language situation of the Ryukyu Islands in the southwest of the Japanese islands are a template for the role of culture and history in endangered language networks (Heinrich, Chapter 10 and Fijya Byron, Chapter 8). This includes traditional music. Gillan (Chapter 11) highlights the challenges for the maintenance of any minority language and poses the question, "how to move beyond very local constructions of identity based on the past, to deal with modern-day issues?" Networking is crucial for policy and strategy, but also for the adaptation of endangered languages to new communicative needs. Suwailai Premsrirat (Chapter 13) deals with this in her elaboration of endangered language speakers networking in Thailand. What are the language supports and what are the impediments to growth? As explained by Jelisava Sethna (Chapter 7) the precise aim of Linguapax as a support organization is to assist in the preservation and revitalization of endangered languages by means of awareness raising but also, fundamentally, to help build networks. How can we build links on the inside, looking for a common discourse that can describe the past and the possibilities of the present, as described by Sachiyo Fujita-Round (Chapter 3) on Miyako Island in the Ryukyus. It seeks to raise awareness of links between language, identity, human rights, and the quest for peace. These wider implications and the entire multiculturalism 'project' is investigated in detail by Katsuragi Takao (Chapter 1).

What metaphors describe the situation of endangered languages in late modernity? The shadow of the mythic Tower of Babel is a lasting metaphor. Babel symbolized the national enterprise of an aggressive community, the pride of an expansionist, urban, imperial capital and the largest metropolitan city of the ancient world. As Hegel shrewdly and approvingly observed, underpinning the Babel story is the common referent: unificationist ideology; where oneness, orderliness, harmony, uniformity was a state of consciousness and an ideal (see Maher, Chapter 5). The inhabitants of the doomed Tower of Babel were thrown out and scattered afar across the world. They were forced to establish their networks and loyalties. Not loyalties to a voracious unificatory empire but loyalty to their newly minted languages. Their bonds were no longer to the emperor but to themselves. In our post-Babel world, networks — as described in these collected papers - proffer evidence of good faith and mutual will. It is the duty of all, the intellectual, the activist, persons in their own community networks who turn their face to the beauty of the language arts to call for a new and more just order. This art that people make in their community is a political declaration, an act of will that challenges rather than confirm the powerful and must forever, as Edward Said "dispute the prevailing norms" (1994:27). Taking a new step is, as Dostoyevsky reminds us in the epigraph, a fearful thing. Pushing back and pushing for language practices that have been actively suppressed and discouraged are fearful things but they are first steps.

The publication of this volume was made possible by the generous support of a research grant from Gakushuin university for which the authors express their sincere appreciation.

References

Bauman, Zygmunt 1988. *Globalization: the Human Consequences*. Cambridge: Polity Press.
Giddens, Anthony 1990. *The Consequences of Modernity*. Stanford: Stanford University Press.
Said, Edward 1994. *Representations of the Intellectual*. London: Vintage.

第1部　理論的考察

Part 1 Theoretical Approaches

第1章

多文化共生(グローカリゼーション)と
マイノリティ(危機)言語復興

桂木 隆夫(学習院大学)

第1節　はじめに

　本章では、マイノリティ(危機)言語復興の議論の背景にある思想的ないし哲学的問題関心について論じてみることにする。

　マイノリティ(危機)言語復興の問題は社会言語学の分野で論じられてきている。だが、マイノリティ(危機)言語に対する日本社会の関心はお世辞にも高いとは言えない。そうしたこともあって、社会言語学の分野では、マイノリティ(危機)言語復興をどのように論じるかの方法論あるいは思想枠組みについて、1990年代以降、言語権的アプローチが採用されるようになってきている。そこには、言語権という考え方が国際的な人権意識の高まりとヨーロッパにおける多言語主義の展開の中で唱えられてきたという事情もあるが、それ以上に、「言語は人間の人格形成にとって不可欠であるから、マイノリティ(危機)言語を母語とする人々はその言語への権利を有する」という強いメッセージを発信することによって、マイノリティ(危機)言語復興への日本社会一般の関心を喚起したいという思いがあるように思う。

　だがそうした思いにもかかわらず、木村が指摘するように、「言語権は日本国民の無関心を克服しえていない」(Kimura 2011: 22)。後述するように、多数の民族と歴史と言語が交錯するヨーロッパの多言語主義という文脈と、日本語(お国言葉あるいは方言を含む)という大きな存在感をもった主要言語があってその周辺に幾つかのマイノリティ(危機)言語(琉球諸語およびアイヌ語等)が存在するという文脈では、言語権という考え方に対する社会一般の受

け止め方に大きな落差が存在する。

　それだけではない。言語権という考え方にはジレンマが含まれているという（Kimura 2011: 27）。もともと言語権は、ナショナリズムが前提とした国民国家の理念、すなわち「一つの国民、一つの国家（言語）」というイデオロギーに対抗する言説として登場した。そしてそれは、脱ナショナリズムの流れの中で、ヨーロッパ各地に存在する地域マイノリティ言語復興をうながし、多言語主義の理論的支柱ともなってきた。だが、それぞれの地域の民族や歴史と不可分であるマイノリティ言語はその集団の母語としての性格を有するがゆえに、排他性をともなっている。一つは、従来のナショナリズムが前提としている国家語に対する自律性（独立性）という意味での排他性と、もう一つは、そのマイノリティ言語の周縁に存在する変異型としての「方言」に対する排他性である。いわば、言語権が主張する地域マイノリティ言語復興は、脱ナショナリズムの流れの中で出てきたにもかかわらず、そのマイノリティ言語の特権性を主張することによって、こんどはその周辺に位置する「方言」に対して新たなヒエラルキーを生み出し、いわばプチナショナリズムともいうべきものと結びついてしまうというジレンマである。

　これとほぼ同主旨のことは、スペインのマイノリティ言語であるカタルーニャ語保全運動を例にとって、寺尾も主張している（寺尾 2014: 122-123）。寺尾によれば、支配言語であるスペイン語の軛を取り払ってカタルーニャ語保全運動を進めるためには、「「一言語、一民族、一領域」というテーゼが保全運動に参加する話者全てに強く共有され」る必要がある。強力な支配言語に対抗するためには、マイノリティ言語自体が強固で一枚岩的でなければならない（プチナショナリズムを含まざるをえない）からである。だがこのことは、マイノリティ言語の保護が必ずしも「言語多様性保全」には結びつかないことを意味する。なぜならば、マイノリティ言語が一枚岩的であろうとすればするほど、マイノリティ言語の周縁の「多様性は、足手まといとなる〈卑しい方言〉として切り捨てられるか、同化させられる運命にある」。ここには、マイノリティ言語の復興運動が、プチナショナリズムと結びつくことによって、言語多様性を抑圧するというジレンマが存在する。

こうしたことを考えたときに、マイノリティ（危機）言語復興にどのような方法論で取り組むべきかに関して、言語権という考え方とは別の考え方（方法論）について、私は以前、「言語権と言語政策について」という小論において、言語政策枠組みということを論じたことがある（桂木2003）。

　これは、マイノリティ（危機）言語復興の問題を、権利の（本質的な）問題としてではなく、政策の（相対的な）問題として考えるのだが、政策のうちで短期の具体的政策と中長期の政策構想とを分けて、中長期の政策構想について政策枠組みという言葉を用いるというものである。短期の政策というのは、具体的な政治的社会的経済的問題に対して解決ないし一定の成果を期待して政策対応する場合のことであり、我々が普通に政策と呼ぶものを指している。これに対して政策枠組みというのは、我々の社会が今後中長期的に見てどのような方向に進むべきかについての基本的な考え方を明らかにするものであり、この政策枠組みは、具体的政策がそれに適うものであるか反するものかに従って取捨選択されるその基準を含んでいる。そしてこの政策枠組みは我々の社会の中長期的な一般的方向性を反映したものであると同時に、その方向性を促進しかつそれに反する要素を除去する志向性を含んでいる。

　このような政策枠組みと具体的政策の例としては、小泉政権の経済政策におけるいわゆる「骨太の方針」とそれに基づいて打ちだされた財政政策や社会保障改革、規制改革などの政策をあげることができる。「骨太の方針」とは、我々の政治経済社会の現実的な認識に立って、今後中長期的に見てどのような方向に進むべきかについての基本的な考え方を明らかにするものであり、この方針に沿ってさまざまな政策が打ち出された。注意しなければならないのは、この「骨太の方針」という政策枠組みが本質的絶対的なものではなく、相対的なものであるということである。それはイデオロギーではない。それは二つの意味で相対的である。それはまず、「骨太の方針」に基づいて打ち出されたさまざまな経済政策が格差の拡大を生み出したことによってそれぞれの政策の修正と見直しがなされたように、「骨太の方針」内部の政策の妥当性について常に再検討の余地があるということであり、さらに中長期的に見れば、この「骨太の方針」に代わる別の新しい政策枠組みとしての新

たな「骨太の方針」が打ち出される可能性が、我々の社会の中長期的な一般的方向性の変動によって、常に存在するということである。

　このように、政策枠組みという考え方は、一方で権利主義的考え方の中にある本質主義的絶対主義的志向性を排しつつ、他方で中長期的観点を組み込むことによって、個別具体的政策が陥りやすい近視眼的利益主義的弊害を是正し、我々の社会の中長期的な方向性を踏まえた公共利益を漸進的に実現しようとするものである。

　このような考え方（方法論）を日本におけるマイノリティ（危機）言語復興に適用する場合、それはどのような言語政策枠組みとして考えられるだろうか。すでに言及したように、多数の民族と歴史と言語が交錯ししかもEUという大きな統合の流れの中にあるヨーロッパの場合は、主に1980年代以降、着実に深まってきた「ヨーロッパは多言語社会である」という人々の意識を背景に、それはいわゆる多言語主義という政策枠組みとして表現される。

　そしてこの多言語主義的政策枠組みにおいては、グローバルな共通語としての英語の積極的受容と各国のナショナルな言語の尊重と並んで、「言語権」という非本質主義的レトリックに基づく地域マイノリティ言語復興のための政策対応が図られることになる。

　これに対して、日本という文脈ではどのような言語政策枠組みが考えられるだろうか？　まず指摘しなければならないのは、日本の言語政策枠組みは、少なくとも現時点では、多言語主義的政策枠組みではないということである。なにより、我々の中に「日本は多言語社会である」という意識が希薄であるという事実が、それを物語っている。この意味で、ヨーロッパの文脈と日本の文脈は異なる。既に述べたように、日本の文脈とは、日本語（お国言葉あるいは方言を含む）という大きな存在感をもったナショナルな言語があってその周辺に幾つかのマイノリティ（危機）言語（琉球諸語およびアイヌ語等）が存在するというものである。

　他方で、日本の文脈とヨーロッパの文脈には重要な共通点がある。それは、日本もヨーロッパも共に、国民国家という枠組み（ナショナリズム）を維持しつつ、グローバリゼーションという大きな流れとそれに対抗するローカリ

ゼーションの流れという三つの要因のせめぎ合いの構図によって規定されているということである。

　この構図の中でヨーロッパは、グローバルな共通語としての英語の積極的受容と、緩やかな国民国家という枠組みの下でのそれぞれのナショナルな言語の尊重、およびローカリズムと非本質主義的「言語権」に基づく地域マイノリティ言語復興という多言語主義の言語政策枠組みを採用してきたように思う。

　これに対して、日本の言語政策枠組みはどうなのだろうか？　私としてはそれについて、可能性としての多文化共生の言語政策枠組みということを考えてみたい。確かに、日本の国民にも政治家にも、「言語権」という考え方のみならず、言語政策枠組みという観念は希薄である。だが我々の共通認識として、偏狭なナショナリズムの言語政策枠組みは採りえないという意識があり、さりとてヨーロッパのような多言語主義の政策枠組みもまた採用しえないという意識もある。そしてもう一つ、ここ十年程の間に、主に国政および地方政治の政策担当者の間で「言語は文化である」という意識が徐々に浸透し、またグローバリゼーションの流れの中で「多文化共生」という用語法がクールジャパンという言葉に重ねられて用いられてきたという事情が存在する。

　もちろんこれだけでは、これからの日本の中長期的な政策構想として、多文化共生の言語政策枠組みを主張するには不十分である。そのことを十分認識したうえで、私はここで、仮説としての多文化共生の言語政策枠組みの背景にあるグローバリゼーションとナショナリズムの対抗関係と、そこから派生的に生じるローカリゼーションの新しい流れとしてのグローカリゼーションという三者の日本的せめぎ合いの構図とこの構図の下でのマイノリティ（危機）言語復興のあり方について考察してみたい。

第2節　ナショナリズム、グローバリゼーション、グローカリゼーション

　言語政策に限らず、日本の中長期的な政策構想を考える場合、ナショナリズムとグローバリゼーションとローカリゼーションの三つの流れがどのようなせめぎ合いの構図をみせているかをみる必要がある。

　日本の場合、大ざっぱに言ってそれは、比較的優勢なナショナリズムが、外からのグローバリゼーションへの対応と、内からの少子高齢化と人口減少による地方の疲弊に対処するための地方活性化（グローバル化に対応しうるグローカリゼーション）の必要性によって、自己変容しつつあるというものであろう。そしてそのことを示すのが、多文化共生という用語法であり、可能性としての多文化共生の政策枠組みである。このことを踏まえた上で、ここではまず、ナショナリズムとグローバリゼーションとグローカリゼーションのそれぞれの現状についてみてみよう。

第1項　ナショナリズム

　まずナショナリズムだが、それは従来、国民国家＝「一つの国民、一つの国家」というスローガンによって象徴されてきた。それには、二つの意味が含まれている。

　第一に、世俗化としての国民国家ということである。国家と宗教を分離する、政教分離ということである。これは元々、中世ヨーロッパの神聖政治（政教一致）の克服に由来するが、現代においてもなお、宗教原理主義（国家の正当化原理としての宗教）という考え方は、イスラム諸国に見られるように優勢であり、ナショナリズムに対して、宗教と政治の関係について再考を促す要因となっている。特に日本の場合、歴史的にみて、キリスト教やイスラム教におけるような一神教ではなく、いわゆる神儒仏習合の多神教的多宗教的背景の下で日本人の宗教意識が形成されてきた。それが、明治維新以後、日本のナショナリズム（国民国家）形成が一神教的原理主義的な疑似宗教としての国家神道と結びつくことによって、ゆがめられてきた。そして日本の敗戦によって国家神道が否定されたにもかかわらず、なお、日本のナショナリ

ズムと国家神道の関係が清算できていないという事情があり、それがこれからの日本の開放的なナショナリズム（国民国家）における日本人の多様な宗教意識と政治の関係を考える上で桎梏となっている。

　また、世俗化としての国民国家は宗教原理主義とは正反対の動きによって自己変容を迫られている。それは、世俗化の徹底としての市場主義である。これはすでに、18世紀のJ. J. ルソーが世俗化としての国民国家を論じたときに直面した問題である。ルソーはこれに対して、国民国家の純粋性（正しさ）を守るために市場経済の排除と愛国心の徹底化（市民宗教）を主張したが、それはルソーの意図をはるかに超えて、ウルトラナショナリズムとしての全体主義の悲劇を生み出した。それに対する反省から、現代の国民国家は市場経済が生み出す価値観の多様性と国民統合との折り合いをつけるために、開放的な国民国家という自己変容を迫られている。

　第二に、同化主義ということである。これはネーション・ステイト、「一つの国家は一つの国民から構成されなければならない」という考え方に由来する。だが、現実には大多数の国家が多数の民族からなっており、それぞれの民族意識の興隆に伴って地域分権主義やさらには地域分離主義が台頭し、これもまた開放的な国民国家という方向性の中で、ナショナリズムと国民国家のあり方に再考を促す要因となっている。これは日本の場合、分離主義的なローカリズムと結びつくよりは、それぞれの地域に育まれた歴史と文化を尊重する多文化共生型の開放的なナショナリズムという方向性である。この意味で、多文化共生は欧米の多文化主義とは異なる考え方である。

第2項　グローバリゼーション

　次に、グローバリゼーションについては、それを象徴するグローバルスタンダード（世界標準）という考え方に二つの意味が含まれている。

　第一に、グローバルマーケット、すなわち、経済的世俗化の徹底としての経済至上主義であり、これはすでに述べたように、一方で宗教原理主義（来世における救済の価値の絶対性の主張）に対立すると同時に、他方で国民国家の統合機能を揺るがすものとなっている。実際、1990年代から21世紀の初め

のグローバリゼーションはIMFや世界銀行によるいわゆるワシントンコンセンサスと結びついたアメリカ型の自由貿易主義と金融資本主義をグローバルスタンダードとして世界に広めようとするもので、アメリカナイゼーションと呼ばれ、1997年のアジア通貨危機や1999年のシアトルにおけるWTO閣僚会議に対する反グローバリズム運動、さらには国際的テロリズムを誘発するなど、様々な問題を引き起こしてきた。こうしたアメリカナイゼーションは現在修正されつつあるとはいえ、依然として強い影響力を有している。

　第二に、グローバリゼーションには普遍的人権の理念＝世界市民社会という側面が含まれている。これは、18世紀のI・カントの人権の理念に由来するものであり、現代では普遍的価値としての立憲民主主義と表現される。これはそれ自体としてグローバリゼーションの積極的価値の表明である一方で、実際にはアメリカの建国の歴史と深く結びついた三権分立と法の支配に基づくアメリカ的共和主義の優位（アメリカナイゼーション）を主張するものとなっていて、それぞれの歴史や文化、民族を背景とする各国のナショナリズムと対立すると同時に、それぞれの国民国家の内部における地域分権主義（民族自決主義）とも対立する。

第3項　グローカリゼーション

　グローカリゼーションという考え方は、上述した、偏狭なナショナリズムからリベラルなナショナリズムへの自己変容の流れと、アメリカナイゼーションとしてのグローバリゼーションへの反省の流れから派生的に生じてきたものである。グローカリゼーションは、グローバルとローカルの造語であり、標語として、'think globally, act locally'（グローバルに考え、ローカルに行動する）と表現されるが、更に、'think globally, act nationally'（グローバルに考え、ナショナルに行動する）ということや'think nationally, act locally'（ナショナルに考え、ローカルに行動する）ということも含まれている。

　つまり、ナショナルとグローバルとローカルという三つの視点の競合ということだが、これら三つの視点は均等というのではなく、どの視点が他の視点に比べて比重が大きいかはそれぞれの国の歴史や文化に依存する。いずれ

にせよ、この考え方は三つの視点のバランスを追求するものであり、特定のイデオロギーや原理主義とは相いれない。

　率直に言って、グローカリゼーションは特定の原理に基づく自律的かつ体系的な思想ではないので、ナショナリズムやグローバリゼーションと比較してインパクトが弱いことは否めない。実際、グローカリゼーションは、近年アカデミズムにおいて徐々に主張されるようになってきているとはいえ、少数にとどまっている。しかも現実政治は依然としてナショナリズムやグローバリゼーションによって支配され、グローカリゼーションの政策構想が積極的に採用された例はない。あるいは、ヨーロッパの多言語主義の政策枠組みがヨーロッパ型のグローカリゼーションと解釈しうるけれども、その他は、可能性としての日本の多文化共生の政策枠組みが考えられる程度である。むしろグローカリゼーションは、現時点では、ナショナリズムの排他主義やグローバリゼーションの独断性、またローカリゼーション（地域分離主義）の偏狭性に対して、開放性と寛容性や柔軟性の立場から反省を迫るものと位置づけられる。

　興味深いことは、ウィキペディアによれば、グローカリゼーションという用語法が、「現地化」、「土着化」という言葉に象徴される、アジア市場における日本企業のビジネス実践に由来するとされていることである。このことからも分かるように、日本社会では、開かれたナショナリズム、途上国などの弱者に寛容なグローバリズム、そしてナショナルな価値やグローバルな価値を尊重するローカリズムを支持する姿勢が優勢である。ただし後述するように、日本政府は依然として硬直したナショナリズムに拘泥しているようにみえる。日本政府の視点と日本社会の視点では落差がある。私の考えでは、グローカリゼーションの日本的表現は「多文化共生」だが、日本政府がそれを硬直化したナショナリズムの観点から理解するのか、それとも、より開放的で寛容で柔軟なナショナリズムの観点から理解するのかによって、その意味内容は変わってくる。

　グローカリゼーションは開放性と寛容性や柔軟性の観念を含んでいる。と同時にそれは、ある種の消極的な規範でもある。それは、国家権力を背景と

した体系性と整合性を特徴とする法規範ではない。またそれは、いわゆる社会慣習や習俗といった社会規範でもない。これに関連して、私は以前、消極的規範としての自由社会を論じたときに、それを「ゲームのルール」の概念を用いて説明したことがあるが、消極的規範としてのグローカリゼーションを説明する際にもこの「ゲームのルール」という考え方が適切である（桂木 1990）。

つまり、グローカリゼーションは、ナショナリズムとグローバリゼーションとローカリゼーションの適正な共存を要請する「ゲームのルール」である。ただしそれは、通常我々がゲームについてイメージするような「ゲームのルールが一義的に明確である」とか「ゲームの開始と終了がはっきりしている」ということではない。では「ゲームのルール」とは何なのか。

これについて私は、古典的自由主義の経済哲学者であるF. H. ナイトに依拠しながら、自由社会と民主主義および市場の『ゲームのルール』について論じたが、それをここで、自由社会という言葉をグローカリゼーションに変えて引用してみたい。

> グローカリゼーション（自由社会）において人々は人生の基本的で多元的な諸価値をめぐって競い合う複雑でときに矛盾を含んだゲームに参加している。人々はゲームのルールに従って勝ったり負けたりしながら社会生活を営む。と同時に人々は、そのゲームのルールを絶えず改善し、より良いものにしようと努力する。ゲームのルールに従いつつ、ゲームのルールを改善するために必要とされるのはある種の知性である。
>
> それは、権威（既存のルール）を尊重しつつ、それに盲目的に従うことなく、証拠を比較しつつ様々な意見を批判的に検討し、自分の知り得ない事柄を率直に認めつつ、一歩一歩漸進的に事態を改善しようとする知的努力を意味する。
>
> この知的努力を発揮するためには、我々は良き競技者でなければならない。勝ち負けにかかわらずゲームを楽しみ、勝つためにズルをせず、相手がちょっとズルをして勝っても余り怒ってはならない。そして常に、

ルールに従いそれを実効あるものにするよう努めながら、徐々にルールを改善するよう努めなければならない。その際、心に留めておくべき教えは消極的なものである。すなわち、行き過ぎてはならない。物事を単純化しすぎてはならない、困難な問題に対して安易な解決策を求めてはならない、というような。(桂木 1990：154-155)

ここでは、「ゲームのルール」の四つの要素が語られている。すなわち、ルールの多元性、ルールの柔軟性（修正可能性）、漸進主義、そしてフェアプレイの精神である。そしてそれらはまた、グローカリゼーションという思考法に含まれる要素でもある。

第3節　グローカリゼーションと多文化共生の言語政策枠組み

　グローカリゼーションの「ゲームのルール」という観点から、中長期的ビジョンとして、日本の多文化共生の言語政策枠組みを考えてみると、基本的方向性として以下の三つの点を指摘することができる。
　第一に、言語はグローバルな、そしてナショナルなコミュニケーションの手段であると同時に、ローカルな生活文化を構成する基本的要素であるという視点が重要性だということである。
　確かに、近代語としての現代日本語は明治期以後、ナショナルなコミュニケーションの手段として形成され、それが時の経過とともにナショナルな文化の表現としても優勢となる中で、日本各地の生活文化を表現するローカルな日本語やマイノリティ言語を次第に駆逐し、その結果、「同質社会日本」という神話が生み出されてきた経緯がある。
　けれども、グローカリゼーション（多文化共生）の「ゲームのルール」という観点から考えるならば、日本社会はナショナルなコミュニケーション手段および文化表現としての共通日本語と日本各地のローカルな生活文化の表現としての日本語（方言）およびマイノリティ言語（沖縄諸語やアイヌ語等）が共

存する多文化共生社会である。

　このような視点に立つならば、グローカリゼーション（多文化共生）の言語政策の例として、日本社会の開放性（多元性と柔軟性）を国際的にアピールするために、たとえば2020年の東京オリンピックパラリンピック招致の際に話題となった「おもてなし」という言語表現に関して、ナショナルな文化表現としての「おもてなし」という日本語表現の重要性を認識しつつ、「おもてなし」に相当する日本各地のローカルな生活文化表現に着目し、いわば「おもてなし」に関わるローカルな言語表現群と生活文化の再活性化を支援するといったことが考えられる。

　また、少子高齢化と人口減少社会の急速な進展や東日本大震災によって、ローカルなコミュニティの消滅が深刻になりつつある中で、コミュニティの再構築の問題がそれぞれのローカルな生活文化と深く関わっていることが認識されてきている。このローカルな生活文化について考えたとき、それはたとえば祭りである。それは日本人に特徴的な宗教意識、現世における「ご利益（りやく）」を説く現世宗教と正直の倫理に基づく「無病息災、家内安全、五穀豊穣、商売繁盛」といったローカルな生活文化と深く結びついている。このように考えるならば、グローカリゼーション（多文化共生）の言語政策をより広い視野で捉えて、ローカルな生活文化を象徴する祭りを活性化し、周年行事としての祭りに関わるローカルな言語表現群と生活文化を活性化することがローカルな日本語（方言）とマイノリティ言語の再活性化につながると考えることもできよう。

　第二に、グローカリゼーションに含まれるオープンなローカリゼーションとは、グローバリゼーションを受容しつつ、そこに本来含まれるべきセーフティネットをより広範に整備し、セーフガードをより実質的に保障するということである。セーフティネットとは、グローバリゼーションが各国に求める構造改革にともなう様々な起業活動から生じるリスクや不安を軽減するための安全網の整備ということであり、また、セーフガードとは、行き過ぎたグローバリゼーションに自制を促し、特にローカルな生活文化を侵食し破壊する明白な危険がある場合には、それを防止するためにグローバリゼーショ

ンの動きに一定の制限を設けるナショナルな政策対応のことである。

　そして、グローカリゼーション（多文化共生）の言語政策としてより広範なセーフティーネットを整備するとは、たとえば、マイノリティの生活文化（マイノリティ言語）の再活性化のための起業活動のナショナルなレベルでの財政支援と再チャレンジの安全網の整備が考えられる。また、より実質的なセーフガードとは、危機的な生活文化（マイノリティ言語）のナショナルなレベルでの保護や、グローバルなレベルでのマイノリティの生活文化の価値に関する共通認識の構築などである。この意味でグローカリゼーションは、ナショナルな言語政策のレベルでのマイノリティ言語の再活性化のための起業活動の支援や、更には、国際機関と協働した危機的なマイノリティ言語の保護の必要性について啓蒙活動の推進などを含んでいる。

第4節　おわりに

　グローカリゼーションという考え方は、日本の生活文化と親和的である。たとえば、グローバルな経済活動とローカルな生活意識ということを考えた場合、グローバリゼーション（日本人のグローバルな経済活動）とローカルな（日本人の）宗教意識との習合的共生が認められる。前述したように、日本の習合信仰は、来世における救済を説く来世宗教ではなく、現世における「ご利益」を説く現世宗教であり、その場合の「ご利益」とは、正直の倫理に基づく「無病息災、家内安全、五穀豊穣、商売繁盛」といったローカルな生活文化に根差した経済活動の成果を指す。この意味で、グローバリゼーションと日本の現世利益を説く習合信仰は親和的であり、少なくとも排他的関係に立つものではない。

　また、グローバリゼーションと日本の生活文化との親和性ということについては、「グローバリゼーションとナショナルな文化およびローカルな生活文化との共生」に関して、最近、クールジャパンということが叫ばれるようになってきている。そして、クールジャパンと日本の言語政策の関連性に

ついて、私は以前、N.ゴットリーブやJ.マーハを引用しながら、日本の多文化共生という考え方を、欧米の政治的多文化主義political multiculturalismと区別して、生活多文化主義aesthetic multiculturalismと性格づけつつ論じたことがある（Katsuragi 2011）。

その前提にあるのは、「日本政府の近代主義への思い入れにもかかわらず、日本人は、近代主義からみずからを解き放ち、多文化社会ニッポンの現実と徐々に向き合い始めている」という認識である。これに関連して、ゴットリーブは日本語と日本人のアイデンティティーという論点について、次のように特徴づけている。「日本人は、国語そのものの内部の多様性を心地よいものと感じている。もっともそれは、日本が多言語主義を受け入れるということではないけれども」（Katsuragi 2011: 209）。

マーハはこのような日本人の言語意識について、「寛容な民族性metroethnicityとクール」という表現を用いて説明している。「寛容な民族性metroethnicityは都会的で、曖昧で、気軽に身に纏える民族性である。寛容な民族性は民族の伝統的主体からの脱中心化を合んでいる。もはや、由緒ある民族だけが権力と権威と正統性を主張しうるのではない。アイヌ語を知らない、イタリア語を話すアイヌがいても構わないのである」。また、クールということについては次のように述べられている。「クールとは、ある種のポスト民族国家であって、そこでは、日本人と民族的マイノリティが、より良い生活のために、様々な民族性を楽しむのである」。つまり、「寛容な民族性とクール」が表現しているのはある種の多文化的距離感覚であり、それは民族的絶対主義と正反対のものである。マーハによれば、「もし標準語がその政治的権力性によってクールでないとすれば、方言のあるものもまた、クールとは言えない。方言絶対主義はクールにになりえない」（Katsuragi 2011: 209）。

N.ゴットリーブやJ.マーハが示唆しているように、日本の社会は現在、新しい多文化主義への移行期にある。ただし、日本の多文化主義は、文化的自律性と民族対立の様々なエピソードを含む西洋の多文化主義とは異なり、相対主義的で、寛容でかつ文化的に習合的である。それは、政治的多文化

主義というよりも、むしろ生活多文化主義aesthetic multiculturalismである（Katsuragi 2011: 211）。

　もっとも、この生活多文化主義に問題がないわけではない。というのはそれは、自律的というより自生的で、状況依存的であり、したがって、多民族的アイデンティティー（そのようなものがありうるとして）を主張する独立した社会運動にはなりえないからである。それゆえ、「寛容な民族性とクール」が持続的なライフスタイルの基礎となり得るかどうかを予測するのは時期尚早であり、まして、それが日本政治を左右するほどの力強い社会運動となり得るかは不明である。マーハ自身は、「クール」現象が一時的な流行とは違うものの、相対主義のもろさを有しており、また自己規律と批判的精神が欠けていることを認めている。マーハも指摘するように、「寛容な民族性とクール」という文化現象がどのくらい広範囲に、またどのくらい速やかに生活多文化主義の社会的寛容の精神を生み出し、それが新しい立法と結びつき、また多文化共生の教育改革をもたらすのかは分からない。だが、「寛容な民族性とクール」が日本のマイノリティ（危機）言語の文化的価値を高める上で重要な役割を担っていることだけは、確かなように思われる。

参考文献
桂木 隆夫（1990）『自由社会の法哲学』、弘文堂。
桂木 隆夫（2003）「言語権と言語政策について」、桂木（編）『ことばと共生、言語の多様性と市民社会の課題』、三元社。
寺尾 智史（2014）『欧州周縁の言語マイノリティと東アジア、言語多様性の継承は可能か』、彩流社。
Gottlieb, N. (2005) *Language and Society in Japan*, Cambridge: Cambridge University Press.
Katsuragi, Takao (2011) "Prospects and prerequisites for a Japanese third-way language policy in Japan," in P. Heinrich & C. Gelan (eds.) *Language Life in Japan, Transformation and prospects*, New York: Routledge.
Kimura, Goro C. (2011) "Language rights in Japan: what are they good for?" in P. Heinrich & C. Gelan (eds.) *Language Life in Japan, Transformation and prospects*, New York: Routledge.
Maher, J. C. (2005) "Metroethnicity, language, and the principle of Cool," *International Journal of the Sociology of Language*, 175/176.

Abstract, Chap.1
Glocalization and Minority Language Revitalization

Takao Katsuragi (Gakushuin University)

What is the philosophical background of the revitalization of minority languages? Since the 1990s, the problem of minority language revitalization has been discussed in the field of sociology of language with specific emphasis on the idea of linguistic human rights, which goes hand in hand with a growing concern about international human rights as well as the development of European multilingualism.

In the Japanese context, in particular, there seems to be a strong feeling that sending a message that language is culture and the foundation of personal identity would be necessary for ordinary Japanese to recognize the urgency of the minority language crisis and the importance of minority language revitalization. And this feeling also seems to affect our theorizing about linguistic human rights.

However, as Kimura indicates, 'language rights could not yet overcome the indifference of the general public in Japan.' Moreover, the idea of language right has a dilemma within itself. Historically, it has emerged as a counter-ideology against nationalism or the ideology of 'nation-state,' that is, 'one nation, one national language.' As counter-ideology, it has promoted multilingualism and revitalization of regional minority languages. Meanwhile, as regional minority language closely connects to its own ethnicity and history, it sometimes shows exclusiveness against other minority languages. Thus, language rights and regional minority language revitalization, in spite of their origin beyond nationalism, have turned themselves into petit-nationalism by asserting their privilege against other minority languages and producing a new hierarchy among them.

Seeing public indifference and the dilemma concerning language rights, we need to reconsider the philosophical basis of minority language revitalization. In place of the essentialism of language rights, the relativistic idea of a language policy-framework with long-term perspective could be an approach to dealing with minority language revitalization problems more adequately. Policy-frameworks are not themselves policies to cope with concrete social problems in the short-term perspective. Rather, they show policy attitudes or directions in our society in the long-term perspective.

In the case of Europe, which is characterized by ethnic, historical and linguistic diversity with the development of European integration in the name of the EU, a language policy-framework is expressed as multilingualism. It is a long-term policy package involving the acceptance of English as a common language, the respect for the national languages of each countries and the revitalization of minority languages with non-essentialist rhetoric. It is also supported by the general consciousness of European people that Europe is multilingual society.

What about a Japanese language policy-framework? It is not multilingualism. The conception that Japan is multilingual society is hardly at all shared by the Japanese general public. But it is not the monolingualism of exclusive nationalism either. It is somewhere in between. In these days, it is called 多文化共生 tabunka-kyosei in Japanese. It literally means multicultural living-together, and is also closely related to the recent symbolism of 'Cool Japan.'

多文化共生 *tabunka-kyosei* or 'Cool Japan' is a syncretism of nationalism, globalization and localization. Japanese nationalism was formerly exclusive nationalism with the pseudo religious (monotheistic) underpinnings of national Shinto-ism. After World War 2, Japanese nationalism has become more liberal, especially among ordinary Japanese. However, it still bears some political connections with national Shinto-ism, which hinders the Japanese government from becoming more open-minded to religious and cultural diversity.

Secondly, globalization bears the key concept of global standard. The concept of global standard has two aspects. One is the idea of the global market which is symbolized by Americanization: with the so-called 'Washington Consensus'. It strongly asserts neo-liberalism and financial capitalism, but has been severely criticized because of its widening the gap between rich and poor. The other is the idea of universal human rights. This is expressed as constitutional democracy with the separation of three powers and rule of law, which is in itself universal value. However it is peculiarly connected to American constitutional republicanism which often produces friction with the nationalism of other countries: history, culture and ethnicity. In case of Japan, although Japan has consistently committed itself to globalization, there is ambivalence towards globalization as Americanization because of Japanese conceptions of equality and liberal nationalism.

Thirdly, in contrast to nationalism and globalization, localization is neither complete or universal. It shows diversity rather than uniformity. It functions as catalyst to make nationalism liberal and to transform globalization to moderate.

Thus, 多文化共生 *tabunka-kyosei* or 'Cool Japan' is a syncretism of liberal nationalism and moderate globalization with catalytic localization. It is newly termed as 'glocalization.' Interestingly enough, according to Wikipedia, the word 'glocalization' has been derived from Japanese business practices of 現地化 genchi-ka which means global localization.

Glocalization has its catchphrase 'think globally, act locally.' It also contains the idea, 'think nationally, act locally.' Thus, it asserts a competitive balance between global, national and local perspectives. Glocalization is a kind of passive norm with openness, toleration and elasticity, which is against ideology or fundamentalism of any kind.

Now, a Japanese language policy-framework, embodying 多文化共生 or glocalization, has two characteristics. First of all, it acknowledges that language is culture and the tool of communication as well. From this viewpoint, the 祭り *matsuri* or local, Japanese religious festivals through the year has a lot of linguistic features in local or minority languages. Thus, glocalization policy for the revitalization of 祭り or local religious festivals could lead to the revitalization of local or minority languages.

Secondly, 多文化共生 or glocalization contains the idea of open localization which means accepting globalization while setting up a safety net to rebuild local life, as well as securing safeguards to protect minimal conditions for community. The enactment of a safety net in glocalization language policy-framework means financial support by national government to promote entrepreneur activities for the revitalization of local life culture (and local or minority languages), as I referred above. The safeguard is the national protection of endangered local life cultures and minority languages through glocalization educational programs. It also entails global enlightenment activities by international agencies to build up a common understanding of the importance of protecting endangered minority cultures and languages.

There is affinity between glocalization and Japanese cultural life. As indicated, glocalization means the mediation of the global economy and local life world. Japanese cultural life is also characterized by the close connectedness of global economic activities and local religious consciousness. The essence of this connectedness is the Japanese idea of 御利益 *go-riyaku*. *Go-riyaku* has its religious phrase, '無病息災 *mubyousokusai* healthy life, 家内安全 *kanaianzen* family safety, 五穀豊穣 *gokokuhōjō* agricultural harvest, 商売繁盛 *shōbaihanjo* business prosperity.' It expresses a kind of economic interest but not the utilitarianism of Western economics. It is religious but shows a secular spirituality, not the divine spirituality of transcendent religion.

These days, the affinity between glocalization and Japanese cultural life has gained the another name of 'Cool Japan.' John Maher relates 'Cool Japan' with contemporary Japanese linguistic consciousness and describes it as 'metro-ethnicity and Cool.' He states, 'cool is a kind of post ethnicity state whereby both Japanese and ethnic minorities play with ethnicity (not necessarily their own) for aesthetic effect.' As Maher suggests, Japanese 多文化共生 *tabunka-kyosei* (multicultural living-together) is different from Western multiculturalism which contains a lot of episodes of cultural autonomies and ethnic conflicts. *Tabunka-kyosei* is aesthetic multiculturalism, rather than political multiculturalism.

We are not yet sure about how fast and extensive the Japanese cultural phenomena of 'metro-ethnicity and Cool' or *tabunka-kyosei* develops itself into policy-framework and produces public spirit of toleration which promotes new legislation for a *tabunka-kyosei* educational program. One thing certain is that 'metro-ethnicity and Cool' or *tabunka-kyosei* will enhance the cultural value of endangered minority languages in Japan.

第2章
多様性の承認と高等教育
多言語教育のもう一つの社会的役割

数土 直紀（学習院大学）

第1節　問題の所在

　本稿の目的は、社会関係資本の構成要素の一つである一般的信頼に注目することで、多言語・多文化教育の社会的な役割を明らかにしようとするところにある。もちろん、多言語・多文化教育のもっとも重要な役割は、私たちの世界における言語的・文化的多様性の生成・維持にあるだろう。そして、多くのマイノリティ言語が消滅の危機にさらされ、そうした言語とともに固有の文化が失われようとしているなか、そうした流れに抗して、"消滅の危機にさらされているマイノリティ言語を保全し、言語にともなう固有の文化を守る"ことの重要性はどれほど強調してもしすぎることはない。しかし、本稿で議論されることは、多言語・多文化教育のそうした直接的な効用についてではなく、多言語・多文化教育が可能にするもう一つの異なる効用を明らかにすることなのである。そしてそのためには、まず社会関係資本論における一般的信頼の議論（Putnam 2001; Putnam 1995; Putnam, Leonardi and Nanetti 1993; 稲葉 2007; 稲葉 2011）を思い起こさなければならない。

　R. パットナムによれば、「互酬制の規範」、「社会ネットワーク」、そして「一般的信頼」によって構成される社会関係資本は、その社会の福祉を充実させ、その社会の生産性を向上させ、そしてその社会のガバナンスを強化する。したがって、もし多言語・多文化教育にその社会の一般的信頼を高める効果を認めることができるならば、多言語・多文化教育はその社会の一般的信頼を強化することで、社会全体に対して大きな利益をもたらすことができ

る。実際に、多言語・多文化教育は"多様性の受け入れ"を基盤としており、いわばその成否に"多様性の受け入れ"を可能にする価値観の育成がある。そのような価値観を醸成することが一般的信頼の生成・強化につながるならば、多言語・多文化教育にその社会の一般的信頼を高める効果を期待することはあながち荒唐無稽なこととはいえないはずである。

　しかし一方で、多言語・多文化教育に力をいれることが、意図せざる結果として社会全体に対してさまざまな問題をもたらす可能性を否定することもできない。いくつかの先行研究は、言語的・文化的な多様性の増大が社会統合を難しくし、結果として一般的信頼を低下させてしまう可能性を指摘しているからである（Bjørnskov 2007; Coffé and Geys 2006; Hooghe 2007; Kesler and Bloemraad 2010; Stolle 1998）。もしそのような説明が成り立つのだとするならば、多言語・多文化教育は社会の多様性の増大を促すことで、社会全体にさまざまな不利益をもたらすことになりかねない。しかしこれは真実だといえるのだろうか。実際に多くの研究は、このような単純な説明に対して少なからず留保を与えている（Glanville and Paxton 2007; Gundelach 2014; Hooghe et al. 2009; Stolle 1998; Tsai, Laczko and Bjørnskov 2011）。

　つまり、多言語・多文化教育が一般的信頼に与える効果がどのようなものであるかを明らかにすることは、多言語・多文化教育に対するこうした誤った理解をただし、それがもっている社会的な意義を正しく伝えることに寄与する。これこそが、本稿が目的にしていることである。

　本稿では、多言語・多文化教育の一般的信頼に対する効果を正しく評価するためには、一般的信頼を二つに区別して考える必要があることを主張する。このように一般的信頼を二つに区別することで、多言語・多文化教育が一般的信頼のどの部分に対して効果をもち、そしてどの部分に対しては効果をもたないのか、そしてその効果をトータルで考えたときにはいったいどのようなことがいえるのか、議論をより精密に展開することが可能になるだろう。

　また本稿では、データの制約上から、多言語・多文化教育の効果を直接的に測ることは断念している。本稿では、高等教育と民主主義的な価値観との関係を明らかにすることで、間接的に多言語・多文化教育の効果を問題にす

ることになる。

　ここで、本稿が検証すべき仮説を明らかにしよう。ひとくちに他者を信頼するといっても、その信頼を導く価値観はひとによって異なる。"多様性を受け入れることを是とし、だからこそ価値観の異なる他者を積極的に受け入れるために、まず相手を信頼する"ことを選択するようなタイプの信頼を考えることができる。このような信頼を民主主義的な価値にもとづく信頼だと考えることにしよう。またそれとは別に、"伝統的な価値観が共有されていることに対する信頼があり、だからこそどのような他者も仲間として受け入れられる"と考えるようなタイプの信頼を考えることができるだろう。そして、この二つのタイプの信頼は、社会によってどちらのタイプが優勢なのかといった違いはあったとしても、一つの社会の内部に混在していると考えられる（Sudo 2014; Sudo 2015; 数土 2013b）。これをまとめると、次のようになる。

> **仮説1**　その社会の一般的信頼は、民主主義的な価値観にもとづく信頼と権威主義的な価値観にもとづく信頼の二種類の信頼によって構成されている。

　さらに、この二種類の信頼の生成・維持は、それぞれ異なる社会的なメカニズムによって可能になっていると考えられる。特に民主主義的な価値観にもとづく信頼に注目するならば、この民主主義的な価値観にもとづく信頼は、自律的な思考能力の育成を助ける高等教育によって強化・維持されると考えることができる。つまり、すでにある既存の価値観の伝承を目的とした初等・中等教育ではなく、柔軟な思考能力を育てることを目的とした高等教育は、多様性を受け入れる民主主義的な価値観にもとづいた一般的信頼を強化する効果をもつ（数土 2013a）。これをまとめると次のようになる。

> **仮説2**　高等教育は、民主主義的な価値観にもとづく信頼を強化することで、社会の一般的信頼を高める。

次節以降、本稿がここで立てた仮説が実証的な妥当性をもつのかどうか、そしてこの二つの仮説が成り立つとするならば、そこから多言語・多文化教育についてどのような含意を引き出すことができるのか、これらのことを順次検討することにしよう。

第2節　データと変数

第1項　データ

　ここでは、本稿で分析にもちいられる社会調査データについて説明することにしよう。本稿で分析にもちいられる社会調査データは、SSP-W 2012調査（2012年「格差と社会意識についてのWeb調査」）である（ウェブ調査実施部門 2012）。SSP-W 2012は、吉川徹（大阪大学）をリーダーとしたSSPプロジェクト（http://ssp.hus.osaka-u.ac.jp/）による社会調査の一つであり、実際の調査の実施は轟亮（金沢大学）がおこなった。SSP-W 2012はいわゆるWeb調査であるが、地域的な偏りをなくすためにまず全国から市区町村単位で250の地点を抽出し、抽出された地点ごとに年齢が25歳から59歳までの調査会社登録モニターに対して調査依頼をおこなっている。SSP-W 2012は2012年2月に実施され、目標数3,000に達した段階で調査を終了した。さらにその後、回収されたケースのうち、重要な属性項目に回答していないもの、あるいはDK回答率が高いものを除き、2,839を有効回収数としている。

　SSP-W 2012は登録モニターを対象としたWeb調査であるから、無作為抽出法をもちいて実施される全国調査とは異なっている。調査の実施にあたっては地点の割り当てをおこなうなどの工夫を施しているものの、母集団はあくまでも調査会社の登録モニターであるから、SSP-W 2012データにもとづいた分析結果によって日本社会全体の姿を直接的に語ることは難しいだろう。実際に、調査を実施した轟ら（轟 2015; 轟 and 歸山 2014）によっても、通常の全国調査と比較して高学歴者が多く含まれているなど、サンプルの構成に偏りがあることが確認されている。しかしそれと同時に、轟ら（轟 2015; 轟 and

帰山 2014)によれば、SSP-W 2012データによって示される変数間の関係・構造は同時期におこなわれた全国調査と比べてもよく似たものになっている。したがって、人びとの意見分布を明らかにすることを目標とするのではなく、変数間の背後にある構造の解明を目標にするのであれば、SSP-W 2012データを全国調査データの代わりにもちいることも十分に正当化されうるだろう。

第2項　分析戦略

　本稿でもちいられる分析手法は、構造方程式モデリング (SEM) である[1]。構造方程式モデリングは、多変量解析の一つであり、変数間の複雑な関係を明らかにしようとするときに有効となる分析手法である (Fox 2006)。本稿では、寛容と一般的信頼や、権威主義と一般的信頼といった意識変数間の関係を扱うためにこの構造方程式モデリングを利用することが好都合であるが、調査分析の専門家でないものにとっては手法の理解自体が容易ではないかもしれない。そこで本稿では、詳細な分析結果は付録で示すことにし、本文では得られた分析結果の要点のみを紹介することにする[2]。こうすることで、必ずしも分析手法について専門的な知識をもっていなくとも十分に内容が理解できるようになるはずである。

　本稿で検証すべき仮説の一つは、"その社会の一般的信頼が民主主義的な価値観にもとづく信頼と権威主義的な価値観にもとづく信頼の二種類の信頼によって構成されている"というものであった。したがって本稿では、SEMをもちいた分析によって、一般的信頼が民主主義的な価値観（多様性の承認）と権威主義的な価値観（権威ある人々への敬意）の二つの変数に影響されていることを確認する。また本稿で検証すべきもう一つの仮説は、"高等教育は、民主主義的な価値観にもとづく信頼を強化することで、社会の一般的信頼を高める"というものであった。そこで本稿では、やはりSEMをもちいた分析によって、高等教育が一般的信頼に影響を与える経路の、とくに民主主義的な価値観（多様性の承認）を介した経路の特定を試みる。さらに本稿では、一般的信頼の分析に加えて、社会のしくみに対する信頼の分析もおこなう。一般的信頼に加えて社会のしくみへの信頼を分析することで、民主主

義的な価値観にもとづく信頼と権威主義的な価値観にもとづく信頼との関係をよりよく解明することが期待できるからである。

第3項　変数

本稿の分析でもちいられる変数を説明しよう。

まず、一般的信頼に関する変数として取り上げたのは、「ほとんどの人は信頼できる」(以下、「信頼できる」)、「ほとんどの人は他人を信頼している」(以下、「信頼している」)、「たいていの人は、人から信頼された場合、同じようにその相手を信頼する」(以下、「信頼の相互性」)の3つの質問項目である。調査票では、回答者にこれらの質問項目を「1．そう思う　2．ややそう思う　3．あまりそう思わない　4．そう思わない」の4段階で評定させている。そこで、そう思う＝4点、ややそう思う＝3点、あまりそう思わない＝2点、そう思わない＝1点と直して、分析にもちいた。つぎに、社会のしくみへの信頼に関する変数として取り上げたのは、「中央官庁」、「地方自治体」、「政府」、「裁判所」の4つの質問項目である。調査票では、まず「次にあげる1〜7について、あなたはどのくらい信頼していますか。」と尋ねたうえで[3]、回答者にそれぞれの質問項目について「1．とても信頼している　2．少しは信頼している　3．あまり信頼していない　4．まったく信頼していない」の4段階で評定させている。やはりこれも、とても信頼している＝4点、少しは信頼している＝3点、あまり信頼していない＝2点、まったく信頼していない＝1点と直して、分析にもちいた。

次に、一般的信頼および社会のしくみへの信頼を説明する変数として取り上げたのは、以下の2つの質問項目である。まず、「違った考え方を持った人がたくさんいるほうが、社会にとって望ましい」(以下、「寛容」)である。この変数は、民主主義的な価値観を表明する質問項目だと解して、分析に利用した。次に、「権威のある人々にはつねに敬意をはらわなければならない」(以下、「権威主義」)である。この変数は、権威主義的な価値観を表明する質問項目だと解して分析に利用した。これらの質問項目は、いずれも「あなたはつぎのような意見についてそう思いますか、それともそうは思いませんか。あ

てはまるものをお答えください。」と尋ねたうえで、回答者にそれぞれの質問項目について「1．そう思う　2．ややそう思う　3．どちらともいえない　4．あまりそう思わない　5．そう思わない」の5段階で評定させている。そこで、そう思う＝5点、ややそう思う＝4点、どちらともいえない＝3点、あまりそう思わない＝2点、そう思わない＝1点と直して、分析にもちいた。民主主義的な価値観についても、権威主義的な価値観についても、1つの質問項目のみで測定している点は、分析の問題点として指摘できるかもしれない。これは、分析にもちいたデータによる制約である。

　そのほか回答者の基本属性として、「学歴」、「性別」、「年齢」を変数として分析にもちいた。「学歴」については、選択肢を「中学校」から「大学院博士課程」までの11カテゴリーを用意し、それらの中からあてはまるものを選択させている。11カテゴリーすべてを区別して分析をおこなうと煩雑になるので、本稿ではいわゆる高等教育として「大卒以上」であるかいなかに注目した。回答者の学歴が大卒以上であるならば「大卒」とし、それ以外の学歴と区別している。「性別」と「年齢」については、特に操作せず、そのまま分析にもちいている。

第4項　変数の特徴

　分析にもちいられる変数の記述統計を確認する。表1は、分析にもちいられる変数の平均・標準偏差・最小値・最大値を示したものである。

　一般的信頼に関する3つの変数についてみてみると、「信頼できる」、「信頼している」の2つは平均が2.5を下回っており、ややネガティブな方に評価が寄っていることがわかる。それに対して、「信頼の相互性」は平均が2.5を上回っているので、この変数についてはポジティブな方に評価が寄っていることがわかる。また、社会への信頼に関する4つの変数をみてみると、「裁判所」を除く3つの変数の平均が2.5を下回っている。その下回り方は、一般的信頼に関する変数よりも大きく、人びとの「中央官庁」、「地方自治体」、「政府」に対する信頼は、人びとの周囲の人に対する信頼よりもかなり低い。したがって、社会のしくみに対する信頼は、身の回りの人びとに対する信頼

表1　変数の記述統計

変数名	平均	標準偏差	最小値	最大値
一般的信頼				
信頼できる	2.26	0.77	1	4
信頼してる	2.20	0.75	1	4
信頼の相互性	2.77	0.76	1	4
社会への信頼				
中央官庁	1.89	0.71	1	4
地方自治体	2.18	0.71	1	4
政府	1.66	0.70	1	4
裁判所	2.54	0.76	1	4
寛容	3.63	0.82	1	5
権威主義	2.53	0.97	1	5
年齢	42.43	10.02	25	59
性別（女性＝1）	0.50		0	1
学歴（大卒＝1）	0.47		0	1

よりも低いことが、調査回答者の信頼の特徴だといってよいだろう。

　次に、寛容と権威主義をみてみよう。寛容については平均が3.0を上回っており、少なくとも回答者についていえば多様性を承認しようとする傾向が比較的強いといえるかもしれない。それに対して、権威主義については平均が3.0を下回っており、反権威主義的な傾向がやや強いといえるだろう。SSP-W 2012データは高学歴者を多く含むデータとなっているので、高学歴者を多く含んでいることがこうした傾向を生んでいる可能性がある。実際に、年齢と性別については大きな偏りはみられないが、学歴については0.47となっており（つまり、大卒以上が47%となっており）、きわめて高い数値となっている。ちなみに、文部科学省がおこなっている学校基本調査（文部科学省 2015）によれば大学進学率がはじめて50%を超えたのは2009年度のことであり、1970年代から1980年代にかけて大学進学率は20%台で安定していた。したがって、SSP-W 2012データは、厳密に無作為抽出をおこなった全国調査のデータと比べると、高学歴者をより多く含むデータになっているといえ

る。

第3節　分析結果

　それでは、寛容と一般的信頼の関係がどうなっているのか、そして権威主義と一般的信頼の関係がどうなっているのか、構造方程式モデリングをもちいた分析の結果を確認することにしよう。

　まず図1を確認してほしい。この図は、分析の結果を簡潔にまとめたものである（分析の詳細な結果については、章末表を参照のこと）。四角で囲まれたテキスト（「年齢」、「大卒」、「女性」、「寛容」、「権威主義」、「信頼できる」、「信頼している」、「信頼の相互性」）は、分析にもちいたSSP-W 2012データの変数を意味している。一方、丸で囲まれているテキスト（「一般的信頼」）は、実際にはSSP-W 2012データには含まれていない変数だが、隠れた変数としてその存在を仮定した変数である。またテキストとテキストを結んでいる矢印は、変数間の関係を示している。たとえば、寛容から一般的信頼にむけて実線の矢印が引かれており、矢印に「＋」の符号が付されているが、これは寛容と信頼にはポジティブな関係があり、寛容が高まることで一般的信頼が高まることを意味している。逆に、もし矢印が点線で、かつ「－」の符号が付されていれば、寛容と信頼にはネガティブな関係があり、寛容が高まることで一般的信頼が低くなることを意味することになるだろう。また、大卒と女性の間には「－」の符号が付された点線が引かれているが、これは大卒であることと女性であることの間に負の相関関係が存在することを意味している。つまり、大卒には女性が少ない（いいかえれば、女性には大卒が少ない）ということである。逆に、もし矢印が実線で、かつ「＋」の符号が付されていれば、今度は大卒であることと女性であることの間に正の相関関係が存在することになる。その時は、大卒に女性が多い（いいかえれば、女性に大卒が多い）ということになる。ちなみに図1で示されている変数および変数間の関係は、分析した

図1

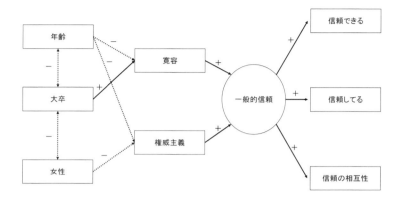

データとの適合度がきわめて高かった。したがって、隠れた変数として「一般的信頼」を想定することも、矢印によって示されている変数間の関係を想定することも、統計的にみて十分に妥当といえる。

　図1からまずわかることは、寛容が一般的信頼に対してポジティブな影響を与えていることと同時に、権威主義も一般的信頼に対してポジティブな影響を与えていることである。ちなみに、寛容と権威主義との間には何も矢印が引かれていないので、この二つの変数は互いに関係はない。このとき、寛容と権威主義がそれぞれ独立にもっている一般的信頼へのポジティブな影響は、"一般的信頼は、民主主義的な価値観にもとづく信頼と権威主義的な価値観をもつ信頼の、二つの信頼によって構成されている"という本稿の仮説の正しさを示唆するものといえる。つまり、多様な考え方をみとめる寛容さによって引き上げられる一般的信頼は民主主義的な価値観にもとづく信頼に相当しており、その一方で権威ある人への敬意を求める権威主義によって引き上げられる一般的信頼は権威主義的な価値観にもとづく信頼に相当しているといえる。

　では、人びとの属性（年齢、性別、学歴）が、寛容と権威主義に対してどの

ような影響を与えているかをみてみよう。年齢をみると、寛容と権威主義のそれぞれに対して「−」の符号が付された点線が引かれている。これは、年齢が高くなるにつれ、多様な意見を受け入れることに抵抗を示すようになり、その一方で権威主義的な態度は弱まっていくことを意味している。次に性別をみると、女性から権威主義に向けて「−」の符号が付された点線が引かれている。これは、女性の方が男性と比べて権威主義的態度が弱いことを意味している。最後に学歴をみると、大卒から寛容にむけて「＋」の符号が付された実線が引かれている。これは、高等教育を受けた者の方がそうでない者と比べて多様な意見を受け入れようとする傾向があり、寛容であることを示している。一方、大卒から権威主義にむけて何も線が引かれていないので、高等教育を受けていることと権威主義的な態度との間には関連はない。先行研究では高等教育と権威主義との間にネガティブな関係があることが指摘されてきたので（吉川 1998; 吉川 and 轟 1996）、これに先行研究と反する結果といえる。先行研究と一致しない傾向が現れた理由として、高等教育の大衆化、あるいは社会状況の変化などが考えられるが、いずれにしても注意すべき結果といえる。

　以上のことをまとめると、高等教育と寛容が一般的信頼の育成にどのような影響を及ぼしているのかがわかる。

　高等教育を受けるということが、必ずしも直接的に一般的信頼を高めるわけではない。図1をみると、「大卒」と「一般的信頼」との間に矢印が存在しないからである。しかし、「大卒」と「一般的信頼」との間に「寛容」をおくと、「大卒」と「一般的信頼」とが二つの矢印によって結びつけられていることがわかる。つまり、高等教育を受けることで多様な意見を受け入れるという寛容さが強められ、そして今度は寛容さが強められることで民主主義的な価値観にもとづく信頼が高まっていく。その結果、高等教育を受けた者は、そうでない者と比較してより強い一般的信頼をもつことになる。このことを図にしてまとめると、図2のようになるだろう。

　ちなみに、ひとくちに一般的信頼といっても、そこには民主主義的な価値観にもとづくものと権威主義的な価値観にもとづくものとがあった。高等教

図2

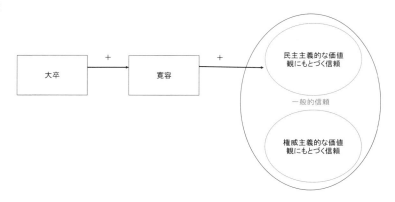

育が寛容さを介して一般的信頼を強化するというときの信頼は、とうぜん権威主義的な価値観にもとづく信頼ではなく、民主主義的な価値観にもとづく信頼なのである。

 次に、今度は寛容と社会への信頼との関係がどうなっているのか、そして権威主義と社会への信頼との関係がどうなっているのか、やはり構造方程式モデリングをもちいた分析の結果を確認することにしよう。

 今度は図3を確認してほしい。この図は、社会への信頼について分析の結果を簡潔にまとめたものである（分析の詳細な結果については、章末表を参照のこと）。図3のみかたは、図1のときと同じである。図1のときは隠れた変数として「一般的信頼」を想定していたが、図3では隠れた変数として「社会への信頼」を想定している。人びとの間に「社会に対する信頼」があり、そのような「社会への信頼」があって「中央官庁」「地方自治体」「政府」および「裁判所」に対する信頼が高められていると考えている。詳しい説明は省くけれども、図1のときと同様に、図3で示されているモデルもSSP-W 2012データとの適合度が高く、十分に現実を反映したものとして受け入れることができる。

 図3からわかることは、社会に対する信頼の規定構造と、一般的信頼（人

図3

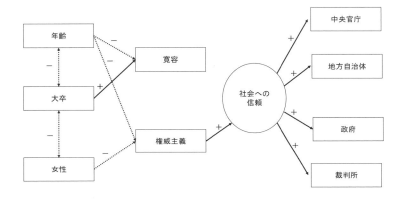

に対する信頼）の規定構造が大きく異なっていることである。これは、"その社会を生きている人びとを信頼できる"ということと"その社会のしくみを信頼できる"ということの間に大きな距離が存在するということである。実際に、社会への信頼（「中央官庁」、「地方自治体」、「政府」）をみると回答が信頼できない方に大きく寄っていた。つまり、私たちは身の回りの人びとを信じるほどには「中央官庁」、「地方自治体」、「政府」を信頼していない。そして、"人びとによって、身の回りの人びとに対するほどには、社会のしくみが信頼されていない"理由は、私たちの社会のしくみの特徴にあったと分析結果から推測できる。

　図3をみると、「権威主義」から「社会への信頼」に向けて「＋」の符号が付された実線の矢印が引かれているけれども、「寛容」から「社会への信頼」に向けては何も矢印が引かれていない。これは、権威主義的な態度が強まれば社会への信頼が高まる一方で、多様な意見を尊重する寛容な態度が強まっても、そのことでは社会への信頼は変化しないということである。つまり、私たちの社会のしくみは、権威主義的な価値観にもとづく信頼によって支えられており、民主主義的な価値観にもとづく信頼によっては支えられていない。民主主義的な価値観をもつ人びとに十分に支持されていないがため

に（いいかえれば、私たちの社会のしくみが十分に民主的でないために）、社会のしくみは人びとから十分な信頼をえることができないのである。

そして、「寛容」が「社会への信頼」に対して統計的にみて意味のある影響をもっていないために、高等教育も「社会への信頼」に対して影響をもつことができない。一般的信頼の場合には、高等教育は「寛容」を介して「一般的信頼」に影響を与えることができた。しかし、社会への信頼の場合には、いくら高等教育によって寛容さを高められても、私たちの社会のしくみがそうした寛容さに支えられていないために、「社会への信頼」に何かよい影響を与えることができないのである。ここで注意しなければいけないことは、だからといって教育が重要な役割を果たしえないわけではないことである。問題は、私たちの社会のしくみが民主主義的な価値観に支えられているのではなく、権威主義的な価値観に支えられていることにあった。もし社会のしくみを民主主義的な価値観に支えられるものにかえていくことができるならば、そのとき高等教育は人びとの間に民主主義的な価値観をもたらすことで、社会への信頼を高めることにも寄与できるはずなのである。

社会における多様性の増大について、先行研究では異なる見解が示されてきたことを冒頭において確認した。"多様性の増大は人びとの一般的信頼を低下させ、そして社会統合を難しくする"という主張がある一方で、"多様性の増大によってむしろ一般的信頼は強まり、より民主的な社会に向かっていく"とする主張もあった。おそらくこの二つの立場は、社会のしくみを支えている信頼のタイプの違いに注目することで両立させることができる。

社会への信頼が権威主義的な価値観にもとづく信頼に支えられている場合には、多様性の増大は人びとの間に利害の葛藤を生み、一般的信頼を低下させ、社会統合を難しくするだろう。この場合には、前者の立場が妥当することになる。しかし、もし社会への信頼が民主主義的な価値観にもとづく信頼に支えられていれば、多様性の増大はその社会の寛容さを高めることにつながり、さらに一般的信頼を強化し、そして社会統合を強めるはずだ。この場合には、後者の立場が妥当することになる。そして、このプロセスを実現するためには、高等教育が重要な役割を担うことになる。

第4節　考察

　ここまでのSSP-W 2012データをもちいた分析によって、本稿がたてた二つの仮説がいずれも支持されることを確認することができた。仮説の一つは一般的信頼の構成にかかわるものであり、もう一つは一般的信頼と高等教育との関係にかかわるものであった。

　社会関係資本論は、社会関係資本の構成要素として一般的信頼を重視してきた。しかし、ひとくちに一般的信頼といっても、その一般的信頼がどのような価値観を背景にして成立しているのかに注意する必要がある。本稿では、一般的信頼が民主主義的な価値観にもとづく信頼と権威主義的な価値観にもとづく信頼とによって構成されていることを仮定し、そして社会調査データをもちいた分析によってもその仮定が支持されることを明らかにした。

　このとき、特に注目したいことは、本稿で一般的信頼を構成する民主主義的な価値観として取り上げた変数が「違った考え方を持った人がたくさんいるほうが、社会にとって望ましい」といった多様性の承認にかかわるものであったことであり、いわば異なる意見・立場への寛容に民主主義的な価値観の根拠を求めていたことである。なぜなら、この点に危機言語の復興とそのためのネットワーキングの探求をテーマとする本書に対して本稿がなしうる貢献の中心があると考えられるからである。

　危機言語の復興・保全をめぐる本書の背後には、基本的な価値観として"文化的・言語的多様性の積極的な承認"がなければならない。とうぜん、そうした価値観は、すでにそれ自身が目標であり、そしてそれ自身にすでに価値があるといえるだろう。しかし、本稿で主張したいことは、それに加えて"民主主義的な価値観の一つである文化的・言語的多様性の積極的な承認は、その社会の人びとに対する信頼を強化することになる"ということであった。つまり、"多様性の承認"は、その社会の一般的信頼を、そして一般的信頼に構成されるところの社会関係資本を強化することで、社会全体の生産性を向上させもするということである。

　"多様性を受け入れるという寛容が、その社会の一般的信頼を強化する"

という関係は、一般的信頼を民主主義的な価値観にもとづく信頼と権威主義的な価値観にもとづく信頼とに区分することでみえてきた関係である。たとえば、その社会の一般的信頼が民主主義的な価値観ではなく主に権威主義的な価値観にもとづいている場合には、多様性の承認が一般的信頼を強化するという関係はみえにくいものになるはずである。むしろ、権威主義的な社会では、"多様性の承認"を求める意識・態度はその社会の支配的な価値観と相容れない可能性が高く、価値観の葛藤によってかえって一般的信頼を低下させてしまうこともあるからである（Sudo 2014; Sudo 2015）。しかし、かりにそのようなケースがありうるにしても、そのことは"多様性の承認"それ自身が人びとの一般的信頼を毀損させたり、あるいは社会統合に対してネガティブに作用したりすることを意味するわけではない。もしそのようなことが起きたとするならば、それはその社会の一般的信頼のタイプが民主主義的な価値観にもとづくものではなく、権威主義的な価値にもとづくものであったことを意味するのである。

　このように一般的信頼を民主主義的な価値観にもとづく信頼と権威主義的な価値観にもとづく信頼とに区別して考えることで、私たちは一般的信頼に及ぼす高等教育の影響を積極的に評価できるようになる。

　本稿では、"高等教育は、そのひとの寛容（多様性の承認）を高めることで、人びとへの信頼を強化する"という仮説をたて、この仮説がデータの分析結果と矛盾しないことを確認した。通常、一般的信頼には民主主義的な価値観と権威主義的な価値観の双方が入り混じっているため、高等教育と一般的信頼の直接的な関係は弱いものとしてしか観察されず、そのため高等教育が一般的信頼に対して積極的な影響を与えていると主張することが難しくなる。しかし、一般的信頼を民主主義的な価値観にもとづくものと権威主義的な価値観にもとづくものとにしっかり区別し、高等教育と民主主義的な価値観にもとづく信頼との関係に焦点をあてれば、確かに高等教育と一般的信頼との間に強い関係をみいだすことが可能になる。本稿が明らかにしたのは、このことである。つまり、高等教育は人びとの間に文化的・言語的多様性の承認を導くような寛容的な意識・態度をもたらすことができ、そしてそれは一般

的信頼を強化するという形で社会全体にさらなる利益をもたらしうる。もちろん、ここで注意しなければいけないことは、本稿の分析ではデータの制約から"実際にどのような内容の高等教育を受けたのか"までは問題にできていないことである。けっきょくのところ、ここでいう高等教育は、大学まで進学したかいなかということであり、その意味できわめて粗い基準でしかない。ただそれでもなお強調しなければならないことは、高等教育一般に人びとの寛容的な意識・態度を醸成する効果があるということである。とうぜん、教育内容まで考慮することができれば、たとえばその教育に多言語的・多文化的な要因が含まれているかどうかを分析に加えることができれば、観察された高等教育のポジティブな効果はより強いものになりこそすれ、弱いものになることはないはずである。

　もちろん、多言語教育あるいは多文化教育の直接の目的が、その社会の信頼の強化にあったり、あるいは生産性の向上におかれたりすることはないだろう。そこで直接的に目標とされることは、とうぜん文化的・言語的多様性の生成・維持であり、そこから外れるものではない。多くのマイノリティ言語が消滅の危機にさらされ、そうした言語とともに固有の文化が失われようとしているなか、そうした流れに抗して、"消滅の危機にさらされているマイノリティ言語を保全し、言語にともなう固有の文化を守る"ことの意義が忘れられてはならない。しかしだからといって、多言語・多文化教育の社会的な効用として信頼の強化や生産性の向上を挙げること自体に問題があるとは思われない。多言語・多文化教育は人びとの民主主義的な価値観によって支えられるはずだが、そのような教育を通じて今度は新しい世代の民主主義的な価値観を育成・強化することになる。いわば、それは、多言語・多文化教育のもう一つの社会的役割だといってよい。

　一般的信頼を高めるといっても、高められる信頼は権威主義的な価値観にもとづく信頼ではなく、民主主義的な価値観にもとづく信頼である。多言語・多文化教育が普及するためには異なる文化や価値観を受け入れることを可能にする民主主義的な価値観（多様性の承認）が必要となるが、逆にそのような教育が普及することで多様性を承認する民主主義的な態度を人びとの間

に呼び起こすことが可能になる。いわば、多言語・多文化教育と民主主義的な価値観は、互いが互いに影響を及ぼしあう相互的な関係にあるといっていいだろう。教育という世代と世代をつなぐ営みは、多様性の承認に支えられる信頼と信頼にもとづいた社会の成長を同時に可能にする。多様性を受け入れることは、社会に何か犠牲を強いることではない。それは、私たちの社会を強い信頼に支えられたよりよい社会へ変えていくための原動力となる。

謝辞　「2012年格差と社会意識についてのWeb調査」データは、SSPプロジェクト（http://ssp.hus.osaka-u.ac.jp/）の許可を得て使用しています。

註

1　ちなみに、分析にあたってもちいた統計ソフトウェアは、Rのsemパッケージである。
2　分析手法について関心のないものは本文だけを読めばよく、分析手法に関心があり、分析結果の詳細を知りたりものは、さらに付録をみればよい。
3　ちなみに、7つの質問項目のうち取り上げなかった3項目は、「国会議員」、「都道府県議会議員」、「市区町村議会議員」である。これらは、社会のしくみへの信頼であるよりは、むしろ"議員"という人への信頼に相当すると考えたからである。

参考文献

Bjørnskov, Christian (2007) "Determinants of generalized trust: A cross-country comparison." *Public Choice* 130(1-2):1-21.
Coffé, Hilde, and Benny Geys (2006) "Community Heterogeneity: A Burden for the Creation of Social Capital?" *Social Science Quarterly* 87(5):1053-72.
Fox, John (2006) "Teacher's Corner: structural equation modeling with the sem package in R." *Structural Equation Modeling* 13(3):465-86.
Glanville, Jennifer L, and Pamela Paxton (2007) "How do we learn to trust? A confirmatory tetrad analysis of the sources of generalized trust." *Social Psychology Quarterly* 70(3):230-42.
Gundelach, Birte (2014) "In diversity we trust: the positive effect of ethnic diversity on outgroup trust." *Political Behavior* 36(1):125-42.
Hooghe, Marc (2007) "Social capital and diversity generalized trust, social cohesion and regimes of diversity." *Canadian Journal of Political Science* 40(03):709-32.
Hooghe, Marc, Tim Reeskens, Dietlind Stolle, and Ann Trappers (2009) "Ethnic diversity and generalized trust in Europe A cross-national multilevel study." *Comparative Political Studies* 42(2):198-223.

Kesler, Christel, and Irene Bloemraad (2010) "Does immigration erode social capital? The conditional effects of immigration-generated diversity on trust, membership, and participation across 19 countries, 1981–2000." *Canadian Journal of Political Science* 43(02):319-47.

Putnam, R.D. (2001) *Bowling Alone*: Simon & Schuster.

Putnam, Robert D. (1995) "Bowling alone: America's declining social capital." *Journal of Democracy* 6(1):65-78.

Putnam, Robert D., Robert Leonardi, and Raffaella Y. Nanetti (1993) *Making Democracy Work : Civic traditions in modern Italy*: Princeton University Press.

Stolle, Dietlind (1998) "Bowling together, bowling alone: The development of generalized trust in voluntary associations." *Political Psychology*:497-525.

Sudo, Naoki (2014) "The Complicated Relationship between Generalized Trust and Democracy." in *XVIII International Sociological Association World Congress of Sociology*. Yokohama.

— (2015) "Social Networks of Trust Based on Social Values." in *The 8 th International Network of Analytical Sociologists Conference*. Cambridge, MA.

Tsai, Ming-Chang, Leslie Laczko, and Christian Bjørnskov (2011) "Social diversity, institutions and trust: A cross-national analysis." *Social Indicators Research* 101(3):305-22.

ウェブ調査実施部門 SSPプロジェクト（2012）『SSP-W2012 コード・ブックおよび基礎集計表』SSPプロジェクトウェブ調査実施部門。

稲葉 陽二（2007）『ソーシャル・キャピタル：「信頼の絆」で解く現代経済・社会の諸課題』、生産性出版。

――――（2011）『ソーシャル・キャピタル入門：孤立から絆へ』、中央公論新社。

吉川 徹（1998）『階層・教育と社会意識の形成：社会意識論の磁界』、ミネルヴァ書房。

吉川 徹and轟 亮（1996）「学校教育と戦後日本の社会意識の民主化」教育社会学研究 58:87-101。

轟 亮（2015）「SSP-W調査について」『社会意識からみた日本：階層意識の新次元』、数土直紀（編）、有斐閣、pp. 109-12。

轟 亮and歸山 亜紀（2014）「予備調査としてのインターネット調査の可能性：変数間の関連に注目して」社会と調査（12):46-61。

数土 直紀（2013a）「一般的信頼と高等教育の重層的関係 2005年SSM調査データをもちいた分析から」、第86回日本社会学会大会、日本社会学会。

――――（2013b）『信頼にいたらない世界：権威主義から公正へ』、勁草書房。

文部科学省（2015）『学校基本調査』、文部科学省。

表A-1　人に対する信頼の規定構造

総数 2,645

			Estimate	S.E.	z value	Pr(>|z|)
Structural						
一般的信頼	<---	寛容	0.113	0.017	6.801	0.000
一般的信頼	<---	権威主義	0.091	0.014	6.411	0.000
寛容	<---	年齢	-0.006	0.002	-3.552	0.000
権威主義	<---	年齢	-0.010	0.002	-5.459	0.000
権威主義	<---	女性	-0.116	0.037	-3.105	0.002
寛容	<---	大卒	0.211	0.032	6.608	0.000
Mesurement						
信頼できる	<---	一般的信頼	1.000		(constrained)	
信頼している	<---	一般的信頼	0.943	0.030	31.059	0.000
信頼の相互性	<---	一般的信頼	0.607	0.024	24.873	0.000
Covariance						
女性	<-->	大卒	-0.067	0.005	-13.382	0.000
年齢	<-->	大卒	-0.540	0.095	-5.679	0.000
Variance						
信頼している	<-->	信頼している	0.155	0.013	12.052	0.000
信頼できる	<-->	信頼できる	0.173	0.012	14.669	0.000
信頼の相互性	<-->	信頼の相互性	0.420	0.012	33.706	0.000
一般的信頼	<-->	一般的信頼	0.416	0.019	21.759	0.000
寛容	<-->	寛容	0.666	0.018	36.359	0.000
権威主義	<-->	権威主義	0.929	0.026	36.359	0.000
年齢	<-->	年齢	101.577	2.794	36.359	0.000
女性	<-->	女性	0.250	0.007	36.359	0.000
大卒	<-->	大卒	0.250	0.007	36.389	0.000

AGFI = 0.971
RMSEA = 0.054
CFI = 0.958

表A-2　社会に対する信頼の規定構造

総数 2,528

			Estimate	S.E.	z value	Pr(>|z|)
Structural						
社会への信頼	<---	権威主義	0.154	0.014	10.963	0.000
寛容	<---	年齢	-0.006	0.002	-3.863	0.000
権威主義	<---	年齢	-0.011	0.002	-5.796	0.000
権威主義	<---	女性	-0.120	0.038	-3.111	0.002
寛容	<---	大卒	0.193	0.033	5.895	0.000
Mesurement						
中央官庁	<---	社会への信頼	1.000		(constrained)	
地方自治体	<---	社会への信頼	0.777	0.020	38.396	0.000
政府	<---	社会への信頼	0.793	0.020	39.920	0.000
裁判所	<---	社会への信頼	0.584	0.023	25.425	0.000
Covariance						
女性	<-->	大卒	-0.066	0.005	-12.834	0.000
年齢	<-->	大卒	-0.536	0.096	-5.576	0.000
地方自治体	<-->	裁判所	0.078	0.008	10.130	0.000
Variance						
中央官庁	<-->	中央官庁	0.065	0.008	8.102	0.000
地方自治体	<-->	地方自治体	0.238	0.008	28.646	0.000
政府	<-->	政府	0.213	0.008	27.327	0.000
裁判所	<-->	裁判所	0.432	0.013	33.717	0.000
社会への信頼	<-->	社会への信頼	0.424	0.016	27.107	0.000
寛容	<-->	寛容	0.674	0.019	35.546	0.000
権威主義	<-->	権威主義	0.931	0.026	35.546	0.000
年齢	<-->	年齢	98.850	2.781	35.546	0.000
女性	<-->	女性	0.249	0.007	35.546	0.000
大卒	<-->	大卒	0.251	0.007	35.574	0.000

AGFI = 0.981
RMSEA = 0.040
CFI = 0.980

Abstract, Chap.2

Higher Education and Tolerance of Social Diversity: The Social Role of Multicultural and Multilingual Education

Naoki Sudo (Gakushuin University)

This essay aims to clarify the social role of multicultural and multilingual education by examining studies on 'generalized trust.' Generalized trust is one component of social capital in society. Generating and preserving cultural and linguistic diversity is the primary role of multilingual education. With the impact of globalization, the importance of preserving minority cultures and minority languages cannot be overstated; globalization has threatened the viability of many cultures and languages across the globe. This essay, however, discusses another potential role that multicultural and multilingual education may play that is separate from the generation and preservation of cultural and linguistic diversity. This role is related to the concept of generalized trust in studies on social capital.

According to Putnam's theory of social capital, social capital consists of reciprocity norms, social networks, and generalized trust. Social capital in society can contribute to improving social welfare and strengthening governance. In other words, when multicultural and multilingual education contributes to strengthening generalized trust among people in society, all of society reaps substantial benefits as a result of rising levels of generalized trust among people.

On the other hand, it cannot be denied that multicultural and multilingual education may unintentionally give rise to social problems. Some studies on the relationship between social trust and social diversity have pointed out that an increase in ethnic diversity can hinder social integration and reduce levels of generalized trust in a society. If this is true, the promotion of multicultural and multilingual education, by reducing levels of generalized trust among people, may induce detrimental social effects. However, is this notion actually true? Although certain studies have shown that social diversity negatively affects social integration, other studies have insisted the opposite—that social diversity positively affects social integration.

Thus, clarifying the effects of multicultural and multilingual education on generalized trust among people can rectify misunderstandings and elucidate what is positive about multicultural and multilingual education. This is the aim of this essay.

In this essay, in order to properly evaluate the effects of multicultural and multilingual education on generalized trust, I argue that two types of generalized trust among people must be distinguished: the authoritative and democratic types of generalized trust. To ensure correct assessment, the effects of multicultural and multilingual education were investigated in regard to these two distinct types of generalized trust.

Unfortunately, I was not able to assess the effects of multicultural and multilingual education on generalized trust because of data limitations. As an alternative, I indirectly assessed the effects of multicultural and multilingual education on generalized trust by clarifying the relationship between generalized trust based on democratic values and higher education. Higher education can be considered inclusive of education for social diversity; in this analysis, I examine higher education as a substitutive variable for multicultural and multilingual education by using data from one social survey.

This paper has several hypotheses. As aforementioned, the two types of generalized trust differ in terms of basic values. I assumed that tolerance of diversity is premised on social trust among people with different values, as the recognition of others is based on trust. This type of trust can be considered generalized trust based on democratic values. I also assumed that the acceptance of social norms is premised on social trust among people within a society (or a community), because social norms are not obeyed in the absence of trust. This type of trust can be regarded as generalized trust based on authoritative values. In addition, I assumed that these two types of generalized trust can coexist within a society. In other words, some people may exhibit generalized trust based on democratic values while others may at the same time exhibit generalized trust based on authoritative values. From these assumptions, the following hypothesis was derived.

Hypothesis 1: Generalized trust in society comprises two types of generalized trust; generalized trust based on democratic values and generalized trust based on authoritative values.

In addition, I assume that each type of generalized trust is generated and maintained by different social mechanisms. In particular, I assume that generalized trust based on democratic values is generated and strengthened by higher education, because higher education improves people's ability to think autonomously. In other words, people learn the basic norms in primary and secondary education that enable them to coexist with others in a society; through higher education, people acquire social intelligence to think through problems more flexibly. Moreover, we can say that this intelligence enables people to accept others with different values. From these assumptions, the following hypothesis was derived.

Hypothesis 2: Higher education increases levels of generalized trust among people in a society by strengthening generalized trust based on democratic values.

I tested my hypotheses by using data from SSP-W 2012 (a web survey on stratification and social psychology in 2012, N=2,839), as this data manifest numerous variables related to social trust. By using structural equation modeling (SEM), I analyzed the relation between social values, social trust and education. Results of the analyses indicated that generalized trust in society can be categorized into two types; democratic and authoritative. Furthermore, the results show that higher education has a positive effect on generalized trust based on democratic values, but no effect on generalized trust based on authoritative values. Thus, my hypotheses in regard to the two types of generalized trust were empirically supported.

Tolerance of social diversity can strengthen generalized trust in a society. This fact is only evident when generalized trust based on authoritative values and generalized trust based on democratic values are distinguished. Conceptualizing generalized trust in a society as based on authoritative rather than democratic values would make it difficult to observe whether there was a positive relationships between generalized trust and social diversity. Tolerance of social diversity may contradict dominant values in strongly authoritative societies; conflicts due to differences in social values can reduce the level of generalized trust in such societies. However, even in such cases, it is not tolerance of social diversity itself that negatively affects generalized trust among people and social integration. The reason why social diversity reduces the level of generalized trust in a strongly authoritative society must be found in the interaction with authoritative values. When social values are democratic rather than authoritative, the negative effect of social diversity disappears and a positive relationship between generalized trust and social diversity can be ascertained.

Thus, by distinguishing the two types of generalized trust into two types—authoritative and democratic—the positive role of social diversity can be determined and the effects of higher education on generalized trust in a society can be assessed. Ordinarily, in societies where authoritative values coexist with democratic values, higher education may not exert positive effects on generalized trust as in such societies, higher education and generalized trust do not have a strong relationship. In analyzing such societies, distinguishing generalized trust based on democratic values from generalized trust based on authoritative values and focusing on relationships between higher education and generalized trust based on democratic values can enable observation of strong relationships between higher education and generalized trust. Higher education facilitates tolerance of social diversity among people; in turn, tolerance of social diversity facilitates a high level of generalized trust based on democratic values throughout entire societies. Because of data limitations, I was unable to add variables related to the content of higher education in my analysis. However, when higher education curricula include multicultural and multilingual components, higher education can be observed to exert stronger and more positive effects on generalized trust based on democratic values.

Although the direct aim of multicultural and multilingual education is to sustain cultural and linguistic diversity, it may be said that the strengthening of generalized trust based on democratic values among people and the improvement of social productivity are its positive byproduct. Many minority languages and unique cultures are in danger of disappearing and we cannot overemphasize the significance of preserving them. However, it must also not be overlooked that preserving minority languages and unique cultures may cultivate tolerance of social diversity, which in turn can strengthen generalized trust based on democratic values. Multicultural and multilingual education, supported by democratic values in society, fosters democratic values among new generations by facilitating tolerance of social diversity. This role—separate from the preservation of linguistic and cultural diversity—is another role played by multicultural and multilingual education.

第3章
消滅危機言語コミュニティから日本の言語教育政策を観る
宮古島の経験から

藤田ラウンド 幸世（立教大学）

第1節　はじめに

　言語教育政策は、往々にして政策を決定する側の言語教育のニーズやその言説に左右されるものである。言語教育に対するニーズ、また、その言説とは、言い換えれば、国家の新たな「未来像（vision）」、経済状況の変動、日本の「教育危機」の語り、過去に後ろ髪を引かれるかのような忠誠心などの、Williams（1977）のいう「急ごしらえのイデオロギーの寄せ集め」だともいうことができる（Fujita-Round & Maher 2008）。

　日本の言語政策に関わる中で、現実とかけ離れた想像の共同体として浮かび上がる二つの目印がはっきりとしている。一つは「日本語」が国家の言語（国語）となっていること、もう一つは「英語」が国際化[1]を担う優れた媒体となっていることである。これらを支えるものとは、日本が驚くべき「単一言語」で「単一文化」の国であるとするモダニストたちの比喩である。事実は、もちろん、そうではない。日本から、また、日本への移民の存在、地理的な再編成（北海道や琉球）による文化の行き来、日本のアジアにおける植民地時代の経験などにより、日本には何世紀にもわたり、多言語、多文化が共存している（Gottlieb 2012; Maher and Yashiro 1995; Maher and Macdonald 1995; Sugimoto 2003; 山本 2000）。

　本稿では、今後の日本の言語教育政策を考える上で、言語の多様性、および、20世紀の「言語」をめぐる歴史を振り返る試みを行いたい。

第2節　ミクロの視点から読み解く

第1項　宮古島の中学生から投げかけられた問い

　筆者は2012年から沖縄県宮古島市でフィールドワークを行っている。きっかけは、共同研究者の善元幸夫[2]が、2010年から年に一度、宮古島市の一つの小学校で国際理解教育の枠組みで行っていた教育実践であった。そこでの善元の教育実践の隠れたシラバスは、宮古島の子どもたちが自分たちの島を誇りに思うために、島の外からみた島の歴史や「いいところ」をいかに子どもたちに認識してもらい、自尊感情、つまり、島の文化を前向きに内面化することで自信を持つようになってもらいたいというものであった[3]。

　善元の授業を受けて4年目の約40人の中学1年生のインタビュー中で、一人の男子生徒が筆者の突っ込みに、とっさに答えた発言があった。このインタビューでは、毎年1回の特別授業を行う教師としての「善元先生」について、また、授業の内容、感想、振り返りを生徒たちに直接聞いていた。

　「あのぉ、宮古の歴史は教科書とかにも全然出てこないし、ほとんど日本のことで、沖縄の話は全然出てこないから、沖縄の歴史はわからなかったから、(特別授業で)先生に教えてもらってよかった」

　　　　　　　　　　　　　　　　　　　　　（注：括弧は筆者の補足）

　ここでは中学一年生の自らのことばで、宮古島と沖縄、日本の三者間の関係性が明確に言語化されている。

第2項　国の歴史、地域の歴史

　この中学生の意味する教科書とは学校教育法に則った社会科の国定教科書のことである。国家としての「日本」が中心に書かれ、義務教育の学習内容として、日本の歴史が主となっているだろう。教科書で学ぶ内容は、学力を量るための評価が伴うことから、全国共通の内容となる。片や、この中学生の現実、日々の生活をしている自分たちの生活に密着したローカルな歴史や

文化については、総合学習や地域学習などで現場の先生方の裁量に任されている。

つまり、中心は日本の歴史で、自分たちの生まれ育った島の歴史は学校では「正式に」学ばないということを無意識のうちにこの生徒はわかっている。自分の地元（ローカル）の宮古島の歴史は、「国」で決められているメインの教科書には書かれていない、13歳の認識である。

東京から来た「善元先生」が特別授業として自分たちに宮古島の詳しい歴史について教えてくれなければ、学校という「正式」な場で自分たちのローカルな歴史を学ばなかったかもしれないという疑問、もしくは、本土の東京からきた先生から自分たちの、地元の歴史を習うという違和感があったのかもしれない。しかし、なぜ、自分たちにとって一番身近な「歴史」を「学校」で学ぶことができないのか。

第3項　祖父母世代のことば、「みゃーくふつ（宮古語）」

宮古島は、沖縄本島からさらに南に300km先の先島諸島（さきしま）にある。飛行機では沖縄本島から宮古島までは40分ほどである。詳しくみると、宮古島といっても、宮古島群島は、宮古島、池間島、大神島、来間島、伊良部島、下地島、そして多良間島と水納島の8つの島からなるのだが、2005年に、宮古島から下地島までの6つの島が合併され、宮古島市となった。2015年11月現在の宮古島市の人口は54,472人である。その中で、インタビューを行った地域は、宮古島市全体では約2パーセントにもみたない1,000人前後の集落である。この集落に通ううちに、子どもたちの祖父母世代が「みゃーくふつ[4]（宮古語）」を第一言語としていたことがわかった。また、宮古語が孫の世代には継承されていない事実もだんだんとわかってきた。

宮古島に生まれ育つのに、学校では地域のことばを使わずに、「日本語」で教育を受け、どのように日本語だけで生活をすることになってしまったのか、どうして日本語と宮古語のバイリンガルが可能ではないのだろうか、という問いが筆者の中で立ち上がる。

次節では、宮古島を一端、離れて、世界に広がる言語の多様性に目を向け

る。

第3節　マクロの視点から捉える言語の多様性

第1項　世界の現用語

　Crystal（1987）は、言語と方言との境界をどこに置くかを決めることが実際に難しいことから、言語学者によってはそれぞれ言語数の数え方が異なり、3,000から10,000の幅で言語の全体数を捉えるのが無難だろうと説明する[5]。Lewis, Simons and Fenning（2015）「エスノローグ（Ethnologue）」[6]によると、地球上の言語話者は7,106,865,254人、現用語は7,102言語とある。次の図1でその内訳を示そう。

　まず、エスノローグでは、世界の国々を大陸や地域として大きく5つ、アジア、アフリカ大陸、南太平洋、南北アメリカ大陸、ヨーロッパに分けている。それぞれの現用語は、アジア地域は2,301言語（32%）、アフリカ地域は2,138言語（30%）、南太平洋地域は1,313言語（19%）、南北アメリカ地域は1,064言語（15%）、ヨーロッパ地域は286言語（4%）と構成されているという。ヨーロッパは、地図上、ロシア連邦を含み、広範囲の面積を占めるように見えるものの、それぞれの国が公用語や標準語を定めているため現用語は全体の4%にしか満たない。ここでは「面積の広さ」と言語数とは結びつかない。それに対して、アジアやアフリカには、国家による統一された言語はあったとしても、それ以上に、いまだに少数言語や少数民族、先住民族といったコミュニティごとの言語が現存しているということをこの数値は示している。同時に、アジアとアフリカを合わせると全体の62%となることから、地球上の言語の半分以上が地理的にアジアとアフリカに、つまり、言語の多様性がそうした地域に現存しているといえよう。

第2項　話しことばとしての言語

　実際には「言語」といっても、主に地域共同体や家庭における機能に限定

図1 世界の現用語

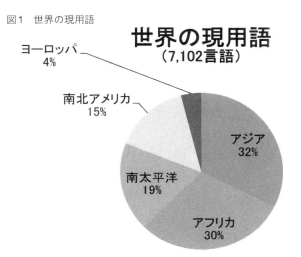

Source: Ethnologue, the 18th edition. http://www.ethnologue.com/world

されている言語が大半であることもここでは留意しておかねばならない。世界の言語における話者の中央値は五、六千人に過ぎず、言語の85パーセント近くは10万人以下の話者しか持たないといわれている[7]。その点、日本語は話者数が1億8千万人で2015年には世界の話者数の推計上では9番目に話者が多い言語[8]であると位置づけられている。

　また、必ずしもすべての言語が、日本語のように「話しことば」と「書きことば」の両方を持つわけではないことに着眼することがここでは必要である。書きことばがない言語も存在するということだ。オング (1991) は、世界の言語の中ではむしろ書きことばのない言語の方が多く、言語とは基本的に声に依存するものだという。オングは、1980年代に実際に話されているおよそ3千の言語のうち、文学をもっている言語はわずか78であると指摘する[9]。言い換えれば、言語は「話される」ことの方が圧倒的に多く、先に挙げた世界の言語は3,000から10,000だと推計されるという場合も、その大半は話しことばとして機能する言語のことを指すといってもいいだろう。

第3項　言語と生物の多様性

　ネトルとロメイン（2001）の挙げる言語密度という概念も言語に対する新たな視点を提供してくれる。ネトルが1998年にまとめた言語密度の推計では、1マイル平方あたりの言語数を指標としたところ、世界地図上の比較的わずかな地域内に高密度帯域があることがわかった。高密度の地域は、ほぼ熱帯地域に集中している。逆に、赤道から南北の両極に移動をするにつれて言語密度は低くなる[10]。つまり、先に挙げた言語の多くが、地図上の熱帯諸国で話されている可能性が高い。また、熱帯に言語話者が多く住むとすれば、ヒトが自給自足をしやすい環境のある場所に、コミュニティを作り、生活をし、そこで「言語」が使われることのほうが世界で多数なのではないかと推測される。

　さらに、言語密度という点で、もう一点挙げておくと、世界の言語の密度の高い言語帯域は、アフリカと東南アジアから太平洋に加えて、ブラジル、中米、オーストラリアの国々にかかり、これらの地域は言語の密度が高いだけではなく、世界の動植物の種が非常に多く生息する熱帯林のある場所でもあるという点である。この森林地域は、世界の言語と同様に、全地球の50から90パーセントに当たる動植物の生息地である。言語の多様性が、話者のヒトを介して、動植物の多様性と結びつく。さらに、ネトルとロメイン（2001）が主張するのは、この言語と生物の相関関係は偶然ではなく、共通の成因を持つと同時に、共通の脅威に直面しているということである[11]。

　地球上の言語の多様性を考えるときには、熱帯地域に位置するアジアやアフリカは言語密度が高く、一方で、温帯から北に位置するヨーロッパは言語密度が低いということが際立つところである。

第4項　消滅危機言語とは

　ここで日本の言語の多様性に戻ろう。エスノローグ（Lewis, Simons and Fenning 2015）は、日本国内で使われている現用語として、日本語、アイヌ語、韓国・朝鮮語、日本手話、喜界語、北奄美大島語、南奄美大島語、徳之島語、沖永良部語、与論語、国頭語、中央沖縄語、宮古語、八重山語、与那国

語、合わせて15言語を挙げる。この中には、沖縄県の11言語、琉球諸語[12]が含まれている。

一方、ユネスコ（2003）は、消滅危機言語のガイドラインを2003年に作成し、その後、2009年に世界の消滅危機言語地図（UNESO Endangered Languages Atlas）をインターネット上で公開した[13]。それによると、日本国内では、8つの消滅危機言語があるという。次の図2は、ユネスコの地図の「日本」に関わる部分である。

北から、アイヌ語、八丈語、奄美語、国頭語、沖縄語、宮

図2　ユネスコ消滅危機言語地図上の日本

引用元：ユネスコ消滅危機言語地図
（UNESO Endangered Languages Atlas）

古語、八重山語、与那国語であり、これらは北海道、東京都、沖縄県で話されている。しかし、2050年にはこれらの言語が消滅する危機にあるといわれている[14]。ユネスコの判断度合いの基準は、以下の6段階である。第一段階の「安全」、第二段階の「脆弱」、第三段階の「危険」、第四段階の「重大な危機」、第五段階の「極めて深刻」、第六段階の「消滅」である。図2に挙げられた8言語は、それぞれ、アイヌ語が第五段階の「極めて深刻」、八重山語と与那国語が第四段階の「重大な危機」、そして八丈語・奄美語・沖縄語・国頭語・宮古語が第三段階の「危険」とある[15]。

図2の地図上で、再度、確認すると、北から南に点在している8言語は、日本の首都（中央）からみると周縁地域で話されている言語である。日本語は、国内で話者数が最も多い「社会言語」であり、「標準語」である。それに対して、消滅危機言語の8言語すべてが、日本の地図の上で、中央に対す

る「周縁」という位置関係に置かれている意味は何か。重要な点は、この8言語が話されている場所は、置かれた位置が、日本の国の境界でもあるという点であろう[16]。

第4節　近代化された「日本語」

　マーハ（1994）によると、日本語は「縄文（紀元前8000-300年）、弥生（紀元前300-紀元300年）、古墳（300-7世紀）の各時代には、南方や大陸から比較的連続的に人々が移住することによる、さまざまなアルタイ系やマラヤ・ポリネシアン言語が混合を重ねた結果、もたらされたもの」だという[17]。また、7世紀以降の読み書きの能力として、当時の国際共通語である中国語や漢語を学び、当時の学者たちは、サンスクリット語から中国語に翻訳された仏教関連、医学、哲学の本を勉強しており、加えて、日本語においては話しことばと書きことばの差が大きく、大正時代に新しく作られた口語体である「文学用口語体」を用いた小説が現れるまで狭まることはなかったと指摘する[18]。つまり、21世紀現在の私たちが使っている日本語が成り立つのは、明治時代からの近代化を経てということがわかる。

第1項　日本の「標準語」とは

　1868年の明治維新を日本の近代化の起点とすると、日本が国家政策として採用した言語教育政策、つまり、「東京」の山の手ことばを基盤とした「標準語」を採用したことが、まず初めに挙げられるだろう（Carroll 2001）。この日本の言語教育政策では、中央集権化のアプローチが採られ（Gottlieb 2005）、知識階層の政策立案者たちは、ヨーロッパの帝国主義と同様の言語と国家主義を調合した方式をとり、これを台湾や朝鮮に同化政策として実施したことが知られている（Heinrich 2012; イ 1996）。「標準語」は、こうして言語教育政策を通して、「国語」としての役割を担うことになった。日本の近代化の初期に、日本語を「標準語」とし、「国語」と位置づけた言語教育政策は、国

家の建立と植民地化の歴史に密接につながっている[19]。

　上田万年は1895年に「標準語」について、「標準語に就きて」と題された講演の中で「一日も早く東京語を標準語とし、此言語を厳格なる意味にていふ国語とし、これが文法を作り、これが普通辞書を編み、広く全国到る処の小学校にて使用せしめ、之を以て同時に読み・書き・話し・聞き・する際の唯一機関たらしめよ」[20]と述べている。東京語の山の手ことばを基準とした標準語をあらゆる言語活動の唯一の道具にしようとしたのである。ここでイ・ヨンスクは、「国民」は標準語形成の過程にはまったく参加できず、受動的立場に置かれたままであったとも指摘する。このように、明治期の言語教育政策を概観した時に、国家側の政策として「標準語」が制定され、「国語」という形になるプロセスを辿ることができる。

　モーリス＝鈴木（2014）は、徳川時代のアイヌ同化政策にも日本語を教える試みもあるとしながら、明治時代の日本語の国家語としての制度化が同化の中心的要素となり、日本中の多様な地域方言も含め、既存の日本文化の地域的な多様性の多くを統合したと指摘する[21]。明治時代に「標準語（東京語）」は、教育現場で、日本国内の言語や方言（アイヌ語と琉球諸語、また日本各地の方言）を「標準語としての日本語」に同化させようとする役目を担った。ここで、「標準語化」された日本語の教育である「国語」は、植民地化のために朝鮮半島と台湾をターゲットとしていたばかりか、国民教育を通して国内の言語の統一も意図していたといえる。

第2項　「標準語」での教育：アイヌと琉球

　アイヌの地は1869年に「北海道」という新たな行政単位に組み込まれ、琉球王国（当時は「琉球藩」）は1879年に沖縄県になった[22]。

　モーリス＝鈴木（2014）によると、18世紀の半ばにアイヌの領土は幕府の直轄下に置かれ、その当時の政府は、「アイヌに『野蛮な』肉食の習慣を放棄し、髪を切って、日本風の髪型にし、農業を採用し、日本語を学び、〈和人に変化〉するよう奨励する必要性に言及していた」という。当時、徳川社会では、社会の中では髪型の違いが明確な身分標識であったため、社会秩序

を守るために、アイヌや琉球の人々に対しては、言語よりもむしろ、その髪型、装身具、アイヌの女性たちの刺青が問題だとされた。しかし、1890年代後半に「旧習を保存する」政策から同化主義教育へと劇的に変化を遂げることになる[23]。

例えば、樺太の「土人学校」[24]の場合は、明治時代に入ってからの学校令が発布された1886年以降には、日本の尋常小学校の場合は就学期間が6年間であったものが4年間の教育のみで、その教育の中では正座や礼などの公式の日本人の行儀作法を習得させるための訓練もあった。日本語の教育は「土人学校」のもっとも基本的な機能のひとつであると考えられ、唱歌、暗唱、その他の直接的な手法が生徒に国家語を流暢に話せるようにさせる手段として推奨されたという。

一方、1872年に始まる琉球処分により、琉球は日本の近代国家の中に組み込まれ、日本政府による同化政策が推し進められた。教育の中では方言札を利用した「標準語励行運動」が推進された。沖縄における教育の目的は、日本人としての自覚を促すため、標準語の励行と天皇への忠誠心を育てることが強調された。1889年「大日本帝国憲法」発布と共に、天皇・皇后の御真影が全国の学校に下付され、翌1890年に「教育勅語」も発布された。1937年の日華事変以降は皇民化教育、標準語励行が強化された。地方語である「方言」は、皇民化教育には不要とされ、方言撲滅のため、「方言札」が作られたという[25]。『宮古島市史』には、方言札の大きさは、縦20センチ、横10センチ、板もしくは紙に紐をつけてとあり、方言を使用した生徒の首に架けられたわけである。この時の「子ども」たちは、現在、すでに80歳代、90歳代の、先に挙げた中学生の祖父母世代になる。

第3項　20世紀の近代化の問い直し

言語話者から、地理から、歴史から観るのか、その観点により「言語」という概念はさまざまな意味合いを持つことになる。

イ・ヨンスク（2009）が「ことばを通してひとびとや世界と交感するという喜ばしい現実が一方にあり、ことばを通じて差別や抑制が行われるという

残酷な現実が他方にある」(p.10)というように、特定の「言語」が「標準語」になる一方で、標準とされない「言語」は方言として下位に置かれ、またそれだけではなく、同化を迫られることもある。これは世界各地で起きていることだが、日本の場合は、近代化において日本語が「標準語」そして「国語」となることでそうした体験をしたのである。

徳川幕府の終わり頃には、「日本語」という単一言語の環境だけではなかったということは明白であり、明治時代からの20世紀の近代化の中で「日本語」も近代化されたわけである。言語の力関係やイデオロギーについては、特に言語教育政策の歴史として、21世紀に向けた言語教育政策を考える上で、まだまだ丁寧に問い直す必要があるのではないだろうか。

第5節　言語の多様性に関わる21世紀への課題

21世紀現在、グローバリゼーションという国境を越えた概念が日本社会を揺り動かしている。桂木 (2009) は、グローバリゼーションとは、本来、経済のグローバル化だけではなく、多様な生活の豊かさの実現を目指すべきものだという[26]。このグローバリゼーションを解き明かすことは、近代世界の抱え込む課題をも明らかにする作業であるがゆえに[27]、国民国家が作られてきたプロセス、近代化が引き起こした事象、つまり、21世紀の課題の前に、20世紀からの近代化に関わる課題を、それぞれの国がそれぞれの文脈で丁寧に明らかにする必要があるとも考えられている[28]。

経済上の効率が求められ、学歴や技術が就職のパスポートとなる場合、言語の「書きことば」が重視される。しかし、ヒトが生きるという営みに目を向けた場合、生まれ育つ中で身につける「話しことば」はそのヒト（話者）のルーツであり、アイデンティティともなる。先にみたように、消滅危機言語とみなされる言語が、文字通り消えるとなれば、「言語」という言語体系（システム）ばかりか、その「言語」の使用に付随している、言語話者たちの築いてきた生活の営み、或いは固有の文化としての「言語」も消滅すること

になる。すると、そうした言語話者にかかわる個人のルーツやアイデンティティはどうなるだろう。

　宮古島に舞台を戻すと、フィールドワークで、80歳代の祖父母世代に「標準語」導入時の「子ども」としての経験を話してもらうことがある[29]。こちらが尋ねてもその口は重い。それがどのような意味を持つのかを無言で伝えている。何よりも「教育」を通して、学校で、ルーツに関わる母語を標準語に置き換えられた政策が行われたことが個人の心の「痛み」として残っているといえる。また、家族の中で、孫と祖父母が言い合いになるときに、祖父母は宮古語になってしまうので、孫は理解できず、世代間の言語の意思疎通ができない時があると中学生の親世代の人から聞いた。ここには、まだ声になっていないミクロレベルでの歴史が個々人の胸の中に深く眠ったままに存在している。ネトルとロメイン（2001）は言語が危機に陥るのは「家庭で両親や世話をする人々によって、言語が自然なかたちで子どもたちに伝達されない場合である」というが、ここで問題となるのは、なぜ子どもたちに伝達しないかである。そこには多くの複雑な要因が絡み合っている。

　ローカルな場では、様々な形で宮古島のことばや文化への再評価、保存や拡張が試みられている。地元の島の人たちが自分たちの手で「方言大会」をはじめとする行事も継続して主体的に行っている。2015年度の夏に宮古島市の毎年恒例の「方言大会」[30]を聞きに行った時には、フランス語母語話者で、宮古語の研究を志す若い大学院生が優勝をした。ユネスコの2003年度の勧告を契機に、琉球大学や京都大学をはじめ、研究者や学生たちが現在は琉球諸語の研究を行い、その成果が形になりつつある過程にあるのかもしれない[31]。しかし、学校に通う子どもたちに「みゃーくふつ」を伝えるとしたら、それだけでは十分ではないだろう。

　言語教育という場合、日本では外国語教育や英語教育の教授法や実践に役に立つという言説で語られる場合が多い。しかし、久保田（2015）が「日本における言語教育は、地域や世界で広がり続けている民族的・言語的多様性に十分目を向けていない」[32]というように、また、ニュージーランドの研究者のMay（2014）が「多言語への転換（multilingual turn）」[33]を言語教育に関わ

る学問領域である第二言語習得、TESOL、バイリンガル教育の分野に要請し、多言語の背景を持つ「話者」に目を向ける必要性を強調するように、日本の言語教育政策においても、新たな視点が必要である。例えば、「文化言語背景の異なる地球市民が民主的に共存していくことの大切さ」(久保田 2015, p.20-21) を教育現場で教えるとすれば、世界の言語の多様性として、日本国内にも多様な言語があり、宮古語もその一つであると「教科書」で読むことが可能になるかもしれない。地球市民として、宮古島、そして、宮古語をルーツに持つ「自分」が、沖縄本島や本土の「他者」と対等にコミュニケーションがとれる、それも日本の言語教育政策の、21世紀のリテラシーともいえる技能の目標となりうるのではないだろうか。教育現場での「多言語への転換」も一つの道となる。

　加えて、言語の多様性というときには、そこでは言語が同等に並列しているわけではないという理解も必要となる。日本の言語政策から近代化を読み解くときに、「国際語」と位置付けた英語や「標準語」あるいは「国語」と位置付けた日本語の言語教育政策はいわば表の顔である中央政府の政策である。本稿のはじめに述べたように、日本では近代化の言語をめぐる政策のアイコンとして、「国際語」や「標準語」といった社会的価値、あるいは社会の言説をそれぞれ英語と日本語という特定の言語に付したわけである。しかし、その一方で、そうしたアイコンの影響下で日本国内には21世紀に「消滅危機」言語と位置付けられるようになった第三の「言語」も浮上した。拡げればみゃーくふつだけに限らず、21世紀現在の、実際に生活を営み、文化的実践として使っている言語、また、そうしたコミュニティや家族内での言語実践をミクロなまなざしから観て、マクロの文脈を捉え直す。そうした「ことば」に対する複眼的な視点（まなざし）を持つことが今後の言語教育政策やその実践における課題となろう。

註
1　本稿では国際化に関わる批判については論じることができなかった。詳しくは、Fujita-Round & Maher (2008), p.393, 402-403、または、藤田ラウンド (2013), p. 153-156を参照。

2 　善元幸夫は1970年代に中国残留孤児の家族として来日した中国をルーツに持つ子どもたちに日本語教育を教えて以来、外国出身の子どもに第二言語としての日本語を公立小学校で教えてきた、少ない小学校教諭のベテラン教員であった。
3 　善元の実践および宮古島でのフィールドワークは藤田ラウンド（2015）の研究ノートに詳しい。
4 　「みゃーくふつ」は宮古語で「宮古語」の意味であるが、以後、本稿では宮古語とする。
5 　Crystal (1987), p.284参照。
6 　Lewis, Simons and Fenning (2015) *Ethnologue*, the 18th edition. http://www.ethnologue.com/world (accessed 30/12/2015). エスノローグは、アメリカ合衆国に本拠地を置くSIL（The Summer Institute of Linguistics）という、海外派遣を実施している最大のプロテスタント伝道団体の刊行物の名称である。現在はインターネット上でも、データベースを公開している。各地に派遣した伝道者から言語の情報を集め、詳細に記録を集めていることから、その数と記録の精緻さで言語学者に信頼を得ている。この団体のもともとの目的は世界の諸民族のために聖書を提供することであった。ネトル＆ロメイン（2001）, p.10を参照。
7 　ネトルとロメイン（2001）, p.47を参照。
8 　Lewis, Simons and Fenning (2015) *Ethnologue*, the 18th edition. http://www.ethnologue.com/world (accessed 30/12/2015).
9 　オング（1991）は、Edmonson (1971, pp, 323,332)を援用している。オングが区別をした、声の文化（orality）と文字の文化（literacy）の詳細については著書を参照。
10 　地図と言語密度の詳細はネトルとロメイン（2001）, p.48-49を参照。
11 　ネトルとロメイン（2001）, p.50を参照。
12 　琉球諸語とは、琉球にある言語の数々という意味で用いる。これまで言語学上では琉球語は日本語と音声や文法のカテゴリーが対照をなし、同じ日本国内であることから日本語の下位の「琉球方言」として位置づけられてきた。近年では、琉球の島々のことばの扱いとして、それぞれ固有の言語の集まりとみなし、「琉球諸語」として見直しが行われている。実際に日本語と琉球諸語のそれぞれは相互理解ができないほど異なっていることも、見直しの一因となった。Shibatani & Kageyama (2015)、田窪（2013）に詳細がある。
13 　ユネスコの消滅危機言語地図についてはブレツィンガー（2014）, p.78-82を参照。
14 　Moseley (2010)は、6,000の現存する言語のうち、21世紀末までにはその半分の3,000になると予測している。今世紀で3000近くの言語が消滅に瀕しているという推測である。詳しくはUNESCO Publishing Online version: http://www.unesco.org/culture/en/endangeredlanguages/atlas (accessed 30/12/2015)。
15 　ユネスコによる危険度の基準は、以下のユネスコのドキュメントに記述されている。本稿では筆者がこれを訳出している。http://unesdoc.unesco.org/images/0018/001836/183699E.pdf (accessed20/5/2016)
16 　モーリス＝鈴木（2000）を参照。
17 　マーハ（1994）, p.38を参照。
18 　マーハ（1994）, p.39を参照。
19 　これらの研究蓄積についてはFujita-Round & Maher (2008)で文献紹介をしている。
20 　イ・ヨンスク（1996）, p.137を参照。

21　モーリス＝鈴木 (2014), p.35を参照。
22　モーリス＝鈴木 (2014), p.29を参照。補足として加えれば、第一次の琉球処分が1872年、さらに1879年の第二次の琉球処分ともいわれる廃藩置県のときに、沖縄藩から本格的に沖縄県として日本に再編入された。
23　モーリス＝鈴木 (2014), p.24-25, 33を参照。
24　北海道では、アイヌの和人学校への統合は1920年から1930年代にかけて行われ、「土人学校」は閉鎖されていった。この「土人」ということばは1997年に「旧土人保護法 (1999年成立)」が「アイヌ文化振興法」にとって代わられるまで、しかし、存在していた。詳しくは、モーリス＝鈴木 (2000), p.147-150を参照。
25　宮古島市教育委員会 (2012), p.292-293を参照。
26　桂木 (2009), p. 23を参照。
27　伊豫谷 (2007), p.19を参照。
28　20世紀を振り返るということでは、西川ら (2000) では多言語・多文化主義を問い直すという議論を多面的に行っており、本稿はこの議論に触発される形で生まれた。
29　宮古島のフィールドワークのノーツの断片、また景色の写真、動画を研究用のウェブサイトで公開している。http://multilingually.jp/category/asia_jp/okinawa_jp (accessed 20/5/2016)
30　ここでは「方言大会」がすでにこのイベントの呼称となっている。
31　例えば、報告書類としては木部 (2013) らのチームが勢力的に講演録も含め記録化している。また、英語で出版された P. Heinrich, S. Miyama & M. Shimoji (2015)、日本語では、ハインリッヒ、松尾 (2010)、田窪 (2013)、下地、ハインリッヒ (2014) などがある。
32　久保田 (2015), p.21を参照。
33　May (2014), p.1-2を参照。

参考文献

Carroll, T. (2001) *Language Planning and Language Change in Japan*, Curzon Press.

Crystal, D. (1987) *The Cambridge Encyclopedia of Language*, Cambridge University Press.

Fujita-Round, S. & Maher, J. C. (2008) 'Language Education Policy in Japan' in S, May & N, Hornberger (eds.) *Encyclopedia of Language and Education (2nd edition)*, Volume 1, Springer.

Gottlieb, N. (2005) *Language and Society in Japan*, Cambridge University Press.

Gottlieb, N. (2012) *Language Policy in Japan*, Cambridge University Press.

Heinrich, P. (2012) *The Making of Monolingual Japan*, Multilingual Matters.

Lewis, M. Paul, Gary F. Simons, and Charles D. Fennig (eds.) (2015) *Ethnologue: Languages of the World, Eighteenth edition*, Dallas, Texas: SIL International. Online version: http://www.ethnologue.com.

Maher, J.C. & Macdonald, S. (eds.) (1995) *Diversity in Japanese Culture and Language*, Keagan Paul International.

Maher, J.C. & Yashiro, K. (eds.) (1995) *Multlingual Japan*, Multilingual Matters.

May, S. (2014) 'Disciplinary divides, knowledge construction'in S. May (ed.) *The Multilingual Turn*, Routledge.

Moseley, Christopher (ed.) (2010) *Atlas of the World's Languages in Danger, 3rd edition*, Paris, UNESCO Publishing. Online version: http://www.unesco.org/culture/en/endangeredlanguages/atlas

Shibatani, M. and Kageyama, T. (2015) 'Introduction to the Handbook of Japanese Language and Linguistics,' in P. Heinrich, S. Miyama & M. Shimoji (eds.) *Handbook of the Ryukyuand Languages: History, Structure, and Use*, De Gruyter Mouton.

Sugimoto, Y. (2003) *An Introduction to Japanese Society*, Cambridge University Press.

Williams, R. (1977) *Marxism and Literature*, Oxford University Press.

マティアス・ブレンツィンガー（訳　新垣友子）（2014）「日本の琉球諸語と韓国の濟州語の国際標準に向けて」下地理則、パトリック・ハインリッヒ編著『琉球諸語の保持を目指して』ココ出版。

藤田 ラウンド 幸世（2015）「学校教育の中で言語継承への気づきを育てる――沖縄県宮古島市での自尊感情につなげる教育実践」『教育研究』(57)、国際基督教大学教育研究所。

藤田 ラウンド 幸世（2013）「国際結婚家族で母語を身につけるバイリンガル――社会言語学と言語発達の視点から捉える」、加賀美 常美代編著『多文化共生論』、明石書店。

パトリック・ハインリッヒ、松尾慎編著（2010）『東アジアにおける言語復興』、三元社。

伊豫谷 登士翁（2007）『移動から場所を問う』、有信堂高文社。

桂木 隆夫（2009）「言語政策の第三の道」、田中 慎也・木村 哲也・宮崎 里司（編著）『移民時代の言語教育』、ココ出版。

木部 暢子（編）（2012）『消滅危機方言の調査・保存のための総合的研究　南琉球宮古方言調査報告書』、国立国語研究所。

久保田 竜子（2015）『グローバル化社会と言語教育』、くろしお出版。

イ・ヨンスク（1996）『「国語」という思想』、岩波書店。

イ・ヨンスク（2009）『「ことば」という幻影』、明石書店。

ジョン・マーハ（1994）「消えゆく言語――環境言語に向けて」、『新しい日本観・世界観に向かって――日本における言語と文化の多様性』、国際書院。

宮島 喬・鈴木 江里子（2014）『外国人労働者受け入れを問う』岩波ブックレット916、岩波書店。

宮古島市史編纂委員会（2012）『宮古島市史　第一巻　通史編　みやこの歴史』、宮古島市教育委員会。

テッサ・モーリス＝鈴木（2000）『辺境から眺める』、みすず書房。

テッサ・モーリス＝鈴木（2014）『日本を再発明する』、以文社。

ダニエル・ネトル、スザンヌ・ロメイン（2001）『消えゆく言語たち』、新曜社。

西川 長夫（2000）「序　多言語・多文化主義をアジアから問う」、西川 長夫・姜 尚中・西 成彦編著『20世紀をいかに越えるか』、平凡社。

オング、W. J.（1991）『声の文化と文字の文化』、藤原書店。

下地 理則、パトリック・ハインリッヒ編著（2014）『琉球諸語の保持を目指して』、ココ出版。

田窪 行則（2013）『琉球列島の言語と文化――その記録と継承』、くろしお出版。

山本 雅代編著（2000）『日本のバイリンガル教育』、明石書店。
〈参考資料ＵＲＬ〉
エスノローグ
　　　　https://www.ethnologue.com/world (accessed 30/12/2015)

Atlas of the World's Languages in Danger, 3rd edn. Paris, UNESCO Publishing. Online version:
　　　　http://www.unesco.org/culture/en/endangeredlanguages/atlas (accessed 30/12/2015)

ユネスコ消滅危機言語アトラス
　　　　http://www.unesco.org/new/en/culture/themes/endangered-languages/ (accessed 20/5/2016)

宮古島　伝承の旅
　　　　http://miyako.ryukyu (accessed 30/9/2016)

Abstract, Chap.3

Japanese Language Education Policy from the point of view of an Endangered Language Community: the Miyako Island experience

Sachiyo Fujita-Round (Rikkyo University)

The formation of language education policy is normally guided by a combination of needs and needs-discourse: a new 'vision' of the state, economic shift, talk of 'crisis in education', and residual loyalties to the past or, conversely, to what Raymond Williams (1977) terms 'emergent ideological assemblage' (Fujita-Round & Maher, 2008).

This paper is an attempt to view Japanese language education policy, which has been formed in step with modernization in Japan, by exploring language diversity around the world.

First, an analysis of the total number of languages (7,102 according to Ethnologue, 18th edition) is shown in Figure 1. When looking at the map, it is striking that the number of countries of Europe, including Russia, does not match its number of languages. This is due to language standardization. In Asia and Africa, however, there still exist many minority and indigenous groups who maintain hold of their own languages. Altogether, Asia and Africa have 62% of the world's languages.

The majority of languages function within the home and in the immediate community; an average number of 5,000 to 6,000 speakers; 85 % of languages have less than 100,000 speakers. Japanese on the other hand is rated as having the ninth biggest number of speakers, approximately 128,000,000 (Ethnologue, 18th edition, 2015).

UNESCO (2003) published a guideline to Endangered Languages and released its Endangered Language Atlas on the internet in 2009. On the map of Japan, there are marked eight endangered languages. The location where each language is spoken is shown in a peripheral region of the country. In Japan, the Japanese language is the 'standard' language in society and therefore is the prestigious language, whereas these endangered languages are regarded as inferior, or categorized as 'dialects'.

According to Maher (1994), during the early history of Japan, groups of people from the south of the continent of Asia migrated Japan, and as a result the Japanese language can be described as a hybrid of these speakers' languages, that is, of Altaic languages and Malayo Polynesian languages. Also, in relation to the written form of Japanese, 7th century scholars studied Buddhism, medicine and philosophy by reading textbooks written in Chinese. Maher points out that the unification of the spoken and written forms of Japanese had to wait until the Taisho period (1912-1926) when the colloquial use of the language was established by modern novels. Therefore, the current Japanese language dates from the period of rapid modernization in the 20th century.

In 1886, after the first school education policy was formulated, the Japanese government adopted the '*Yamanote* variation' of the Tokyo dialect as *hyojungo* (standard language) for the nation (Carroll, 2001). For the implementation of this policy, a centralist approach to the issue of standardization was applied (Gottlieb, 2005). The policy-makers and intelligentsia of Japan adopted the formula of language and nationalism employed by the empires of Europe and pressed this into service, first, in the colonies of Taiwan and Korea (Lee, 1996; Heinrich, 2012). This is the beginning of *kokugo* (national language), which caused the dilemma of whether the Japanese language in the educational domain means only the 'national language' of Japanese nationals or includes Japanese as learned by non-Japanese nationals.

The second stage was the assimilation of Japan's language diversity into the Japanese national language. The land of the Ainu was officially embedded into Hokkaido in 1869. Until the 1890s, local governments encouraged the Ainu to behave like Japanese, but also had a policy to respect and preserve their customs. This changed dramatically at the turn of the century to a policy of assimilating them into Japanese society. The Ainu people had to attend school where they recited and sang Japanese songs. In particular, there was education and training, showing how Ainu should bow and follow Japanese manners.

In the case of the assimilation in Okinawa, according to the Education Authority of Miyako Island (2012), the government encouraged the use of 'standard

Japanese' and loyalty towards the emperor. The Ryukyu Kingdom was first reconfigured as Okinawa-*han*, a feudal domain (*han*) in 1872, then as Okinawa prefecture in 1879 at the point of the social restructuring of Japan. When the Meiji Constitution was established in 1889, a picture of the emperor and empress was hung in each school. After the second Sino-Japanese war (1937-1945), the educational movement towards respecting the Japanese emperor and changing to Japanese standard language was intensified. The "language tag (*hogenfuda*)" came into use in schools. The language tag, as reported in Miyako Island, was 20 cm by 10 cm, and made of either wood or paper with a string to hang around the neck of a child. It was used as a punishment for speaking in the mother tongue. Those children who experienced wearing the language tag are now in their 80s and 90s.

Just as there are diverse languages throughout the world, so are there diverse languages in Japan, and many are now marked as endangered languages. Looking at the history of the Japanese language, we can discern the process of how it was formulated as the national language and also how it was unified to become current spoken and written Japanese. The process of modernization in the 20th century mirrors the development of the Japanese language. Understanding this historical process and its implications for the Japanese language is essential for understanding Japanese language education policy. I will connect my reflection on the 20th century to the 21st century language education policy. The approach which Maher (1994) suggests is the ecological point of view, and this current paper's historical and local approach, should help contextualize Japanese language education policy. To envision what language education policy means, perhaps 'place (local)' and 'time (history)' are key terms.

The age of globalization, with the challenges it presents to national borders, has shaken Japanese society. As Katsuragi (2009) argues, the goal of globalization includes not only economic success but enrichment by the diversity of human life. To achieve this goal is obviously a complex process and in order to achieve it we have to unfold the rich context of each country, its process of modernization in the 20th century, before we go on to address the issues of the 21st century.

When seeking economic success, educational qualifications and skills are accounted as important, and this is related to 'written language'. When we turn our eyes to human life, however, the 'spoken language' which we acquire in the home and community, relates more closely to our roots and identity. If the languages labelled as "endangered" disappear, the speakers of those languages will be left behind.

I started my interviews with 40 junior high school pupils on Miyako Island in the south of Okinawa prefecture in 2012. One male pupil last year reacted abruptly to one of my questions by saying, "The history of Miyako! Why can't I read about Miyako's history in our school textbook? Our school textbook talks mostly about Japanese history, Okinawan history is not included, so I did not know anything about Okinawan history, I am grateful to Mr. Yoshimoto (who came from Tokyo to deliver a special class) for teaching us." This 13 year old boy, a first grader at junior high school, pointed out the hierarchy between Miyako, Okinawa and mainland Japan. I also interviewed elderly people in a local community of 1,000 inhabitants. When I asked them about their experience of being forced to learn 'standard Japanese' at school, although they trusted me and had invited me over for a cup of tea, they were not willing to speak but often stayed silent. It showed how they did not feel comfortable recalling the experience.

Generally in the discourse of language education in Japan, pedagogy and how-to practices in Japan and the field of foreign language (i.e. English) education are foregrounded. Kubota (2015) pinpoints the fact that in language education in Japan, at both the local and national levels, ethnological and linguistic diversity is not paid enough attention. Also, May (2014) articulates the term the 'multilingual turn' to encompass the fields of second language acquisition, TESOL and bilingual education, to contexualize multilingualism, not monolingualism. Language education policy in Japan perhaps needs to grasp the recent trends in Applied Linguistics, to understand how other countries are dealing with globalization.

One suggestion is to teach about language diversity. For Japanese people to become global citizens, language diversity can be a key to learning about the world and also about their own country in more depth. The endangered languages of Japan are part of the rich language diversity of Japan.

In the discourse of language diversity, it is necessary to have an understanding of the fact that languages are not always equal. As this paper describes, as part of their drive to modernize Japan, the Japanese government formulated a language education policy presenting English and Japanese respectively as 'the international language' and 'the national language'. This reductive labeling achieved an iconic status that still defines Japanese government language education policy today. As a consequence, a third label, 'the endangered languages', has emerged in the 21st century. It is essential that future language education policy and practice face the challenge presented by this triangulation of 'international language', 'national language' and 'endangered languages' and not ignore 'the third label'. For this the micro context of actual language use in families and close knitted communities needs to be woven into the macro context of society, if we are to reformulate a language education policy that reflects the culture and meets the needs of the Japanese people.

第4章
欧州少数言語における文字の重要性、ケルト諸語の事例から

原 聖（女子美術大学）

第1節　欧州における文字化と文字伝統

　なぜ私が少数言語における文字の問題を重要に思うようになったかというと、それは、西欧の少数言語の復興にとって、言語教育がもっとも重要であり、教育のためには教科書が必要であり、教科書作成のためには標準的書きことばが不可欠だからである。

　西欧の少数言語の特徴のひとつは、近代化の時点で、ないしはすでに中世から書きことばをもっていたことである。なぜかといえば、それは欧州全域ですでに古代から書きことばの伝統があったからである。

　私は2013年4月から3年間にわたって、科研費プロジェクト「書記伝統のなかの標準規範に関する歴史的東西比較研究」を主導してきた。このプロジェクトは、ラテン語に象徴される、非常に長い書きことばの伝統をもつ欧州キリスト教文化圏（これをとりあえずラテン語文化圏と呼んだ）と、漢字という、これもまた長い伝統を形成してきた東アジア文化圏（こちらを漢字文化圏と名付けた）とをその標準規範形成に関して比較してみようという壮大な企画である[1]。

　ここで判明した重要な事実のひとつは、文法から書体にいたるまで、両文化圏において、書記言語誕生の時点ですでにある程度の規範的書きことばが成立していたということである。古代の書きことばは、書記官という多くは世襲によるごく少数の集団によって維持されていた。そこにおいては、定まった書法・用字法があり、これが現代的には標準的書きことばと同等に考

えられるのである。
　この面に関する最新の研究によれば、文字化のプロセスには、話しことばをただ単に転写するのではなく、韻律を伴う口頭伝承が維持されるなかで、文字化が起こり、まさに韻律文が文字化とともに成立する場合があったということである（Wagner et al. (eds.) 2013）。したがって、文字化には、単なる「転写的書記化」と、第2段階である「韻律書記化」があり、こちらの場合は、かなり進んだ標準化・規範化を伴うのである。たとえばドイツ語では、転写的書記化が8世紀に起こり、韻律書記化は10世紀に始まったとされる。この時点でかなりの程度の標準化が行われたと考えられる。これは、本稿で事例として取り上げるケルト諸語で見られたことでもある。

　本稿は、ケルト諸語の文字史を、欧州における文字史のなかに位置づけ、欧州全体の文字史のなかでのケルト諸語の位置を確認する試みでもある。欧州の書きことばはラテン語が最初ではない。欧州での最古の書きことばとしては、紀元前3000年頃からの、エーゲ（ミノア）文明による、クレタ象形文字とクレタ線文字があげられる。いわゆる線文字Bのみがこれまでに解読され、これが紀元前1500年頃のギリシア語の古い形と判明した。この線文字はその後継承されなかったので、文字伝統からは除外していいだろう。
　文字史から重要なのはフェニキア文字である。フェニキア人は、もとはといえば、中東パレスチナ地方に暮らしていたカナーン人だったようだが、紀元前12世紀以降、地中海地域をまたにかける海洋民族として知られるようになり、前8世紀頃に成立するイタリア半島のエトルリア文字、同時期成立のギリシア文字も、フェニキア文字を借用したものであった。

第2節　古代ケルト諸語

　ケルト学研究の最新の成果によれば、最古のケルト語は、イベリア半島西南部、現在のスペイン、アンダルシア地方からポルトガルにかけて、前8世

紀以降栄えたタルテッソス王国のタルテッソス語とされる（これには異論がある）。フェニキア人は前10世紀には地中海から大西洋地域まで活動の輪を広げていたようで、前7世紀から前6世紀にかけて95点ほどが確認されているタルテッソス語はすべてフェニキア文字で書かれている。

イベリア半島のケルト語は、このほか、前3世紀から前1世紀にかけての200点ほどの碑文があるケルト・イベリア語、紀元後1世紀から2世紀にかけての5点の碑文がその証拠とされるルシタニア語があるが、いずれもラテン文字であり、タルテッソス語との関係も判明していない。

ヒベルニア（エール／アイルランド）には、「エール来寇の書」という渡来起源伝説があり、それによれば、建国の神々と最初の人間集団は、南方のイベリア半島から渡来したということになっているが、比較言語学的にイベリア半島のケルト語とヒベルニアのケルト語の近い親縁性を明かす証拠はなく、考古学的にも渡来を明かす物質的類似文化も見出されてはいない。

文字史から興味深いケルト語は現在のフランス地域で広範に碑文が発見されているガリア語である。

ガリア語は、前6世紀前半（前575頃）から紀元後3〜4世紀にかけての700点に上る碑文が確認されているが、その初期、前6世紀から前2世紀にかけてはエトルリア文字であり、その後、前3世紀から後1世紀にかけてはギリシア文字、前1世紀から後4世紀にかけてはラテン文字になる。おそらくその時代のもっとも進んだ文明の文字が採用されて、こうした変遷を辿ったと考えられる。ケルト語は文字を持たなかった、ないし無文字をよしとした文明と喧伝される場合があるが、むしろ中心的文明の影響を常に受けた、一種の周辺的文明だったと、このガリア語の事例が教えてくれるように思う。

現イタリア北部のアルプス山麓地域で前7世紀〜前4世紀にかけて見られるレポント語は、ガリア語の初期段階と考えられるが、初期エトルリア文字の一種ルガノ文字を採用している。エトルリア文字はフェニキア文字の一種であり、これも中心的文明の影響であろう。

前3世紀から後4世紀にかけて、現トルコにガリアからの移住により成立したと考えられるガラティア語はギリシア文字を採用しており、この場合も

まさに先進文明の影響である。

　前4世紀から1〜2世紀の2点の碑文が知られるのみのノール語は、現オーストリア、スロヴェニア地域であり、これもガリアからの移住により成立したとされる。

第1項　ケルト諸語と周辺の諸言語
　このように古代のケルト諸語はいずれの場合にも中心的文明の影響を受けた周辺的文化と考えられ、その文字文化は墓碑銘など、ごく限られた用途の転写文字にすぎず、本格的な文字文化をもったとはいえない。

　ラテン語には文化的権威があった。ただし、紀元後2世紀まではギリシア語の権威のほうが圧倒的に高かった。ローマ帝国でキリスト教が公認されるのが313年（さらに国教化が392年）だし、ローマにおけるキリスト教典礼がギリシア語からラテン語に変わるのはやっと4世紀後半である。したがって、4世紀後半以降、キリスト教の浸透とともに、文化的権威を獲得しつつあったラテン語の使用が、ガリアのようなローマ人の移住者の地域で生活言語として継承されたと考えられる。

　4世紀末、ゲルマン人の一派西ゴート人が「同盟者（フェデラーティ）」としてローマ帝国内への定住が認められ、5世紀末には「フランク王国」として足場を固める。ゲルマン系のフランク語は文字に代表される文化的権威を持たず、ラテン語の方に権威があったので、短期間でラテン語に同化した。移住地のフランク人は兵士として単身で入植し、総勢3万人程度で「少数派」でもあり、ガリアで地元の女性と家庭をもったためガリア語に同化したと以前は説明されたが、最近の説はこの文化的権威（Cultural Prestige）を重視し、支配者の言語であっても、文化的権威がない場合は、被支配者の言語に同化するという考え方が有力になりつつある（原2015: 142-144）。

第2項　ブリテン島とガリア
　「ドゥルイデス［ドルイド］の教義は、まずブリタンニア［ブリタニア／ブリテン］で発見され、そしてそこからガリアに移入されたと考えられている。そ

れで今日でも、この教義をいっそう深く研究しようと志す者は、大抵ブリタンニアに渡って、修業を積むのである」（カエサル『ガリア戦記』第6巻）とあるように、前3世紀にはガリアとブリテン島とで交流があり、それを明かすのが、ガリア語とブリトン語の類似性だとされる。これは、移住を伴わない文化伝播の事例である。

伝統的考え方としては、前6世紀、ないしそれ以前に、ガリアからブリテン諸島に移住があったとされたが、それを証明する考古学的証拠がなく、現在ではむしろ、前2000年紀ないしそれ以前からの、移住を伴わない交流の結果（原 2008: 152）とされる。前3世紀以降の交流もこの時代に突如開始されたというよりも、それ以前からの、長期的な文化交流を継承するものと考えられる。

ブリテン島のラテン語は、後1世紀の入植期から4世紀始めの撤退にいたるまで、存続期間が長いとはいえず、なおかつ支配者の書きことば・行政語としての意味しかなかったため、生活言語として定着することはなかった。

ブリテン島のケルト人の多くが、このようにラテン語化することはなかったが、5世紀以降のアングロ・サクソン人の侵入により、文化的にアングロ・サクソン人に同化する場合があった。この場合は、文化的権威によるわけではなく、数的に少数派だった地域、すなわち現在のイングランドに散在したブリトン人の集落がアングロ・サクソン人に同化したと考えられる。そうした考古学的証拠が存在するのである（青山吉信『アーサー伝説』参照）。

ちなみに、移動しつつあったゲルマン人のなかでも、5世紀に「西ゴート王国」を形成するゲルマン人は、短命に終わるこの5世紀のガリアにおける西ゴート王国の時代にすでに自らのゲルマン語を放棄し、ラテン文化に同化していたとされる。

第3節　オガム文字

ケルト語に関して文字史から興味深いのは、3世紀末から8世紀にかけて

のオガム文字である。ヒベルニア（アイルランド）のゴイデル族（ゲール人）が最初に使用したとされ、その碑文はこの一族が居住した西南部ケリー州にもっとも多い。ヒベルニアで350点確認されているが、主に墓標、記念碑であり、ほとんどが人名である。したがって、いわゆる転写的書記化であり、この文字自体が本格的書きことばの導入につながったとはいえない。

　3世紀末以降、ゲール人がブリタニア島に侵入し、アルバ（スコットランド）、ワリア（ウェールズ）、ケルノウ（コーンウォール）、マン島でもオガム文字が使用された。ヒベルニア以外でもっとも多いのは、ワリア南西部であり、ラテン語とのバイリンガル版はブリタニア島のみである。これは、オガム文字の習得が主にヒベルニアで行われていて、ほかでの習得が難しかったためと考えられる。

　文字というよりも、秘儀的な幾何学的記号であり、その音声体系は、初期エール（アイルランド）語の音韻に基づいている。すなわち、15の子音と5つの母音が、5×4（＝20）の数え方に基づいて整備されているのである。神聖な木であるイチイの木に、ドルイドが占トを行うためにオガム文字を用いたとされ、文字自体が神聖性をもち、秘匿されるべき暗号として保持された可能性が高く、キリスト教文化に対する抵抗の意味合いがあったと思われる。

　最初の2文字と区切りになる5番目の文字名から、アルファベットは「ベイス・スイス・ニン」と呼ばれ、それぞれ「木」の名称がつけられている。オガム文字についての詳細が知られているのは、そのための解説書があるからであり、それは、14世紀末の写本「レアール・ワイレ・ア・ウォータ」（Leabhar Bhaile an Mhóta、英語では「バリモートの書」Book of Ballymote）に含まれ、「アウライケプト・ナ・ネケス」（Auraicept na n-Éces、「賢者の心得」Scholars' primer）と題される。そこには、この解説書が7世紀の学者ケン・ファエラッド（Cenn Faelad、英語でキニアリKinealy）の執筆によるものという記述があり、ラテン語に対するエール語の優位が説かれている。その真偽は不明とはいえ、ダンテの『俗語論』に先んずること600年、こうした書物が存在したかもしれないということは注目に価する。後で見るように、このエール語については、7世紀にラテン文字による書記規範がすでに成立していた可能性は高い。

第1項　オガム文字とルーン文字

　オガム文字と比較して注目すべき文字が、北方スカンジナビアのゲルマン人が編み出したとされるルーン文字である。最古の碑文は2世紀ないし3世紀、オガム文字より出現はやや早いともいえるが、ほぼ同時期である。成立は1世紀、北イタリアが有力ということで、こちらの場合も、ラテン・アルファベットがそのモデルとなった可能性が高く、なおかつキリスト教文化に対抗するための考案という点も類似すると考えられる（ページ1996参照、ただし最近では、成立はもっと古く、紀元前6世紀から前3世紀はじめ、ラテン文字ではなく、フェニキア文字がもとになったという説も有力。Oppenheimer 2006: 369-371）。

　ルーン文字でさらに興味深いのは、5世紀ころからブリテン島に侵入するアングロ・サクソン人がこれを用いたことである。しかも、最近の研究では、650年以前のルーン文字とそれ以降では、Hの横棒が前者では1本であるのに、後者では2本になるなどの違いがあり、おそうく7世紀半ばを境に、系統の異なる集団の進出があったのではないかという。

　7世紀半ば以前の移住者は、ユトランド半島以北、スカンジナビアからの人々であり、これ以降は、系統の異なる、おもにアングル人、すなわちユトランド半島の付け根部分からやってきた人々だったのではないか、と最近の遺伝子研究を踏まえ、文明史家オッペンハイマーは述べる（ibid.: 380-381）。さらに言うと、このアングル人が日常的にはローマ字を用い始めたという。

　イングランドでは、5世紀以降、アングロ・サクソン人による七王国（ヘプターキー）が建設され始め、6世紀後半には、ヒベルニア（アイルランド）から聖コルンバにより、また6世紀末には大陸からカンタベリの聖アウグスティヌスにより、キリスト教化が開始される。これによって、ヒベルニアのエール語の場合と同様、アングロ・サクソン語にラテン文字が流入することになった。代表的なのが9世紀後半のウェセックス王アルフレッド大王の治世であり、アングロ・サクソン語による法律の整備、ラテン語古典のアングロサクソン語翻訳が行われたのである（原2015: 150）。

第4節　ブリタニア島からアルモリカ（ブレイス／ブルターニュ）へ

　3世紀後半以降のローマ帝国の危機により、ガリア北西部とりわけアルモリカ地方（現ブレイス／ブルターニュ）には、「政治的経済的文化的空隙」（原 2008: 157）が生じた。また、450年頃、ピクト人討伐のためのブリトン人の王によるサクソン人傭兵の要請がきっかけとなり（8世紀のベーダによる）、クローヴィスとその子ヒルデベルト1世が、ブリトン人のアルモリカへの移住を容認した（7世紀の歴史家フレデガリウスによる）。これにはフランク王ダゴベルト1世とブリトン人の王ジュディカエルの協定（同）があったともされる（原 2003参照）。いずれにしても、3世紀後半以降、5世紀後半、ないし6世紀に至るまで、ブリタニアとアルモリカとの関係は緊密であり、ブリタニアからアルモリカへの移住の社会的条件は十分にあったと考えられる。

　4世紀から7世紀に至る、ブリタニアからアルモリカへの移住を明かす証拠はほかにもある。まずは、ワリア（ウェールズ）、ケルノウ（コーンウォール）とアルモリカとの地名の共有である。ブリトン語で「ラン」（lan＝「聖地」）、「トレ」（tre＝「居住地」）「ロク」（loc＝「場所」）をもつ地名が多数あり、さらに5世紀後半以降を舞台として、8〜9世紀に作成された60件を超える、ブリタニアからアルモリカへの渡来聖人伝と合わせて考えると、少なくとも、5世紀後半から7世紀にかけて、聖人の布教に関わる渡来とそれに付随する、ブリトン人のアルモリカへのかなりの人数の移住があったと推計される。

　ただし、7世紀までのブルターニュは伝説の時代であり、たとえば「ブルターニュ建国の武将」コナン・メリアデクスが、4世紀末（384年頃）アルモリカで支配者となったとされ、聖女ウルスラを娶るなど「コナン伝説」として数々のエピソードを残しているが、史実として歴史的に承認される武将が登場するのは、9世紀になってからであり、その始めがノミノエである。ノミノエは、842年、北イタリアのロタールに対し、西フランク王と東フランク王が協力を誓った「ストラスブルクの宣誓」に、西フランク王シャルル禿頭王の忠臣として立ち会っている。845年には、シャルル禿頭王に反旗を翻し、「バロンの戦い」で彼を撃破した。

書きことばに関して考えると、8〜9世紀の聖人伝がすべてラテン語だったように、8世紀以降になると、おそらくキリスト教との関係で、文化的権威をもつラテン語文化が書きことばの面では主流になっていたと考えられる。4世紀から7世紀にかけての移住の経緯を考えると、渡来聖人という文化的権威をもつブリトン人の文化がガリアのラテン系文化に同化・吸収されるということは考えられない。現にそうしたことが起こらず、ブリトン語の後衛であるブレイス語は現在にまで生き延びることになった。

第5節　書記文化とブレイス語

　さてそのブレイス語だが、8世紀末から12世紀に至る古文書（おもに土地の証文など391点のラテン語文書）をまとめる『ルドン修道院記録集』など、8世紀末以降のラテン語文書は大量に現存する。そこには人名や地名などケルト語で解釈できる固有名詞が頻出する。ブルターニュの研究者ベルナール・タンギは、ケルト系の人名2100点、地名8000点を列挙したが、かなりその綴りは均質的である（cf.: Tanguy 1998）。これは、地名・人名を文字に転写する規範がすでに存在したということを示しており、ブレイス語には少なくとも、9世紀という歴史的に実在が証明されている領主のもとで、転写（書記化）規範が存在したということができる。

　おそらく、話しことばでは、ブレイス語圏の領主でも11世紀までは常用語はブレイス語だったと考えられている。9世紀〜10世紀のブルターニュは、北方の民（いわゆるヴァイキング）の襲来による混乱の時代だったが、10世紀のノルマン人による「ノルマンディー公国」の成立ののち、とりわけ11世紀の「ノルマン・コンクウェスト」により、落ち着きを取り戻すと同時に、権威をもつフランス文化の支配がはじまることになる。ブレイス語を話せた最後の領主は、コルヌアイユ（ケルネ）家（ブルターニュ西南部を支配）の「鉄人王」アラン4世（治世1084〜1112年）といわれている。この12世紀は、イングランドとフランス南西部（アキテーヌなど）が一つの王国となるへ

ンリー2世による「アンジュー帝国」の時代である。それは国王をはじめとする宮廷社会が書きことばを身につけ出す時代でもあった。「アーサー王伝説」のもとになる、ジェフリー・オブ・モンマスの『ブリタニア列王史』の成立が1136年頃であり、フランス語（アングロ・ノルマン語）によるワースの『ブリュ物語』が1155年頃である。広大な「アンジュー帝国」の領地を中心に、読書能力をもつ宮廷社会が広がり始めたのである。実際に、英仏の王が識字能力を獲得するのはこの12世紀以降とされる。この識字能力は、当然ながら、当時の宮廷の話しことばであるフランス語によるということになる。13世紀には、現在のフランスばかりでなく、イングランド、ドイツ、フランドルの宮廷でも、話しことばはフランス語だったのであり、14世紀になると、宮廷人はフランス語による読み書き能力も獲得するようになる。

　こうした流れに沿う形で、1213年以降、ブルターニュの公文書が、ラテン語に代わってフランス語になっていく。14世紀になると、ブルターニュ公も読書能力を獲得する。その1番手が、フランス王国の貴族でもあったブロワ伯シャルル（治世1341〜64年）である。

　ブルターニュは、1536年にフランス王国に統合され、政治的な独立を失うが、文化的言語的にはその遥か以前、12〜13世紀にはフランス語文化圏に統合されていたということになる。フランスでは、この後、公文書のフランス語を規定する「ヴィレール・コトレ法」が1539年に発布され、書きことばにおけるラテン語の地位が最終的に剥奪されるが、ブレイス語圏での公文書の完全なるフランス語化は、17世紀以降になる。公文書のフランス語化はすでに書いたように13世紀には開始されたが、このように遅々として進まなかったのは、教会においてラテン語使用がなかなか途絶えなかったことが大きいだろう。教会では、ブレイス語も書きことばとして、とりわけ17世紀以降のカトリック宗教改革以降用いられたが、これはフランス語の文化的権威が実はそれほど高くなかったことがその原因だろう。

第6節　他のケルト諸語の書きことば

　書きことばの形成それ自体に規範化が伴う、標準化は避けられないということが近年とみに主張されている。古代においては、読み書き能力を有するのは書記官（Scribe）という職人層が主であり、ギリシャ・ローマでは、これに特権階級である市民・貴族層が加わった。書きことばの獲得には学習が不可欠であり、このことが規範化を促す要因ともなったと考えられる。

　近年主張されるもうひとつの重要点は、この規範化には2段階ある、ということである。すでに第1節で記したことだが、そのひとつが転写的書記化であり、これはたとえばガリア語の墓碑銘やブレイス語の人名などの場合である。

　もうひとつが、韻律書記化である。この場合には、すでに口頭伝承として韻律文が発達していて、それを前提として書記化が行われるので、こうした韻律を書きあらわすための規則的綴字法が必要とされたのである。

　ケルト語圏でこれに当てはまるのが、エール（ニベルニア／アイルランド）語とカムリー（ウェールズ）語の事例である。

　エール語では、6世紀に遡るとされる「コルムキル（聖コルンバ）頌歌」があり、年代記、法律文書もその大元は6世紀に遡るという。法律文書で現存するのは12世紀はじめが最古であり、「ナ・ヌイドレ書」（1106年頃）、「ラグネッヘ書」（1160年頃）などがある。言語史の研究者によると、600年頃から10世紀始めまでの古期エール語は非常に均質で、つづり字の統制がとれており、この後1200年頃まで乱れ、それ以降1600年頃まで規範が健固の時期が続くという（EDEL 2003: 353）。世俗の法律文書集である『センハス・モール』は8世紀前半の成立と考えられるが、そこには、「伝統的法律が謳うように（amal arindchain in fénechas）」としばしば書かれるという（ibid.: 355）。これはまさに、口頭による韻律文の伝統が以前から形成され、それが書記化につながったことを物語る表現である。

　カムリー語についても同様であり、「アネイリン」「タリエシン」という武勲詩の創作年代は6世紀まで遡る。現存カムリー語文書は13世紀が最古だが、

エール語と同様、法律文書でも起源は9世紀に遡ると推定される文書がある（「善王ハウェルの法律」）。

ケルノウ語についても、11世紀から12世紀頃のケルノウ語ラテン語の対訳語彙帳（約3000語）、14世紀の聖史劇「オルディナリア」の写本など、古い文献が結構ある。

第7節　欧州での「俗語」の書きことばの成立

ケルト諸語とその周辺の諸言語の歴史的状況を比較しておくと、ケルト諸語の書きことばの欧州における位置が見えてくる。フランスの言語史家バッジオーニは、欧州の「俗語」、すなわちラテン語以外の現在の諸国語の原型となる言語について、最初は、ローマ帝国の周辺部とその隣接地帯においてラテン語を範にとる形で、独自の文字作成による書きことばが成立した。それが、ブリタニア諸島の3世紀末から8世紀にかけてのオガム文字であり、ドイツ北東部の4世紀のゴート文字であり、スカンジナビアの2世紀のルーン文字であった。オガム文字、ルーン文字についてはすでにみたが、いずれもラテン文字ないしはその元になった文字に対する抵抗的意味合いがあった。オガム文字のところで解説したように、この文字自体が、エール語文化の教養を象徴する意味合いがあり、そうした教養がラテン語ギリシア語文化に対抗するものだった。

欧州では、古代末期の4世紀以降は、キリスト教とラテン語がその中心的文化として結合する形で、まさに欧州文化の中核をなしていく。その中心的国々であるイタリア、フランス、スペイン、ドイツではその国語の書きことばとしての成立がむしろ遅れる。フランス語についてみると、最初の書きことばである「ストラスブールの宣誓」（842年）は転写的書記化であり、最初の文学「ローランの歌」（1098年頃）、すなわち11世紀末か12世紀が韻律的書記化の開始と考えることができる。

これに対し、英語の前身アングロ・サクソン語では「ベオウルフ」（8世紀

初め)という韻律的書記化と考えられる文学があり、ブリテン諸島のケルト諸語とまったく同時代に書記化が始まったとみなすことができる。

ちなみに、12世紀の段階では、政治権力はパリのフランス王国ばかりでなく、イギリスで大王国（ノルマン王朝）を築くノルマンディーにもあり、フランス語においては、ノルマン・フランス語がもうひとつの規範を形成していた。さらに南フランスのオック語も「トルバドール」という詩人たちによって権威を保持していた（11～13世紀）。おそらくこうした複数規範の状況が、ほかの地方にも影響を与え、フランス全体でのフランス語規範化（おそらくこれはいわゆるアカデミー・フランセーズとともに、すなわち17世紀に始まる）以前に、地方ごとの規範的書きことばが存在したのである。これは「地方的書記言語 (regional scripta)」と呼ばれる。

東ブルターニュの「ガロ語 (gallo)」、ノルマンディーの「ノルマン語 (normand)」（ノルマンディー半島とチャンネル諸島、ジャージー島とガーンジー島）、ピカルディー地方の「ピカール語 (picard)」が代表的であり、こうした言語には現在復興運動が存在する。1980年代には「オイル諸語使用擁護推進委員会 (Défence et promotion des langues d'oïl)」という交流団体が結成され、復興運動が進められている。ピカール語はベルギーの一部にも使用地域があり、こちらでは公的認知が行われ、国をあげた復興運動が始まっている。

こうしてみてくると、ケルト諸語は、欧州の古典語を除く諸言語のなかで、たいへん早い段階で、書きことばを獲得していた言語だということがわかる。

第8節　ケルト諸語の少数言語化

「近世以降、国語化した言語との戦いに敗れ」た言語が少数言語だと指摘したのは、ピーター・バーク (2008参照) だが、欧州におけるその典型的言語がケルト諸語だということができる。

ケルノウ語の話されていたケルノウ（コーンウォール）地方は、1337年、コーンウォール公領となり、行政単位としては、イングランドの一部となっ

た。したがって、政治的な独自性は14世紀という早い段階で消滅し、行政言語は英語だけということになった。こうしてケルノウ語は、18世紀後半には言語コミュニティーを喪失し、最後の話者が1777年に亡くなるとともに、言語としても死滅したとされるのである（原 2012参照）。

　ブリテン島とヒベルニア（アイルランド）島との間のアイリッシュ海に位置するマン島は、5世紀以降、ヒベルニアからの移住者によってゲール（エール）語化したが、8世紀から12世紀にかけて、北方の民（ヴァイキング）の支配を受けた。ただし、この間の支配は間接的で、「ティンヴァルド」という北欧起源の独自の議会をもちつつ、ケルト系言語が失われることはなかった。1405年、このマン島はイングランドのスタンリー家の領地となり、以降、その子孫のダービー伯領を経て、1765年、英国王室領となった。この間も自治議会が続いていて、マン語は失われなかった。島として地理的に独自性を保持しやすかったことも好条件だったはずである。これは14世紀以降、行政言語が英語のみとなる、イングランドとまさに地続きのケルノウとの大きな違いである。したがって、20世紀始めまで言語共同体が維持された（原前掲書参照）。

　ブレイス（ブルターニュ）地方は、1532年、フランスへ併合されるが、三部会地方として、課税権などかなり大きな自治権を確保しつづけた。行政言語はもっぱらフランス語で、この面でブレイス語はまったく用いられなかったが、いわゆるブレイス語圏（ブルターニュの西半分の地域）ではカトリック教会が教会運営言語として使用し続けた。これは20世紀始めまで継続され、これが1902年の教会でのブレイス語使用禁止（またブレイス語カテキズムの禁止）という条例につながった（原 前掲書参照）。

　宗教面での言語使用が言語の擁護・保存に直結するのは事例が非常に多い。とりわけキリスト教圏ではこれが最大の拠り所となることがしばしばある。

　1536年にイングランドに併合されるカムリーの場合がまさにそうである。ウェールズ大公という大きな称号により、地域としての独自性を保持し続けたが、行政言語としてカムリー語は用いられず、政治的なプレスティージュはまったくもなかった。しかし、18世紀、カムリーで宗教的な主流派とな

るプロテスタントのメソジスト派が布教用言語としてカムリー語を採用したため、日常的使用において活力をとりもどした。19世紀後半以降、ケルト的な文化イヴェントとして復活した「アイステズヴォット」(カムリー語詩歌・歌謡祭)が文化的権威の向上を後押しし、言語的な大きな後退を免れることになる。

1707年の連合法によって、スコットランド王国とイングランドが連合し、グレート・ブリテン連合王国が成立する。スコットランドは、言語的にはブレイスの場合と同様、ケルト系のゲール語(ハイランド地方)と英語(ローランド地方)に2分される形で、伝統的言語文化圏を形成してきた。ブレイスとの違いは、宗教的なまとまりがあまりないことである。16世紀以降プロテスタント系が中心的勢力だったが、カトリックも勢力を保った。いずれの場合も、布教言語・日常的言語としてスコットランド・ゲール語が用いられたのはごくわずかな地域に限られたので、19世紀以降、早くから消滅の危機を迎えた。

1801年、アイルランドは英国に併合される。すでに16世紀のヘンリー8世による支配等、英国による侵略は以前から始まっていたが、言語文化的にはその侵略の程度はそれほど進展していなかった。19世紀以降、とりわけ、1840年代のジャガイモ飢饉による経済力の低下により、米国への移民が急増し、それとともに英国の支配も強まる。こうした事態はほかのケルト諸語文化圏ではなかったことである。これが、ほかの地域にはない民族主義の高揚を19世紀末以降もたらすことになったと考えられる。宗教的にはスコットランドと異なり、カトリックがエール(アイルランド)のアイデンティティーであり、これが北アイルランド紛争の核心部分を構成することになる。これとアイルランド民族主義、そしてその文化的独自性の象徴としてのエール語が結びつき、政治性が高まることになるが、19世紀までは言語文化的には衰退を余儀なくされつつあった、というのが実態である(原 前掲書参照)。

第9節　ケルト諸語の復興

　少数言語というのは国語に敗北した言語であり、その復興ということがあるとすれば、それは政治的な復興すなわち民族主義の高揚と結びつく。欧州における民族主義は、オーストリア・ハンガリー帝国からの独立を目指す運動に典型的に見られるように、自らの言語を中核とする民族主義である。

　ケルト諸語文化圏では、すべての地域でこの種の運動が存在した。ただし、それが大衆的な支持を得て民族的運動として広がり、ついには独立を達成するという政治的な勝利に至ったのは、エール（アイルランド）だけである。1893年結成の「ゲール同盟」はゲール（エール）語文化の振興とその政治的権利の主張を全面に打ち出し、これに加わる人々を中心とする1916年の「ダブリン蜂起」、1922年の「エール（アイルランド）自由国」の設立に至るのである。とはいえ、独立後、エール語文化復興が順調に進んだかというと、けっしてそうとはいえない。おそらく経済的な貧困さゆえに、国家的事業はまずは経済面が優先され、文化振興の原則が独立当初から打ち出されていたとはいえ、財政的な裏打ちがなく、思うようにことが運ばなかったというのが実情だろう。真の言語文化政策が打ち出されるようになるのは、1990年代以降なのである。

　ブレイスでは、政治的運動は地域主義（1898年結成の「ブルターニュ地域主義連合」）という、独立を目指す民族主義より一段レベルの低い、地方的独自性・地方自治を要求する運動として始まり、そのあと民族主義政党が誕生する（1911年結成の「ブルターニュ民族主義党」）が、こうした政党はごく少数の知識人による運動にとどまる。そうした状況は第二次大戦後まで継続する。これに加えて、ブレイスでは民族主義派の知識人の一部がナチスと協力するという局面があったため（第二次大戦中の対独協力派）、大戦後は独立運動が「対独協力」という戦後の不可侵の「タブー」と重なり、民族主義自体も1980年代までタブー化するという状況が続いた。これはケルト諸語文化圏では、ブレイスのみの特殊状況だが、フランスでは、アルザス、フランドル、コルシカで同じような地域的民族主義タブー状況が少なくとも1970年代まで残

存した。

　1970年代以降の言語復興は、民族主義とは別のレベルの政治性を背景とするようになる。その一つが環境保護（エコロジー）である。環境破壊を食い止めるための地方分権、また環境保護の一つとしての生物的多様性の擁護、その関連として文化的多様性の擁護が、1990年代以降、強く主張されるようになり、これが少数言語復興の追い風となったのである。また、人権の一つとして言語権も主張されるようになった。こうした言語的文化的多様性の主張の一環としての少数言語復興は、「異なることへの権利」として1970年代以降主張されるようになり、これが少数言語復興の最も重要な手段としての「幼児教育運動」につながったのである。カムリー語では両大戦間期から、ブレイス語でも第2次大戦直後から幼児教育運動があったが、「異なることへの権利」を意識した教育運動はやはり1970年代以降と考えていいだろう。この教育のために標準的書きことばがたいへん重要だったのである。

第1項　復興運動の前提としての標準的書きことば

　すでに何度か指摘したように、言語が文字を獲得する時点で、ある程度の規範化が行われるのが普通であり、とりわけ韻律書記化を経る場合には規範化が避けられない。ところが学校教育（それには近世における神学校での教育も含まれるが）が開始されると、文字が大衆化し、そのなかでいわば「規範の乱れ」が生じるのである。

　エール語で1000年頃から1200年頃まで綴字法に乱れが生じたというのは、北方の民の侵入による乱れだが、1600年以降、再度それが始まるというのは、まさに神学校による文字の「大衆化」によると考えられる。

　ブレイスにおいても、カテキズムなどの印刷出版物をみると、17世紀半ば以前は方言による印刷もなく、その綴字法もたいへん均質だが、これ以降、方言による印刷が始まり、綴字法も一定ではなくなる。この画期となったのが、17世紀カトリック宗教改革のブレイス語圏における立役者ジュリアン・モノワールによる『イエズス聖学校』という、紛らわしいがブレイス語の文法書辞書の刊行（1659年）である。これによって、ブレイス語書きことばが

「大衆化」したのである。大衆化といっても、それは多くの司祭・聖職者が使えるようになったということであり、けっして文字通りの大衆化ではない。ブレイスでは「司祭のブレイス語（brezhoneg ar beleg）」という、あまり出来のよくないブレイス語を蔑む言い方があるが、そうしたブレイス語が登場することになったのである。

　こうした状況を改善することになったのが、19世紀の文法家たちであり、その筆頭がルゴニデック（アル・ゴニデック）である。彼の『文法書』（1807年）、『辞書』（1821年）は、ブレイス語史では、近代的文法書の開始を告げるものとされる。ただし、彼はプロテスタントだったため、残念ながらその著書がブレイスで広まることにはならなかった。19世紀ブレイスの代表的知識人で『バルザス・ブレイス』（1839年）で有名なエルサール・ドラ・ヴィルマルケ（ケルヴァルケール）が自著でその文法書辞書を再録する（1847〜50年）ことで、その真価が認められ、19世紀末以降のフランソワ・ヴァレによるブレイス語教科書（『ブレイス語文法基礎講座』1902年、『ブレイス語40課』1907年以降7版）につながるのである。

　ちなみに現在のブレイス語綴字法は、第2次大戦中に考案されたものが基準となっていて、それゆえに一部では政治的な対独協力派の影響を持ち出して、使用を控える向きもあったが、現在ではそう考える人たちはほとんどいない。

　プロテスタント圏では、ルターによるドイツ語訳聖書のように、自言語訳の聖書が綴字法の基本としての役割を果たす場合が多いが、ケルト諸語圏では、カムリー語だけがこれに該当する。カムリー語聖書（1588年）は、いわゆる俗語訳聖書のなかでも初期にだされたものの一つだが、19世紀以降の言語復興のなかで、絶大な権威力を発揮し、聖書由来の綴字法はほとんど問題視されることがなく、現代にまで継承された。ただし、1980年代以降、いわゆる「生きたカムリー語（Cymraeg fyw）」という運動のなかで簡素化された綴字法も提示されているが、基本的には16世紀のものが土台になっていると言っていい。

　聖書と綴字法との関わりを一般的にいえば、カトリック圏では、4世紀の

ラテン語ウルガタ聖書が定番で、いわゆる俗語訳が異端視される場合が多く、聖書の翻訳自体が遅れた。1960年代の第2バチカン公会議以降、ようやく公認されるようになり、エール語訳聖書は1981年に公認聖書が刊行された。それ以前のものはほとんどがプロテスタント系の聖書・祈祷書である。1690年のアルバ（スコットランド・ゲール）語聖書、1767年の同新約聖書、1775年のマン語完訳聖書、1827年のブレイス語聖書（これはルゴニデックの手になるもの）などはすべてプロテスタント派のものである。とはいえ、カテキズム（教理問答）や讃歌集、祈祷書、聖人伝などは多数が翻訳・出版され、こうした書物が言語擁護に果たした功績は大きい。

結びにかえて

　本稿でケルト諸語を事例にあげて検討したように、少数言語の復興・擁護に果たす書きことばの役割は大きい。ケルト諸語においては、その書記化自体がたいへん長い歴史をもっており、これが復興運動においても大きな自負を形成していると考えられる。欧州における少数言語においては、実はこうした事例は少なくなく、それが欧州的特徴をなしているということがいえるだろう。
　こういった少数言語における文字史の長い歴史を検証することは、逆に大言語の文字史を相対化する。すなわち歴史の長い文字を持つものが国語や世界的言語を形成したとはいえず、少数言語でもこうした長い歴史をもつ言語がある。さらにいえば、こうした長い歴史をもったとしても、政治的な力がなければ、少数言語の地位に甘んじざるをえなかった言語も存在するということである。
　ところが現代では、そうした政治力に関係なく、まさに文化的多様性こそ人類文化の核心であるという認識のもと、言語的多様性が主張され、少数言語・危機言語の復興が叫ばれるのである。このことも認識しておく必要がある。

注

1　科研報告書は2016年3月に刊行された。日中英の3言語で出版されたが、著作権や翻訳の問題で、各言語版に収録される論文にかなりの異同がある。原聖（編）（日本語版）『書記伝統のなかの標準規範に関する歴史的東西比較研究』女子美術大学、324頁。原圣、包联群（編）（汉文版）『书写传统之标准规范的历史性东西方比较研究』女子美術大学、181頁。Hara Kiyoshi, Heinrich Patrick (eds.), English version, *Standard Norms in Written Languages—Historical and Comparative Studies between East and West—*, Joshibi University of Art and Design, 304p.

参考文献

青山 吉信（1985）『アーサー伝説』、岩波書店。
カエサル（1994）『ガリア戦記』、講談社学術文庫。
ピーター・バーク（2008）『近世ヨーロッパのことばと社会』、岩波書店。
原 聖（2003）『〈民族起源〉の精神史』、岩波書店。
原 聖（2008）『ケルトの水脈』、講談社。
原 聖（編）（2012）『ケルト諸語文化の復興』（『ことばと社会』別冊4、三元社）。
原 聖（2015）「言語接触と文化移転」、東北史学会ほか編『東北史を開く』、山川出版社、139-154頁。
レイ・ページ（1996）『ルーン文字』、學藝書林。
Edel, Doris (2003) 'The Status and development of the vernacular in early medieval Ireland', in: Mchèle Goyens, Werner Verbeke (eds.), *The Dawn of the Written Vernacular in Western Europe*, Leuven University Press (Belgium).
Oppenheimer, Stephen (2006) *The Origins of the British*, London, Robinson.
Tanguy, Bernard et al. (eds.) (1998) *Cartulaire de l'Abbaye Saint-Sauveur de Redon*, Rennes.
Wagner, Esther-Miriam et al. (eds.) (2013) *Scribes as agents of language change*, Walter de Gruyter.

Abstract, Chap.4
The Importance of Written Languages in European Minority Languages : examples from Celtic Languages

Hara Kiyoshi (Joshibi University of Art and Design)

Having a written norm is very important for language survival, especially for the revival and revitalization of the minority or endangered languages. European minority languages were destined to decline, mainly because of the compulsory education of national languages.

In most European languages, even among minority languages, the alphabet has been employed since the Middle Ages and early modern times, supporting the long tradition of written literature. This long tradition of written language is a major support for the reconstruction of these languages today. In this paper, I discuss European minority languages, especially Celtic languages; their long written history, comparable to European national language. I note that Latin, which is thought to have absolute authority as a written language, has mere relative authority as written language, and that when considering the pre-Christian tradition of the alphabet in Europe, minority languages are not so different from other European national languages.

The most important language in pre-Christian Europe was the Phoenician language, which had hegemony in the Mediterranean of 12th century BC, and which, in the 10th century BC, had advanced to the Atlantic coast region. Etruscan in Italy adopted this Phoenician alphabet in the 8th century BC, and Greek language also adopted this as first written alphabet in the same period.

Some researchers have argued that languages must have been more or less standardized at the time of the formation of written language, although the standard language is said to have been formed in modern times, at the creation of grammars and dictionaries.

European written languages were introduced from the outside, and kept by a small number of experts (possibly hereditary) in most cases. Some German researchers introduced the concept of prosody standardization (*Verschriftlichung*: language norm which has prosody formation, and poetic literature) to distinguish it from the introduction of a mere alphabet (literalization: *Verschriftung*); prosody standardization is decisive as a written norm but necessary also in the oral tradition. In this paper, by introducing this concept, I discuss the formation of the alphabet in the Celtic languages.

As for the Celtic languages, the alphabet seems to have been formed in the 6th century in *Gaeilge* (Irish) and in *Cymraeg* (Welsh), although there are only indirect historical documents. This long tradition is one of the major positive backdrops for the language revival movement of modern times.

The language of Tartessos Kingdom which flourished in the southern part of the Iberian peninsula in the 8th century BC (present Portugal and Andalusia) adopted the Phoenician alphabet. This language has been claimed recently to be a member of the Celtic family. 95 inscriptions from the 7th century BC to the 6th century BC have been confirmed. Lepontic, the oldest of Celtic languages in northern Italy in the Alps foothills, from the 7th century BC to the 4th century BC, is written in Lugano alphabet, a language related to Etruscan.

Interesting when viewed from written language history is the Gaulish language, which has more than 700 inscriptions from the first half of the 6th century BC to the 3rd and 4th centuries AD. This language adopted the Etruscan alphabet from the 6th to the 2nd century BC, Greek alphabet from the 3rd century BC to the 1st century AD, and Latin alphabet from the 1st century BC to the 4th century AD. Thus, we consider that the change of these alphabets reflects the influence of the neighboring prestigious cultures: Phoenician, Etruscan, Greek and it became Latin at the turn of BC and AD period.

As we can see now, the authority of written Latin became obvious from the turn of BC-AD period. This was associated with Christianity only from the 4th century AD at the time of the Christianization of the Roman Empire. Moreover, French and other Roman languages (Italian, Spanish, etc.) were confirmed as written languages much later in the 9th century, the successor languages of Vulgar Latin. Furthermore, even in the 5th -8th centuries in Europe, Latin did not have sole authority as a written language: there were other written alphabets, Runes (2nd -6th centuries) in the North Germanic language, Ogham (3rd -8th centuries in Celtic language), Gothic (4th century or later) of the northeast German, and Anglo-Saxon alphabet invented a prosody norm in the 8th century.

In addition, in the late 8th century, in Breton there is indirect evidence that literalization by the Latin alphabet was carried out, and there is a vocabulary book of the 11th century in the Cornish language. Prosody standardization was performed in these languages, as early as French or German. Therefore, we can say that in the Celtic languages, in the Middle Ages, the written language was introduced as early as the other European national languages.

However, from the late period of the Middle Ages, the decline of these languages had already begun. *Kernewek*, the Cornish language, since it was not used at all in Christianity (at least in missionary activities), was forced to disappear at the end of the 18th century. *Brezhoneg*, the Breton language, was no longer used in the higher social classes, nobles and royal court already at the beginning of the 12th century, but it was used in the Catechism (a Christian primer), so it survived to the modern times. *Cymraeg*, the Welsh language, maintained prestige even in the 19th century, because the Bible was translated into this language in the 16th century. Methodism, a major Christian sect in Wales, used this language actively in their mission since the 18th century. In Alba (Scotland), *Gaighlig*, Scottish Gaelic was only used in the so-called Highlands, the northen part of the region, from the Middle Ages. Because the Christian missionaries did not use this language actively after the 16th century, it began to decline in the 19th century. The situation was the same in Éire (Ireland): *Gaeilge*, the Irish language, which had a long literary tradition from the early Middle Ages, declined in the 19th century as well. Potato famine in the middle of the 19th century accelerated this situation.

In these circumstances, in the late 19th century, the revival movement started in Éire, combined with political nationalism. After independence in the first half of the 20th century, Éire began to make efforts towards linguistic reconstruction as a national policy. In other Celtic languages also, the language revival movements began in the 19th century, even though they did not have such a strong political motivation. At the end of the 19th century, *Brezhoneg* had such a revival movement combined with the political regionalism movement.

In Cymru (Wales), the Celtic revival movement, which had Celticity as its main identity, in the general stream of European Romanticism, symbolized by the "Eisteddfod" (Welsh festival of literature, music and performance) since the middle of the 19th century. This competition became the core of the Cymraeg revival movement.

However, real linguistic revival movements began in the 1970s, because the situation of decline became serious. In addition, together with the reconsideration of the theory of the nation-state, regional cultures were re-evaluated, and among others, minority and regional languages began to receive attention. Since the 1990s, cultural diversity has become increasingly focused. Linguistic pluralism and the re-evaluation of regional languages has begun. This has led to the current revival situation.

Chapter 5
Liberating Babel, Notes on Imperialism, Language and Dystopia

John C. Maher (International Christian University)

> *The question of the tower of Babel, built without God, was not to mount to heaven from earth but to set up heaven on earth.*
> Fyodor Dostoyevsky, *Brothers Karamazov*, 1950, pages 25-26)
>
> *That gibberish he talked was city speak, gutter tclk. A mishmash of Japanese, Spanish, German, what have you. I didn't really need a translator, I knew the lingo, every good cop did.*
> Rick Deckard, *Blade Runner* (Dir. Ridley Scott, 1982).

1. Introduction

The traditional explanation holds that the story of Babel is the Edenic problem of human disobedience before a jealous God. It is a miserable story in which a selfish and human God appears unable to share space with the men and women he has created. With such an interpretation, the story of the Tower of Babel is mostly reviled by linguists. According to that version, the languages of the world are humankind's punishment, bilingualism a curse. The metaphor of the Tower of Babel in the Hebrew Bible has been a powerful and destructive image in the history of nationalism and the state management of language. It seems to suggest that monolingualism is our natural state. It seems to suggest that knowing other languages is abnormal. Monolingual is pure and trustworthy, dialects are inferior, regional languages are unpatriotic. There is one pure accent, one pure variety that we should aspire to, one beautiful tower reaching to the sky.

Emptiness lay at the heart of Babel. The emptiness described in Fritz Lang's (1927) film 'Metropolis' has its own Tower of Babel. The empty space combines with the emptiness offered of the false-Maria, the robot who symbolizes the ethically hollow force of Babel's power. If the purpose of the Tower of Babel is thought-control, language then speech control is its vehicle — as Orwell's novel *1984* described. By contrast, the post-Babel world radically argues that human speech does not transmit thinking —the thoughts of the powerful. Rather the goal of speech is to accomplish thinking. Language is not the dress of thought but its very body.

The interpretation advanced here is that Babel was a struggle over ultimate political truth, a divine critique of cultural (linguistic) homogeneity and the hubris of empire. The building of the Tower of Babel was a sign of imperial anxiety. The massive structure signaled a fear of cataclysmic decline. Underpinning its construction was a typical colonial referent: unification with, unsurprisingly, a 'united' one language policy. Babylon was the seat of empire, a powerful port, capital of the vast Babylonian empire, and the largest metropolitan city of the ancient world. The Tower of Babel symbolized the national enterprise of an aggressive and expansionist community.

Babel was a not-good place, a dystopia, an imaginary community, characterized by linguistic and cultural oppression right at the centre of the capital of empire. The goal of Nimrod — ruler of the Empire — was territorial unity (the city), and language unity. However, such policy contravened the human situation specifically envisioned and promoted by the God of Creation (Genesis 9.19): "And you, be ye fruitful, and multiply; bring forth abundantly in the earth, and multiply therein."

The Babel story has been destructive in the narrative of language in society. Babel is a warning about 'multilingualism.' Ultimately, the King cannot permit it. Babel implies a rejection of multilingualism in the modern nation state. It is an ancient myth groomed for the modern age. It was the guiding myth when the United States declared war on Germany in 1917 and pursued war at home on America's second language, German, and on other 'foreign tongues'. It did so under the banner of the "Babel Proclamation" (1918). In this, German was proscribed, "immigrant languages went into decline and the there was a precipitous drop in the study of foreign languages in US schools" (Barron 2014:1; Frese 2005). Theodore Roosevelt, commending the "Babel Proclamation" stated: "America is a nation — not a polyglot boarding house. . . . There can be but one loyalty — to the Stars and Stripes; one nationality — the American — and therefore only one language — the English language" (Barron: ibid). Roosevelt's words are echoed in today's English-Only movement in the USA. Likewise, in the Babel of 16th-17th century Europe only selected languages would be permitted to survive the wrath of God, namely, dominant national languages. There would be no room for convivial co-existence with smaller non-national or even national languages, languages of the periphery, languages of the indigenous.

The event at Babel was a confrontation about the nature of society. It depicts God throwing down empire, overturning a tried-and-tested policy of cultural and linguistic conformity. Powerful states have a long coercive tradition involving the suppression of local languages and cultures. After Babel, the policy is reversed. The world is returned to multilingualism.

The analysis of a myth must, of necessity, be bifocal. It must focus on both the historical background that underpins it and at the same time look at how the myth has functioned as a cultural product. This interpretation reverses the traditional tropes of Babel towards a postcolonial and liberationist perspective.

The language-diversity-as-punishment exegesis is here reversed to become a story of existential liberation. This is in accord with the biblical God's declared creative purpose for humankind: to populate the earth and contribute to it richness. God subverts the hubris and introversion of the Tower of Babel — through the instrument of language. Destroying its uniformity of purpose and language practice God forces humankind to go out to embrace a diverse world. Babel was indeed a symbol of national unity, language unification, the 'architecture' of community purpose. Hegel (1835) commended Babel for the 'corresponding sensuous presence' of an inner vision "rising into the clouds." This vision was 'dissolved unity' of individuals. Theirs was a common purpose – where the individual no longer exists, no longer 'objective to itself.' Rather the 'form and shape' of Babel was the realization of a new and wider-one: the state 'the holy, absolute unifier of men.' The outward sign of an inner language that the tower of Babel represents is a false vision that must inevitably fail. Communities of action are diverse: horizontal rather than vertical. A creative presence of a multiplicity of voices and translations is the divine purpose toward the construction of truly human community.

2. Build Higher

2.1. A Purer Air

Imperial states seek a purer air. They build higher. The Pantheon, the Empire State Building, the Arc de Triomphe. Go bigger. Like Edward Lutyens' rebuilding of New Delhi, fit for the greatest empire on earth. Build more. The ziggurats of Babylon. Babel. Build stronger. States construct roads and plazza and monuments to themselves. They build factories, do good things, establish schools named after national heroes and write their own history.

Empires do not strike back. They decline and fall. By c. 612-320 BC, after the fall of the Assyrian Empire, Babylon was a populous trade city of 200,000 people estimated to be the largest city in the ancient world, on the banks of the river Euphrates, beautifully adorned by king Nebuchadnezzar. It had geo-political significance in Mesopotamia and throughout the powerful Babylonian Empire — the most powerful state of the ancient world. Even after the overthrow of the empire by the Persian king Cyrus the Great (539), the Babylonians never forgot that they had once been rulers of the world.

The capital of the province of 'Babil' is the now the city of Hillah which lies opposite the ancient city of Babylon (لباب), on the Euphrates river. Until recently, Babylon was an elegant ruins in central Iraq, a proud tourist site in Babil province' south-west of Baghdad: relic of mighty conflict and the inevitable demise of empire.

On the American invasion of Iraq in 2003, the US army converted Babylon into a military depot with 2000 ground troops, munition dumps and hundreds of vehicles over a period of two years. (Note 1) The 2,600-year-old brick pavement was crushed by military vehicles, "archaeological fragments scattered across the site, and trenches driven into ancient deposits, vast amounts of sand and earth, visibly mixed with archaeological fragments, were gouged from the site to fill thousands of sandbags and metal mesh baskets, contaminating the site for future generations of archaeologists, cracks and gaps where people had tried to gouge out the decorated bricks forming the famous dragons of the Ishtar Gate" ('Babylon Wrecked by War' The Guardian 2005: Jan.15 and Bajjaly, Joanne Farchakh. 'History lost in the dust of war-torn Iraq.' *BBC News*. 2005-04-25.). One empire installed above another.

A decade later, in 2015, ISIS continued the war on Iraq, bulldozing the ancient Assyrian city of 'Nimrod,' capturing its archeological treasures for sell-off and now ISIS' own army is poised at the gates of the ancient capital Babylon.

2.2. Nimrod. Ruler of the High Air

Nimrod was grandson of Ham, great-grandson of Noah who established his kingdom in Babylon (Gen. 10:10-11). Extra-biblical traditions (Dailey 1998;) associate this mighty ruler with the Tower of Babel whose power led him into conflict with God (in addition to Flavius Josephus, this is found in the Talmud (Chullin 89a, Pesahim 94b, Erubin 53a) and later midrash (van der Toorn, K. van and van der Hosst 1990).

> *Nimrods were again deployed to the Middle East as part of the British contribution to the US-led invasion; missions in this theatre involved the Nimrods performing lengthy overland flights for intelligence-gathering purposes. On 2 September 2006, 12 RAF personnel were killed when a Nimrod MR2 was destroyed in a midair explosion..following an onboard fire over Afghanistan* 'Nimrod' (military aircraft). *Wikipaedia*

Imperial states make language laws, define borders and describe their territory with maps. When new territory is invaded, or occupied, new place names replace the old, according to the prevalent angle of power: toponymic cleansing.

The slaves who serve these places hold different dreams — sometimes complacent, comfortable thoughts, sometimes visions of resistance and independence, or escape

> *We know where we're going*
> *We know where we're from*
> *We Leaving Babylon-*
> Bob Marley, *Exodus*

The 'problem of Babel' was that humankind frantically sought transcendence — higher and bigger — when a reasonable answer lay, in fact, on solid ground beneath their feet. In the messiness of culture, the ambiguities of language, the daily work of translating who we are in the minds and lives of others. Being grounded.

Perhaps this was the import of Kafka's suggestion in the story 'The Pit of Babel' (*Der Schacht von Babel* 1930): we must no more build a Tower of Babel but rather dig a hole in the ground.

3. Living Speech, Dead Words

3.1. The Social Soul

Babel builders belong to various ideologies of power. Dostoevsky warned that capitalists, communists, fascists are all zealots for mastery of the skies: but only in order to bring it down and make it subject to their own material goals.

> *The question of the tower of Babel, built without God, was not to mount to heaven from earth but to set up heaven on earth.*
> Fyodor Dostoyevsky, *Brothers Karamazov*, 1950, pages 25-26.

Babel builders reach forward and up. Theirs is a social eschatology. They manufacture the soul anew: in their own image.

In the structuring of the cities of Babel, downtown towers block the sun, walkways send people in directions they don't like to go, high rises make tunnels of wind, giant housing slums growl, bleed, smoke on the outskirts of cities. A metaphor for something lost? But what? What are the metaphors that make the Babel story so compelling.

Babel was modernity's first urban enterprise. It was built as a sign that the past no longer mattered (God, society, covenant with the earth, language). It was built to predict the future. How so? In Jung's term's modernity's humankind: was now lost from ancient roots. Even more terrible it could not see properly tomorrow and so 'modern man' was "at the very edge of the world, the abyss of the future before him' (Jung, 1976).

Perhaps, then, a large tower will improve our vision? This was the import of Franz Kafka's narrative comparison of two structures 'built' in Babylon and China more or less the same time. More than this was Kafka's argument that Babel was the sign of the impossibility of human restraint. "Human nature, essentially changeable, unstable as the dust, can endure no restraint; if it binds itself it soon begins to tear madly at its bonds, until it rends everything asunder, the wall, the bonds, and its very self" (the Great Wall and the Tower of Babel).

3.2. A Place of Dead Words

Babel was not a home. It purpose was to remain empty. A permanent sign of emptiness. Not too far from the territory of old Babylon, Dubai boasts the tallest building in the world. Burj Khalifa was opened in 2010 at 830 meters. Almost 3 times the height of Tokyo Tower. It cost 1.5 billion U.S. dollars Babel was not a home. It was a temporary place. It that lonely place there was only one version of reality, one culture, one language. Burj Khalifa has 900 apartments: 825 apartments remain empty.

Does the monolingualism of the spirit create its own destruction? It hears only itself. It speaks one language. This spirit is unkind. It brings fire not light. It hears only one voice, one thought. For a thousand years Babel has been a quiet ruins: a tourist site in the province of Babel, south of Baghdad. The US-led Western coalition stays and ISIS push forward. Does Babel call again? Does it beckon, again, to the worship of a single voice that listens only to itself? A voice that leads inexorably to banal self-destruction.

> *The Tallest Building in the World: Burj Khalifa!*
> *The asking price for a one-bedroom apartment is at Dh120,000, while two bedrooms are advertised for Dh220,000. Similar offers can be found at Bayut or Propertyfinder. According to Better Homes (Dubai) sales adviser Laura*

Adams, about 825 of 900 apartments in the Burj Khalifa are still empty, some nine months after the tower's launch (Zainab Fattah, Bloomberg 2010).

3.3. Handing Back the Living Tongues

The language of the world of Babel was pristine, all one thing. This language consisted of dead words in a tower of already constituted meanings. The masters of Babel knew that in order to pursue their Orwellian project that thought and language must be united ("And the whole earth was of one language, and of one speech"). Babelic was near-death language constructed and patrolled by speakers themselves.

No interrogations of meaning could be heard in the corridors of Babel. No silences of doubt and the ambiguity of past, present and future. Babelic was dogmatized, institutionalized language, ready-made and limiting human experience. Employing Merleau-Ponty's fecund concept we might say that Babelic was 'sedimented language' (*le langage parlé*) or the 'the stock of accepted relations between signs and familiar signification." We presume that by 'taking down' Babel without actually destroying it, God's action handed back to society a living tongue (*le langage parlant*). This living, authentic speech, creates and recreates itself in expressive acts 'sweeping me on from signs to meanings' (Merleau-Ponty).

The living tongues recovered in post-Babel world were far from the tight replicant speech of a linguistic norm. The living tongues were not a social duplication, the desire for speech control by an authority. The post-Babel world recognized that human speech does not transmit thought — there is no transfer cable in the speaking head. The goal of speech is to accomplish thinking. Language is not the dress of thought but its very body.

4. Emptiness: a Tale of Two Babels

Was baust Du?
Ich will einen Gang graben.
Es muß ein Fortschritt geschehen. Zu hoch oben ist mein Standort.
Wir graben den Schacht von Babel.

Kafka Der Schacht von Babel (1931/Glatzer 1995)

4.1. Kafka and Babel

Was the Tower of Babel built to recreate an original unity of community? Franz Kafka believed so and also that the tower aimed at ultimate truth. Kafka concluded however that this was folly, that community and unity could be achieved by doing the opposite. Digging a hole. Kafka concluded that the way to reconnect humanity after Babel would be to dig a hole (see also Kafka's 'Der Turm zu Babel'):

> What are you building? I want to dig a passage. A progress has to happen. My position is too elevated. We are digging the pit of Babel (*The Pit of Babel*, 1931/ Glatzer 1995 p.35).

What makes Tower of Babel different from a Pit of Babel? The essential difference is darkness. Going deeper means going ever darker. To go higher is achieve light and perspective — a Promethean enterprise. And yet, what unites the hole and the tower is surely is their emptiness.

Kafka's notes and parables on Babel seem to be about emptiness. The creation of absence through which we can know emptiness. Paradoxically, it is emptiness that must be excavated in order for humanity to communicate. To examine the meaning of Babel consider two cinematic examples of emptiness — an unwanted condition in which we are empty of spirit - that explicitly draw upon with Babel themes in the city.

4.2. 'Metropolis' (1927)

In the rarified high tower complexes of Fritz Lang's Metropolis (1927) we are presented with the 'New Tower of Babel,' the social metaphor of futurism. This German expressionist sci-fi epic describes the attempts of the wealthy son of the ruthless ruler of the city and a poor worker, Maria, to deal with, to overcome their class differences. In the shadow of the towers, the film's protagonist Maria explains to the abused workers who toil at the machines underground the meaning of their work. She speaks of the biblical Tower of Babel in order to emphasize the disjunction between the city's ruling class and the workers who have built it. The delusional scientist Rotwang seeks to undermine this message and builds a duplicate woman, fantasizing robot-Maria as the 'Whore of Babylon' riding a dragon.

We are forced to conclude from Metropolis that the ideal builder of the future is actually a fiction. Not a real person at all. In fact, Rotwang's laboratory is designed just for that artificial purpose: to build a Machine Man that can replace the human workers of Metropolis. Maria knows this and therefore in her sermon in the basement of the city, she subverts the biblical tale. In Maria's version, God does not destroy Nimrod's tower. The brutalized worker-slaves destroy it. Was that in God's mind how it should be?

Having conceived of Babel, yet unable to build it themselves, they had thousands to build it for them. But those who toiled knew nothing of the dreams of those who planned. And the minds that planned the Tower of Babel cared nothing for the workers who built it (Maria in Fritz Lang's 'Metropolis').

In 'Metropolis,' the ruined Tower of Babel has become a hollow shell. We see, shockingly, that from the beginning, the building was only a surface, a façade, a container of interior spaces. We see, finally, that as Laurence Bird's insightful analysis shows, the new city of Babel permitted a "concordance of depth and shallowness that enables Lang's translucent opacities, his blazing shadows, his machines with phantom flesh, to be both there and not there, the most substantial and the most insubstantial of things" (2011:20). The robot was found to be hollow. Robots always are.

4.3. 'Blade Runner' (1982)

Babylon turns up again in Los Angeles in 2019: a rubble of high rise structures of glass, metal, concrete, Above it, the skies glow with fire, smoke, and industrial rain. The emigration of the elite to utopian "off-world" planets leaves an imperial capital filled with 90 million well-monitored people with complicated lives. Replicants do the dirty work. In fulfillment of the hope in 'Metropolis.'

LA 2019 lacks the civility and continuity of well, say, Helsinki. The debris of the past mingles and layers with the new technologies. In this noir film of social despair and ambivalent fantasies, Blade Runner (1982), there emerges in the first scene a 700-storey pyramid. Babel. Where is God's hand in this pharaonic imagery? Judith Kerman (2012) in her analysis of the biblical images of Blade Runner notes how both Babel and Los Angeles pervert Jacob's ladder (Genesis 28: 13) where the angels go up and down. Replicants do the dirty work.

What makes LA not Babylon is its multilingualism. It is a seething mess of edgy creoles. It is first-world and 3rd world. The culture of the streets is hybrid, a Japanified Babel, as if the 90s Japanese economic bubble never burst but rather took over the world.

> *That gibberish he talked was city speak, gutter talk. A mishmash of Japanese, Spanish, German, what have you. I didn't really need a translator, I knew the lingo, every good cop did* (Rick Deckardt in *Blade Runner*, Scott Ridley,1982)

With robots at the gates whither language? With replicants to replicate language what do the inhabitants of Babel 2019 have left to say? Do the replicants keep daily diaries, write poetry? Is theirs a living authentic speech that can express so many shades of human passion. Rick, together with Merleau-Ponty, would agree that this is not the case. It will soon be revealed that their language is as empty as Babel itself. Emptiness is the physical core of Babel — its bricks and mortar — surround the emptiness of Rotwang's and Nimrod's ambition. The hollowness of the robot — the false Maria — is startlingly revealed as her shell burns off in the fire. This is meaning of Walter Benjamin's lament that with mechanical reproduction there is a corresponding loss of aura, in other words the loss of soul.

5. The Story of Babel

In the narrative of the Hebrew Bible, Genesis 11:1-19, the citizens of Babylon set themselves to build a high tower to touch heaven, "in order to make a name for ourselves." God sees their activity as potentially dangerous, threatening ("nothing they plan to do will be impossible for them"). And so they build the tower of Babel. "Babel" is composed of two words, "baa" meaning "gate" and "el," "god." Hence, "the gate of god."

The Babel story, as told in the Hebrew Bible (Book of Genesis (11:19) was based around the building of *Etemenkanki*, the great ziggurat of Babylon (in Sumerian: "temple of the foundation of heaven and earth"). 'Babel' was the place-name (Eng.'Babylon') for the metropolitan capital of the Babylonian and Assyrian empires in the 2nd millennium BC. (Akkadian: *Bābili or Babilim*; Arabic: لبابل, *Bābil*; the Greek *Babylṓn Βαβυλών* is a transliteration of the Akkadian) By mistaken etymology in the Hebrew Bible the meaning was taken from the Hebrew verb balal ("to confuse", i.e. confusion of languages) from the verb לבלב *bilbél*, "to confuse." In other words, (only) the related word in Hebrew, "balal" means "confusion."

The Babel narrative runs thus (Authorized King James Version, 1611):

The Tower of Babel

1. And the whole earth was of one language, and of one speech.
2. And it came to pass, as they journeyed from the east, that they found a plain in the land of Shinar; and they dwelt there.
3. And they said one to another, Go to, let us make brick, and burn them thoroughly. And they had brick for stone, and slime had they for morter.
4. And they said, Go to, let us build us a city and a tower, whose top may reach unto heaven; and let us make us a name, lest we be scattered abroad upon the face of the whole earth.
5. And the Lord came down to see the city and the tower, which the children of men builded.
6. And the Lord said, Behold, the people is one, and they have all one language; and this they begin to do: and now nothing will be restrained from them, which they have imagined to do.
7. Go to, let us go down, and there confound their language, that they may not understand one another's speech.
8. So the Lord scattered them abroad from thence upon the face of all the

earth: and they left off to build the city.

9. Therefore is the name of it called Babel; because the Lord did there confound the language of all the earth: and from thence did the Lord scatter them abroad upon the face of all the earth.

Genesis 11: 1-9 Authorized King James Version

We point out here that the Babel story in Genesis is similar to and different from the rabbinic midrashic literature. The Babel story can usefully set beside the (neglected) story recounted in The Book of Jubilees sometimes called Lesser Genesis the Jewish religious text of of 50 chapters (VanderKam 2001, Endres 1987). Jubilees is considered canonical (also known as the *Book of Division — Ge'ez:Mets'hafe Kufale dating from the 15th centuries*) by the Ethiopian Orthodox Church and by Ethiopian Jews . The was quoted extensively by Church Fathers such as Epiphanius, Justin Martyr and Origen and is known as the pseudoepigraphia in the Catholic and Protestant as well as Eastern Orthodox Churches.

Whilst it is clear from text of Genesis that the sin committed by the builders of Babel is not named. Jubilees however, adds that the builders exclaimed '*Come, let us go up in it into heaven*' (Jub. 10:18), with the implication that they indeed wanted to claim heaven.

"God has no right to choose the upper world for Himself, and to leave the lower world to us; therefore we will build us a tower, with an idol on the top holding a sword, so that it may appear as if it intended to war with God" (Gen. R. xxxviii. 7; Tan., ed. Buber, Noah, xxvii. et seq.).

Zvi Ron in his exegesis on Babel (2014) notes that this idea is found in TB *Sanhedrin* 109a as well as in later rabbinic literature. He adds that "*Pirkei de-Rabbi Eliezer* (chapter 24) states that Nimrod instigated the plan as a way to invade God's "power base," the heavens. Importantly, he also notes that Based on the plain reading of this verse, Saadiah Gaon explains that their sin was wanting to stay in one area and not filling the earth as God commanded, which led Him to disperse them " (p.42). (See also Note 1).

Book of Jubilees

1. For they departed from the land of Ararat eastward to Shinar; for in his days they built the city and the tower, saying, 'Go to, let us ascend thereby into heaven.'
2. And they began to build, and in the fourth week they made brick with fire, and the bricks served them for stone, and the clay with which they cemented them together was asphalt which comes out of the sea, and out of the fountains of water in the land of Shinar.
3. And they built it: forty and three years [1645-1688 A.M.] were they building it; its breadth was 203 bricks, and the height (of a brick) was the third of one; its height amounted to 5433 cubits and 2 palms, and (the extent of one wall was) thirteen stades (and of the other thirty stades).
4. And the Lord our God said unto us: Behold, they are one people, and (this) they begin to do, and now nothing will be withholden from them. Go to, let us go down and confound their language, that they may not understand one another's speech, and they may be dispersed into cities and nations, and one purpose will no longer abide with them till the day of judgment.'
5. And the Lord descended, and we descended with him to see the city and the tower which the children of men had built.
6. And he confounded their language, and they no longer understood one another's speech, and they ceased then to build the city and the tower.
7. For this reason the whole land of Shinar is called Babel, because the Lord did there confound all the language of the children of men, and from thence they were dispersed into their cities, each according to his language and his nation.
8. And the Lord sent a mighty wind against the tower and overthrew it upon the earth, and behold it was between Asshur and Babylon in the land of Shinar, and they called its name 'Overthrow'.

The building of tower temples was an important work of the Babylonian empire. Greek historian Herodotus described an enormous tower-temple in Babylon in the 5th century BCE:

In the middle of the [sacred precinct of Jupiter Belus] there was a tower of solid masonry, a furlong in length and breadth, upon which was raised a second tower, and on that a third, and so on up to eight. The ascent to the top is on the outside, by a path which winds round all the towers. When one is about half-way up, one finds a resting-place and seats, where persons can sit for some time on their way to the summit. On the topmost tower there is a spacious temple, and inside the temple stands a couch of unusual size, richly adorned, with a golden table by its side. There is no statue of any kind set up in the place, nor is the chamber occupied of nights by any one but a single native woman, who, as the Chaldeans, the priests of this god, affirm, is chosen for himself by the deity out of all the women of the land (Histories 1.181).

6. Interpretations

6.1. Storming Heaven

Kugel summarizes the traditional interpretation of Genesis 11: 1-9. thus: "The real crime involved in the building project was the tower itself, which was intended for the purpose of "storming heaven" or some related evil desire. For this plan and the arrogant attitude underlying it the builders were punished. Their leader was Nimrod. He himself was a wicked giant and a rebel against God; he may have been aided by other giants. As a result of this deed, the people themselves were scattered and their great tower was cast down to the ground" (1998, p. 234 quoted in Strawn 2105).

The 'Tower of Babel' is an ancient story with iconic status that deals with —as I shall explain — the theme of Bob Marley's song - Babylon. Babel is thematized in poetry and literature from Dante and John Milton to Dostoevsky and Pierre Emmanuel. It was the subject of artistic representation in the renaissance and of contemporary theological and critical literary discourse. Placed at the beginning of the Tanakh, the canon of the Hebrew Bible, Babel narrates a dramatic struggle between God and humankind (Genesis 11:19). The traditional interpretation holds that Babel is the story of humankind storming heaven. Its symbol is architecture: the building of a ziggurat, one of the many temple-towers in the Tigris-Euphrates valley.

6.2. Pentecost: Reversing Babel

The Babel drama ends with terrible dénouement. In the wake of the fury of God, the work of the Tower must cease; the population is stricken by a 'confusion of tongues.' The conventional reading of the story's ending is straightforward: cultural diversity is a curse. The Babelic community is now torn apart by differences of language. 'Difference' is divine punishment.

As we see in Thomas Aquinas and Christian philosophy the tragedy of Babel is ultimately redeemed. At Pentecost, Jesus' disciples, in order to preach the Gospel, are given enhanced powers of language — bilingualism — the ability to speak in many tongues. And they do.

In classical hermeneutics, to understand a text we are invited to read backwards, to interpret in light of what particular events may become rather than conjecture meaning from text at the time of construction. Thus, one line of Christian interpretation of Babel has connected the story in Genesis with the story of Pentecost in the Acts of the Apostles: from the Hebrew bible to the New Testament. Pentecost has been termed 'the reversal of Babel' (Guthrie 1971: 71). What does this mean and does Pentecost shed light on the interpretation of Babel? The Pentecost text runs as follows,

> When the day of Pentecost came, they were all together in one place. **2** Suddenly a sound like the blowing of a violent wind came from heaven and filled the whole house where they were sitting. **3** They saw what seemed to be tongues of fire that separated and came to rest on each of them. **4** All of them were filled with the Holy Spirit and began to speak in other tongues[a] as the Spirit enabled them. **5** Now there were staying in Jerusalem God-fearing Jews from every nation under heaven. **6** When they heard this sound, a crowd came together in bewilderment, because each one heard their own language being spoken. **7** Utterly amazed, they asked: "Aren't all these who are speaking Galileans? **8** Then how is it that each of us hears them in our native language? **9** Parthians, Medes and Elamites; residents of Mesopotamia, Judea and Cappadocia, Pontus and Asia,[b] **10** Phrygia and Pamphylia, Egypt and the

parts of Libya near Cyrene; visitors from Rome 11 (both Jews and converts to Judaism); Cretans and Arabs — we hear them declaring the wonders of God in our own tongues!" **12** Amazed and perplexed, they asked one another, "What does this mean?" **13** Some, however, made fun of them and said, "They have had too much wine." *Acts of the Apostles* 2: 1-13

According to the 'Pentecost connection' in the presence of God, there are no foreigners. This is the Christian message of Pentecost. Belief in God is no longer the property of one ethnic group, one chosen people one language, one nation. Rather, the awareness of God, as depicted in Pentecost, transcends boundaries. The implication is that Christians at Pentecost saw themselves as the new global citizens.

In the mind of the writer of this 5th book of the New Testament (traditionally attributed to Luke), the metaphors of Pentecost (tongue of fires) and the magnificence of a polyglottal world might be intended to show that we are not cultural prisoners bound by a language and culture. We are not either/or. We are not Jews or Gentiles, Roman or Greek. We have different voices within, different faces. This Christian idea was liberation from the Upper Room, liberation from the Tower, the liberation of voices that were suppressed in the Tower of Babel.

It is quite possible that the Pentecost story signals a shift in awareness from local to global, from inside to outside, from fear to confidence. The Pentecost text speaks, excitedly, of the new communication now among, "Romans and Arabs," among people from Egypt, Crete, Libya and Asia. The gospel of Jesus is a lingua franca for all. The Orthodox Church, the Roman and Anglican Churches recite the Nicene Creed (325) in their services: "We believe in the holy Catholic church.' 'Catholic' means universal.

After the death of Jesus of Nazareth, his disciplines whisper among themselves in local Galilean dialect in a room. The next day they are empowered to become world citizens. They will stand in the middle of Jerusalem a world capital: communicating with peoples and cultures from around the world. Today they are trapped in an upper room. Immobile, paralysed with fear. Tomorrow, they will be confident, ready to engage with life, with society. Their new strength is symbolized by tongues of fire above their heads. With these tongues in their mouths they are given the power of speech. The Holy Spirit gives them a new ability to respond to the world. Pentecost is conceived, therefore, as reversing Babel. Languages that once confused and alienated humankind were now combined to new purpose.

7. Reinterpreting Babel

7.1. The Tragedy of Babel

The myth of Babel is troubling to linguists and the story is reviled by them. In that story, the result of language diversity turns language into a weapon of intimidation and destruction. Babel serves as a proto-explanation for how mutually unintelligible languages in the world came into being. However, its iconic message has only served as the talisman of the negative notion that multilingualism is a social problem. Einar Haugen, Norwegian-American pioneer of postwar sociolinguistics summarises the problem in 'The Curse of Babel,'

> "Those of us who love languages and have devoted our lives to learning and teaching them, and who find in language a source of novel delights and subtle experience, find it hard to put ourselves in the right frame of mind to understand the conception of language diversity as a curse" Einar Haugen, 1973: 47)

7.2. Reinterpreting Babel: Cultivating Heteregeneity

In this paper I suggest an alternative reading to traditional interpretations. The proto-myth is not, in the first instance, a tragic 'explanation' of language diversity. In fact, the reverse. The story of Babel is a critique of tribalism, homogeneity, and the hubris of nation. This critique thereby replaces a 'tragic Babel' and its confounded victims with a 'liberated Babel.' Following the tower's demise, its inhabitants are "dispersed," enjoined to embrace the world, a larger and less uniform cultural world, beyond the gates of Babylon. The tower of Babel drives out persons away from the true nature of humanity, everything — thinking, language — is subsumed into a whole, the burning bricks of desire for conformity.

The traditional interpretation does not suit everybody. Dostoevsky, confronting the shadow of an emerging state in 'The Brothers Karamazov,' rejected this interpretation. 'New society' wants to create a heaven on earth and it will kill to get it. Just like in the old days.

The symbolism of Babel is that the tower was the pride of an expansionist, urban, imperial capital. As Hegel shrewdly and approvingly observed, underpinning the story is the common referent: unificationist ideology where oneness, orderliness, harmony, uniformity was a state of consciousness and an ideal. Babylon was a powerful port, capital of the Babylonian empire, and the largest metropolitan city of the ancient world. The Tower of Babel symbolised the national enterprise of an aggressive and expansionist community.

The monolingualism of Babel is the key to an understanding of the project. Language must be shaped, directed, managed. Military mayhem and murder are named by the state — according to its wishes.

Thus, the destruction of Babel throws down empire and its suppression of local languages and cultures. It is a postcolonial perspective and liberationist perspective. Language in Babel is slavery. It serves the needs of the state, the system not the will of the person. The aim is the destroy the good that was there in the beginning.

> The forgotten principle is that the machine
> Should always destroy the maker of the machine
> Being more important than the maker
> Insofar as man is more important than
> God Words also reflect this principle.
>
> *Tower of Babel*, 1953, Thomas Merton.

The cataclysmic divine intervention in the story of Babel was directed at the hubris and introversion of a community — symbolized by its 'one language' (monolingualism). Divine action challenged Nimrod, the city and its inhabitants (i.e. 'the world') holding out the prospect of a post-Babel condition of greater existential and social freedom, in the wider world, beyond the gates of Babylon. The Tower of Babel represented a false vision that must break down. In its place emerged the complex notion of diversity.

The divine challenge to Babel was in accord with God's declared creative purpose for humankind — to populate the earth and contribute to its richness. In fact, this divine manifesto, a warning about the impending conflict was reiterated in the text (Genesis 9:7) immediately preceding the story of Babel. No longer could the narrow ideology of Babel be sustained. It had to topple.

Communities of action are diverse: horizontal rather than vertical. A more sympathetic reading of the Babel myth sees that the creative presence of a multiplicity of voices and translations is closer to the divine purpose. From the fearful but proud corridors of the tower of Babel, humankind is enjoined to reject the homogeneity of culture and language and place, rather to participate in the construction of a truly human community. Making Genesis happen.

Babel appears to be yet another 'Fall' from true existence from the intention of God. Adam and Eve fell from Paradise itself. The builders of Babel fell from another height — a construction of their own making. The builders of Babel were confused (linguistic confusion) by their own monolingualism not by separate tongues (i.e. linguistic diversity). This aligns with Metropolis' Maria that "All the people spoke the same language but they did not understand each other."

> *La langue*, conceived of as the common, unitary, unifying, and creative core, is distinguished from *langues*, whose plurality is portrayed as punishment. This theme of a universal language (*langue*) and multiple languages (*langues*) that manifest it but also occult it and muddle its purity…is magnificently represented by the mythical sequence of the tower of Babel
>
> Julia Kristeva *Language the Unknown* 1989: 98.

Robert's (2012) states "to me the great tragedy of Babel will always lie in the narrative motif of the loss of the 'holy tongue.' The Talmud states, after all, that Babel is the root of all our forgetting…The tragedy of Babel is that the people once *did* speak the holy tongue; that they had "a way of elevating the mundane to the sacred" (Beck, 1995 p.15 quoted in Roberts 2012a, p.85. Thus, the intervention at Babel was on behalf of cosmopolitanism rather than a metropolitanism.

NOTES

Note 1. The images in this chapter are reproduced from the definitive reconstruction of Metropolis (1926) by the Friedrich Wilhelm Murnau Foundation: Metropolis (New York: Kino International/Transit Films, 2002 ; videorecording).

Note 2. 10.26 in Charles ed., Apocrypha and Pseudepigrapha of the Old Testament. Cf. also Midrash Rabba to Genesis, and sources in Ginzberg, Legends III. 35 in which it is said that "the Lord sent a mighty wind against the tower and overthrew it upon the earth."

Note 3. Note the translation 'one language and the same words' as well as the somewhat more contemporary term population 'dispersal' (rather than more tendentious 'scattered') provided in the English Standard Version (ESV) an "essentially literal" translation of the original (Hebrew, Aramaic and Greek).

The Tower of Babel (Genesis 11: 1-9)

1 Now the whole earth had one language and the same words. **2** And as people migrated from the east, they found a plain in the land of Shinar and settled there. **3** And they said to one another, "Come, let us make bricks, and burn them thoroughly." And they had brick for stone, and bitumen for mortar. **4** Then they said, "Come, let us build ourselves a city and a tower with its top in the heavens, and let us make a name for ourselves, lest we be dispersed over the face of the whole earth." **5** And the Lord came down to see the city and the tower, which the children of man had built. **6** And the Lord said, "Behold, they are one people, and they have all one language, and this is only the beginning of what they will do. And nothing that they propose to do will now be impossible for them. **7** Come, let us go down and there confuse their language, so that they may not understand one another's speech." **8** So the Lord dispersed them from there over the face of all the earth, and they left off building the city. **9** Therefore its name was called Babel, because there the Lord confused[a] the language of all the earth. And from there the Lord dispersed them over the face of all the earth.

References

Alvara, Don Fernando de. *Obras Historicas* (Mexico, 1891), Vol. I, p. 12.

Augustine of Hippo, *On the Literal Meaning of Genesis (De Genesi ad litteram)*, VIII, 6.12 and 13.28,BA 49,28 and 50-52; PL 34, 377; cf. idem, De Trinitate, XII, 12.17; CCL 50, 371-372 [v. 26-31;1-36]; *De natura boni 34-35. On the Literal Meaning of Genesis (De Genesi ad litteram, De Trinitate XII and De Natura Boni)*, VIII, 4.8; Bibliothèque Augustinniene 49, 20

Bhabha, Homi. (1994) *The Location of Culture*. London: Routledge.

Brawn, Brent A. (2105) *Holes in the Tower of Babel*. Oxford Biblical Studies. http://global.oup.com/obso/focus/focus_on_towerbabel/ Date of Access, May 23, 2016.

Daniel I. Bock, "The Role of Language in Ancient Israelite Perceptions of National Identity", *Journal of Biblical Literature* 103.3, Sept 1984

Brooker, Will. (2012) *The Blade Runner Experience: The Legacy of a Science Fiction Classic*, Columbia University Press.

Brueggemann, Walter. (1982) *Genesis: Interpretation*. Atlanta: John Knox,

Certeau, Michel. (1986) *Heterologies: Discourse on the Other*. University of Minnesota Press.

Endres, John C. (1987) *Biblical Interpretation in the Book of Jubilees* (Catholic Biblical Quarterly Monograph Series 18). Washington: Catholic Biblical Association of America.

Dailey, Stephanie et al. (1987) *The Legacy of Mesopotamia*. Oxford, Oxford University Press.

Derrida, Jacques. (1987) *Des Tours de Babel. In Psyche: Inventions de !'autre, tomes I et II*, Paris: Editions Galilee Jacques Derrida, "Des Tours de Babel," (*Difference in Translation*, ed. Joseph F. Graham 178-9 Ithaca: Cornell University Press, 1985).

Edwards, J. (1994) *Multilingualism*. Harmondsworth: Penguin.

Garbini, GIovanni (2011) *History and Ideology in Ancient Israel*. McGill/Queens University Press. Chora: Intervals in the History of Architecture, Volume 631-42.

Guthrie, D., et al. (1970, 91) *The New Bible Commentary Revised*. Michigan: Wm. B.Eeerdmans.

Good, Edwin M. (2011) *Genesis 1–11: Tales of the Earliest World*. Palo Alto: Stanford University Press.

Hiebert, Theodore. "The Tower of Babel", *Journal of Biblical Literature* 126.1, Spring 2007.

Haugen, Einar. (1973) The Curse of Babel. *Daedalus* Vol. 102, No. 3, Language as a Human Problem (Summer, 1973), pp. 47-57

Hannah Lammin (2013) A paradoxical architecture: Babel, and the founding of community through the confounding of tongues. *Zetesis*. Vol. 1 No. 1, The Cruelty of the Classical Cannon, pp. 79–87.

Hegel, W.F. (1835) *Aesthetics. Lectures on Fine Art*, trans. T.M. Knox, 2 vols. (Oxford: Clarendon Press, 1975)

Hiebert, Theodore "The Tower of Babel and the Origin of the World's Cultures," *Journal of Biblical Literature* 126 (2007): 29–58.

Jung, C., (1976) The Spiritual Problem of Modern Man. In: J. Campbell, ed. *The Portable Jung*. London: Penguin, pp. 456-479.

Kafka, Franz. *The Complete Stories*. Eds. Nahum Norbert Glatzer and John Updike. New York: Schocken, 1995.

Kristeva, Julian. (1998) *Language the Unknown* (Le Langage, cet inconnu, Editions du Seuil, Paris, 1981). Translated by Anne M. Menke, Hertfordshire: Harvester Wheatsheaf.

Kugel, James L. (1998) *Traditions of the Bible: A Guide to the Bible As It Was at the Start of the*

Common Era. Cambridge, MA: Harvard University Press, 228–242.

The Collected Poems of Thomas Merton. Vol. 1. 1 vols. New York: New Directions, 1980.

Moosavinia, Sayyed Rahim. (2015) Global Translation: The Dream of a Translation Tower of Babel. Translation Directory. Com and Empire and Apocalypse: Postcolonialism and the New Testament (Sheffield, U.K.: Sheffield Phoenix Press, 2006).

O'Sullivan, Colleen Ann. (2006) *Merton, Thomas and The Towers of Babel*. Australian Catholic University, Ph.D. Thesis

Purdy, Daniel L. (2011) On the Ruins of Babel *Architectural Metaphor in German Thought*. Signale: Modern German Letters, Cultures and Thought. Cornell University Press.

Roberts, Kathleen Glenister. (2012) *Alterity and Narrative: Stories and the Negotiation of Western Identities*. SUNY Press.

Russell E. Gmirkin, *Berossus and Genesis, Manetho and Exodus: Hellenistic Histories and the Date of the Pentateuch* (LHB/OTS 433).

Said, Edward. (1993 *Culture and Imperialism*, New York, Knopf, p.336.

Saadiah Gaon, quoted in Adin Steinzaltz, *Bible Commentary in Responsa Literature* (Jerusalem: Keter, 1978) p. 8 (Hebrew).

Sawyer, J.F.A. Babel. *The Encyclopaedia of Langauge and Linguistics*. Elsevir. 295-6.

Steiner, George. (1975) *After Babel*. Oxford, England: Oxford University Press.

VanderKam, James C. (2001) *The Book of Jubilees* (Guides to Apocrypha and Pseudepigrapha). Sheffield: Sheffield Academic Press.

van der Toorn, K. van and van der Hosst. "Nimrod before and after the Bible" *The Harvard Theological Review*, Vol. 83, No. 1. (January, 1990), pp. 1–29

Zvi Ron. (2015) The Book of Jubilees and the Midrash Part 3: The Tower of Babel. *Biblical Quarterly* 42.
http://jbq.jewishbible.org/assets/Uploads/423/jbq_423_zvironjubileesbabel.pdf. Date of access June 5, 2105.

第5章　要約

バベルの解放
帝国主義、言語、ディストピアについての覚書

ジョン・C・マーハ（国際基督教大学）　　　　　　　　　（崎山拓郎訳）

　メトロポリタンかコスモポリタンか？　虚空なる支配か地に足をつけるか？　帝国に鎮座する巨大な帝国の記念碑（塔）を建造するのか、はたまた世界の国々へ住み着き、管理するのか？　多言語主義／言語多様性か、それとも単一言語による言語の純粋性なのか？
　伝統的な解釈では、バベルの物語を、妬む神の前での人間の不従順という（エデンの園における）問題であると考える。わがままで人間らしい神が、自ら創造した人間と共存できないようにみえる、悲惨な話である。そうした解釈によって、バベルの塔の物語は、言語学者からたいてい、悪しざまに罵られている。この解釈の文脈からは、世界の諸言語は人類の罰であり、二言語併用は呪いである。

バベルの塔

1. 世界中は同じ言葉を使って、同じように話していた。[1]
2. 東の方から移動してきた人々は、シンアルの地に平野を見つけ、そこに住み着いた。
3. 彼らは、「れんがを作り、それをよく焼こう」と話し合った。石の代わりにれんがを、しっくいの代わりにアスファルトを用いた。
4. 彼らは、「さあ、天まで届く塔のある町を建て、有名になろう。そして全地に散らされることのないようにしよう」と言った。
5. 主は降って来て、人の子らが建てた、塔のあるこの町を見て、
6. 言われた。「彼らは一つの民で、皆一つの言葉を話しているから、このようなことをし始めたのだ。これでは彼らが何を企てても、妨

7. 我々は降って行って、直ちに彼らの言葉を混乱させ、互いの言葉が聞き分けられぬようにしてしまおう。」
8. 主は彼らをそこから全地に散らされたので、彼らはこの町の建設をやめた。
9. こういうわけで、この町の名はバベルと呼ばれた。主がそこで全地の言葉を混乱（バラル）させ、また、主がそこから彼らを全地に散らされたからである。

（『欽定訳聖書』「創世記」11章1節から9節）

　ナショナリズムの歴史と言語の国家管理において、ヘブライ語聖書におけるバベルの塔の隠喩は、力強く破壊的なイメージであった。単一言語のみの使用は我々の健全な国家を暗示し、他の言語を知ることは異常事態を暗示している。単一言語のみの使用は、純粋で信頼に値するが、方言は劣っており、地域言語は非愛国的である。唯一つの純粋なアクセント、希求すべき唯一つの純粋なバラエティ、天まで届く唯一つの美しい塔が存在する。ジュリア・クリスティヴァが書いていたように「単一的、統合的で創造的な共通基盤と解された場合の言語（La langue）は、罰として複数形で表わされる諸言語（langues）とは区別される。普遍言語（langue）と、これを明示も隠蔽もし、その純粋性をもつれさせもする複数言語（langues）というテーマ（中略）はバベルの塔の神話連環に見事に表されている」（『言葉、この未知なるもの』1989: 98）[2]。

　バベルの中心は空虚である。フリッツ・ラング（1927）の映画「メトロポリス」で描かれた空虚は、それ自体のバベルの塔を持つ。このバベルの塔を備えた空虚は、ロボットのマリアが示す空虚と結合する。ロボットは、バベル権力の倫理的に空虚な支配力を象徴化しているのである。言語と文化は社会と発話の複製にすぎないのだろうか？　メトロポリスの完全なロボットやリドリー・スコットが描くディストピア「ブレードランナー」に登場する「レプリカント」は、この考えが妥当である可能性を暗示している。バベ

ルの塔の目的が思想統制の言語であるとすれば言論統制はその手段である——ちょうどオーウェルの小説『1984』に描かれているように。それに対して、ポスト-バベルの世界では人間の言論は思考——権力の思想——を伝達しないとラディカルに論じられている。むしろ言論の到達点が思考の達成となる。言語は思想の衣装ではなく実にその身体である。

行動の共同体は多様である。並行というよりむしろ垂直である。バベル神話のより共感的読解は、多種多様な声と翻訳は創造的な現前であり、神の目的にいっそう適うとみなす。すさまじくも壮麗なバベルの塔の回廊から、人類は文化と言語と場所との同一性を拒絶し、むしろ真の人間の共同体の構築に参加するよう命ぜられた。創世記の創造が起こったのである。

バベルはどうも、依然として神意より生じる真の実在からのもう一つの「堕落」のようだ。アダムとイヴは楽園それ自体から落ちた。バベルの建築者たちはもう一つ別の高み——自らの手で成した建造物——から落ちたのである。バベルの建築者たちは、自らの単一言語の使用によって混乱（言語的混乱）に陥ったのであって、別々の舌（すなわち言語的多様性）によってではない。これは、メトロポリスのマリアが言うところの「皆が同じ言葉を話すが人々は互いに理解し合わない」と軌を一にしている。

ここで一歩踏み込んだ解釈は、バベルが、最終的な政治的真理を巡る係争地、文化的（言語的）同一性と帝国の傲慢に対する神の批判であった、というものである。バベルの塔の建造は帝国における不安の兆候である。豪壮な建物は大変動による破局に対する恐怖を表わしている。その建造物の土台を支えているのは典型的な植民地支配の指示対象であった。すなわち、統一化であり、驚くにあたらないが、植民地支配による統一化は「統一された」単一言語という政策を伴うものであった。バビロンは帝国が鎮座する所、強大な港、広大なバビロニア帝国の帝都、古代世界におけるもっとも広大なメトロポリタン的都市であった。バベルの塔は侵略的で拡張主義者的共同体による国家事業を象徴化したものだったのである。

バベルは不正の場、ディストピア、想像の共同体であり、帝都真っ只中での言語的、文化的抑圧を特徴としていた。ニムロデ——帝国の支配者——

の最終目標は領土統一（都市）、そして言語統一であった。しかしながら、そのような方針は明らかに造物主が構想し、助成する人間のあり方に抵触する。（創世記9章7節）：あなたたちは産めよ、増えよ、地に群がり、地に増えよ。バベルの物語では、社会において言語が演じる役割は破壊的であった。そのように引き合いに出されると、バベルは「多言語の使用（multilingualism）」に対する警告となる。最終的に、王は多言語の使用を許すことができない。バベルはこうして近代国家にあっては多言語使用の拒絶を含意していた。それは近代に仕立てられた古代神話であり、言語破壊の文脈で繰り返し引用された。この近代のバベルは、1917年、アメリカがドイツに宣戦布告した際に国民を先導する神話となり、アメリカの第二言語であるドイツ語、またはその他の「外国語」の故郷に向け戦争を突き進めたのである。戦争はそのように「バベル宣言」の旗印の下でおこなわれた（1918）。バベル宣言によりドイツ語は禁止を言い渡され、「移民の言語は影をひそめ、アメリカの学校における外国語研究は急転直下で凋落した」（Barron 2014: 1; Frese 2005）。「バベル宣言」を称賛するセオドア・ルーズヴェルトは、次のように明言している。「アメリカは一つの国家である。多言語が飛び交う下宿屋ではない。（中略）唯一つの忠誠心さえあればよい——ただ星条旗だけに。国民はひとつ——アメリカ人——、それゆえに唯一の言語は——英語である」。ルーズヴェルトの言葉はアメリカにおける今日のイングリッシュ・オンリー運動にも響いている。同様に、16世紀から17世紀に及ぶヨーロッパのバベルにおいて選ばれし諸言語は、神の怒りを免れ生き延びることを許されたであろうもの、すなわち支配者の国語なのである。そこではより規模の小さな非−国語はおろか、国語ですら、周辺言語や土着の言語にあっては、和気藹藹たる共存の余地はなかったであろう。

　多様性は、実に、神の創造行為の明らかなしるしであった。バベルでの出来事は社会の本質をめぐるせめぎ合いである。それは、神が帝国を投げ落とし、多くの試練に耐えてきた文化的な——言語的なものも含む——慣習行動についての国家政策を覆したことを示している。強大な国家は地域言語や文化に対する弾圧を含め長い圧政の伝統を持っている。バベルの後、この支配

は逆転する。世界は多言語使用に戻されるのである。

　神話分析は必然的にバイフォーカルでなくてはならない。神話の土台となる歴史的背景に焦点を当てると同時に神話が文化的産物としてどのように機能しているかにも注意を払わなければならないのである。この解釈は、ポストコロニアル論者やフェミニズム的観点による従来のバベルの隠喩とは、真逆のものである。

　罰と解釈された言語的多様性は翻って実在的解放の物語となる。これは神に宣言された人類の創造的目的にも一致する。その目的とは、地上で暮らし、地上の豊饒に対して寄与することである。神は人の思い上がりとバベルの塔の内側とをひっくり返す――言語という道具を通じて。バベルの塔における人類の意志と言語実践の統一を破壊することで、神は人類に言語と文化の多様な世界を受け入れ、塔から出て行くよう強いる。バベルとは国家統一、言語の統一化、共同体の指標となる「建造物 (architecture)」の象徴であった。ヘーゲルはバベルを「雲にそびえる」内的ヴィジョンと対応する「感覚的現前の一致」と称賛する。このヴィジョンでは個々人の統一は溶解される。その状態が共通の目的だったのである――そこではもはや個は存在せず、「客体それ自体」が存在しない。むしろバベルの形姿は新しくより大きな個の実現である。それは国家、すなわち「神聖で絶対的な人間の統一体」であった。バベルの塔が表象する内なるものの外的象徴と内なるもの及び言語との一致は、不可避に失敗し、倒壊しなくてはならない偽りのヴィジョンである。行動の共同体は多様である。垂直的というよりは平行的である。多種多様な声と翻訳は創造的な現前であり、真の人間的共同体の構築へ向けた神の目的なのである。

訳者注
1　以下聖書からの引用は、日本聖書協会『聖書　新共同訳』(日本聖書協会、1990年)に拠った。
2　訳文に関しては、ジュリア・クリスティヴァ『ことば、この未知なるもの』(谷口勇・枝川昌男訳、国文社、1983年)150頁を参照し、必要に合わせて修正した。

Chapter 6
Cam's Linguapax Adventure — Helping children learn about languages of the world through an online audio and graphic novel

Dr. Olenka Bilash, Ms. Alanna Wasylkiw (University of Alberta, Canada)

1. Introduction

As linguists confront the growth of endangered and disappearing languages, advocates for languages struggle to compete with other social justice issues. Bilash (2012: 25) claims that "language use and language rights have not yet been included in the social justice agenda". To bring issues to the public eye requires researchers to mobilize knowledge at multiple levels in society simultaneously. While Linguapax Asia and Linguapax Africa have focused on academic research relating to language loss and language growth, Linguapax Central America and Linguapax North America have also attempted to reach both an academic and youth audience, the former by publishing stories in first nations' languages and the latter by creating a website about world languages This paper focuses on this website. It begins with a description and rationale for the content and design of the website, is followed by results of a small study with youth users of the first two modules of the website, and concludes with recommendations for future endeavours.

2. The website

The main component of the website consists of a story about a young boy named Cam, who is trying to save the languages of the world in the year 2153. It is presented in the form of a series of comics, like a graphic novel, with audio recordings of the text. The storyline follows Cam to eleven countries on six continents on his mission to "light up a globe" and defeat his menace, the Evil Lopran and his minions, who have begun to destroy the languages of the world by attacking people's capacities to speak their mother tongues. With the guidance of his father, an anthropological linguist, Cam collects meaningful artifacts at each destination to help create an antidote which they hope will save Carla, Cam's mother from losing her language. Students help defeat Lopran by collecting an artifact (for example, legends, proverbs, ways of seeing the world, traditions and linguistic rights), learning to count to ten in a variety of languages and completing quizzes for each of the eleven countries Cam visits. After collecting artifacts from two countries a continent lights up on the globe.) See overview in Table 1.

Table 1. Overview of the website

Country	Artifact	Sample Concepts	Some Languages
Canada	Indigenous Game - Lacrosse ball	Bilingualism; multiculturalism; antidote; anthropological linguist; aboriginal languages; plurilingualism	English, French, Ukrainian, Cree
Mexico	Legend	Cognates, proto-indo-european (PIE) languages; bilingual schools	Spanish Nahuatl
Japan	Tea cup – connection to nature	Names and showing respect; meaning of place names	Japanese, Korean, Tagalog, Ainu
India	Value - hospitality	Diaspora	Punjabi, Hindi
Australia	Memories Dream	Prejudice; language loss; conscious-unconscious; connection to land	Greek, Cantonese, Yolngu, ,
Uganda	Fable	Official languages; ubuntu;	Acholi, Zulu
Morocco	Proverb	UN	Arabic, Berber
France	World view-Joie de vivre	World view	French
Netherlands	Education system	Dialect	Dutch
Brazil	Ecological knowledge-Herbal medicines	Ecological knowledge	Portuguese Italian German
Chile	Linguistic rights	Constitution	Mapuche

Site design

The website design falls within the domain of edutainment, a term coined by White in 2003, but with a history that dates back to WW2 (Van Riper, 2011) and includes television (e.g. Walt Disney family movies), radio (e.g. NHK, CBC and BBC broadcasting), educationally oriented media programming in film (e.g. documentaries by National Geographic), museums (e.g. science centres), and computer games (e.g. learning about subject content, historical events or concepts and learning a skill while playing)[1]. As the name suggests, edutainment emphasizes learning alongside "fun" or entertainment, and in more recent years also encompasses serious games (Adamo-Vilani et al., 2012).

The linguapax website is intended for use at home and in school. As such, its design considered a number of factors: the entertainment factor (EF) and sustaining interest; literacy; motivating and interactive tasks; and balancing new information with presumed prior knowledge.

EF

The creation of this website drew on the coveted research of game developers in the area of affect, pleasure or *fun* in sustained activities such as computer games (Malone 1980; LeBlanc 2004; Hunicke, LeBlanc, & Zubek 2008; Lazzaro 2011). The IT industry fully acknowledges EF and has taken the lead on discerning types of fun or engagement:

> A critical consideration in the development of any video game, serious or otherwise, is whether the finished game is fun, or at the very least, compelling. This factor is what makes a serious game a game rather than a simulation or an interactive lesson. It is the "fun" factor that distinguishes serious games from other pedagogical approaches in that the learner is compelled to learn not necessarily due to the subject matter's intrinsic appeal, but rather due to the entertainment value of the gaming activity with which the subject matter is associated. The player of a serious game is motivated to play the game, and in so doing continues the lesson, much longer and with greater attention than he or she would using traditional learning techniques. (Adamo-Vilani et al. 2012)

As early as 1980 Malone identified three heuristics of games: challenge, fantasy and curiousity. LeBlanc's Taxonomy of Game Pleasures expands this to "eight kinds of fun" to maximize and sustain user interest (Hunicke, LeBlanc, & Zubek 2008) and are summarized in Table 2. The taxonomy explains how a game like *Charades* is designed to develop Fellowship, Expression, and Challenge while games like *Quake* are designed to experience Sensation, Challenge (competition) and Fantasy.

Table 2. LeBlanc's Taxonomy of Game Pleasures

Type of Fun	a.k.a.	purpose
Sensation	Game as sense-pleasure	anything involving the joy of experiencing with the senses.
Fantasy	Game as make-believe	the pleasure of imaginary worlds, and imagining yourself as part of it.
Narrative	Game as unfolding story	the pleasure of experiencing the unfolding of events.
Challenge	Game as obstacle course	the pleasure of solving problems in a game.
Fellowship	Game as social framework	Developing Friendship, cooperation, community
Discovery	Game as uncharted territory	Seeking and finding something new
Expression	Game as soap box	Expressing yourself and creating things (games that let you design characters, etc).
Submission	Game as mindless pastime	Allowing yourself to be swept up in the rules and experiences of the game.

Nicole Lazzaro, founder and CEO of XEO games, a major game development company, describes fun in four categories: 1. The **hard fun** of challenge and mastery; 2. the **easy fun** of exploration, role play, and storytelling; 3. The **serious fun** that emerges from feelings such as frustration or relief associated with experiencing real world issues and contexts (e.g. fire fighter simulations or eco games); and 4. **people fun** that renders amusement, laughter, social mechanics, and bonding while playing. Lazzaro (2011) claims that the most successful games on the market use at least three of these four factors, such as *World of Warcraft* or the *Simms* or *Myst*. Although educators avoid terms like *fun* in the academy, "learning something worthwhile should always be at least a little bit fun" (Jack 2010).

Literacy

The site is designed for a number of audiences including students in grades 4-8, 9-12 and parents/teachers. The component described in this paper targets the first user group. Considering the variability of literacy levels of this audience and their more limited background knowledge about language concepts such as cognates, scripts, language loss, and plurilingualism, we chose to convey the information through a narrative and to tell the story through comics. Weinschenk (2011: 76) claims that "people process information best in story form…[because]… stories are the natural way people process information". She reminds us that "stories aren't just for fun. No matter how dry you think your information is, using stories will make it understandable, interesting, and memorable" (78).

Hogan (2013) and Schwarz (2002) decribe the value of comics or graphic novels as a scaffolding device for higher-level thinking "(T)he reading of graphic novels may require more complex cognitive skills than the reading of text alone" (Schwarz 2002: para. 4). In addition, Wolstat (2013: para. 2) has reported the "near-instantaneous impact" that a teacher's lessons have had by incorporating Marvel comics. In our "increasingly visual culture, literacy educators can profit from the use of graphic novels in the classroom, especially for young students" (Schwarz 2002: para. 1); they both "promote literacy" (para. 3) and "introduce students to literature they might never otherwise encounter" (para. 3). It is thus not surprising that there is a "burgeoning scholarships in comics" that explore the space in which the scientific and literary study of language combine (Prevoo, n.d. quoted from Bramlett 2012: 1).

Comics also lend themselves to bolded and coloured words, thus drawing attention to and providing support for the acquisition of significant vocabulary and concepts in a story. This is a popular strategy within graphic novels such as *Geromino Stilton*, *Thea Stilton*, and *Diary of a Wimpy Kid*. Having certain words and phrases delineated and highlighted in this manner will aid readers to infer the meaning that the comic book creator is hoping will transact in the author-reader interchange.

> The human brain processes written language in several ways at once. For example, you probably aren't sounding out each word in this paragraph as you read. Instead you grab words, and even phrases, in chunks. One way you do that is by perceiving the exterior shape of the words, and the shape of the spaces between words. Therefore your choices regarding the case of the lettering have an impact on the reader's experience (Abel & Madden 2008: 89).

Thus, the highlighting of words is especially effective for readers unfamiliar with the comic book format or at-risk readers who will appreciate the additional reading clues. It will also allow for quicker reading experiences, much in the same way that *manga* texts are created with shorthand clues built into the illustrations and texts. With the proven impact of the graphic novel as a narrative and for the conceptual and linguistic highlighting its format offers, it was well suited for the narrative of Cam's Linquapax Quest.

Motivating and interactive tasks

The majority of the site was developed and constructed on volunteer time. In the absence of a high-tech budget the activities for the site were limited. However, the tasks are meaningful for students: they learn to count to ten in many languages, gain immediate feedback after completing quizzes, and report long term benefits to their own studies, as will be reported later. Furthermore, the original artwork is engaging, the voices are that of professional actors, and the user friendly site was built as a part of a Masters in Education degree.

Balancing new information with presumed prior knowledge

The storyline is simple and risks being considered what novelist Chimamanda Ngosi Adichie's would call the danger of a single story. (See: http://www.ted.com/talks/chimamanda_adichie_the_danger_of_a_single_story). But rather than intending to be stereotypic, it considers the cognitive load of the content and seeks to balance the storyline with the concepts to be learned with the counting tasks and

Figure 1. Strategies for learning to count to ten in different languages

<u>Here are some tips to help you learn more quickly:</u>

1. Listen for cognates- words that seem the same in English and Spanish (eg. *seis* and *six*)
2. Make associations with words you already know to help you remember (eg. *cinco* (5) sounds similar to the French *cinq* (5). Or *ocho* (8) is a bit like ouch!
3. Review often so you do not forget
4. Find extra YouTube clips to practice:

This is a really good site. It might also help you practice. And then you can play the games on the right hand side of the screen:

http://www.bbc.co.uk/schools/primarylanguages/spanish/numbers

Figure 2. Reflection on learning

When you can do it continue on to the next slide.

What helped you learn and remember?
Was it easier or more difficult than learning to count in French or Ukrainian?
Why do you think so?
Did the music help you?
Did you use your fingers to help you count?
Did you repeat after the speaker?
How many times did you repeat before you could remember?
Can you remember how to count in French and Ukrainian?

Practice so you don't forget!

the EF.

The bulk of the site was created by second language (SL) educators at various stages of their careers. Hoping to reach a North American audience and aware that SL learning is not compulsory in many parts of this continent, we sought to expose students to a variety of SL. With Canada being an officially multicultural country and the United States a land of immigrants, we also intended to increase awareness about and give local legitimacy to both first nations languages and the places, languages and peoples who have come to this continent (settlers). Thus, we integrated language learning into the site as well as a number of strategies for learning to count in multiple languages: song, repetition, visual cues, multiple voices. See Figure 1. Embedded in the links are tips about developing language awareness. See Figure 2

3. Website Development

The website was developed in several stages: composing the text, selecting additional support information such as videos, maps and websites, creating visuals for the comics, selecting a domain name, constructing the website, testing the site with student users, and revising the website. Considerable technical preparation was required — formatting all of the comic panels for the website, changing fonts, resizing characters, expanding or reducing speech bubbles to fit the text proportionately, adding the audio and formatting the navigation bar. In several instances one panel had to be made into two because it contained too much text. Finally, it was decided that no more than 150 words would be placed on one page. It was also decided that all guest characters in each unit would be in colour whereas the five main characters in each unit — Cam, Cam's father, Cam's mother, Lopran, and the minion — would remain in black and white for consistency. See Figures 3 and 4 for examples. The audio accompaniment was created for the comics by trained actors and actresses who also volunteered their time.

In *Create Top Level Navigation Tabs*, Nick Beresford Davies (n.d.) suggests that information from eye tracker studies shows that often users of a website read in an 'F' pattern, thus advising the main navigation to be developed along the top

Figure 3. Panel 11 from the Canada unit.

Figure 4. Certain words are bolded and coloured for emphasis and reader engagement.

portion of the site with less important sub-categories on the left side. However, for the purposes of this site it was thought that two different menus would confuse students and its absence would lend more space to content on the main screen which was where the content was located. This supports one of Nielsen's five quality attributes of usability: satisfaction or how pleasant it is to use the design (Nielsen 2012).[2]

4. Using the site

The ultimate goals of the website can be seen on the *Welcome* page of the site. After students read the *Welcome* page they are taken to *Navigation Tips* followed by *Help Find the Antidote!* where the goals of the website story have been outlined for the user. Next, the student is given the introduction, containing background information to the story before he/she begins to read the story in comic format. After the introduction and before the first page of the comics the student is introduced to the country that Cam will visit. This page displays an image of where that country is located on a world map[3], an image of the continent it is on, and the country's flag. The page for the Canada unit can be viewed in figure 5. By controlling for image size students can scroll down quickly to see all of the images before they get to the NEXT button.

Figure 5. Welcome panel from Canada unit.

Once the user has read the introductory pages, he/she is guided to begin the first unit of the website where Cam travels to Canada. Each comic page is on an individual page of the website and the user navigates through the comics using buttons labelled "previous" and "next". The first page of the Canada unit can be seen here. Some pages of the comics have additional information, hyperlinks, and external links for the student to clarify meanings of words that may be unknown and to expand learning on certain topics. For example, see the second page of the Canada unit. An important element of the site, on both the educational and game sides, is exposing students to different languages. See an example of learning to count to ten in over twenty languages throughout the site. After the student has read each of the comics page by page, visiting links as desired, a review page is provided of all of the comics on one page. Once the student has read through the comics and additional information for a second time, they complete a quiz. The Canada review and quiz can be seen here.

5. Student feedback

Four youth participated in a user study of the website: two females (one in grade seven and another in grade five), and two males in grade five. They shall be called A, B, C, and D respectively. After ethics approval and parental consent and student assent were obtained, each student was invited to navigate the website for a period of one hour.[4] Their interaction with the site was recorded through Screencast-O-Matic and analyzed later. Once the student began using the site s/he was not interrupted but a researcher was present to answer any questions. After the hour, students answered fifteen questions orally regarding their experience with the site. From this, we hoped to confirm the user-functionality and goals of the site for the intended target audience, and then be able to improve the site accordingly. In total each student dedicated approximately an hour and a half to the study. Results are reported according to observations of student navigation as well as interviews.

All four student participants reported that they were aware of the countries visited and that there were more countries to visit. When asked to explain the purpose of the site in their own words, and something that they learned, students replied as follows:

- A-The purpose of the website was to teach you about different cultures and that it is important to use and never forget your language...I learned that there are about 7100 languages in the world. Also I learned how to

count to ten in Spanish..
- B-The purpose was to learn a little about the countries and to learn about languages...I learned how to count in different languages and different stories.
- C-The purpose is to help students from grades 5-8 to learn about different countries around the world...Canada has a game called lacrosse which was created by aboriginals over 1000 years ago.
- D-For the navigator of the website to learn things about other countries in a fun way...Mexico has many indigenous cultures, and they all have to be preserved.

All students reported that the website was easy to use, noting clear instructions and the value of the audio component:

- A-It was easy to use, and it was explained well how to use it. It was more educational than fun, but if it did have maybe more games it would be more fun.
- B- Yes, it was easy to use because of the instructions. And it was fun to use because it was fun to read and listen to the comics.
- C- Yes it was fun. The comics and the audio made it easy to get through and there wasn't any boring and uninteresting information.
- D- Yes. The comics and audio made it easy to go through, and there wasn't too much boring info that I had to read.

Although all students responded "no" when asked if there was anything they would change about the website to make it easier to use, they also all offered some tips for improvement. Please see Appendix A.

The value and enjoyment of comics or the graphic novel narrative format expressed by Wolstat (2013) was confirmed by all students who agreed that "it made the website feel more like an adventure." Similarly, the addition of audio contributed to comprehension:

- A-Sometimes the comics would skip something but then I would catch

on (in the storyline). And I liked the audio.
- B- The comics were easy to understand and the sound was helpful.
- C- The comics were easy to understand but at one point the audio needed to be improved. Most of the time the audio made it easier and clearer.
- D-Sometimes the people said a bit too much, but the audio fixed that.

All of the students in grade 5 felt that looking over the comics a second time helped them understand the story and answer the quiz.

- A-Not really but it was a great review and a useful reference when doing the quiz at the end.
- B- Yes, because when you would do the quiz it was a lot easier to scroll up.
- C- Yes it did. It made me understand what they were talking about.
- D-Yes. I could review all of the information as I was going to the next slide or starting the quiz.

All students also agreed that both sets of comics should remain — the first page-by-page with extra information, and the second with continuous comics on the same page. The latter "was useful for the quiz at the end." (Student D)

The students clearly enjoyed the edutainment dimension of the site, and recognized that the quizzes were a part of the narrative adventure. About enjoying completing the quizzes their comments follow:

- A-Yes, but it did say I got a hundred percent even when I didn't finish the quiz.
- B- Yes, it was a good review.
- C- Yes. They were easy and they were good.
- D-The quizzes were too easy, but other than that they were good.

All participants felt that the amount of text per page was "about right", although they noted how the audio helped when there was sometimes "too much on some pages, and too little on others." Having recorded student users in action the points of audio, visual or technical confusion were noted and can easily be revised. (See Appendix A) Three of the four participants reported that they would be interested in exploring this website further in the future "to find out more about other countries to use for school. For example, next year in grade eight I will be learning about the Aztecs and I could use this as a reference." Both males wanted "to see Cam explore more countries and defeat Lopran." The younger female said that she "already learned about the website".

The site is intended for multiple visits and each student took just over one hour to complete two modules. For the most part students felt that the one hour was engaging but that they might have taken a break if they were not a part of the study. After one hour the students were at these points in the site:

- Student A: Mexico Review and Quiz, full quiz completed
- Student B: Mexico Review and Quiz, question two of the quiz completed
- Student C: Mexico 11 (stand-alone page)
- Student D: Mexico 11 (stand-alone page)

All students asked to finish to the end of the two units, even after the one hour timeline. The following are the times that students required to complete to the end of both units:

- Student A: 1:00:17
- Student B: 1:04:47
- Student C: 1:11:00
- Student D: 1:12:34

These similar times likely reflect the fact that not all students visited all of the proposed links. However, with multiple visits being possible, they could always revisit another time. They all listened to the full audio for the page-by-page comics, but just scrolled through the review comics. None of them listened to the comics for the second time on the review pages; however they did use that page to find answers to the quizzes through the text for both units. The quizzes proved to be successful in getting students to review and confirm learning.

Students C and D (the two boys) sang along with videos, specifically the French and Spanish counting sing-alongs. They both replayed them numerous times to sing along . Neither of the girls sang along at any point, nor counted aloud. Student C repeated the name of the warrior, Popocatepetl, under his breath after hearing this pronounced in the comics. If students were participating in this site in their leisure, without the watchful eye of a researcher, they might feel more relaxed to sing along or repeat the numbers while learning to count. If a teacher was using the site with students in a classroom this could also be encouraged.

6. Closing comments

Taking into account researcher observations of the students navigating the site and re-watching the recordings, along with student feedback, the small study confirms the following eight successes.

1. All of the students were engaged by the comics and the audio and they demonstrated comprehension of the story through the combination of both.
2. All of the students enjoyed the quizzes as part of the interactive website "game". They answered all questions on the quizzes and went back to find answers in the comics to make sure they were correct. The quiz motivates students to pay attention to the comics and to help "overcome the evil Lopran."
3. Integration of videos is helpful for teaching students to count. Short videos enabled students to watch multiple times for counting practice.
4. Counting videos with singing or sing-a-longs proved especially engaging.
5. It is helpful to have comics appear in two forms, especially as support for answering the quiz.
6. All four students indicated that they learned from the site. Although it is difficult for students to convey how they learned, or even what they

learned, the fact that they suggested they did is promising. All students also said that they had fun and three of the four would like to explore more of the site.

7. All four students offered helpful technical feedback that will be acted upon in the revisions. See Appendix B.

8. In returning to Leblanc's taxonomy, we see that the website applied six of the eight types of fun: sensation (use of colour and sound; the boys even sang along); fantasy (students comfortably entered/imagined the futuristic story); narrative (the unfolding game/adventure); challenge (the pleasure of solving problems to help Cam overcome Lopran); fellowship (one can imagine children going through the website together or comparing perspectives of characters, or counting together in different languages); and discovery (users were learners who discovered many new things about language and culture).

The numerous other topics that can be explored on the site through extra information and links makes it a valuable resource for parents and teachers to increase the learning opportunities for students.

7. Future endeavours

In addition to attending to all of the student-participants' observations and suggestions, we intend to make the site more interactive. See details in Appendix B. The ultimate goal of the site is to have students complete five steps of activities relating to languages and social justice and then be awarded a Linguapax certificate. The five steps will include accompanying Cam on his adventures (learning to count in many languages, completing the quizzes); supporting plurilingualism; learning what a language means to someone through a personal interview; identifying and sharing projects that would bring language into the social justice arena; and finally, completing an individual or collective social action project based on everything they have learned. It is further hoped that with the site going public, funding will be found to support a new narrative for grades 9-12 as well as a teacher guide.

8. Limitations

Results of this study were limited by the following:
1. student performance may have been affected because the students knew it was a research study.
2. Since a researcher was watching them as they navigated the site, they might have been nervous which could have affected their actions.
3. One hour is a long time for youth to be on the site in one sitting, so this could also account for varying results .

Note
1. In Africa, and now beyond, edutainment refers to educational theatre.
2. Usability is defined by **5 quality components**:
   - **Learnability**: How easy is it for users to accomplish basic tasks the first time they encounter the design?
   - **Efficiency**: Once users have learned the design, how quickly can they perform tasks?
   - **Memorability**: When users return to the design after a period of not using it, how easily can they reestablish proficiency?
   - **Errors**: How many errors do users make, how severe are these errors, and how easily can they recover from the errors?
   - **Satisfaction**: How pleasant is it to use the design?
3. World Atlas gave approval to use their maps so long as their logo was kept on the image. Any other images in the site that are not original drawings were verified as free to use in the public domain through Wikimedia Commons.
4. The requests were kept simple in order to insure sufficient volunteers for the research. Parents and youth were told that the student would be filmed as to observe how they navigated through the site and completed the two units of comics for one hour, and then asked 15 questions one on one about their experience with the website.

References
Adamo-Villani, N., Oania, M., Brown, J. Whittinghill, D. & Ccoper, S. (2012) "Building a

serious game to teach secure coding in introductory programming courses" *Proceedings of Eurographics 2012* - Educators, Cagliari, Italy. EG Digital Library.

Abel, J., Madden, M. (2008) *Drawing Words & Writing Pictures*. New York: First Second.

Beresford Davies, N. (n.d.). *Create Top Level Navigation Tabs*. Retrieved from http://www.using-dreamweaver.com/building-a-website-using-dreamweaver/create- navigation-tabs.html

Bilash, O. (2012) "Factors Contributing to Current Aboriginal Language use in Canada: A Call for Social Justice" *Citizenship Education Research Network Peer Review Collection*, 2 (1), 62-75. (URL: http://www.ubc.ca/okanagan/education/__shared/assets/2912CERNCollection35953.pdf

Hogan, J. (2012, August 30) "Ghost of a Chance: How One Teacher Explores Comics in the Classroom" [Web log post]. Retrieved from http://www.20somethingreads.com/features/articles/2012/08/30/ghost-of-a-chance-how- one-teacher-explores-comics-in-the-classroom

Hunicke, R., LeBlanc, M. & Zubek, R. (2004). *MDA: A Formal Approach to Game Design and Game Research*. Proceedings of the Challenges in Game AI Workshop, Nineteenth National Conference on Artificial Intelligence. Retrieved June 10, 2012 from http://www.cs.northwestern.edu/~hunicke/vitae.html

Jack, M. (2010) Independent http://www.independent.co.uk/life-style/history/edutainment-is-there-a-role-for-popular-culture-in-education-1869105.html

Lazzaro, N. (2011) The 4 Most Important Emotions for Social Games. Retrieved June 10, 2012 from http://www.slideshare.net/NicoleLazzaro/gdc-4-emotions-social-games-lazzaro-slides-100311

Lazzaro, N. (2010) Big Think Interview With Nicole Lazzaro. Retrieved June 10, 2012 from http://bigthink.com/ideas/19131

LeBlanc, M., ed. (2004a) "Game Design and Tuning Workshop Materials," *Game Developers Conference 2004*. Available online at: http://algorithmancy.8kindsoffun.com/GDC2004/

LeBlanc, M. (2004b) "Mechanics, Dynamics, Aesthetics: A Formal Approach to Game Design" Lecture at Northwestern University, April 2004. Available online at: http://algorithmancy.8kindsoffun.com/MDAnwu.ppt

Malone, T.W. (1980) "What Makes Things Fun to Learn?: Heuristics for Designing Instructional Computer Games" *Proc. SIGSMALL '80*, ACM Press, NY, USA, 162-169.

Nielsen, J. (2012, January 4) *Usability 101: Introduction to Usability*. Retrieved from http://www.nngroup.com/articles/usability-101-introduction-to-usability/

Prevoo, J. (n.d.) "Linguistics and the Study of Comics" [Web log post]. Retrieved from http://blog.comicsgrid.com/2012/09/linguistics-study-of-comics-review/

Schwarz, G. (2002) *Graphic novels for multiple literacies*. Retrieved from http://www.readingon-line.org/newliteracies/jaal/11-02_column/

Van Riper, A. B. (2011) *Learning from Mickey, Donald and Walt: Essays on Disney's Edutainment Films*. Jefferson, North Carolina: McFarlane and Company.

White, R. (2003) *That's edutainment*. Retrieved May 15, 2012 from: http://www.whitehutchinson.

com/leisure/articles/edutainment.shtml Weinschenk, S. (2011) *100 things every designer needs to know about people*. Berkeley, CA: New Riders.

Wolstat, R. (2013, October 6) "Using comics to teach literacy has Marvel-ous results" *Toronto Sun*. Retrived from http://www.torontosun.com/2013/10/05/using-comics-to-teach- literacy-has-marvel-ous-results

Appendix A: General feedback

The following is general feedback from students during their website use and conversation after the formal interview questions:

Videos

- "In the Cree video with the little girl, I couldn't understand her. It should be like the Ukrainian one with the girl counting to ten."
- "Some videos were too long, like the lacrosse video and the Cree video."
- "It would be better if the long videos could be shortened."
- "The video after the little girl video in the Cree section was sort of weird and silly, younger kids may like it more."
- "There are too many videos about the exact same counting."
- "The Spanish and French videos were really fun. The sing-along helps me remember better."
- "When I was in Kindergarten I learned to count in Spanish (the student sings them for me) because it was in a song."

Quizzes

- "In Quiz 2, I didn't know where to go to get to Google translate."
- "When I took quiz two then back to the cognates chart and then back to the quiz I had to retype answers that I had put in. They got deleted when I went to the new page."
- "With the quiz it was convenient to scroll up and have all of the comics to help answer the questions."
- "Great review of going through the comics a second time."

Audio
- "The voices are good. There is one different voice and bad quality."
- "Definitely better with the voices."
- "One was missing an MP3 file."
- "I like Lopran's voice the best. The minion was high pitched, like it wasn't human" (then the student tried to imitate the voices).
- "It is better with audio, easier to follow. If there was a word I didn't know how to pronounce the spelling it is better to have someone saying it the right way for me to hear."
- "The Introduction would be better with a voice. I can't remember if I even read the whole thing."

Amount of information
- "Good information but way too much, it loses the flow of comics. Or at least make it shorter."
- "There is too much information with the part on the cognates."
- "A little too much text, would be better balanced, more minimal."
- "If there was too much I just skipped it. I would read half maybe and then skip the rest."
- "It could be summarized smaller."
- "The extra information was useful."
- "On the first page, I just pressed next without reading anything else. Kids won't read it, they will just press next."
- "I like the comics page by page and then review as I can understand more."
- "If there was too much information that would be good for the teacher to know."

Other
- "I liked that the special characters were coloured. I didn't even notice that there was no colour in the other three."
- "I did not like the questions that said "did you use your fingers…" because you can't answer that. Just in your head. I think most kids will skip that. And there is too much text. I read a couple then skipped the

rest."
- "In the first page there are words underlined, it looks confusing like it is supposed to be a link."
- "I understood the story of the comics."
- "I think it is too easy for grade five up or grade six up. Even grade three could start with it."

Appendix B: Revisions

In addition to attending to all of the student-participants' observations and suggestions, we intend to make the site more interactive. The following changes have already been made:

1. Use a vodcast for the first page. The students confirmed that they skimmed over this page but did not read it. A video explaining all of the information in writing would be more user friendly. To support this recommendation, Weinschenk (2011) says that "you can remember things that you see (visual memory) better than words" (p. 54) and that a solution for this is to "reduce [the] cognitive load by increasing a visual or motor load" (p. 67). In this case the students are filtering information because they do not want to read the text. Weinschenk suggests that "if you think people are filtering information, use color, size, animation, video and sound to draw attention to what's important" (p. 98).
2. Take away the underlining of text and just leave bold. Students tried to click on many titles and words that were underlined, believing that it was a hyperlink, when it was not.
3. External links were only clicked on about half the time. And when they were clicked on, students spent minimal time on the webpage, not reading through information only looking at pictures. This may be more useful to put in the teacher guide section where teachers have this extra information and can lead students through it after the students have gone through the comics on their own first.
4. Instant feedback would be helpful when students are completing the quiz. Currently students input their answers and responses are collected on a

spreadsheet with Google Forms. However, the students wanted to know how they scored immediately. The quizzes serve as motivation to reach the end of the unit. Weinschenk (2011) says that "people are more motivated as they get closer to a goal". This was evident when observing the students continue working past the one hour point required for the study, just so they could finish the quiz. This reward of instant feedback on the quizzes would serve as an intrinsic reward for students, which Weinschenk says are actually more motivating than extrinsic rewards like money or other material items (p. 126).

5. Add a picture of Cam or some type of graphic to the introduction page to get students introduced immediately to the idea of comics and a character. This may pique their interest and get them engaged sooner.
6. Consider shortening the section on cognates to not overwhelm students, or create a simplified version for students and a more detailed one for the teacher guide.
7. Remove videos that are too long. Replace them with shorter ones. Put longer ones in the teacher resources so that teachers can choose to show segments of the film in class.
8. Re-record the audio clip for Mexico 14. A portion of this clip was recorded later (and separately) by the actors, without proper recording equipment. All four students pointed out to me that it sounded off.

第6章 要約
Cam's Linguapax Quest を通じた
グローバル・ハビトゥスの学習

オレンカ・ビラッシュ＆アランナ・ワシルク（アルバータ大学）（崎山拓郎訳）

　2015年母語の日のプレゼンテーションで、アルバータの文化大臣とエドモントン市長は、今や無数の公共サービスで130を越える言語が利用可能だと誇ってみせた。過去10年にわたる進歩はまこと注目に値する！
　それからすぐ後、ビラッシュはエドモントンの英語環境で母語を話すことに伴う不快な感情——反対を示す顔つき、非容認を示すしかめつら、拒絶を示すわずかに頭を振る仕草、お暇を願う態度——について話した。彼女の発言はいつの間にか拍手を呼び起こし、公選された役職者たちを驚かせた。彼らはこの町に浸透する言語的偏見を全く理解していなかったようだ。

　カナダの公共の場で英語以外の言語を話す不快度を計るのは難しく、その不快さを記述するリスクを冒す者はごくわずかしかいまい。とはいえ、バイリンガルまたマルチリンガルが浸透しているこうした空気を打ち消すわけでもなさそうだ。そこにはブルデューが「ハビトゥス」と呼んだものが組み込まれている。「ハビトゥス」とは「社会慣習が永続する性向で人に堆積したもの、あるいは、教育された能力、または、思考、感情、行動を先導し、思考、感情、行動において決定的となる構造化された傾向」である。ブルデューは権力を文化的ないしは象徴的に生み出されるものとみなす。したがって、公の場で顔をしかめたり、肩をすくめたりする仕草は、英語が持つ権力と似姿の創造というメインストリームの欲望とを絶えず再-合法化し、供給するのである。この行為と構造の相互作用はフレイレ（1970）が意識化（conscientization）と呼んだものを通じてのみ変えることができ

る。元々フランス語のconscientiser（Fanon, 1952）に由来するポルトガル語のconscientizaçãoは、世界と世界の仕組みに対する意識的な自覚の発達と不平等に対して行動を起すこととの両方の意味を持っていた。『被抑圧者の教育学』(1970) においてフレイレは教育者たちを誘う。子供たちに「世界を読み取りなさい」と教え、予め決められた知識や情報を空き瓶のように子どもたちに詰め込むだけ（「銀行教育」）にならないようにと。「世界を読むこと」はハビトゥスに意識的になること、ハビトゥスを批判的に吟味すること、その不平等なところを変革するため行動を起こすことである。

　この論文では、フレイレが定義するところの「心」を取り上げ、9～12歳の児童が、電子物語による冒険への参加を通じて、自身のハビトゥスについて意識化し、変えてゆく可能性を探求する。『キャムのリンガパックス・クエスト (Cam's Linguapax Quest)』は、言語（と権力と振る舞い）についてのウェブサイトである。世界中の全大陸、11の国で起る11のモジュールを通じて獲得される認識は、公立学校の大半の児童にとってまず出会うことのないものである。このウェブサイト[1]は、合わせて7時間から10時間の作業時間で完了するように企図されており、「言語使用と言語の権利（とその権利を掲げた）社会正義のアジェンダ」を擁護する試みである。個人の言語権は、世界人権宣言の4つの条項[2]で規定されているが、その他多くの権利と同じく、個人の言語権を私的空間と公的な場へ適用するには大変な困難が生じる。ゆえに社会はハビトゥスに潜む言語的偏見を認識し、受け入れるという困難に直面することになる。その結果生じたのは、カナダまたは世界の、とりわけファーストネイション（訳注：「先住民族」をさすカナダ独自の用語）の人びとにおける急速な言語消失である。カナダにおける民族移民のグループもまた、カナダのフランス語を話す人々と同じく、高い割合で世代間言語喪失を経験している (Chronopoulus 2008; Lupul 2005; Guardado 2009; Palladino 2006; Salegio 1998; Schaarschmidt 2008)。たとえ彼らがカナダ人権憲章によって擁護されている追加の言語権を持つにせよ、そうなのである (Clément, Noels, Gauthier 1993; Gaudet & Clément 2009; Lafontant & Martin 2000; Landry & Allard 1988; Moulun-Passek 2000)。そのため、ハビトゥスを自覚して、言語の再活性化と言語の趨

勢を覆す必要を理解するのに、このウェブサイトが貢献することが望まれているのである。言語の再活性化における最終目標は、共同体の中であるべき位置へと言語の名誉を回復することに等しい（Crystal 2000; Tremblay 2005）。

　本論文は、そのウェブサイトを紹介したアランナ・ワシルクの予備研究（教育学修士論文）（Wasylkiw 2014; Bilash & Wasylkiw 2014）を手がかりにして、ウェブサイトの概要を伝え、教育学的基礎を入念に分析・抽出した後、さらに研究を進める。本論文では、「言語の本質、および、人間生活における言語の役割に対する感受性と意識的知覚」（James and Garrett, eds. 1991, p. xi）を言語意識（LA）がどのようにもたらすかについて、年少者を対象にして論拠を示す。さらに、諸言語に対する意識、並びに「文化が、守るべき風習、習慣、慣習、儀礼といった外的要素のみならず、その文化の中で生活する人々が保ち続けている観念、振る舞い、信念や概念体系といったような内的側面を含む」様（Dufva 1994, p. 22）に対する意識をテクノロジーがどのように高めるかについても、年少者を対象にして論拠を示す。本論の結論は改善点と今後の展望についての提言で結んでいる。

　論文中にはサイトのスクリーンショットを含めている。グラフィックノベルの物語を通じて、二言語の使用、複数言語の使用、多言語の使用、世界観、同族言語、方言、環境知識などの言語的概念が年少者に対してどのように導入されていくかを明示するためである。「物語は人が情報を処理する適切な方法である」（Weinschenk 2011, p. 76）。物語はただ楽しいだけではない。伝えようとする情報がどれほど無味乾燥に思われても、物語を使えば、理解可能で、興味深く、記憶に残るものとなる。したがって、そのウェブサイトは、キャムという名の若者が世界の言語救出に着手する2153年に始まる物語から出来ている。この物語はグラフィックノベルのようなコミック・シリーズの形式で、テキストの音声記録を伴っている。つまり、マルチモードであり、ユニヴァーサルデザインの原理に忠実に従っているのである。物語は、キャムが「地球に火を灯し」、彼の敵、邪悪なロップランとその手先たちを倒すミッションのため6大陸11ヶ国を巡るという筋書きである。ロップランとその手先たちは、人びとの母語を話す力を攻撃することで、世界の言語を壊

し始めている。人類学的言語学者である父の導きに従い、キャムは解毒剤を作る手助けをするため、方々の地にある意義深い人類の所産を集める。その解毒剤が、言葉を失ってしまったキャムの母を救うであろう頼みの綱なのである。児童は人類の所産（例えば、伝説、箴言、世界の見方、言い伝え、言語権）を集め、多様な言語で10まで数えることを学び、キャムが訪れたそれぞれの国の設問にしっかり答えることで、ロップラン打倒に手助けをする。二ヶ国から人類の所産を集めた後、地球上で大陸がひとつ輝き始める。話者の数が少ない言語ほど意図的に物語へ加えられているのは、ユーザーが非国際言語について意識を高め、深く理解するためである。したがって、G7の内キャムが訪れるのはわずか3ヶ国である（G20なら5つ）。

加えて25を超える言語について数字を10まで数える方法を学び、児童は新しい語彙習得を補助する学習方法（例えば、歌、チャンツ、含蓄、同族言語、繰り返し（復唱）と反省）について意見を述べる。予備研究で、ある男子児童は「映像がマジで面白いんだよ。みんなで歌うと覚えやすくなるし」と報告している。

その「ウェブ」は年少者の言語や文化の探求に多種多様な形で応える。キャムのリンガパックス・クエストでは、無料で利用可能な大量の素材をまとめているが、それらの素材は通常年少者がアクセスしやすいものではない。本研究は、年少のユーザーが自らの局所的なハビトゥスを批判的に反省し、世界中全ての人及び言語に対する同情を育む助けとなる物語の力を明らかにする。年少者は私たちの教師であり希望である。「このサイト、先生たちが知っておいたらいいと思いますよ」（女子児童）。

注
1 このサイトの最終目標は、言語と社会正義に関する5つのステップによる活動を完成させ、生徒がリンガパックスの証明書を受け取ることである。5つのステップはキャムの冒険についていく事（数多くの言語で数を数えることを学び、いくつかの設問に適切に解答すること）、複言語の使用を支持すること、パーソナルインタヴューを通じ言語が人にとってどんな意味を持つかを学習すること、社会正義の領域へ言語を導入する計画を確認し、共有すること、そして最後に、生徒たちがひとつひとつ学んできたことに基づいて、個人的、集団的社会行動の計画を完成させること、である。

表1. ウェブサイトの概要

国	人類の所産	テーマ一覧	言語
カナダ	土着の競技—ラクロスボール	二言語の使用、多文化主義、解毒剤、人類学的言語学者、アボリジニーの言語、複言語の使用	英語、フランス語、ウクライナ語、クリー語
メキシコ	伝説	同族言語、インド・ヨーロッパ祖語、バイリンガルの学校	スペイン語、ナワトル語
日本	茶碗—自然との関わり	敬称 土地の名称	日本語、韓国語、タガログ語、アイヌ語
インド	価値—ホスピタリティ	ディアスポラ	パンジャブ語、ヒンディー語
オーストラリア	思い出、夢	偏見、言語喪失、意識—無意識、土地との関わり	ギリシャ語、広東語、ヨォルング語
ウガンダ	寓話	公用語、ウブントゥ	アチョリ語、ズールー語
モロッコ	箴言	国連	アラビア語ベルベル語
フランス	世界観—生きる喜び	世界観	フランス語
オランダ	教育体制	方言	オランダ語
ブラジル	環境知識—ハーブの薬	環境知識	ポルトガル語、イタリア語、ドイツ語
チリ	言語権	制度	マプーチェ語

2 　第2条——すべての個人は、言語による差別を受けない権利を宣言され、これを享有する。
　　第10条——個人は公正な裁判を受ける権利を享有し、これは一般に、もし個人が刑事法廷における手続きの言語、または刑事告発で使用される言語を理解していない場合、通訳を持つ権利を含むと認められる。個人は、通訳者に法廷文書を含め法的手続きの翻訳をしてもらう権利を持つ。
　　第19条——個人は表現媒体としてどのような言語でも選ぶことのできる権利を含め表現の自由を有する。
　　第26条——すべて人は、適切な教授媒体の言語によって、教育を受ける権利を有する
3 　ウェブサイト開発期間中、10歳（grade 5）と12歳（grade 7）の年少者4人にサイト上で毎日1時間過ごすよう求めた。彼らは、そのサイトで改良の余地がある点について数えきれないほどの助言をくれ、彼らの言葉を受けてサイトバランスを改善した。
4 　この人類の所産のリストは未完である。よってこのリンガパックスシリーズの続編で、追加価値、箴言、そして食べ物、ダンス、伝統的な衣裳の名前の意味とその回復へのアプローチなど別の要素や他の概念の統合が図られるだろう。

Chapter 7
Language for Peace: Linguapax in Asia

Jelisava Sethna (Director, Linguapax Asia)

*"I am always sorry when any language is lost,
because languages are the pedigrees of nations."*

Samuel Johnson

"Wer fremde Sprachen nicht kennt, weiß nichts von seiner eigenen."

Johann Wolfgang von Goethe

1. Introduction

Why should we care about endangered languages? This question was put at the start of the roundtable discussion which completed the latest Linguapax Asia symposium on 13th September 2014, at Gakushuin University in Tokyo. The reasons for the preservation of endangered languages, given by the expert in language revival Ghil'rd Zuckermann, were three fold - ethical, aesthetic and utilitarian. The ethical argument posits that, in the past, many languages were 'killed' by imperialistic expansion (aboriginal languages in Australia, Irish, Ryukyuan, to name a few), so the wrongs committed in the past should be rectified. Language death means not only the loss of cultural autonomy, but also spiritual and intellectual sovereignty. It follows that language rights should be part of fundamental human rights. The aesthetic reasoning is that the world is beautiful in its cultural and linguistic diversity. Languages store the cultural practices and beliefs of an entire people as well as their unique way of thinking and expressing ideas. Through language maintenance these important cultural practices and concepts can be kept alive. The utilitarian explanation asserts that language reclamation may provide speakers with better mental health, empowerment and general well-being by helping them develop a sense of connection with their cultural heritage and tradition, and thus giving them a strong sense of pride and identity (Zuckermann 2013).

Linguapax Asia, which represents the Asian branch of the NGO Linguapax International, makes the support for the preservation and revitalisation of endangered languages one of its prime objectives. Other goals include advocacy of bilingual and multilingual education, facilitating intercultural understanding and fostering respect for linguistic diversity and linguistic heritage. Through its activities, Linguapax seeks to raise awareness of the links between language, identity, human rights, and the quest for peace, hence the name linguapax, lingua "language" and pax "peace". The above objectives are consistent with the recommendations that were first put forward at the inaugural Linguapax meeting in Kiev in 1987[1]. The result of the conference was the so-called Kiev Declaration, entitled Linguapax, which was unanimously accepted by the participants (see Dennis Cunningham, 2010, for a full text of the declaration). Linguapax became a UNESCO sponsored project which was developed through annual workshops[2]. In 1998, the Linguapax International Committee was formed which was later renamed the Advisory Committee for Linguistic Pluralism and Multilingual Education with Felix Marti elected chair. The original aim of promoting language education for peace was expanded to include efforts to maintain linguistic plurality around the world and to protect endangered languages. In the year 2001, coinciding with a growing awareness of the loss of the world's linguistic heritage, the UNESCO Center of Catalonia decided to continue the project, to give it its own structure and establish the headquarters in Barcelona, Spain. On 21st February 2006, on the occasion of the celebration of the International Mother Language Day, Linguapax officially established an international network, which now continues as an independent NGO Linguapax International with seven delegations on five continents, including Linguapax Asia.

2. The Evolving Philosophy of Linguapax

What is the philosophy, the *raison d'être* behind the Linguapax project? The Kiev Declaration which was addressed to teachers of languages and literature as well as to relevant NGOs, specialised institutions of UNESCO member states and to the Director-general of UNESCO, recommended, to the teachers, among others, to increase "the effectiveness of teaching foreign languages with a view to enhancing mutual understanding, respect, peaceful co-existence and co-operation among nations in accordance with UNESCO's principles", and to the Director General "to contribute in every possible manner to a more extensive study of less widely taught languages and their respective cultures" (Cunningham 2010: 25,26). The focus of the original Linguapax manifesto was, thus, on foreign language instruction which "gives students broader perspectives on the world, breaks national egocentricity and contributes to international understanding and solidarity" (Siguan 2010: 15), while urging the institution not to forget about the lesser taught languages and their respective cultures.

In the next decade, the philosophy and objectives of Linguapax evolved and expanded. In 1995, Joseph Poth, director of the Language Division at UNESCO, identified the further priority of the Linguapax project the "provision of a specific contribution of a linguistic nature to conflict areas and to identify ways and means by which foreign language teaching and teaching of mother tongues might promote peace, democracy and human rights. " (Cunningham 2010: 26)

In 1996, Félix Martí, a prominent figure in the Linguapax project, listed the three objectives of Linguapax to be: to advise governments of member states of UNESCO, on the planning of linguistic policies; to protect linguistic diversity; and to help educators, especially those working in the field of languages, with methodologies for the education of peace, tolerance and international understanding, by creating adequate pedagogical materials (Martí 1996b: 2). These objectives also embraced political and legal aspects, urging language teachers to take up the role of activists, who believe that an education favoring cultural and linguistic diversity is timely and feasible. Through their work teachers were encouraged to promote a vision that peace is desirable and is possible in all conflict situations, thus replacing "the culture of war with the culture of peace" (Marti, in Cunningham 2010: 28). In this formulation, linguistic diversity was not viewed as an obstacle to be eliminated in order to facilitate understanding among peoples, but rather the opposite: it was seen as wealth that must be preserved and the only way to do so was to increase awareness and mutual understanding (Siguan 2010: 16). The Linguapax International Committee, which was formed in 1998 within UNESCO with Felix Martin as chair, defined Linguapax as a "language-related philosophy and ethics" (Marti 2010: 41) which provides a general framework for all UNESCO's language-related activities. The committee established five areas of work: linguistic heritage protection; language policy reform; expansion and improvements to multilingual education; the development of sociolinguistic information and communication; and the use of new technologies in the service of linguistic diversity and multilingual education. The committee produced a white paper on languages that could be used as a reference document for all stakeholders that work to preserve linguistic diversity. The paper, titled 'Words and Worlds', described the international linguistic scene, studied the situation of risk affecting most of the six thousand languages that currently spoken and presented a series of recommendations to protect humankind's most valuable heritage. Due to "its contents being too critical of the language policies of some member states" (Marti 2010: 43), UNESCO decided not to publish the paper. It was eventually published by Multilingual Matters in 2005 under the title 'Words and Worlds: World Languages Review'.

Linguapax VIII, held in Kiev in 2000 was the last congress that fell within the UNESCO framework. In 2001, an NGO Linguapax Institute was created with its headquarters at the UNESCO Centre of Catalonia, in order to continue with the programmes that UNESCO stopped leading. Linguapax became a network formed by sociolinguists, language community experts, officials from national and international organisations concerned with the lives of languages and people, and representatives of organisations dedicated to teaching languages or to facing global challenges. It began to promote actions tailored to the needs of the different continents and to create local and international events in favor of linguistic diversity as a way to contribute to democracy, human rights, sustainability and peace. Linguapax activities and involvement spread around the globe. In 2005, Linguapax helped the National Commission on Bilingualism in Paraguay to prepare a draft law on languages for the Republic of Paraguay; and participated in an advisory mission to the Chinese government promoted by the State Ethnic Affairs Commission with the collaboration of the Norwegian Centre for Human Rights. The first Linguapax Africa conference took place in 2006 in Cameroon to coincide with the African Year of Languages. In the same year, a network of delegations around the world was created to include Linguapax Europe, Linguapax Africa, Linguapax Asia, Linguapax Eurasia, Linguapax Latin America, Linguapax North America and Linguapax Pacific.

Since 2002, Linguapax honours contributors to the preservation and promotion of linguistic diversity worldwide with the annual International Linguapax Award. Prominent recipients to date include Joshua Fishmann, Tove Skutnabb-Kangas, and Robert Phillipson.

Felix Marti (2010b: 51) succinctly describes the aspirations of the Linguapax project henceforth. "We want to build societies that intelligently manage their own linguistic diversity. We must create conditions that do not require any language community to abandon their language and replace it with supposedly prestigious linguistic practices. ... Old rivalries and aggression among language communities should be replaced by a new 'linguistic sympathy' that is an essential component of the sociolinguistic ethics that we desire. We aspire to a world of linguistic harmony". Linguistic harmony can be achieved through the "recognition that all languages are the heritage of humankind, and that the life and health of each language is not solely the responsibility of the language community that speaks it and of the state to which that community belongs, but of the entire human race" (51). Through this awareness the current trend toward the extinction of many of the 7,000 languages that make up our most valuable intangible cultural heritage, can be averted. To reverse this trend toward a loss of linguistic diversity, Linguapax activities should strive to establish new self-esteem in language communities, make changes to state language policies and strengthen international cooperation.

3. Linguapax Comes to Asia

The first time the Linguapax project was introduced in Asia was at the JALT

(Japan Association of Language Teachers) international conference in Hiroshima in 1996 on the theme of "Crossing Borders". The official UNESCO Linguapax delegation included Félix Martí, President of the International Linguapax Committee, Denis Cunningham, organiser of Linguapax V in Australia, Albert Raasch, organiser of Linguapax III in Germany, Madeleine du Vivier, President of the International Association of Teachers of English as a Foreign Language (IATEFL), FIPLV Honorary Counsellor Reinhold Freudenstein, and Andrea Truckenbrodt, newly appointed Convener of the AFMLTA (Australian Federation of Modern Language Teachers Associations). The participation included a keynote address by Félix Martí on the theme of 'Language Education for World Peace'; daily Linguapax workshops, which introduced conference participants to Linguapax principles and practice in promoting education for international understanding; a Linguapax colloquium on the theme of 'Language Teaching and Peace Education'; as well as a public forum in Hiroshima City on the theme of 'Peace through Education', conducted with Japanese peace educators. Through these activities, teachers were not only informed about the Linguapax project but also encouraged to rethink the aims of their teaching (see Cornwell et al 1997 for details). As a result, an informal Linguapax Asia Network was formed to work through JALT's Global Issues in Language Education SIG, headed by Kip Cates, to publicise and promote Linguapax ideas for furthering peace and international understanding through language teaching. However, the movement did not seem to pick up at this time.

It was another six years, before a group of academics got together to start promoting the ideas of Linguapax in Japan in earnest. The group was headed by Frances Fister Stoga, a professor at the University of Tokyo, whose commitment to the ideals promoted by Linguapax propelled the movement forward in top gear. In the first year, the objective was to gather as many interested academics as possible to form a core action group. Members were recruited through a network of colleagues whose interests coincided with the Linguapax objectives. Especially fortunate was the inclusion of a renowned Japanese sociolinguist and an expert on revitalisation Tasaku Tsunoda who was a professor at the University of Tokyo at that time. Contact was made with the United Nations University who agreed to holding the inaugural Linguapax Asia symposium in April 2004. The UNU acted as co-organizer of the event. Rotation of venues for symposia became a practice that Linguapax Asia has continued to this day. In early April, Prof. Tsunoda was interviewed by The Daily Yomiuri, the then English version of the Yomiuri Shimbun, the largest daily newspaper in Japan, in which he introduced the concept of language ecology[3] (Mark 2004a). Linguapax Asia adopted the term as the theme for its inaugural symposium which took place on 17th April 2004.

3.1. Linguapax Asia Symposia

The Linguapax Asia inaugural symposium at the United Nations University (UNU) had as its theme "Language Diversity/Language Ecology". The opening address was given by the rector of UNU Dr. H. van Ginkel, while Dr. Felix Marti of the Linguapax Institute became a keynote speaker. John Maher introduced the Ainu linguistic community in Japan, and Dr. Tasaku Tsunoda together with his wife Dr. Mie Tsunoda presented their extensive work in documenting the last native speaker of Warrongo and their project in passing on the language to younger generations. Two experts on language minorities from Europe, Koloman Brenner and Herta Mauer Lausegger talked about linguistic minorities of Hungary and Austria. They were joined by Shinji Yamamoto of the Tokyo University of Foreign Studies who introduced Slovenian minorities in Italy. Case studies of linguistic situations in

Table 1 Linguapax Asia Symposia 2004 - 2013

Symposium	Date	Place	Theme
Linguapax Asia I	17 April 2004	United Nations University	Language Diversity/ Language Ecology
Linguapa Asia II	11 June 2005	Canadian Embassy, Tokyo	Language in Society and Classroom: Preserving Heritage and Supporting Diversity
Linguapax Asia III	7 October 2006	University of Tokyo	Who Owns Language?
Linguapax Asia IV	21 October 2007	University of Tokyo	Language, Religion, and Ethnicity
Linguapax Asia V	26 October 2008	University of Tokyo	Language and Propaganda
Linguapax Asia VI	14 June 2009	University of Tokyo	Language and Human Trafficking
Linguapax Asia VII	3 December 2011	International Christian University	Literacy for Dialogue in Multilingual Societies
Linguapax Asia VIII	13 September 2013	Gakushuin University	Endangered Languages Networking

Thailand, the Philippines and Palau were also presented and ESL/Bilingual education in California schools as well as native American language programs unveiled by Dr. Melvin Andrade and Cary Duval respectively. The keynote speaker was Felix Marti of the Linguapax Institute who came from Barcelona to observe the event and who by the end of the symposium gave his enthusiastic approval to the newly established Linguapax Asia team. The symposium was also reported on The Language Connection page of The Daily Yomiuri (Mark 2004b).

The following year (2005), The Embassy of Canada hosted a symposium on "Language in Society and the Classroom: Preserving Heritage and Supporting Diversity". The symposium had four featured speakers, including John Maher (Rethinking Multilingual, Multicultural Japan), Tasuku Tsunoda (Attempt to Revive the Warrongo Language of Australia), Hideo Oka of The University of Tokyo (Issues in Bilingual Education with Special Reference to the Japanese Context) and Charles Mann of the University of Surrey (Issues of Language Diversity and Languages of Education in Africa: Illustrations from Nigeria). Three colloquia on Heritage Language Education and Language Preservation, Bilingual and Intercultural Education and Diversity and Harmony in Teaching and Learning, engaged 11 speakers/experts in their field of work. Kip Cates, who was the key person in bringing Linguapax to Asia in 1996, showed parallels between language, language education, and global understanding. Also impressive was the sponsorship and support of the external organisations, which included United Nations University, Linguapax Institute (UNESCOcat), Delegation of the European Commission in Tokyo, Embassy of the Republic of Austria, Embassy of Canada, Embassy of the Republic of Slovenia, Embassy of Spain, Embassy of the United States of America, Teachers College, Columbia University, Japan and Four Seasons Hotel Tokyo at Marunouchi. Linguapax Asia became recognised as an innovative, alternative approach in language teaching and awareness raising of socio-linguistic issues in the globalised world.

"Who Owns Language?" was the theme of the 2006 symposium at the University of Tokyo. Charles de Wolf, professor at Keio University and an expert on East Asian and Oceanic languages, set the agenda by discussing multilingualism and multiculturalism. Can one have multiple identities? This issue was addressed by Mong Lan, artist and poet, in presenting poems highlighting her Vietnamese and American background. From another point of view, Saran Shiroza from the University of Tokyo described a variety of English developing in Japan and its impact on both Japanese and standard English. Arudo Debito, an activist and human rights campaigner in his home in Hokkaido, addressed the topic of language and nationalism, while Fernand De Varennes, a prominent lawyer and language rights expert, revealed how language can be a source of conflict and language protection legislation in Asia. Olenka Bilash, University of Alberta, discussed "What happens When No One Takes Ownership of Language?". The symposium closed with final remarks by Felix Marti, Honorary President of the Linguapax Institute.

Links between language, religion and identity were explored in the 2007 symposium, "Language, Religion and Ethnicity". The connection between mythology and ethnicity was discussed in William Gater's presentation on "Nordic Mythology, the Runes, and Ethnic Revivalism", and in Cary Duval's "The Sense of the Sacred in Navajo Language". The relationship between the scripture and the spoken language was addressed by Charles De Wolf in his "Biblical and Liturgical Japanese", by Rabbi Henri Noach in "The Relationship Between the Hebrew Bible and the Hebrew Language" and by Jelisava Sethna, Tokyo University of Foreign Studies, in "The Freising Manuscripts, The Birth Certificate of the Slovene Language." Identity issues were introduced by Marek Kaminski in "An Urban Japanese-Ainu Identity Dilemma" in which he also presented his project to collect Ainu folk tales as a means of the revitalisation and study of language. The symposium was concluded by conductor and composer Steven Morgan with his analysis of "Janacek's Glagolitic[4] Mass".

The 2008 symposium on "Language and Propaganda" saw a wide range of papers detailing the connection of language with political propaganda. The "Theory and History" session included a presentation by Shinji Yamamoto on the linguistic communities in the Friuli area of Italy and how they were politicised during Fascism. John Spiri discussed "The Fallacies and Perils of Patriotism", while William Gater analysed G.A.Henty's novels and the language of colonialism. In the Socio-Cultural Issues session, Robert Stuart Yoder discussed how class groups are described in his "A Pattern of Class and Youth Deviance in Japan", while human rights activist Arudou Debito's visually-enriched paper showed how linguistic propaganda works to stigmatise the foreign population in Japan by making it the 'Other'. In the Pedagogy session, Donna Tatsuki, Kobe City University of Foreign Studies, looked at how textbooks portray gender and various ethnic groups in Japan, Stephanie Houghton, University of Kitakyushu, discussed how to overcome bias and propaganda in foreign language education and Frances Fister Stoga presented ESL texts in the German national socialist era. In the final session "Language of Art", the use of film combining language, sound, and image to control populations was the subject of Kyoko Hirano's paper on US policy on Japanese cinema after World War II. The symposium's emphasis on language and propaganda was supported by the performance of Harold Pinter's play *Mountain Language* directed by Cyrus Sethna which depicts what ensues when a language is banned from public use.

The symposium was the best-attended Linguapax Asia event to date which was in part due to a renewed collaboration between Linguapax Asia and JALT (Japan Association of Language Teachers) based on a bilateral agreement signed between the two entities in 2007. As a result, several speakers presenting at the symposium were recruited from the JALT membership.

The 2009 symposium developed the connection between language in various forms of human trafficking which, according to the then estimates, afflicted 900,000 victims annually. Defining human trafficking and the Polaris project to report cases of trafficking was the topic of the introductory talk by Daniel Garrett, former human rights officer at the Embassy of the United States in Tokyo. How human trafficking has been described historically in biblical sources and slave narratives was presented by Stewart Dorward and Ann Jenkins in her reading of slave narratives by Olaudah Equiano and Frederick Douglass. William Gater and Charles Cabell introduced Japanese literary works which describe both labor and sexual human trafficking, while Marek Kaminski addressed the topic of human trafficking and diplomacy. Activists and researchers Patricia and Jason Aliperti gave an account of their investigation and documentation of trafficking of children in India and the role language and education can play in eliminating the problem.

In November 2010, collected proceeding of Linguapax Asia Symposia from 2004 to 2009 were published under a title 'Linguapax Asia: A Retrospective Edition of Language and Human Rights Issues'.

The year 2011 brought about significant changes for Linguapax Asia. The

Tohoku Earthquake, also known as the 'Great East Japan Earthquake' in March of 2011 and the ensuing Fukushima nuclear disaster caused a postponement of the symposium planned for May of that year. In the same year Linguapax Asia director Frances Fister Stoga who had been the inspiration and driving force behind the Linguapax activities moved to Europe and later resigned from her post. A report from the Linguapax Institute in Barcelona indicated an imminent closure of UNESCOcat (The UNESCO Centre of Catalonia) which had been a staunch supporter of the Linguapax project and had shared its offices with the Linguapax Institute. In spite of the above mentioned drawbacks, the planned symposium on "Literacy for Dialogue in Multilingual Society" went ahead in December at the International Christian University, supported by the ICU Institute for Educational Research and Service (IERS), the ICU Social Science Research Institute (SSRI), and ICU UNESCO Club. The attendance of Linguapax delegations from India and Malaysia, which were now joined under the Linguapax Asia umbrella, made this the first true pan-asian event. Following the symposium, Linguapax Asia reorganized itself; John Maher, a leading sociolinguist in Japan and an expert on Ainu, became Research Director, while Jelisava Sethna, who had been an active participant in the Linguapax Asia project from its conception, took up the reins as Director.

The symposium "Literacy for Dialogue in Multilingual Societies" highlighted current issues and changes in the nature of literacy in multilingual societies, with multi-literacy seen as encompassing both multilingual and multimodal literacy. Presentations dealt with literacy issues involving social empowerment, development, the digital divide, language policy, historical perspectives on literacy and writing systems. Joo Young Jung presented a Tokyo-based study of internet connectedness and civic action in a critical situation, such as the 2011 Fukushima nuclear disaster in Japan, while a study of cyberspace and the possibility of maintenance of a threatened language in the Philippines was discussed by Francis Dumanig and Maya Khemlani David. Joseph DeChicchis investigated multimodal literacy in the Mayan areas of Guatemala and how success is possible in effecting language policy decision. Kayako Hashimoto examined the current situation of second language education at the tertiary level in Australia and explored the values and meanings underpinning that education. The paradox of English language hegemony in foreign language education in schools in Japan and how to introduce a language diversity experience in schools was considered by Atsuko Koishi. The keynote speaker Lachman Khubchandani, a long-time member of the Linguapax project, argued that, in the era of communication, dispersed cultural groups in diaspora, sharing a common heritage, can explore space through convenient modes of mobility and electronic networking. Shaun Malarney elaborated on the innovative strategies launched in revolutionary Vietnam to teach reading and writing to the masses, while Patrick Heinrich revealed how the dominance of one language over others depended on the extent to which a written tradition existed and how, in the Ryukyu Islands, language activism turned to writing in order to support the Ryukyuan language revival. Lunch-time screening of a documentary film on Sami linguistic minorities titled *Suomi tuli Saamenmaahan* (Finnish Came to Samiland) was introduced by Eija Niskanen, University of Helsinki.

In 2012, Linguapax Asia engaged in a joint project with the Research Institute for Oriental Cultures at Gakushuin University on endangered languages in Asia. Several Seminars were organised as part of the project which culminated in the symposium Linguapax Asia 2014 on the theme of "Endangered Languages Networking: Values and Benefits for the Future" with Takao Katsuragi of Gakushuin University as the symposium Chair. The purpose of the symposium was to frame the emergence of endangered language networks by political and sociological theory and to present case studies of such networks as part of the process of language revitalisation, to connect experts of language maintenance and revitalization, and to share experiences and transfer knowledge among all participants of the symposium. Fija Byron, an activist and teacher of the 'Uchinaa Okina-wan' language, opened the program with a traditional Okinawan song accompanied on the sanshin Okinawan string instrument. He gave an account of how he became a language activist and of his efforts at preserving his mother tongue. Matt Gillan, International Christian University, introduced the Ryukyuan music tradition which has been one of the most important contexts for the preservation and dissemination of disappearing Ryukyuan languages. Moving to the northern part of Japan, Katayama Kazumi described the role of Internet Telephone Services such as Skype, and other visual-based learning sites that she has used, to facilitate Ainu language learning in a variety of new ways. Identification and practical situations of Endangered Languages in China were presented by Xing Huang, Institute of Ethnology & Anthropology, Chinese Academy of Social Sciences, and Lianqun Bao of Oita University, which concluded the morning session. During the lunch break Gabina Funegra, a PhD candidate at UNSW Australia, showed her documentary "Quechua: The fading Inca language". In the afternoon session, Dr. Suwilai Premsrirat, Mahidol University, Thailand, described the community-based language revitalisation model, known as Mahidol Model, which is the result of a 10-year cooperative effort between ethnolinguistic communities, linguists and other specialists in the field of education, botany, public health and culture. How an on-line game can help children learn about the key concepts of language use, language loss and language endangerment was presented by Olenka Bilash, University of Alberta. The main villain in the game Lopra was adopted by the symposium participants as a mascot/symbol for language hegemony and language loss. In a keynote address, Keiki Kawai'ae'a, University of Hawai'i at Hilo, discussed the Hawaiian language revitalisation movement through its 30 years of growth and development to ensure the survival of the Hawaiian language. The discussion that followed brought together some leading experts in the field of revitalisation and reclamation of endangered languages, including Ghil'ad Zuckermann, Nicholas Ostler of FEL (Federation of Endangered Language), Tjeerd De Graaf of Mercator Research Centre, as well as Olenka Bilash, Xu Feng, China Agricultural University, and Fujita-Round Sachiyo, Rikkyo University. The symposium met its goals of presenting and discussing the role of endangered languages networks as part of the process of language revitalization and to connect experts of language maintenance and revitalization. Linguapax Asia hopes that its future symposia will continue to bring together experts in the field of multilingual education and language ecology in cooperation with relevant institutes and organizations in Japan and Asia.

3.2. Linguapax Asia Screenings of Documentaries on Minority and Endangered Languages

Another activity, initiated by Linguapax Asia, that has proved successful in raising awareness of the issues related to language, identity and human rights, includes screenings of documentaries on minority and endangered language communities. The showing of the documentary *Suomi tuli Saamenmaahan* (Finnish Came to Samiland) at the Linguapax Asia 2011 symposium led to a joint project with the Delegation of the European Community in Japan which extended over the next two years. The project involved a series of screenings of documentaries on the minority communities and peoples of Europe and Japan with the purpose to raise awareness of the existence of particular minorities, their historic biopics and the issues that arise in such predicaments.

In the first session in April 2012, the documentary *Suomi tuli Saamenmaahan* was shown together with two puppet animations from *Mire Bala Kale HIn* (Tales From the Endless Roads) directed by Katariina Lillqvist which introduced the Roma minority in Europe and in Finland in particular. Before the screening, a short introduction to the films was give by Eija Niskanen, while the discussion that followed after the screening further illuminated the issues presented in the films. This arrangement proved very successful and was repeated in subsequent screenings. Linguapax made contact with the Centro Espressioni Cinematografiche in Udine, Italy which had organised festivals of minority languages films in the past. Their introduction by the director of Friulian descent, Christiane Rorato, led to the next screening in the series, at Europa House, of her documentary *Vuerirs the gnot...su lis olmis dai Benandans* (Warriors of the night... on the Benandanti's tracks) which shows the director returning to the home of her parents in Friuli in search of her roots and to explore the legend of Friulian warriors Benandanti. Professor Shinji Yamamoto of Tokyo University of Foreign Studies, who has been researching the Friulian language, gave a short introduction to the film and the Friulian community.

In December of 2012, Linguapax participated at the 13th IALL conference in Chiang Mai, Thailand, on "Language Rights, Inclusion and the Prevention of Ethnic Conflicts" with three documentaries, the Sami documentary mentioned above and two films by the director Robert Alaux *Le Derniers Assyriens* (The Last Assyrians) and *Seyfo L'elimination* which portray the Syriac Assyrians Chaldeans, one of the oldest Christian communities in Turkey and Iraq[5].

The following screening in the series at Europa House introduced the Okinawan communities in the south of Japan. Two documentaries produced by the National Broadcasting House NHK were shown. *Okinawa within Japan* (1962),

Table 2 Linguapax Asia Screenings of Documentaries on Minority and Endangered Languages

Title of Documentary	Date	Place	Language
Suomi tuli Saamenmaahan Finnish Came to Samiland	4 April 2012	Europa House, Tokyo	Sami
Mire Bala Kale HIn Tales from the Endless Road	4 April 2012	Europa House, Tokyo	Roma
Vuerirs the gnot...su lis olmis dai Benandans Warriors of the night... on the Benandanti's tracks	11 October 2012	Europa House, Tokyo	Friulian
Le Derniers Assyriens The Last Assyrians	15 December 2012	13th IALL Confer. Chiang Mai, Thailand	Syriac Assyrian
Seyfo L'elimination Seyfo Elimination	15 December 2012	13th IALL Confer. Chiang Mai, Thai	Syriac Assyrians
Suomi tuli Saamenmaahan	15 December 2012	13th IALL Confer. Chiang Mai, Thailand	Sami
日本の素顔　日本の中の沖縄 Nihon no Sugao: Nihon no naka no Okinawa Okinawa within Japan	11 June 2013	Europa House, Tokyo	Okinawan
長老の風車　山田政心と150人の一族, Choro no Kazaguruma: Yamada Seishin to 150-nin no ichizoku The Windmill of the Old Man	11 June 2013	Europa House, Tokyo	Okinawan
Quechua: The Fading Inca Language	13 September 2014	Gakushuin University	Quechua

introduced a whole range of social, historical and political questions regarding the postwar history of Okinawa, and *The Windmill of the old Man, Yamada Seishin and his 150 member-family (1984)* documented the 97th birthday of the main protagonist Yamada, who represents the epitome of the modern history of Okinawa. The films were introduced by Prof. Yasuhiro Tanaka of ICU, himself of Okinawan origin, who gave a running commentary in English throughout the screening.

Quechua: The Fading Inca Language was presented during the Linguapax Asia 2014 symposium by the director Gabina Funegra. The documentary captures Gabina's family journey to the town of Huallanca, high in the Peruvian Andes.

They travel to this remote village to discover their mother's language, a fading Quechua language, and find resilience in this indigenous community.

4. Conclusion

Linguapax project was initiated almost 30 years ago by UNESCO with the purpose of promoting language education as a means to enhance mutual understanding, respect, peaceful coexistence and co-operation. The original objectives were later expanded to include efforts to maintain linguistic plurality around the world and to protect endangered languages. Linguapax philosophy was built on the premise that peace can be achieved by the implementation of human rights that affirm one's own linguistic identity and by promoting understanding and sympathy towards other linguistic communities (Marti et al 2005: xiv). At present, Linguapax International elucidates its values, as follows:

— Languages express the rich cultural pluralism of the human species and its preservation is a major contribution to peace and international understanding.
— All languages are considered as part of the world heritage and, as such, are equal in dignity regardless of their demographic, political, economic and legal aspects.
— Multilingual education is a necessary option in a world affected by globalization processes, which favors both the psychological development of people and the economic, social and sustainable progress of communities.

(Linguapax International Website, 19/7/2015)

The above proclamations correspond to the ethical, aesthetic and utilitarian motives for the preservation of endangered languages, as put forward by Zuckermann at the opening of the roundtable discussion that completed the Linguapax Asia 2014 symposium. It also highlights the principles and norms put forward by UNESCO on cultural diversity, safeguarding of intangible cultural assets, as well as the protection and promotion of the diversity of cultural expressions.

Linguapax Asia activities to date, as reviewed in this paper, are underpinned by the above philosophy. The symposia organized between 2004 and 2014 dealt with the issues of language ecology; language in society and classroom; language, religion and ethnicity; language ownership; language and propaganda; language and human trafficking; literacy in multilingual societies; and endangered languages networking. The purpose of these symposia has been to bring together experts, academics and activists from Asia and from around the world in order to discuss, share and propose solutions to, as well as raise awareness of, the issues related to language ecology in the increasingly complex globalized world. Some 7000 languages exist in the world today, out of which about 1,900, or 32%, of all languages are spoken in Asia alone[6]. It is estimated that, if nothing is done, more than 50% of all world languages will disappear by the end of the 21st century, due to globalization, homogenization and "Coca-colonization" (Zuckermann 2013). With the disappearance of languages, humanity will lose not only cultural wealth but also important ancestral knowledge embedded in those languages. However, this process is neither inevitable nor irreversible. Concerted efforts of all stakeholders, including teachers, linguists, experts, activists, and speaker communities, as well as NGOs, government officials and international institutions, can help avert and stop this imminent disaster. As part of these efforts, officials are encouraged to create "well-planned and implemented language policies that can bolster the ongoing efforts of speaker communities to maintain or revitalize their mother tongues and pass them on to younger generations" (UNESCO 19/7/2015). Linguists and researchers, on the other hand, are prompted to exercise cultural liberty which goes beyond the limitations of modernist ideologies anchored in power and inequality; and solidarity with the 'others' whereby truly multicultural and multilingual societies will emerge and be sustained through mutual care, concern and responsibility (Heinrich 2012: 182).

Note

1   The topic of the conference was "Teaching Foreign Languages for Peace and Understanding". Participants from 14 different countries included experts appointed by UNESCO in ad-

dition to representatives from the International Federation of Language Teacher Associations (IFLTA) and the European Bureau for Lesser-Used Languages (EBLUL).

2   Linguapax II in 1988 Stiges, Linguapax III in 1990 In Saarbrucken, LInguapax IV in 1994 in Barcelona, Linguapax V in 1995 Melbourne. These were the golden years of Linguapax, through the support of the UNESCO Director-General Federico Mayor (1987 to 1999) and the "enthusiastic devotion" of Joseph Poth, director of the newly formed Language Division.

3   Haugen (1972) first introduced the term language ecology to define a new ecological study of the interrelations between languages in both the human mind and in multilingual communities.The study includes such topics as the maintenance and survival of languages, the promotion of linguistic diversity, language policy and planning, language acquisition, language ideology, language rights, the ecology of (multilingual) classroom interaction and the ecology of literacy, among others.

4   The Glagolitic Alphabet was an early Slavic alphabet, the predecessor of the modern Cyrillic alphabet.

5   Seyfo refers to the genocide of the Syriacs, together with the Armenians, in 1915 by the Ottomans, after which many fled to Europe and the United States. Some 400,000 Chaldo-Assyrians remain in Iraq where they are threatened by Islamic extremists.

6   European languages, which are commonly taught as second, foreign languages in Asia, represent only 3% of all world languages.

References

Cornwell, S., Rule, P., Sugino, T.(Eds.) (1997) *On JALT°6: Crossing Borders*, Tokyo: Japan Association of Language Teachers.

Cunningham, D. (2010) FIPLV and Linguapax: A Quasi-autobiographical 23 Account. In Cru, Joseph & Lachman Khubchandani (Eds). *Linguapax Review 2010*, 23-35.

Dobovsek-Sethna, J., Fister-Stoga, F., Duval, C., (Eds.) (2007) *Linguapax Asia: A Retrospective Edition of Language and Human Rights Issues*. Tokyo. Linguapax Asia.

Haugen, E. (1972) *The Ecology of Language*. Stanford University Press.

Heinrich, P. (2012) *The Making of Monolingual Japan*. Bristol: Multilingual Matters.

Linguapax Asia website http://www.linguapax-asia.org (29.7/2015)

Linguapax International website http://www.linguapax.org/english (19/7/2015)

Maher, J., Dobovsek-Sethna, J., Duval, C. (Eds.) (2012) *Literacy for Dialogue in Multilingual Societies: Proceedings of Linguapax Asia Symposium 2011*. Tokyo: Linguapax Asia.

Mark, C. (2004a, April 15) Lost languages a loss for world. *The Daily Yomiuri*, p. The Language Connection.

Mark, C. (2004b, April 22) Linguapax speakers urge protection for minority languages. *The Daily Yomiuri*, p. The Language Connection.

Marti, F., Ortega, P., Idiazabal, I. et al (Eds) (2005). *Words and Worlds: World Languages Review*.

Clevedon: Multilingual Matters.

Martí, F. (2010a) Defending Linguistic and Cultural Diversity. In Cru, Joseph & Lachman Khubchandani *Linguapax Review 2010*, 11-13

Martí, F. (2010b) Materials for a history of Linguapax. In Cru, Joseph & Lachman Khubchandani *Linguapax Review 2010*, 36-51.

Siguan, M. (2010) The Beginning of Linguapax. In Cru, Joseph & Lachman Khubchandani *Linguapax Review 2010*, 14-16.

UNESCO website http://www.unesco.org/new/en/culture/themes/endangered-languages/ (19/7/2015).

Zuckermann, G. (2013) *Historical and moral arguments for language reclamation*, http://hiphilangsci.net/2013/06/26/historical-and-moral-arguments-for-language-reclamation/ (10/7/2015).

第 7 章 要約

言語と平和
リンガパックス・アジア

イェリサバ・セスナ（リンガパックス・アジア　ディレクター）（崎山拓郎訳）

　この論文はユネスコ（UNESCO）が創始したプロジェクト、リンガパックスがどのようにアジアで確立していったか、その経緯の報告である。最初にリンガパックスの起源とその思想及び目的を論ずる。次にシンポジウム、フィルム上映、出版物を含めたリンガパックス・アジアの活動に焦点を当てる。

　リンガパックス・アジアはNGO「リンガパックス・インターナショナル」（'Linguapax International'）のアジア支部を代表し、その最大目標の一つは、絶滅の危機にある言語の保存と再活性化の支援である。このことは、絶滅危惧言語のネットワーク構築をテーマに、東京都の学習院大学で開かれた直近のシンポジウムでも表明された。また他の目標として、二言語教育及び多言語教育の擁護、異文化間理解の促進、言語多様性や言語遺産に対する敬意の育成を含む。そうした活動を通じて、リンガパックスは、言語、アイデンティティ、人権、平和追求、それぞれのつながりに対する意識向上を目指す。それゆえ、その名は、lingua（言語）と pax（平和）でリンガパックスである。

　以上の目的は、1987年キエフにおける「平和と理解のための外国語教授」と題する会リンガパックス発足の議で初めて発表された提言とも一致する。キエフ宣言は、リンガパックスを冠し、ユネスコの基本方針に基づく国家間の相互理解、尊敬、平和的共存と協調を進める観点から外国語教授の有効性拡大に向けた尽力を推奨した。平和のために言語教育を促進するという根本目標には、後に世界中の言語複数性の維持や絶滅危惧言語の保護に対する取り組みも盛り込まれ、さらなる広がりをみせた。このリンガパックスの定式化においては、言語の多様性は人々の相互理解の促進を妨げる排除すべ

き障害とはみなされない。むしろ逆である。つまり言語多様性を言語の豊かさと捉え、その豊かさは意識向上と相互理解の増進によってのみ維持されると考えるのである。2001年はちょうど、世界的に言語的遺産の喪失に対する認識が強まりつつあった時期であり、カタルーニャのユネスコセンターは、リンガパックスの枠組みを作り、本部をバルセロナに設立するため、リンガパックスの計画継続を決定した。2006年、国際母語デーの祝いの折に、リンガパックスは国際ネットワークを公式に樹立した。それは、リンガパックス・アジアを含め、5大陸に7つの代表団を持ち、独立したNGO、リンガパックス・インターナショナルとして今日も続いている。リンガパックスは、毎年インターナショナル・リンガパックス・アワードで、世界中の言語多様性の保存と促進に対する貢献に対して表彰をする。

リンガパックスの価値は以下のように要約できる。

- 言語は人類の豊かな文化的複数性を表わし、多様性の保存は平和と国際理解に対し重要な貢献となる。
- 全ての言語は世界遺産の一部とみなされるべきである。それゆえ、全ての言語は、人口的、政治的、経済的、法的面でいかなるものであっても、尊厳を持ち平等である。
- グローバリゼーションの進行によって影響を被る世界において、多言語の教育は必要不可欠の選択肢であり、人びとの心理的発達においても共同体の経済的、社会的な持続可能な発展においても両面で好適である。

1996年広島で「越境」("Crossing Borders")をテーマにしたJALT（全国語学教育学会）国際会議が行われた。この会議で「教育を通じた平和」と題した公開討論と並んで、複数のワークショップと専門家会議が、公式のユネスコ・リンガパックス派遣団のメンバーによってなされ、その時、アジアではじめてリンガパックス・プロジェクトが紹介された。とはいえ、日本で真剣にリンガパックスの理念を振興しようと大学人のグループが集うには、その

後さらに6年を要することになる。グループの代表に選ばれたのは、フランセス・フィスター・ストーガ、当時東京大学の教授であった。リンガパックスの推進する理想にストーガがコミットメントしたことで、運動は一気に加速した。最初の年の目標は、核となる活動グループを形成するため可能な限り多くの大学人の関心を集めることだった。メンバーは、リンガパックスの目標に共鳴する同僚間のネットワークを利用して集められた。特に幸運だったのは、日本の高名な社会言語学者で、言語の再活性化を専門にしていた角田太作教授が加わったことである。当時角田は東京大学でその職に就いていた。2004年4月には、リンガパックス・アジア発足のシンポジウム開催に賛同する国際連合大学（UNU）の大学人にもコンタクトがとられた。UNUはそのシンポジウムで共同組織者を担っていた。シンポジウムの開催指定地のローテーションはリンガパックスが今日まで続けている実践のひとつである。4月初期、角田教授はデイリーヨミウリ、当時の読売新聞の英語版、日本最大の日刊新聞からインタヴューを受け、言語環境の概念について紹介した。

　国際連合大学のオープニングシンポジウムは、「言語の多様性と言語環境」をテーマにし、同時に、学者が集う場を設けるというねらいがあった。それぞれの学者が抱いている見解や現在の研究について意見を交換し、いかにして多言語使用の促進を図るかについてヴィジョンを展開し、マイノリティ言語や絶滅危惧の言語を保護するためである。また、リンガパックスの根本的使命——平和のための言語の促進——を前へ押し進めるためでもあった。アジア、ヨーロッパ、北アメリカからの10人の話し手が、ヨーロッパや北アメリカ、並びに、日本、タイ、フィリピン、パラオ、オーストラリアのマイノリティ言語及び絶滅危惧言語に関する研究やフィールドワークについてプレゼンテーションをおこなった。話し手も聞き手もUNU総長H・ファン・ヒンケル博士とリンガパックス・インスティテュートの会長フェリックス・マルティ博士から歓迎を受け、マルティは新しく設立するリンガパックスのアジアチームに熱烈な賛意を示した。

　続く5年間、リンガパックス・アジアは東京で年次のシンポジウムを開催

することで着実に足場を固めていった。リンガパックス・アジアの2005年大会は「社会と教室における言語——文化遺産の保護と多様性の促進」をテーマにカナダ大使館で開かれた。シンポジウムのプログラムには、日本、ヨーロッパ、カナダの15人の話し手／専門家により交わされた「遺産言語教育と言語保存」「バイリンガルと国際教育」「教授と学習に関する多様性と調和」の三つの専門家会議と並んで、四人のメイン講演者による講演が組まれていた。

2006年から2009年にかけて、リンガパックス・アジアの年次大会は、信望ある東京大学で開催された。言語の所有者とアイディンティに関する「言語は誰のもの？」（リンガパックス・アジア 2006）、「言語、宗教、民族性」（リンガパックス・アジア 2008）、「言語とプロパガンダ」（リンガパックス・アジア2008）、さらに「言語と人身売買」（リンガパックス・アジア 2009）など、言語と人権問題についてヴァラエティに富むトピックが紹介された。2010年の11月、2004年から2009年にかけたリンガパックス・アジアのシンポジウムにおける一連の活動を集録した『リンガパックス・アジア——言語と人権問題についての回想版』が一巻本で出版された。JALTとの共同も2007年の協力同意のサインと共に更新された。

2011年は、リンガパックス・アジアにとって転機となる重要な年だった。「東日本大震災」として知られる東北地方の震災が2011年3月に発生、続く福島の原発事故により5月に予定されていたリンガパックス・アジアの2011年度のシンポジウムは延期されたのである。同年、リンガパックスにインスピレーションを与え、原動力となってその活動を影で支え続けたリンガパックス・アジアの指導者、フランシス・フィスター・ストーガがヨーロッパへ移り、後に彼女のポストを辞任する運びとなった。こうした試練にも関わらず、予定されていたシンポジウムは、ICU教育研究所の支援の下、「多言語社会における対話のためのリテラシー」と題して、12月に国際基督教大学で開催された。そのシンポジウムでは、いろいろな形態のリテラシーを含め、多言語社会におけるリテラシーの本質について現今の問題と変化を強調した。昼の休憩中には、サーミ人における言語マイノリティ Suomi tuli

Saamenmaahan（「フィンランド語のサーミランドへの到来」）というドキュメンタリー映像が上映された。

　続く二年間、リンガパックス・アジアは、マイノリティ共同体が直面する一連の問題に対する意識向上を目的として、日本にいるEU派遣団の協力のもと、多数のマイノリティ共同体とその人びとに関するドキュメンタリー上映を企画した。そのフィルムでは、フィンランドにおけるサーミ人のコミュニティ、ヨーロッパ最大のマイノリティを代表するロマ人、イタリアにおけるフリウリ人のコミュニティが紹介された。イタリアのウディネにある「映画表現センター」（Centro espressioni cinematografiche）は、マイノリティ言語の映画祭を企画しており、この映画表現センターの協力を得て、リンガパックス・アジアはマイノリティ言語映画の監督にコンタクトを取った。フリウリの伝説のヒーロー、ベナンダンティについて制作したクリスティアンヌ・ロラート、シリアのコミュニティについてのドキュメンタリーを制作したロベール・アローなどである。アローのドキュメンタリーについては、タイのチェンマイで開かれた13回IALL（言語法国際アカデミー）大会において、「言語権、多様性の受容、民族紛争の防止」の席で、リンガパックス・アジアが紹介した。

　2013年、リンガパックス・アジアは東京の学習院大学東洋文化研究所と共に、アジアにおける絶滅危惧言語についてのプロジェクトを開始した。2014年、「危機言語復興ネットワーキング――その意義と今後の可能性」をテーマに、リンガパックス・アジアのシンポジウムで最高潮に達したプロジェクトの一環として、いくつかのワークショップが企画された。続くディスカッションでは、ギラード・ツッカーマンやFEL（絶滅危機言語連盟）のニコラス・オストラー、オランダのメルカトル研究センターのチェルド・デ・フラーフを含む絶滅危機言語の再活性化及び再生の分野を牽引する専門家が一堂に会した。将来、リンガパックス・アジアは、世界中に「平和のための言語」を広げる支援をするために、日本やアジア、その他の地域の関連機関と協力関係の強化に努めることになるであろう。

第2部　事例研究

Part 2　Case Studies

第8章
うちなーぐち（おきなわ語）を歴史認識で復興させる試み
カムリー（ウェールズ）語、カタルーニャ語、ハワイ語復興の源、宗教力に代わる力

比嘉 光龍（ふぃじゃ ばいろん）（歌三線者、うちなーぐち〔おきなわ語〕講師）

第1節　はじめに

第1項　うちなーぐち（おきなわ[1]語）復興

　2009年2月、ユネスコ（国際連合教育科学文化機関）は日本に8つの危機言語が存在すると発表した[2]。アイヌ（諸）語[3]と八丈語の2言語と、琉球諸島の6言語、すなわち琉球諸語である。筆者は危機言語となっている琉球諸語中、うちなーぐちの講師をしており、また継承・啓蒙活動もしている。それ故にうちなーぐち復興の参考になることはないか、情報を得ようと世界中の同じ境遇にある少数言語を注視している。その中でも特に筆者が注目しているのが、本稿で扱う欧米の3地域である。その3地域は具体的にイギリスの中の「カムリー[4]（ウェールズ）国（首都を擁するので地域とはいえない）」、スペインの中にある「カタルーニャ自治州」、アメリカの「ハワイ州」である。最初に本稿の要旨を簡単に述べると、ここで扱う欧米3地域の復興運動の原動力となっているのは宗教、具体的に言うとキリスト教の存在だと筆者は分析する。しかし、我がうちなー（おきなわ）地域にうちなーぐち復興運動を支援する宗教は現在のところ存在しないように見受けられる。それならば何かその欧米3地域の宗教力に匹敵するものはないかと、ここ数年悩んできた結果見出したのが、本稿のタイトルにも掲げた歴史認識をきちんと持つことである。つまり、日本側から視た、うちなーの歴史観ではなく、うちなー側から視る、うちなーの歴史観である。それは今後のうちなーぐち復興運動の大き

な原動力になりえると考える。

第2項　ハワイ語復興運動からの影響

　筆者は2010年にハワイ大から招聘を受け講演し、またハワイ語のイマージョン・スクール[5]を視察させていただいた経験からハワイ語の歴史と現状について、多少は知り得ることができた。ハワイでは過去の弾圧をはねのけ、現在、イマージョン・スクールを設立するまでの発展を遂げてきたという、世界中の少数言語話者にとって参考になる経験が豊富にある。ハワイのみならず、イギリスのカムリー（ウェールズ）、スペインのカタルーニャ地域の言語復興運動も盛んである。それらから、現在消滅危機に瀕している地球上の2500もの少数言語[6]を話す人々は大きな刺激を受けることができるだろう。

第2節　日本の少数言語復興を妨げる「国語」と「方言」という語の弊害

第1項　「国語」という語の弊害

　上述した欧米3地域には、それらの言語によるイマージョン・スクールが存在し、復興運動が盛んだが、我が琉球諸語地域には、復興運動と呼べるまでの動きは見受けられないように思われる。復興運動が盛んにならない理由はいくつかあるのだが、まずは、その障害となっているであろう精神的な足かせ、「国語」と「方言」という語について考察を加えてみる。はじめに「国語」という語の弊害から述べる。

　明治維新以降日本は、「日本語」の教科書、すなわち「国語」を学校教育の要として現在も引き続き教育している。けれども「日本語」のことを「国語」と呼ぶ必要はあるのだろうか。1944（昭和19）年に発足した歴史ある「国語学会」という組織が存在するが、そこは2004年に「日本語学会」と改称している[7]。この「国語学」と「日本語学」の違いだが、日本語を自国の言語「国語」と見る立場から研究するのが「国語学」で、日本語を多くの世界言語のうちの一つと見る立場から、その特質を研究するのが「日本語学」

という[8]。また、この「国語」という呼称を用い学校教育で「日本語」のみを学ばされ続けているアイヌや琉球などの少数言語を母語とする人々は、自らの母語を「言語」として認識できなくされてきた。つまり「国語」以外の日本に存在する言語は「方言」という烙印を押されてしまうのである[9]。

第2項　アイヌ人の国語は「アイヌ語」、おきなわ人の国語は「おきなわ語」

その一方「アイヌ語」は「アイヌ方言」と呼ばれて来なかったという反論も考えられよう。それならば「アイヌ語」を「方言」ではなく「言語」と定義してきたからと言って「国語」と同等の権利を日本は保障してきたのであろうか。また、アイヌ人に「アイヌ語」教育を施してきたのだろうか。「アイヌ語」教育どころか1899年〜1997年まで「アイヌ人」を「土人」と日本は法律で定義し差別し、アイヌ人の文化や言語を撲滅していったというのが過去の歴史である[10]。「日本語」を自国の言語「国語」と見る立場から「国語学」が生まれたとの定義を上述したが、アイヌ人にとっての「国語」は「アイヌ語」であり「日本語」ではない。それはもちろん、我々琉球諸島に住む者にとっての「国語」も「日本語」ではなく「琉球諸語」なのである。「国語」という名の下に現在も「日本語」を学ばされ続けている日本の少数言語を母語とする人々は、自らの母語を認識できなくなり、さらに自らの母語は学校教育では教えられない「方言」という価値の低いものだと認識させられていった。

第3項　「方言」という語の弊害

近年ユネスコの発表により琉球諸語を「方言」ではなく「言語」と呼んでいこうという動きが多少ではあるが見受けられるようになってきた。けれども、いままで琉球の各言語は「方言」だと定義され多数の論文や著作が出版されてきた[11]。厳しい言い方になるが、これが弊害となり琉球諸語復興運動の大きな足かせとなっている。それは明確で、色々な学術書や研究、教育現場で琉球諸語ではなく「琉球方言」とされてきた結果、我々琉球諸島に住む者は自らの言語を「方言」だと認識し、それにより「国語」つまり「日本

語」をまず学ぶことが何より大切で、自らの言語は「方言」であり、取るに足らないもので今さら学ぶ必要はないという考えが大多数をしめるようになっている。その大きな証拠が、2015年11月現在、琉球諸島のどの地域の小中高校においても必修科目としての琉球諸語がまったくないことである[12]。あるのは「国語」と、我々の地域とは関係のない「英語」の教科である。

第4項　日本政府に国連：自由権規約委員会より勧告

　ハワイではハワイ語が学校の教科として取り入れられるどころか、ハワイ語イマージョン・プログラムを導入している公立校が20校[13]もあり、2200人あまりの生徒達[14]が自らの言語であるハワイ語を学んでいる。イギリスにおいてはカムリー（ウェールズ）国でカムリー語が義務教育に導入されている。スペインでは700万人以上の話者がいるというカタルーニャ自治州においては行政、教育、マスメディアなどがカタルーニャ語を用い、自治州内はもはやスペインとはいえない様相を呈している。世界の少数言語復興が活発な地域の実例を挙げられても日本とは事情が違うという意見も考えられるが、日本はGDP世界3位の経済大国[15]で、GDPに関していえばイギリスやスペインよりも上なのである。また、途上国援助総額の多い国ランキングで日本は世界5位である[16]。世界の発展途上国などへの支援は惜しまないけれども、国内の少数言語には目も向けようとしないどころか、未だに我々の言語を「方言」と分類し、我々のプライドを傷つけ、公教育への琉球諸語導入推進などは一切みられず、我々の文化や言語に誇りを持てない教育や行政を明治以降ずっと押し付け続けている。さらに重大な事実がある。締約国数は日本を含め168カ国になる自由権規約という国際条約があるが、その委員会である自由権規約委員会より「**法制を改正し、アイヌ、琉球及び沖縄のコミュニティの**（中略）**児童に対する彼ら自身の言葉での教育を促進すべきである**」との勧告を2008年より日本は現在もずっと受け続けているが、未だに何の措置も講じられていないというのが現状である[17]。

第3節　日本の少数言語

第1項　日琉語族

　日本語や琉球諸語は日琉語族に属し、日本語と琉球諸語の祖語は日琉祖語（Proto-Japanese-Ryukyuan）[18]と呼ばれる。その日琉祖語は、日本語派と琉球語派（琉球諸語）に分かれた。ただ、分岐年代は議論されており、奈良時代以前、また以降との意見があり今のところ定説はない[19]。日本語派には現在の「日本語」が含まれる。ユネスコは日本には危機言語が8つあると指定したが、日本国内で危機言語ではない言語は「日本語」のみである。したがって、日本には9つの言語が存在することになる。一方危機言語に指定されている琉球語派には、さらに2つの語派に下位分類でき、6つの言語が属する。まず、北琉球語派には「奄美語」、「国頭語」、「おきなわ語（うちなーぐち）」があり、「北琉球諸語」と呼ばれる。南琉球語派には「宮古語」、「八重山語」、「与那国語」があり、「南琉球諸語」と呼ばれる[20]。

第2項　日琉語族以外の日本の少数言語

　ユネスコの発表する日本の危機言語には日琉語族以外の言語も存在する。東京都八丈島の言語である「八丈語」も系統は不明だが日本国内の言語であり、危機言語だとユネスコは発表した。他には、アイヌ（諸）語もある。アイヌ（諸）語は実は琉球諸語と同じように一枚岩ではない。アイヌ（諸）語には「北海道アイヌ語」「樺太アイヌ語」「千島アイヌ語」などが存在しており、これらは隔絶言語である可能性が高いとの指摘がある[21]。「琉球諸語」も、これまで「琉球語」と呼ばれていたが、上述したようにユネスコは琉球諸島の言語を6つに分類している。それを「琉球語」だというと、琉球諸島には言語が一つしかないという誤解を与えかねない。それゆえに「琉球諸語」という呼称を近年用い始める学者が多くなっている。同じくアイヌの中にも色々な言語が存在する。したがって今後は「アイヌ諸語」という表記を用いれば「琉球諸語」と同じように複数の言語が含まれていると理解できるであろう。さらに、ユネスコは発表していないが、日琉語族以外の日本の少

数言語には「日本手話」もあり、また、「小笠原クレオール英語」という言語も存在する[22]。

第4節　カムリー（ウェールズ）語、カタルーニャ語、ハワイ語への聖書翻訳

第1項　カムリー語復興の源流は聖書

　イギリスのなかのカムリー国の「カムリー語」は1988年[23]、義務教育に組み込まれることにより、復興への大きな一歩を踏み出した。

　「カムリー語」は、1536年〜1543年の「併合法」によりカムリーがイングランドに支配され、その後様々な迫害を受け減少の一途をたどるのみだった[24]。けれども、その生き残りに大きな役割を果たしたのが16世紀のヨーロッパで興った宗教改革以降の教会の活動だった。そのなかでも、カムリー語に翻訳した聖書が1588年に完成したことが、カムリー語復興の萌芽となっているといえるだろう[25]。その理由は、カムリー語聖書が完成した後、17世紀末のキリスト教知識普及協会が設立した慈善学校、また、18世紀に入って広まった巡回学校、また、18世紀末には日曜学校など、教会がカムリー語聖書を用い布教活動を積極的に行ったことが功を奏したからである[26]。その証拠に、1801年時点で、カムリー語話者は、カムリー人口のうち80%を占めていたと見積もられる報告がある[27]。それから20世紀に入り英語がかなり主要な位置を占めるようになり一時期は相当、話者数が減退したにも関わらず、上述したように1988年には、カムリー人の地道な活動が実りカムリー語はカムリー国において義務教育化され、その復興に大きな一歩を踏み出した。

第2項　カタルーニャ語、ハワイ語復興を担う聖書の役割

　カムリーを見てきたように言語復興の要を担ってきたといってよいのがクリスチャン（キリスト教信者）達の活躍だが、その原動力は、聖書に翻訳され

るほど語彙や慣用句などが豊富な自分たちの言語という誇りが根底にあったからではないだろうか。また、他にも近年目覚ましくカムリー語が復活した理由がある。それは、1960年代以降、米国のキング牧師などが中心となり興った公民権運動が世界各地へ伝播し、マイノリティ復権運動となり多大な影響を及ぼしているということである[28]。その運動はカムリーはむろん、カタルーニャやハワイにも広がっていったと考えられよう。

　少数言語のエースと言われるスペインのカタルーニャにも、カタルーニャ語の聖書が存在する。それは1287年～1290年に翻訳された[29]。そのころはカタルーニャ・アラゴン連合王国で、その後スペインのカスティーリャ王国を中心とした国家統一の動きの中で、スペインという国の一地域となる[30]。その間もカタルーニャ語は用いられ続けてきた。しかしその後1939年にフランコがスペインで独裁体制を敷き1975年までの36年間、カタルーニャ語は公的な場で用いることは禁止される。その後、フランコが亡くなると1979年には自治憲章を手に入れ、スペインの他地域に先駆け自治州となり、以後カタルーニャ州では「カタルーニャ語」を州の公用語に指定し、現在では学校教育もカタルーニャ語で行っている。簡単にカタルーニャの歴史を述べたが、現在までのカタルーニャ語復興には、1287～1290年に作成されたカタルーニャ語聖書の存在も大きいが、そもそもカタルーニャ・アラゴン連合王国はキリスト教徒のレコンキスタ（国土回復運動）[31]により誕生した国で、カタルーニャ語とキリスト教徒とは密接な結びつきがある。

　次はハワイ語だが、筆者はカムリー語とカタルーニャ語に関しての聖書の翻訳があるというのは知っていたが、ハワイ語の翻訳聖書も存在するということを知った時に、この論文のタイトルを決めた。ヨーロッパにおいてキリスト教の影響が色濃く反映されていることは周知の事実であろうが、まさか太平洋上に浮かぶ孤立した島ハワイにもその影響があり、しかもハワイ語の聖書まで翻訳されていた事実には驚かされた。その事情は紙幅の都合により詳細は割愛するが、1822年に聖書はハワイ語に翻訳され、さらにハワイ最初の新聞、Ka Lama Hawaiiも刊行されたのである[32]。新聞まで刊行されるに至るとは、やはり聖書という高度な知識と智慧の詰まった書物の翻訳が、

自らの言語に対しての自信につながり、その後のハワイ語の発展、またハワイ王国の発展にも繋がっていったと考えられる。

その繁栄も束の間、悲しいことに、1893年に米国の侵略事件がおこる。それによりハワイ王国は崩壊しハワイ語は禁止されていった。それから1959年にハワイは米国の50番目の州に組み込まれ、1978年にはハワイ州憲法が修正されハワイ語はハワイ州の公用語となる。以後、上述したように、キング牧師などが中心となった公民権運動は米国で興り、それはダイレクトにハワイ語の復興運動へ繋がっていった。ただ、その原動力となっているのは、あくまでも過去にハワイ語への聖書翻訳が存在したからで、それが現在のハワイ語復興運動の萌芽となっていると言えるだろう。筆者は直接ハワイへ行き復興運動の中心メンバーと交流を持てた。そこで知ったのが、彼ら復興運動の中心メンバーは、やはりキリスト教信者だったのである。

第3項　琉球諸語復興には特に関わりのないキリスト教信者

カムリー語、カタルーニャ語、ハワイ語の復興に関して中心的な役割を果たしてきたキリスト教徒たちが翻訳した聖書、この書物の存在が上記3地域の少数言語復興の最大の原動力になっていると筆者は考える。ただし、現代においては必ずしもキリスト教信者が中心となり上記3地域の復興運動の中核を担っているわけではないであろう。ここで述べたいのはあくまでも言語として過去から現在まで認識され、それが継続されてきた歴史を見ると、聖書が果たした役割が大きいという意味だということである。

聖書に関してだが、一応、うちなーぐち訳も存在する。それはイギリス人ベッテルハイム（1811〜1870年）が琉球王国時代に那覇に8年間滞在し訳したものである。背文字には「琉球語新約全書」と表記され、別名「琉訳聖書」とも呼ばれる[33]。ただし、タイトルは琉球語とあるが用いられている言語は、うちなーぐちである。ざっと目を通してみるとかなり日本語直訳が多いが、それでも琉球王国時代のうちなーぐちの片鱗が伺え、ある程度はうちなーぐち資料として参考になり得るだろう。このようなベッテルハイムのうちなーぐちへの注力にもかかわらず、伊波普猷も述べるように、その当時の

琉球王府役人にしつこく付け回され監視され続けた結果、ただの一人もキリスト教信者を獲得することはできず帰国したようである。さらに伊波によると『新約聖書』の三分の一を琉球語（うちなーぐち）に翻訳して上海で出版したとのことである[34]。その後1879（明治12）年、琉球国は日本に侵略され崩壊。沖縄県が強制設置され現在に至るが、特にキリスト教信者が琉球諸語復興運動を行っているということはほとんど聞いたことがない。ただ、文化庁の出している「宗教年鑑　平成26年版」の「全国キリスト教系宗教団体・教師・信者数」の「宗教団体（宗教法人を含む）」の項目を調べると47都道府県中沖縄県の総数は11位であった。並み居る大都市と比べてもキリスト教系宗教団体数は多いのだが、それでも特に琉球諸語には関心はないようである。キリスト教信徒の援助や関心がない琉球諸語には未来はあるのか。

第5節　琉球諸語を宗教力ではなく歴史認識で復興させる

第1項　うちなーぐち復興はうちなー地域全体の課題

　筆者は琉球諸語中、うちなーぐちの講師でもあり、その復興には精力を傾けている。これは筆者個人の問題ではなく、うちなー（おきなわ）地域全体の問題でもあるので、皆で考えるべきであろう。しかしながら、一般の人はあまり関心がないように見受けられる。それではどうやって関心を持ってもらえるか。それには宗教、ここでは「聖書」に変わる何かが必要だと考える。色々と模索中ではあるが、現段階で効果的だと思えるのは、きちんとした「歴史認識」を持つことではないかと最近強く感じる。その一番の核となるのが1609年の薩摩侵略の事件である。この大事件こそが、我々琉球諸島の「歴史」を歪め、「文化」「誇り」などの価値を軽んじる元凶となっているのである。

第2項　琉球処分ではなく琉球侵略

　1609年に薩摩が琉球国を侵略した事件は当然、我々琉球諸島地域に住む

者は教育などで学ぶべきである。それと同様に1879（明治12）年に日本が琉球を侵略した事件も、琉球諸島地域では特に時間を割き教えるよう、文科省は特別教育枠を設けるべきである。現在我々琉球諸島に住む者は米軍基地問題に悩まされ、また、琉球諸語が危機言語となっているという重大な人権侵害を日米両政府より受けている。その元凶は1609年の薩摩侵略に遠因を求めることもできるが、直接的な被害は1879年からである。それほどまで重大な琉球にとっての大事件を物の本では、「琉球処分」と書いているものが多い。「処分」とは「処罰」のことで、上から下に下す命令なども含まれる。少し考えてみれば分かるが、1879年に日本の警察と軍隊を合わせた約560人が首里城を武力占拠し、時の国王を東京へ拉致し生涯軟禁状態に置き、その後、日本は1945年まで、米国、仏国、蘭国などと修好条約を結ぶほど国際的に独立国として認められていた琉球国を占領・支配したのである。この一大事件を「琉球処分」だという訳の分からない言葉を用いごまかすことにより、その後日本の取った琉球諸語の「方言化」、また日本への「同化政策」、さらに「琉球人の徴兵」や「沖縄戦による一般民の死亡」など、数々の我々琉球諸島住民への「暴力」と「文化的ジェノサイド（cultural genocide）」が見えなくなってしまうのである。また、第二次世界大戦後の米国の琉球諸島支配による「人権侵害」や「土地収奪」など、数々の米国の行為も1879年に強制的に琉球国が日本に組み込まれ沖縄県となったがゆえに起こったとも言えるのである。

第3項　新しい琉球・うちなーの歴史観提唱

　タイトルに掲げたように歴史認識を、うちなーんちゅ（おきなわ人）の視点からきちんと捉えることができれば、うちなーぐちを復興させるのは当たり前だと、うちなーんちゅならば考えるだろう。しかし、うちなーぐちの復興、復権運動は我がうちなーではほとんど興っていないと筆者は感じる。1879年までは琉球国の中心となる言語であったうちなーぐちの復興、復権運動はなぜ起きないのか。その要因はうちなーの本当の歴史が教育で教えられておらず、日本人の歴史観のみを1879年以降、うちなーんちゅは学ばされてき

たからだと筆者は考える。根本的にこれだけはおさえておきたい、うちなーの歴史区分をいささか簡単ではあるが下記にまとめてみた。

　　1609年、薩摩は琉球侵略後1872年まで裏から支配する。1609年～
　　　　1872年（263年間）
　　1872年、日本の謀略により琉球藩となる。1872年～1879年（7年間）
　　1879年、日本は琉球を侵略、沖縄県を強制設置し1945年まで支配する。
　　　　1879年～1945年（66年間）
　　1945年、米国より占領支配を1972年まで受ける。1945年～1972年（27
　　　　年間）
　　1972年、日本が再び琉球諸島を支配し沖縄県を強制設置する。1972年
　　　　～現在も継続中。

　これらの歴史観を厳しく、また大げさだと捉える人もいるだろう。けれども400年間薩摩や日本、米国と支配され続け、我々琉球・うちなー側から、支配者を糾弾できる過去は存在したであろうか。1609年以来ここ琉球諸島はずっと何者かに支配を受け続け、それは現在も継続中なのである。このように、我々の抑圧されて来た歴史を直視できてはじめて、我々琉球の言語が「方言」ではないと認識できるだろう。我々の誇りである、700年近くも歴史のある言語うちなーぐち（おきなわ語）は「方言」ではないのである。

第4項　琉球国の歴史は692年

　700年近くと書いたが、これは文献上溯れる数字である。琉球国の正史『中山世鑑』（1650年向象賢編述）に舜天即位（1187年）とある。その後1879年、日本は武力を背景に琉球国を崩壊させる。したがって1879年から1187年を引くと692年という数字になる。これは琉球・うちなー側からみれば当たり前にはじき出される数字だろう。しかし、物の本には第一尚氏が三山を統一した15世紀頃を嚆矢とし、「琉球国は450年の歴史」と矮小化されているとしか言いようのない数字がまことしやかに書かれている。中国や日本もそう

だが、世界には統一されてからの歴史が短い国が存在する。日本で考えると、封建主義を打ち破り民主主義を標榜した明治から建国されたともいえ、150年位の歴史しかない国になる。その国の建国された歴史年をどこに置くかで歴史の見方はまったく異なってくるだろう。

　もう一つ、日本の直接支配について述べたい。琉球国は692年間存在したが、1879年に日本の侵略を受け沖縄県が強制設置された。それから現在まで136年になる。ただし、1945年〜1972年の27年間は日本ではなく米国支配であった。その27年間の米国支配を差し引くと、109年という数字になる。つまり、日本の直接支配は、2015年現在も含めて109年なのである。琉球国の歴史は692年だが、それが109年の日本支配により、琉球諸語は消滅危機に追いやられている。上述した歴史観を直視できる同胞が増えるのを祈るばかりである。

第5項　19世紀に欧米と結んだ条約が歴史を覆す

　琉球国は1609年までは独立国であり、自らの力で国を運営していた。しかし1609年、薩摩侵略により表面上は独立国であったが裏では薩摩、ひいては江戸幕府の支配下に置かれた。表面上独立国の体裁を保っていたので、19世紀頃の欧米諸国には独立国と捉えられ、1854年に米国、1855年に仏国、1859年には蘭国と、左記三国に、強制的ではあるが修好条約を結ばされる。皮肉にもその条約は、国際法上、琉球国は主体性を持っていたとみなされることになり、1879年以降日本や米国に強制的に支配され植民地とされ続けている現状を打破する起爆剤となる可能性がある。しかも、その動きは少しずつではあるがうちなー社会で始まっている[35]。

　もう一つ、あまり知られていない重大な歴史的事実を最近知った。どういうことかと言うと、修好条約を欧米と結び、国際的に独立国として位置付けられた琉球国だが、実は、支配していた側の江戸幕府や薩摩も琉球を独立国として認めざるをえなかった事実があったのだ。時は1854年2月17日以前、日米和親条約を結ぶ際に米国側が幕府に迫った日本の開港だが、その候補地に米国側は「松前（函館）」や「琉球（那覇）」などを提案していた[36]。その際

「琉球は甚だ遠隔の国で、同地の港を開くことは我々の論議しえないところである」と江戸幕府は拒否回答したのである[37]。つまり薩摩や江戸幕府は琉球国を裏で支配していることを欧米に知られることを恐れ、琉球の那覇港は幕府と関わりが無いと返答したのである。だからこそ米国、仏国、蘭国の三国はわざわざ琉球国と、その後独自に条約を結んだのである。

　最後に日本近世史専門の荒野泰典氏の言葉を引用しこの論考を閉じたい。「『蝦夷地』の大部分は現在の北海道、『琉球』は沖縄県だが、そうなるのはこれらの地域が日本の国家領域に組みこまれた近代以後のことだ。近世日本においては、外国、あるいは『異域（いいき）』（日本以外の地）とされており、その地の住民たちは自らの国や地域に対する独自のアイデンティティを持って生活していた」[38]。

琉球諸語言語地図

琉球諸語言語地図（琉球諸語の区分と、区分論）

　2009年2月にユネスコ（国際連合教育科学文化機関）は次の6つの言語を危機言語として発表した。

　地図を参照していただきたいが、北から奄美語、国頭語、おきなわ語、宮古語、八重山語、与那国語である。近年この6つの総称を「琉球諸語」と呼称する学者が増えてきており筆者もそれを採用している。

　琉球の6つの言語の行われている地域と範囲について簡単に記す。

奄美語

　奄美語は奄美大島北部と南部、加計呂麻島、徳之島の言葉などが含まれる。奄美語の北限は奄美大島で南限は徳之島である。

国頭語

　国頭語はおきなわ島北部、伊江島、与論島、沖永良部島、喜界島の言葉などが含まれる。国頭語の北限は喜界島で、南限は、おきなわ島の東海岸の金武町屋嘉から西海岸の恩納村恩納までとなる。

おきなわ語

おきなわ語は、おきなわ島中南部、慶良間諸島の言葉などが含まれる。「おきなわ語」の北限は、おきなわ島東海岸のうるま市石川から恩納村谷茶まで。南限はおきなわ島南端。

宮古語

宮古語は宮古島、伊良部島、池間島の言葉などが含まれる。

八重山語

八重山語は、石垣島、竹富島、黒島、鳩間島、波照間島、西表島の言葉などが含まれる。

与那国語

与那国語は、与那国島のみで話されている。

さて琉球にはいくつの言語があるかということについて少し記しておきたい。琉球諸島の言語を6つに分類したのはユネスコだというのは上記の通りだが、Googleが支援し東ミシガン大学などが作成するThe Endangered Languages Projectでは国頭語が抜けた残り5つを提唱しており、筆者の所属する「琉球継承言語会」会長宮良信詳氏も範囲を同じく5つとすることを提唱しておられる。さらにキリスト教系の少数言語研究団体の作成するEthnologueでは琉球諸語をさらに細かく分類し12もの言語に分けている。沖縄学の父と言われる伊波普猷は7つに分類し、宮良当壮は、The Endangered Languages Projectの見解とは違う区分で同じく5つに分類している。東条操にいたっては、薩南、沖縄、先島という3つのみに分類している[39]。

以上見てきたように、このように琉球諸島には複数の言語が存在するのであるが、それをどこで線引きし、区別するのか、またどこから言語として認めるのか、それらは現在でも定説はない。筆者はユネスコの定義に一応賛同してはいるものの、便宜上はThe Endangered Languages Projectの提唱する奄美語、おきなわ語、宮古語、八重山語、与那国語の5つだと講義や講演で一般の方に理解しやすくなるのではと感じる。しかし、便宜上分かりやすいから、地図上で見た目が分かりやすいということと言語区分は違うものなの

で、琉球諸語が今後5つになったり、もしかしたら細分化し12言語に分かれる可能性もあるだろう。

註

1　筆者は「沖縄」という漢字をなるべく用いたくない。その理由は、薩摩が使い始めたと考えられ、おきなわ人が考案した漢字かどうか不明だからである。1609年、琉球王国を侵略した薩摩は1872年まで263年にわたり裏から支配し搾取し続けた。その薩摩の1629年の文献（本稿掲載歴史年表参照）に「沖縄」という漢字があらわれると『沖縄大百科事典』（沖縄タイムス社）の項目「沖縄」にある。また、1879年琉球王国を侵略・占領した日本は「沖縄県」を強制設置した。この「沖縄」という漢字の出所は上述した薩摩文書だといえ、さらに沖縄県と命名したのは日本政府のようで経緯は不明である。よしんば「県を置くのでその呼称を申し出よ」と問われ、琉球側が「沖縄」という漢字を提示したという資料が見つかったにせよ、暴力的に沖縄県が設置された事実には変わりがない。今後この「沖縄」という漢字についての議論が活発になることを期待し、あえてひらがなで「おきなわ」と書きたい。

2　1.八丈語？　世界2500言語、消滅危機　日本は8語対象、方言も独立言語　ユネスコ（朝日新聞デジタル）　2.消滅の危機にある方言・言語（文化庁ウェブサイト）3.UNESCO Atlas of the World's Languages in Dangerなど。

3　アイヌの人々の言語を今までは「アイヌ語」と称してきたが、アイヌ語の中に複数の言語が存在するとの指摘がある（パトリック・ハインリッヒ＋松尾慎 2010）。

4　イギリスの中には4つの国があり、人口の多い順にイングランド、スコットランド、ウェールズ、北アイルランドの順となるが、イングランド以外の3つの国の言語は元々英語ではなくケルト語派で、その総称はケルト諸語という。その3つの地域の呼称は英語名であり自らの言語呼称は英語名と異なる。それぞれアルバ（スコットランド）、カムリー（ウェールズ）、エーレ（北アイルランドを含むアイルランド全体）という。ここでは、原聖（女子美術大）氏の指摘もあり、ケルト諸語地域の言語を尊重する意味も込めて、カムリー（ウェールズ）という呼称を採用したい。

5　イマージョン・スクール（Immersion school）とはイマージョン・プログラム（没入法）を導入している学校を指す。イマージョン・プログラムとは、外国語なり少数言語なり、学びたい言語を母語などの助けを用いず、その言語のみで教え学ぶ学習法をいう。

6　消滅の危機にある方言・言語（文化庁ウェブサイト）など。

7　日本語学会ウェブサイトのトップに「―日本語研究の進展を願って1944年に『国語学会』として設立され、2004年1月に『日本語学会』に改称しました―」とある。http://www.jpling.gr.jp/

8　小野正弘（明治大学ウェブサイト「国語学・日本語学」）を参考http://www.kisc.meiji.ac.jp/~wonomasa/nsidaijiten.htm

9　榎澤幸広（2009）、86頁。

10　ノエミ・ゴッドフロア（2014）など。

11 例えば、消滅の危機にある方言・言語（文化庁ウェブサイト）には、わざわざ「八重山語（八重山方言）」「沖縄語（沖縄方言）」など、（方言）という表記が併記されている。国の機関が我々の言語を括弧つきではあるが「方言」と定義しているのである。ユネスコやEthnologue、また、米Google支援の「Endangered Languages Project」では明確に「言語」と定義されている。日本政府は国際社会の取り組む少数言語支援が理解できないのだろうか。

12 多少の琉球諸語への取り組みを行っている学校もある。けれども、それは教師個人の裁量によるところが大きい総合学習や、言語はあまり取り扱わない郷土芸能コースなどである。ここで述べたいのは自国語という概念をきちんと持ち、学科として「国語」や「英語」と同時間、もしくはそれ以上の時間を割き、さらに義務教育として学ぶということを筆者は前提にしている。

13 A total of 20 public schools operate the Hawaiian Language Immersion Program. http://www.hawaiipublicschools.org/TeachingAndLearning/StudentLearning/HawaiianEducation/Pages/History-of-the-Hawaiian-Education-program.aspx

14 Hawaiian education http://www.hawaiipublicschools.org/TeachingAndLearning/StudentLearning/HawaiianEducation/Pages/translation.aspx

15 GDPの国際比較（内閣府ウェブサイト）http://www.esri.cao.go.jp/jp/sna/menu.html

16 外務省ウェブサイト世界いろいろ雑学ランキングより。http://www.mofa.go.jp/mofaj/kids/ranking/oda.html

17 『3　自由権規約（市民的及び政治的権利に関する国際規約）』中『同報告に関する自由権規約委員会の最終見解（2014年7月24日）』の26より　（外務省ウェブサイト）、比嘉光龍（2015）など。

18 歴史上初めて、琉球諸語と日本語は姉妹語の関係にあると述べたのはバジル・ホール・チェンバレン（1850-1935）で、彼の著書 *Essay in Aid of a Grammar and Dictionary of the Luchuan Language*（1895）にて発表された。そこには「共通祖語」から「古代琉球語」と「古代日本語」が分かれたと図で示されている。その著書以来、日本語と琉球諸語の共通祖語の名称は、その後の研究者により色々な名称が提示されてはいたが、いまだに統一されていない。けれども、2016年に田窪行則＋ジョンホイットマン＋平子達也（編）『琉球諸語と古代日本語——日琉祖語の再建に向けて』（くろしお出版）という本が出版され、タイトルに「日本語」と「琉球諸語」の祖語として「日琉祖語」を用いている。他にも京都大学からトマ・ペラール（Thomas Pellard）が論文「日琉祖語の分岐年代」（2012）を発表している。個人的には「琉日祖語」といいたいが、今のところ、この「日琉祖語」が琉球諸語研究者間の共通理解を得ているように見受けられるのでとりあえず採用したい。

19 日本語と琉球諸語の分岐年代については、トマ・ペラール「日琉祖語の分岐年代」（2012）の論文中にさらに詳しく論者の論文が引用されている。

20 上述トマ・ペラール論文と山下・渡辺・高田（2011）、104頁。

21 山下・渡辺・高田（2011）、104頁。

22 同上、102頁。

23 The Welsh language in education in the UK| 2nd Edition | mercator http://www.mercator-research.eu/fileadmin/mercator/dossiers_pdf/Welsh_in_the_UK_2nd.pdf#s

earch='welsh+language+1988+compulsory'
24　原聖（編）（2012）、62頁。
25　同上、68頁。
26　ウェールズを知る――ウェールズ概略史
　　http://www.cymru2008.com/historyofwales.html
27　浦田和幸（『拡大EU諸国における外国語教育政策とその実効性に関する総合的研究報告書』平成18-20年度科学研究費補助金プロジェクト））、176頁。
28　松原好次（編）（2010）、6頁。
29　スペインの他の現地語による聖書　カタロニア語http://www.jw.org/ja/%E5%87%BA%E7%89%88%E7%89%A9/%E9%9B%91%E8%AA%8C/wp20140301/%E4%B8%AD%E4%B8%96%E3%81%AE%E3%82%B9%E3%83%9A%E3%82%A4%E3%83%B3%E3%81%A7%E3%81%AE%E8%81%96%E6%9B%B8%E7%BF%BB%E8%A8%B3/
30　沖縄大学地域研究所（2013）、224頁。
31　知恵蔵2015　カタルーニャ自治州。
32　田中（2004）、48頁と http://hawaiitribune-herald.com/news/local-news/old-newspaper-link-hawaiian-history
33　高良倉吉（2006）、解説。
34　伊波普猷（1993）、332頁。
35　例えば、これら修好条約の3原本が沖縄県浦添市美術館で2015年2月から「琉球・幕末・明治維新　沖縄特別展」（琉球新報社、沖縄産業計画主催、浦添市教育委員会共催）と銘打ち開催され一般公開されている。さらに、琉球新報にて2014年より長期連載された「道標求めて――琉米条約160年　主権を問う」（新垣毅記者）は、詳細且つ、うちなーんちゅの視点に立ち歴史修正を迫っている論考である。その連載中、2014年7月11日の琉米修好条約160周年の日の記事は圧巻である。その日の一面トップが「琉球処分は国際法上不正」と大きな見出しで飾られ、それのみならず他面にも大きく日本を糾弾する学者の論調が報じられた。1879年に日本が琉球侵略、その後支配し現在まで、基地問題で日本政府を糾弾する記事は多々あるが、沖縄県強制設置の明治期の日本を批判・糾弾する記事がうちなーのマスメディアで報じられたのは稀有なことであろう。この長期連載は琉球新報社＋新垣毅（編）（2015）『沖縄の自己決定権――その歴史的根拠と近未来の展望』とされ出版された。
36　函館市史デジタル版「幕府の条約草案」（p.11-13）に「2月17日以前に既に5港の開港を要求していた」とある。
37　西里喜行（2010）、73-74頁。
38　荒野泰典（2012）、http://www.nippon.com/ja/features/c00104/（2015年10月6日アクセス）。
39　金城朝永全集（1974）、17-18頁。

参考文献

朝日新聞（2009）「八丈語？世界2500言語、消滅危機　日本は8語対象、方言も独立言語　ユネスコ」、2月20日夕刊1ページ1総合。

新城 俊昭（2010）『沖縄から見える歴史風景』、編集工房 東洋企画。
荒野 泰典（2012）「第4回「四つの口」と長崎貿易──近世日本の国際関係再考のために」、nippon.com。http://www.nippon.com/ja/features/c00104/（2015年10月6日アクセス）
アンナ・ブガエワ（児島 康宏、長崎 郁 訳）（2014）「北海道南部のアイヌ語」、早稲田大学高等研究所紀要第6号、早稲田大学高等研究所。
伊東 治己（2007）「カナダのイマージョン教育の成功を支えた教授学的要因に関する研究」、鳴門教育大学研究紀要、第22巻。
伊波 普猷（1993）『伊波普猷全集1巻』平凡社。
上村 英明（2001）『先住民族の「近代史」──植民地主義を超えるために』、平凡社。
浦田 和幸（平成18-20年度 科学研究費補助金プロジェクト）「ウェールズにおける言語状況と言語政策」、拡大EU諸国における外国語教育政策とその実効性に関する総合的研究報告書。
エホバの証人「スペインの他の現地語による聖書」。
　　http://www.jw.org/ja/%E5%87%BA%E7%89%88%E7%89%A9/%E9%9B%91%E8%AA%8C/wp20140301/%E4%B8%AD%E4%B8%96%E3%81%AE%E3%82%B9%E3%83%9A%E3%82%A4%E3%83%B3%E3%81%A7%E3%81%AE%E8%96%E6%9B%B8%E7%BF%BB%E8%A8%B3/（2015年9月9日アクセス）
浦添市美術館（2015年2月～3月）「琉球・幕末・明治維新　沖縄特別展」。
　　http://museum.city.urasoe.lg.jp/docs/2015022400019/（2015年9月9日アクセス）
榎澤 幸広（2009）「方言話者と法廷」、筑波学院大学紀要第4集、83～92ページ。
小野 正弘「国語学・日本語学」、明治大学ウェブサイト
　　http://www.kisc.meiji.ac.jp/~wonomasa/nsidaijiten.htm（2015年9月8日アクセス）。
沖縄県公文書館（2008）「3月27日沖縄県の設置（1879年）」（2015年9月12日アクセス）。
　　http://www.archives.pref.okinawa.jp/publication/2013/03/130.html
沖縄大学地域研究所（2013）『琉球諸語の復興』、芙蓉書房出版。
沖縄大百科事典刊行事務局（1983）『沖縄大百科事典　上巻　中巻　下巻』。
外務省ウェブサイト「途上国援助総額の多い国」。
　　http://www.mofa.go.jp/mofaj/kids/ranking/oda.html（2015年9月12日アクセス）
外務省ウェブサイト「自由権規約（市民的及び政治的権利に関する国際規約）」
　　http://www.mofa.go.jp/mofaj/gaiko/kiyaku/（2015年9月12日アクセス）
金城 朝永（1974）『金城朝永全集（上巻）』、沖縄タイムス。
国立民族学博物館「世界の諸言語における態（voice）の類型論的研究」。
　　http://www.minpaku.ac.jp/research/activity/project/iurp/06jr092（2015年9月8日アクセス）。
国立公文書館（2007）「琉球藩ヲ廃シ沖縄県ヲ被置ノ件」。
　　http://www.archives.go.jp/ayumi/kobetsu/m12_1879_01.html（2015年9月12日アクセス）。
下地 理則・パトリック ハインリッヒ 編（2015）『琉球諸語の保持を目指して──消滅危機言語めぐる議論と取り組み』、ココ出版。
大学共同利用機関法人 人間文化研究機構国立国語研究所（2011）「文化庁委託事業危機的な状況にある言語・方言の実態に関する調査研究事業 報告書」、4.1.2 琉球方言の独自性、19頁。
高良 倉吉（2006）「解説　琉球語新約全書」、琉球大学附属図書館貴重書展。

http://manwe.lib.u-ryukyu.ac.jp/library/digia/tenji/tenji2006/10.htmlhttp://manwe.lib.u-ryukyu.ac.jp/library/digia/tenji/tenji2006/10.html（2015年9月9日アクセス）。

田中 圭治郎（2004）「多文化社会ハワイ州における教育の実態と展望」、教育学部論集15号、佛教大学教育学部。

トマ・ペラール（2012）『日琉祖語の分岐年代』、「琉球諸語と古代日本語に関する比較言語学的研究」ワークショップ、京都大学。

内閣府「国民経済計算（GDP統計）──GDPの国際比較」
　　http://www.esri.cao.go.jp/jp/sna/menu.html（2015年9月9日アクセス）

西里 喜行（2010）「東アジア史における琉球処分」、『経済史研究』第13号、大阪経済大学、日本経済史研究所。

日本語学会　http://www.jpling.gr.jp/（2015年9月8日アクセス）

ノエミ・ゴッドフロア（2014）「明治時代におけるアイヌ同化政策とアカルチュレーション」、アルザス日欧知的交流事業 日本研究セミナー「明治」報告書。

函館市史デジタル版「幕府の条約草案」、p.11-13（2015年10月6日アクセス）。

原 聖編（2012）『ケルト諸語文化の復興』、三元社。

パトリック・ハインリッヒ、下地 理則（共編）（2011）『琉球諸語記録保存の基礎』東京外国語大学アジアアフリカ研究所。

パトリック・ハインリッヒ＋松尾 慎 編著（2010）『東アジアにおける言語復興』、三元社。

比嘉 春潮（1971）『比嘉春潮全集第1巻（歴史編Ⅰ）、第2巻（歴史編Ⅱ）、第4巻（評伝・自伝編）』、沖縄タイムス。

比嘉 光龍（2015）「琉球及びおきなわ児童の言語教育権：日本政府に国連：自由権規約委員会より勧告」、日本言語政策学会、JALP2015年大会発表予稿集。

文化庁「消滅の危機にある方言・言語」
　　http://www.bunka.go.jp/seisaku/kokugo_nihongo/kokugo_shisaku/kikigengo（2015年9月8日アクセス）。

文化庁（平成26年版）「宗教年鑑」
　　http://www.bunka.go.jp/tokei_hakusho_shuppan/hakusho_nenjihokokusho/shukyo_nenkan/（2015年9月9日アクセス）

松原 好次編著（2010）『消滅の危機にあるハワイ語の復権をめざして』、明石書店。

ソジエ 内田 恵美（2008）「日本の言語政策における統一性と多様性」、早稲田大学政治経済学部教養諸学研究会。

琉球新報社・新垣 毅編著（2015）『沖縄の自己決定権』、高文研。

琉球大学付属図書館貴重書展（2001）「明治政府と琉球処分」。
　　http://manwe.lib.u-ryukyu.ac.jp/library/digia/tenji/tenji2001/m05.html

山下 仁＋渡辺 学＋高田 博行編著（2011）『言語意識と社会』、三元社。

Yoshifumi Nagata「ウェールズを知る─ウェールズ概略史─」
　　http://www.cymru2008.com/historyofwales.html（2015年9月9日アクセス）。

DUNBAR, Robert WILLIAMS, Colin（2007）*Language and Governance*, Cardiff, University of Wales Press.

The Welsh language in education in the UK 2nd Edition mercator
  http://www.mercator-research.eu/fileadmin/mercator/dossiers_pdf/Welsh_in_the_UK_2nd.pdf#search='welsh+（2015年9月9日アクセス）
UNESCO Atlas of the World's Languages in Danger
  http://www.unesco.org/languages-atlas/index.php（2015年9月8日アクセス）
Mid-2014 Population Estimates: Pivot table Analysis Tool for the United Kingdom.
  http://ons.gov.uk/ons/publications/re-reference-tables.html?edition=tcm%3A77-368259（2015年9月9日アクセス）
Ethnologue　Languages of the World Japan.
  https://www.ethnologue.com/map/JP（2015年9月9日アクセス）
Endangered Languages Project
  http://www.endangeredlanguages.com/#/9/23.250/120.578/0/100000/0/low/mid/high/dormant/awakening/unknown（2015年9月9日アクセス）
Hawaii State Department of Education [History of the Hawaiian Language Immersion Program]
  http://www.hawaiipublicschools.org/TeachingAndLearning/StudentLearning/HawaiianEducation/Pages/History-of-the-Hawaiian-Education-program.aspx（2015年9月9日アクセス）
Hawaii State Department of Education [Hawaiian education]
  http://www.hawaiipublicschools.org/TeachingAndLearning/StudentLearning/HawaiianEducation/Pages/translation.aspx（2015年9月9日アクセス）

琉球・うちなーの歴史簡略表

　この「琉球・うちなーの歴史簡略表」を作成するに至る動機を簡単に述べたい。筆者は今から二十数年前にうちなー民謡を始め、その習得にはうちなーぐちが不可欠と考え、努力し習得につとめた。その結果、大学でうちなーぐちを講義させていただくまでになった。さらに、うちなー民謡そのものが生まれた、筆者自身の生まれ島、うちなーの歴史にも興味がわき、独自にうちなーの歴史本も幅広く読み、また蒐集にもつとめた。著名なうちなーの歴史学者から民間の研究者、さらに他都道府県出身者の書くうちなーの歴史本を読んでいくうちにある疑問が生じた。それは歴史の定義、認識である。筆者の思い、考えに合致する、うちなーの歴史定義をする本がほとんどと言って良いほどないのである。日本人ではなく、うちなーんちゅの側から視る琉球・うちなーの歴史定義をまとめる必要があると考え簡略表を作成した。これをもとに大学での講義や講演、執筆を行っている。

琉球・うちなーの歴史簡略表

備考	時代区分	年	「琉球・うちなー」歴史定義の提起と時代背景
一八七一～一八七九まで「六九二年間」、琉球は独立国。一八七九～一九四五の六六年間と、一九七二～二〇一五までの四十三年間を足した、「一〇九年間」が日本の琉球諸島支配年数。一九四五～一九七二の「二七年間」は米国支配。	舜天即位年を琉球国の始めとして、薩摩侵略の年まで「四二二年間」、実質的に琉球は自主独立していた。その後、一六〇九～一八七二の「二六三年間」、薩摩（一八七一年から鹿児島県）は裏で支配し、琉球を表面上は独立国とさせた。一八七二～一八七九の「七年間」、明治政府は薩摩から支配を引き継ぎ、琉球藩とする。それらの合計「六九二年間」が歴史上の琉球国存続年数だといえよう。	一一八七年～（四二二年間）	舜天即位（1187年） 1. 1187年以前には天孫氏という伝説上の王統があり、25代1万7802年間続いたという神話的な数字が琉球国最初の正史「中山世鑑」（1650年編纂）にある。 2. 天孫氏家臣「利勇」、主君を毒殺し中山王を名乗る。(1186年) 3. 1187年に逆心利勇を討った舜天だが、彼は天孫氏一族ではないようであるが、家臣の薦めにより即位し跡継ぎとなる。 4. 舜天は父が「源 為朝」、母は大里按司の妹の子という伝説があるが、その真偽は不明である。
		一六〇九年～（二六三年＋十七年間）	薩摩琉球侵略・裏支配（1609年） 1. 薩摩島津軍三千の兵が1609年3月8日奄美大島、3月21日には徳之島を侵略する。徳之島では2～300人の死者が出た。 2. 薩摩軍侵略を続け、4月1日首里城占拠。5月15日琉球国王「尚寧」、三司官・謝名親方等捕虜となり薩摩へ拉致。 3. 尚寧2年間拉致後、起請文に誓約し1611年帰国許可。 4. 薩摩侵略により1266年琉球入貢の奄美は1611年9月から薩摩直轄地。廃藩置県後も鹿児島県の領土。 5. 1609年薩摩の琉球侵略を「慶長の役」、「島津の琉球入り」と記す本もある。 6. 琉球国は裏では薩摩が支配するが、表面的には独立国として国際的な地位があった。ゆえに欧米との条約も締結した。(1854年米国、55年仏国、59年蘭国、と修好条約を結ぶ)

で「六六年間」、日本が占領・支配する。	一八七九（明治一二）年、日本国は琉球国を侵略し、沖縄県を強制設置する。以後、一九四五（昭和二〇）年まで	一八七九年〜（六六年間）	日本の琉球侵略・占領（1879年） 1. 1879年3月27日、日本の警察約160人、日本の軍隊約400人が首里城を強制的に占拠。その後5月27日に最後の琉球王「尚泰（しょうたい）」は東京へ拉致、軟禁され1901年東京宅にて死去。 2. 1872年〜1879年の7年間を一般的に「琉球処分」という。 「処分」は「処罰」と辞典にあるが、日本は琉球を侵略・占領したのが実態である。 3. 1879年4月4日、日本は一方的に「沖縄県」を強制設置。 4. 1879年8月、日本政府樹立の「沖縄県」に従わない琉球貴族・士族100人余が拉致され拷問。彼らは暴力に屈し恭順を誓約。 5. 薩摩の「琉球国之内知行高目録写」（1629年）に「沖縄」という字があり、それが、歴史上の初見だと考えられる。
		一九四五年〜（二七年間）	米国の支配（1945年〜1972年） 1952年のサンフランシスコ平和条約を米国統治開始とすれば、20年間の支配ともいえる。
	日本国に支配され、二〇一六年現在で「四十四年め」。	一九七二年〜現在	再び日本国の支配（1972年） 日米両政府で勝手に進められた沖縄返還協定に反対する11・10ゼネスト（1971-11-10）が起こり、10万2000人が決起した。(1969年11月の佐藤・ニクソン共同声明で、沖縄を72年に返還する合意がされたが、その内容は核つき・基地自由使用だった)

『琉球・うちなーの歴史簡略表』作成に当たり参考にした文献や資料、図書などは数十冊を数えここで記すことは紙幅上の都合により割愛する。他日を期して記したい。

Abstract, Chap.8

Attempt to revitalize the Ryukyuan languages by historical awareness, not by religious awareness

Byron Fija (Okinawan folk musician, Okinawan Lecturer at Okinawa Christian University)

Six years after their inclusion in the UNESCO *Atlas of the World's Languages in Danger of Extinction* in 2009, the Ryukyuan languages are still without any particular protection from the government of Japan. Also, efforts of revitalization are not particularly developed. This stands in contrast to other cases of language endangerment, where efforts to maintain endangered languages are more developed. When considering the three cases of Hawai'i, Catalonia and Wales, it appears to me that religion has played an important role in language revitalization there. Translating the bible and writing in the endangered language has been important there, but language activists have also been bounded to each other on the basis of religion. In the Ryukyus, however, religion does not serve as a resource to unite people towards a common aim. This is why I think that Ryukyuan language revitalization has to draw on historical awareness. In other words, we need to rethink and rewrite Ryukyuan history. At the present, Ryukyuan history is depicted only from a Tokyo perspective. Hence, there is little awareness, or even no knowledge, how the Ryukyu Kingdom was dissolved and replaced by Okinawa Prefecture by in 1879. Children in school exclusively learn that everyone from Hokkaido to the Ryukyu Islands has Japanese nationality. There is no word, anywhere, that the Ryukyu Kingdom was defeated by force then, and that its ancient government did not want to be part of Japan.

The Tokyo perspective is also all in evidence in the terminology with which these events are delineated, or how language issues in general are discussed in Japan. This is most notably the case with the term 'national language' (*kokugo*). Critically rethinking history from a Ryukyuan perspective involves questioning the legitimacy and continued use of this term in Japan today. Such terminology reflects, in the most obvious ways, an old inward looking ideology and a totalitarian nationalism. It promotes the idea that there is only one language in Japan, that is to say, it claims that other languages of Japan such as Ainu, Ryukyuan and Hachijo languages are either non-existent or erroneously brands these languages as "dialect" of Japanese. It is a sad fact that up to today, articles and books are published which claim that Ryukyuan languages are dialects of Japanese. It must also be clearly stated that such a practice is detrimental to all efforts of revitalizing the Ryukyuan languages. It is also because of the reproduction of such ideologies and such terminology that, at the time of writing this article, Ryukyuan language education is not yet established in any school across the entire Ryukyu Archipelago. Such practical issues aside, it also hurts Ryukyuan cultural pride to have Ryukyuan languages being labeled 'dialects' of Japanese. This is part of a policy which has been implemented with the purpose to undermining the culture of the Ryukyus. This policy was launched right after the annexation of the Ryukyu Kingdom in the Meiji period, and it is still in place to day.

I have myself studied three different cases of successful language revitalizations (Hawai'i, Calatonia, Wales) and found that in every case Christian religion has played an important role, be that by translations of the bible into the endangered language or by the fact that it was Christian believers who mainly pursued language revitalization. The Bible has, as a matter of fact, been translated into Okinawan, one of the six Ryukyuan languages, by Bettelheim in the 19th century. However, Bettelheim never converted a single person to Christianity during his 8 years in Okinawa, and his bible translation was not an important factor, neither for Okinawans nor for the recognition of Okinawan as a language in its own right. Before the idea took root that there is a Bible translation in Okinawan, and before Christianity could have spread, the Ryukyu Kingdom was annexed and a policy installed which downplayed the importance of Ryukyuan languages and cultures. Hence, my belief that Ryukyuan language revitalization can only be based on and depart from a new historical awareness.

Even since the Satsuma Clan invaded the Ryukyus in 1609, the history of the Ryukyus has been distorted in order to hide this coercion from the outside, and this has resulted in negative views on Ryukyuan culture. The term *Ryūkyū shobun* ('disposal of Ryukyu', or more literally 'disciplining Ryukyu') is another example of the lack of Ryukyuan perspectives on history. What actually happened during the so-called *Ryūkyū shobun* was that armed forces counting 560 people, recruited from either the Japanese police or the Japanese military occupied Shuri Castle in 1879. They then abducted the Ryukyuan King, brought him to Tokyo, and placed him under lifelong house arrest there. The effect of misrepresenting the Ryukyus as 'breakaway province of Japan', which needed to be 'disciplined' in 1879, was also felt after the end of WWII. Instead of restoring Ryukyuan independence, the Ryukyu Islands were occupied by the Allied Powers, de facto by the US. This occupation has also been crucially facilitated by the fact that the Ryukyuan languages were branded as 'dialects of Japanese'. There is a dire need to rethink every single aspect of Ryukyuan history from a Ryukyuan perspective. Without confronting the Tokyo perspective on Ryukyuan history, not only Ryukyuan languages are hidden, but also the forced assimilation and the policies which were legitimized by this Tokyo-centered historiography, and so is the death of civilians during the Battle of Okinawa. Up to today issues such as ongoing violence and cultural genocide become invisible or misunderstood if history is not clarified. Invisible also is the forced confiscation of land for the development of military infrastructure, the continuous disrespect of human rights, or all kinds of illegal activities by the United States in Okinawa today.

Language revitalization in the Ryukyus has to depart from de-colonizing Ryukyuan history. Religion is not a ready resource to mobilize people into revitalization activities, as has been the case in other regions in the world. Addressing history and departing from Ryukyuan perspectives is the basis from which a new awareness has to rise. Only on the basis of such a new awareness will it become possible to do something exceedingly trivial but nevertheless utterly important, namely to give one's own regional language priority over all other languages in everyday life.

第 9 章
ネット上のアイヌ・コミュニティにおける
アイヌ語学習

片山 和美（アイヌ語学習者）

第 1 節　アイヌの歴史と現在

(1) アイヌが住んでいた地域

　アイヌ語はアイヌ民族が近世まで使用していた言語である。アイヌ民族は、本州の東北北部、北海道島、クリル（千島）列島、サハリン（樺太）島の北緯50度線付近までの地域に居住してきた事が知られており、アイヌ語の使用圏もおおむねこれに合致すると見られている。より北方ではニヴフ語やツングース諸語に含まれるウイルタ語等が、東方ではイテリメン語等が、南方では日本語が話されており、各言語からの借用語彙が見られるが、どの言語とも系統関係は認められていない。

(2) アイヌ文化の成立

　アイヌ文化は12〜13世紀頃、成立したといわれているが、アイヌ民族は文字を持たなかったこともあり、アイヌ文化成立についての経緯などを十分に知ることは難しい。史料のうえで確認できるのは15世紀頃からで、狩猟・漁労・採集を生活の基盤として暮らしていた。また、和人（アイヌ以外の日本人）やサハリン、大陸の諸民族の人たちと交易も行っていた。

(3) 入植による強制移住と貧困

　1868年以降、政府の植民策が進み、北海道への移住者が増加してきた。

1886年の〈北海道土地払下規則〉や1897年の〈北海道国有未開地処分法〉によって和人に対する大規模な土地の配分が行われるなかで、アイヌは和人の入植地や市街部から離れた〈保護地〉と称する原野に強制的に移転させられた。

先住していたアイヌに対して農業の奨励や教育・医療などの施策も行われたが、施策が十分ではない為に、次第に生活に困窮するアイヌが増えてきた。

(4) 1899年　北海道旧土人保護法 制定

この法律は貧困にあえぐ「北海道旧土人」(アイヌ民族)に対する保護を名目として作られたもので、土地、医薬品、埋葬料、授業料の供与などが定められていた。この法律は「貧困にあえぐアイヌ民族の保護」を名目としていたが、実際にはアイヌの財産を収奪し、文化帝国主義的同化政策を推進するための法的根拠として活用された。

具体的には、

1. アイヌの土地の没収
2. 収入源である漁業・狩猟の禁止
3. アイヌ固有の習慣風習の禁止
4. 日本語使用の義務
5. 日本風氏名への改名による戸籍への編入、

等々が実行に移された。

入れ墨や耳輪などの風習ははっきり禁止令が出たという事実があるものの、アイヌ語については、通達・法令などで禁止されたという事実はない。しかし、義務教育では日本語の学習が強制されたのは事実である。もちろん、仕事や役場での手続きなど、公的な場ではアイヌ語を使うことはできない。そのため、和人が多数派になった社会で、アイヌは生きていくために日本語を覚えなければならなかった。

そして、和人による差別・迫害の中で、アイヌ自身がアイヌ語を家庭で使

うことを断念し、子供を日本語で育てていくことを選択していった。

　「お前たちはアイヌ語など覚えなくていい」「日本語ができないと和人に馬鹿にされるからアイヌ語は覚えなくていい」と親や周りの大人たちに言われながら育った人がたくさんいる。私の曾祖父母や祖母もアイヌ語を話すことができたが、孫や子供の前でアイヌ語を使うことはほとんどなかったと聞いている。

(5) 1997年　旧土人保護法廃止、アイヌ文化振興法が制定

　1997年に「アイヌ文化の振興並びにアイヌの伝統等に関する知識の普及及び啓発に関する法律」（通称「アイヌ文化振興法」）が施行された。この法律は、日本の先住民族、アイヌを固有の民族として初めて法的に位置づけた法律で、「アイヌの人々の民族としての誇りが尊重される社会の実現」を目的に、国と地方自治体の責任としてアイヌ語やアイヌ文化の継承者の育成、調査・研究、国民への啓発などの文化振興策を行うと定めている。アイヌ語の振興は音楽、舞踊、工芸と共に主要な施策の一つに位置づけられ、それまでは北海道内でしか開かれていなかったアイヌ語教室が、北海道外でも開かれるようになった。

(6) 現在のアイヌ語学習の状況

　個人レベルでアイヌ語学習を行っている人はたくさんいるが、まずはアイヌ文化振興法に基づいて、同法に規定された業務を行う日本で唯一の法人として、国土交通省、文部科学省から指定されているアイヌ文化振興・研究推進機構（正式名称：「公益財団法人　アイヌ文化振興・研究推進機構」[アイヌ文化財団]）が行っているアイヌ語の関する講座について紹介する。

　学べる場と頻度
　・アイヌ語上級講座　　　⇒月一回
　・アイヌ語初級講座　　　⇒月一回（北海道のみ）
　・親と子のアイヌ語講座　⇒月二回

・語り部育成事業　　　⇒月一回（北海道のみ）
・ラジオ講座　　　　　⇒週一回（道外はポッドキャストでダウンロード可能）
・その他・・・弁論大会（年一回）、指導者育成事業（二年に一回生徒募集）

第2節　私の取り組み

　私は北海道のむかわ町という小さな町で生まれ育った。小学校の高学年のころから自分がアイヌだということは分かっていたが、中学生の時にアイヌに対する差別を目の当たりにし、自分がアイヌであることを隠すようになった。

　2008年に北海道を離れ東京で働き始め、そこで知り合った同僚に自分がアイヌだということを話した。自分がアイヌであるということを話さないのは、自分を偽っているような気がしたからだが、その人から差別されることはなかった。アイヌであっても差別されない環境もあるのだと知ったことがきっかけで、自分のこと、先祖のことを知るためにアイヌについて勉強するようになった。

　2010年頃から本を読んでアイヌの歴史などを勉強したり、両親からアイヌのことを教えてもらっていたが、アイヌ向けに行っているアイヌ語講座があると知り、2012年4月からアイヌ語上級講座を受講し始めた。

　その数か月後に、ウタリ（仲間）からニコニコ動画という投稿動画配信サイトにあるアイヌ・コミュニティを紹介された。そこでは、北海道に在住し、自身もアイヌである先生がアイヌ語、アイヌの歴史、物語や、アイヌが置かれている現状、他民族の歴史についてなど様々な内容を配信していた。

　アイヌ・コミュニティに参加しネット放送を聞くことで、それまでは月一回だけだったアイヌについての勉強が、多い時には毎日受けられ、アイヌ語に触れる機会が増えた。また、サイトのタイムシフト機能で、一週間以内であれば自分の好きな時間に視聴することができるという点も、仕事をしなが

ら勉強をしている私たちにとってはすごく良かった。それぞれが仕事や家庭を持ちながらアイヌのことを勉強しているため、同じ時間にみんなで集まることが難しいことも多いが、東京で行っている勉強会にスカイプを使って北海道にいる先生に参加してもらうなど、自分たちの出来る範囲で勉強を続けている。

　インターネットを使い、離れた場所に住んでいるウタリと繋がることで、同じアイヌでも置かれている状況も様々だということや、そういったいろいろな人の視点に立ってこれからのアイヌのことを考えていかなければならないのだということが分かった。

　ニコニコ動画のミナミナコタンというコミュニティは、インターネットではよくある匿名でのメンバー登録は行わなかった。必ず氏名や出身地などを明らかにし、アイヌのみが参加し、安心して学べるコミュニティとして存在していた。

　インターネットを使った学習はニコニコ動画以外にもある。

- ・SKYPEを使用したアイヌ語学習・・・月一回の上級アイヌ語講座の後の勉強会で、北海道とのやり取りに使用。
- ・EMAILのやり取りにアイヌ語を使用する。
- ・LINEでアイヌ語学習グループを作成し、知っている単語だけでもいいからアイヌ語でやり取りをする。
- ・TWITTERでアイヌ語を発信する。

第3節　WiPCE2014

　2014/5/18〜2014/5/26までハワイで行われたWiPCE2014に参加してきた。WiPCEでは様々な民族と交流をし、それぞれの民族で行われている取り組みについて発表を聞いてきた。ある発表では、高校の退学率が高いため、学校と生徒が属するコミュニティの橋渡しをしたり、就職のためのワーク

ショップを行っているという話をしていた。また別の発表では、大人に対する言語教育の手法についての発表を行っていた。そういった話を聞くと、アイヌの取り組みがどれだけ遅れているのかを実感し、そこに追いつける日が来るのだろうかと、道のりの長さに気が遠くなる思いがした。それと同時に、やれることをコツコツと積み重ねていくしかないのだとも思った。

　WiPCEでは各民族が自分たちの歌や踊りを披露する時間もあった。ステージに立つ人たちが誇りをもってパフォーマンスする姿を見て、私たちも自信をもっていいんだと勇気をもらった。日本にいると、アイヌであることを知られたらどう思われるか？　と不安になることもあるが、WiPCEでは私が私として、アイヌがアイヌとしている。それだけで、自分や自分たちの文化を誇れる素晴らしい時間だった。

　帰国後、美容室に行きハワイでの話をしたところ、「ハワイは仕事で行ったんですか？」と聞かれた。仕事ではなく、北海道の先住民族アイヌとして参加したと答えたところ、「仕事でないのならそれは趣味ですか？」と言われた。まだハワイで過ごした素晴らしい時間の中から抜け出せていなかった私は、一気に現実に引き戻された気分だった。「趣味ですか？」と聞いてきた人には、もちろん悪気などなく、素直に思ったことを質問しただけである。日本にいればマイノリティーになることのない人たちは、日本人であるということを意識することはあっても、民族を意識することはほとんどないのだろう。私に「趣味ですか？」と聞いてきた人は、アイヌ民族の存在すら知らないようだった。

　この「趣味ですか？」という発言に、現在のアイヌ語学習やアイヌ語復興といった取り組みの問題点が表れていると思う。つまり、現在のアイヌ語学習は、休日を利用したアイヌ個人の取り組みによるものがほとんどで、アイヌ以外の人から見ればそれは趣味でしかないのだ。しかし、アイヌ語学習、アイヌ語復興は個人レベルの活動に留めることなく、アイヌ自身が研究者となり、復興に取り組んでいかなければならい。2013年に北海道により実施されたアイヌの生活実態調査によると、アイヌの大学進学率は、居住市町村43％に対して25.8％と依然として低く、教育面の格差解消が大きな課題と

なっている。教育格差を解消し、アイヌの研究者が増えていくことを望んでいる。

第4節　最後に

　私が小さい頃、親や親せきに怒られるときは必ず「ハイタ！」(日本語で「馬鹿」の意味)と言われていた。当時はその言葉の意味を知らずにいたが、アイヌ語を勉強するようになり、それがアイヌ語だったと知った。
　地元にいた頃はアイヌ語やアイヌ文化を避けてきたと思っていたが、知らないうちにアイヌ語に触れていたと知り、少し嬉しくなった。今後も勉強を続けていけば、昔何となく使っていた言葉が実はアイヌ語だった、と知ることがあるかもしれない。
　言葉を自分たちの手に取り戻すことは簡単なことではないが、アイヌ語を取り戻し、本当の意味で「a=kor itak（私たちの言葉）」と言えるよう、勉強を続けていきたい。

参考文献
大学共同利用機関法人 人間文化研究機構 国立国語研究所　「危機的な状況にある言語・方言の実態に関する調査研究事業報告書」。
北海道ホームページ　「参考資料2　旧土人保護法について」。
常本 照樹（2000）「アイヌ民族をめぐる法の変遷──旧土人保護法から「アイヌ文化振興法」へ」、自由学校「遊」ブックレット。

Abstract, Chap.9
Ainu on the Internet : Learning the Ainu Language in Community

Kazumi Katayama (Ainu Language Learner)

The Ainu people have lived and spoken Ainu from Tohoku in the north to Hokkaido, Sakhalin (Karafuto) and Chishima (the Kurile Islands). However, when 'wajin' settlers (Japanese other than Ainu) migrated to Hokkaido, Japanese became the compulsory language for work and other official purposes.

As a result of continued cultural and political discrimination, the Ainu themselves abandoned the use of the language. The language itself is distinctively different from Japanese both in its lexico-grammar and the fact that it has not had its own writing system. Ainu is transcribed in Romanized form or the katakana syllabary. As fluent mother tongue speakers of Ainu diminished, in the 1980s, a movement arose among Ainu themselves to stem the decline and to make efforts to maintain the Ainu language. With a particular focus on young learners Ainu language classes were established. As a result, Ainu language classes have spread throughout all parts of Hokkaido.

In 1997, a law was enacted in Japan called the 'Law for the Promotion of Ainu Culture and Dissemination and Advocacy of Knowledge about Ainu Traditions.' This set out a policy containing specific measure. The measures included in this ground-breaking document were designed to promote the Ainu language, Ainu music, dance and crafts. Further, this led to the establishment of Ainu language classes in locations outside Hokkaido. Recently, together with the spread of the internet, changes have occurred in language learning styles where Ainu language instructors and learners can assemble in a manner not hitherto seen. This paper describes the role of Internet Telephone Services such as SKYPE, and other visual-based learning sites that I have used, to facilitate Ainu language learning in a variety of new ways.

In 1868 and beyond, colonial policies were pursued by the mainland government of Japan. Immigrants to Hokkaido dramatically increased and in 1886 and 1897 state-owned land allocation reached high levels such that Ainu settlements were overtaken and the Ainu transferred to deserted 'wilderness' areas. The settlers or so-called 'pioneers' from various parts of Japan were assigned preferential treatment in terms of education, agriculture and medical care; even in areas where the indigenous Ainu were living. A spiral of poverty forced the Ainu people to move away from their traditional ways of life.

The notorious 1899 Hokkaido Former Aborigines Protection Act was designed to protect against the impoverishment of the Ainu people but whilst nominal assistance was given, the exploitation of Ainu land and livelihood continued. The new law itself provided the legal platform for a vigorous assimilation policy. Specifically, this involved:

1. confiscation of Ainu land
2. prohibition of fishing and hunting as a source of income
3. prohibition of traditional Ainu customs
4. Japanese language and cultural education in elementary school
5. transfer to family register by renaming into Japanese-style patronymics

Whilst unequivocal prohibitions occurred on such practices as tattoos and earrings there was no specific anti-Ainu language law or regulation. However, in work and public domains the Ainu language was not used — preferential linguistic usage given to Japanese. In order to survive, the Ainu spoke Japanese. The ethos grew that "It's better to speak Japanese. You don't need Ainu." The use of Ainu as a language of the home disappeared — there was little motivation for grandparents to speak Ainu in front of their children. My own great-grandfather and mother and my grandmother were able to speak the Ainu language.

Whereas native speakers of Ainu gradually disappeared by the 1980s, Ainu as a second language instruction started to appear. Classes for children were opened in Hokkaido and elsewhere. In addition, as mentioned above the 1997 "Ainu Culture Promotion Law" led to the promotion of music, dance and crafts together with Ainu-related activity outside Hokkaido itself.

In recent years, with the spread of the Internet, teachers and students committed to learning Ainu have gathered in classrooms to embrace new styles and modes of learning such as the use of the Internet phone service known as SKYPE: a telecommunications software product that employs video chat and voice calls from computers, tablets and other electronic devices (mobile phones also). I describe here the efforts to implement new forms of Ainu language learning.

The current status of Ainu language learning can be summarized as follow:

Learning Location and frequency
- Ainu senior course ⇒ once a month
- Ainu beginner course ⇒ once a month
- Ainu language classes of parent and child ⇒ twice a month
- Radio course ⇒ once a week
- Speech Contest (annually), leadership development business (student recruitment once in two years)

Listening to Internet broadcasting with participants in the Ainu community began slowly once a month and then it went to daily broadcast, increasing the opportunity to reach out to Ainu people. In addition, the time shift function of the site meant that learners could watch it at their own suitable time during the week. For this author, it was particularly helpful – to learn whilst working at home, for instance. It is difficult for a group of learners to gather in one place at a particular time whereas using the Skype sessions in Tokyo from a teacher in Hokkaido lent flexibility to study sessions and participation.

Ainu language learning via the Internet makes it possible to connect with Ainu living in a remote locations. This is a dramatic change from my own previous experience of Ainu. It put me in touch with other Ainu and varieties of views on language and the Ainu community.

As a participant in the World Indigenous Peoples Conference on Education 2014 (WiPC:E) that took place in Hawaii I was party to much exchange among ethnic groups. Highlighted in this gathering was the efforts being made in various ethnic groups to stem the high dropout rate at high school, to make bridges betweens school and community. There were presentations on methods of language education for adults and this brought me to the awareness of how earnestly and diligently must ethnic communities make efforts improving and promoting language education in their communities.

When I was small my parents and relatives would regularly admonish me with the word "Haita!" In Japanese, this means 'baka' (stupid, idiot). At that time I did not know the meaning of the word. However, on starting to learn/study Ainu I came to undertand what it meant. The place where I lived was, in my understanding, a vacuum in which Ainu language and culture was missing or deleted. However, on embarking on the road to learning Ainu 'somehow or other' the language began to percolate into my life. Now, having the opportunity to feel and know the Ainu language (*Ainu kotoba ni furete…to shiri*) I began to feel happy, delighted. If I can continue to learn Ainu, continue to study I may be able to reach an understanding that the language of the past, used in the past was, in fact, Ainu. Needless to say, it is not a simple matter to reclaim — into our own hands — the Ainu language. However, I wish to embrace the real meaning of the term 'a kor itak' (in English 'our language': in Japanese 'watakushitachi no kotoba') and to be able to say it.

Chapter 10
Modernist and ecologist approaches to language and identity — the case of the Ryukyu Islands

Patrick Heinrich (Ca' Foscari University, Venice)

> The freedom to have which characterized […] industrial society has been replaced by the freedom to be. […] In post-material society, there emerges a further type of right, the right to new existence, or rather, to a more meaningful existence. (Karen A. Cerulo 1997: 393)

1. Introduction

Language planning is "nationality planning" wrote Fishman (1973: 31) more than 40 years ago, clarifying thereby that language planning does not simply aim at solving perceived linguistic problems. Language policy seeks to change ideas about belongingness and identity. How people identify has political implications, and for this reason states have played an active role in creating a national identity. As a result, language planning has been one major arena in which processes of directing collective identities has been carried out. Along the lines of modernist ideology, this has usually implied imposing only one language for one nation. Where such policies met with 'success', language planning has thus crucially contributed to the endangerment of other languages.

Smaller languages or non-national languages have become endangered not because people cannot cope with several languages in their daily lives. Rather, these languages have been marginalized by assimilist language policies. These policies are informed by language nationalism, that is to say, the invention of a new imagined community for which one shared language, culture and history is invoked. This invention serves the purpose to create a bond of horizontal solidarity among its members which replaces the hierarchical social order of the feudal age. In order to realize the idea of 'fraternity' between nationals of a modern state, 'equality' tends to thereby become equated with 'homogeneity'. This is the point where the quest for equality following modernist ideology creates problems for linguistic and cultural minorities. The nation is, after all, nothing but a modernist invention. The linguistic diversity within states testifies to the ideological character of this idea. There are over 7,000 language among the 200 states — none of these states is actually monolingual, nor has it ever been. As a result, all those falling between the gap of the 'nation as the invention' and the 'people actually populating the state' risk exclusion from the 'bond of national solidarity' if they do not adapt to the way the nation is imagined. With regard to autochthonous minorities, this results in assimilist language policies (and with regard to migrant minorities to 'integrative' policies). Hence, from a minority perspective, modernist approaches to language policy constitute inequality, because their languages, cultures and identities are not considered, valued and supported, and they are in addition also pressured on ideological grounds to adapt to those of the majority. Treating people who differ 'equally' in the modernist sense amounts to nothing more but imposing 'homogeneity' on those who differ from the majority. In other words, it results in inequality. Different people call for differentiated treatment, and only this results in 'equality' among majority and minorities. This, in a nutshell, is the ecological position.

Adapting linguistic minorities to national identities based on a national language has been perceived to constitute 'progress' along modernist ideology. According to late modern attitudes, however, efforts are made to adapt national identities to the multilingual situation actually present in the state. Hence support for cultural freedom — and not assimilation — is seen to constitute progress. Escaping inequality by giving up heritage languages, cultures and identities was the modernist solution for the creation of national identities. Differentiated treatment allowing the maintenance of differences vis-à-vis language, culture and identity is the ecologist solution.

This chapter discusses these incommensurable two approaches on the case of the Ryukyu Islands. Towards the end of understanding how modernist and ecologist approaches to language and identity affect endangered languages, we will first discuss how language and identity is regimented along the lines of modernist ideology before moving to a discussion of how this ideology is currently being contested by ecological approaches. In order to prepare the ground for these discussion we will first turn to a brief account of language and identity under conditions of modernity.

2. Language and Identity in Modernity

Modernity is often conceived of as a period of time. It might however be much more beneficial to regard it as an attitude which gained prominence in specific regions at a specific point of time. If we do so, then 'modernity as an attitude' manifests in a prioritization of universality, homogeneity, monotony and clarity in a world perceived to be in disorder. 'Disorder' is again the result of a specific idea of what is seen to constitute 'order'. Modernists equate order with universality, homogeneity, monotony and clarity, and hence perceive pluralism, variety, contingency and ambivalence as disorder (Bauman 1992). The latter characteristics are however valued by those we call the ecologists in this chapter. The basis for dissension between modernists and ecologists is thus one of differing views of order and disorder. Accordingly, modernists feel a compulsion of ordering, while ecologists seek to understand and maintain the functionality underlying diversity.

Figure 1: Contested views on order and disorder and their implications

	Modernists	**Ecologists**
Order	homogeneity and clarity	pluralism and ambivalence
Disorder	pluralism and ambivalence	homogeneity and clarity
Actions	imposing order	maintaining functions
Epistemological position	center of power	margins and niches
Language attitudes	assimilate and integrate	maintain diversity
Identity	shared monolingualism	shared values

As can be recognized from Figure 1, the positions of the modernists and ecologists are incommensurable. Both constitute full-fledged ideologies, or worldviews if you want. That is to say, you cannot be in favor of e.g. 'homogeneity and clarity' and 'pluralism and ambivalence' at the same time. Nor can 'diversity' be maintained if 'homogeneity and clarity' are treasured. (We will return to this point below). The view on what constitutes order and what constitutes disorder has therefore far-reaching implications on concrete actions concerning language and identity. This underlines the fact that efforts of maintaining endangered languages must start with refuting modernist attitudes and with embracing ecological attitudes. They must start with what Fishman (2001: 17) famously termed "ideological clarification", that is to say, start with a refutation of those attitudes which have led to language endangerment in the first place.

The list of possible questions to address when studying identity is long and includes issues such as 'how does identity emerge from the countless singular events in one's life?' 'How does a community emerge from the shared events it experiences?' 'How often or how long must one take part in such events in order to share a sense of belongingness with other members of a shared community?' Answering any of these questions is not possible here. However, an awareness that identities are shaped and changed in rather long periods of time, which involve countless events of various lengths — from single speech acts to the completion of school education — allows us to somewhat structure the field of language and identity. It is clear that not the many diverse, specific and individual events can be at the center of attention here, for they cannot — "it takes a village to study a village" (Lemke 2000: 286). Also, the most slowly changing factors affecting identity are quickly dealt with. Geographically, the Ryukyu Islands are at the periphery of the Japanese Archipelago and this implies vast differences in terms of language, history and culture between the Japanese mainland and the Ryukyus (see Katsukata & Maetakenishi 2010). It was only the new institutional organization which accompanied the transition from an agrarian, feudal society to an industrialized, modern society which rendered these differences 'a problem'. Responsible for such perception of linguistic and cultural diversity was a new geographical frame according to which territories were no longer confined by 'frontiers' but by

Figure 2: The frontier model of the Japanese Archipelago

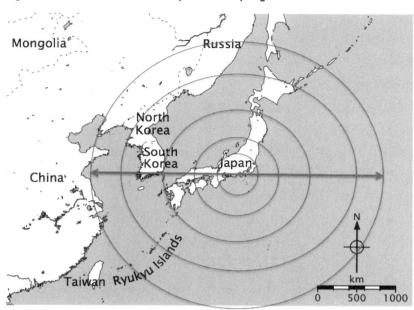

'borders' (Giddens 1990: 14). Frontiers imply that the further one moves away from the center of power, the more diverse the encounters become. Borders, on the other hand, project diversity to the outside in order to invent homogeneity within. This has consequences for those 'outside' upon whom some kind of diversity is first imagined and then projected upon (Said 1978), but also for all those 'inside', because they are imagined to be homogenous even if they, in fact, differ.

In the feudal age, the Ryukyus constituted the center of Ryukyuan culture. The relations between the center of the Japanese Shogunate and the Ryukyuan Kingdom were nevertheless characterized by inequality, with the kingdom being a vassal state and being exploited by the shogunate (Kerr 2000[1958]: 183–419), but this did not affect linguistic diversity. Moving away from the center of power in Edo, the seat of shogunate authority, implied encountering increasing diversity. This was never perceived as 'a problem'. Diversity was seen to be 'horizontal' so

Figure 3: The border model of the Japanese Archipelago

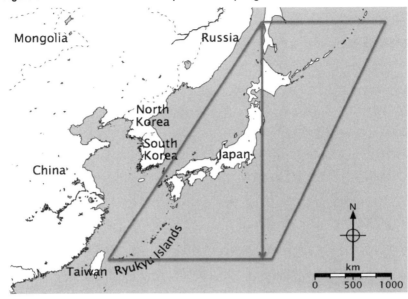

to speak. That language differed according to region and that this difference grew larger with distance was seen to be normal. Hence, it did not call for any kind of intervention. Language diversity was not conceived of as a problem due to (1) a lack of borders, within which (2) homogeneity was projected — a homogeneity confused with (3) constituting equality, and hence (4) made the objective of language planning. The latter is, in a nutshell, the modernist approach. It crucially requires borders in order to function.

It was only after the onset of modernity that the Ryukyu Archipelago became a 'border region' of the Japanese state. Since all Japanese were, at least ideologically, conceived to being equal, and equality was associated with linguistic and cultural homogeneity, diversity, for the first time, constituted 'a problem'. Language planning was meant to 'solve' this problem along modernist lines of thought. Hence, in order to declare linguistic homogeneity where there was none, Ryukyuan languages were declared to be 'greater dialects' (*dai-hōgen*) of Japanese, and since they were the most diverging 'Japanese dialects', efforts were made to replace them by the language of the center, i.e. Tokyo Japanese (Heinrich 2015a). It was no longer sufficient to speak — as one had done in the past — one now had to speak 'a language' and that meant Standard Japanese. Hence, the way of speaking at home was no longer seen of being simply 'regional', now it was perceived to be 'incorrect' and 'inferior' (Yasuda 1999). Language diversity was no longer perceived to be 'horizontal' so to speak — it was seen to be 'vertical'. The greater the diversity from the situation at the center, the worse. On a more theoretical or abstract level, everything contradicting the new ideology of sameness and homogeneity became seen as disorder, and thus calls for intervention in the form of assimilation.

3. Language and identity in the Ryukyus: The modernist position

Identity is the result of a process of identification, that is to say, a process of recognizing aspects of sameness – of seeing each other as being identical. Identification as 'Japanese' did not exist at the onset of modernity in the Ryukyus, nor did an identification as 'Japanese' exist beyond the small elite of Japanese enlighteners then (Gluck 1985). Semiotically speaking, 'Japanese' was a *signifiant* without *signifié*. The concept of the nation was unknown, and so was the idea of Japanese as a national language (Lee 2010). Hence, Japanese enlightenment scholar Fukuzawa Yukichi (1835–1901) famously remarked that "though there is a government in Japan, there is no nation" (quoted from Craig 1968: 118–119).

Language and identity before 1945

Despite the initial absence of a popular identification as 'Japanese' being absent within the entire Meiji state, the case of the Ryukyus differs in that Japanese was not even spoken there before the Meiji Restoration of 1868. Japanese writing had been introduced in the Ryukyus in 1265, and few selected people of the warrior class studied Japanese there in order that the Ryukyu Kingdom could correspond with the shogunate on the mainland (Heinrich 2015b: 593–594). However, Japanese only started being popularly spread through the education system as a foreign language from 1880 onwards. Unsurprisingly, therefore, Japanese language education in the Ryukyus required different textbooks, curricula and teaching methods (Kondo 2014, Yoshimura 2014). Japanese was not seen as a language of identity by the local population then. They termed it *yamatuguchi*, the language of mainland Japan, or *naichigo*, the language of the Japanese inland.

The aim of spreading Japanese in the Ryukyus went much beyond the necessity of closing the communication gap between Japanese mainlanders and Ryukyuans. Japanese was also spread in order to adapt Ryukyuans to mainland Japanese culture and customs, that is, as a means to furnish them with a Japanese identity (Shinzato 2001: 241). Towards this end, a unitary genealogy between mainland and Ryukyuan language and culture was projected into an archaic and imagined past by scholars of Japanese folk studies (*minzokugaku*) or Okinawan studies (*Okinawagaku*) (see e.g. Taniguchi [1970]2008). The construction of a shared origin and history aside, Japanese language spread was another central pillar of Japanese 'national citizen education' (*kokumin kyōiku*) and 'imperial subject education' (*kōminka kyōiku*), which totally ignored aspects of Ryukyuan history, language and culture (Kondō 1995). Assimilation efforts have been characterized as "hysteric" (ODJKJ 1983: 320), and the noted local newspaper columnist Ōta Chōfu (1865–1938) is remembered until today for commenting on these hysterical efforts by saying that is seemed that the people of Okinawa Prefecture were also expected to learn how to sneeze in Japanese (Oguma 1998: 284).

In order to ensure the success of the Japanization campaign, Japanese language spread was accompanied from the very start with efforts of an 'eradication' (*bokumetsu*) of Ryukyuan languages and cultures. The focus on suppressing Ryukyuan languages, rather than emphasizing an improved use of Japanese, is due to the fact that Ryukyuan teachers struggled themselves with the Japanese language (Maeda 2012, 2013). As one of the earliest suppressive measures, the Ryukyuan languages were banned from schools in the so-called 'Ordinance to Regulate the Dialect' (*Hōgen torishimari-rei*) in 1907 (ODJKJ 1983: 443–444). Shortly afterwards, the system of using the infamous 'dialect tag' (*hōgen fuda*) was implemented and spread among an ever-growing number of schools. According to this system, students speaking Ryukyuan languages were humiliated by having to wear a tag around the neck, and those having to wear the tag were responsible for passing it on to the next 'offender' (see Kondō 2005). Assimilist fervor also led to a Japanization of Ryukyuan personal names and toponyms (Bellevaire 2001). Despite such Japanization policy and the many efforts implemented in its support, Japanese remained a foreign language in the awareness of Ryukyuans until the 1950s (Higa 1963: 4), and a large number of Ryukyuans did not easily identify themselves as Japanese. Other than a lingering unfamiliarity with the Japanese language (Anderson 2015), the de-facto colonial status of Okinawa Prefecture and the Amami Islands in Kagoshima (Christy 1993) and the continued discrimination against Ryukyuans from mainland Japanese (see e.g. Rabson 2012, Maeda 2014) played a key role in having Ryukyuans maintain a distinct identity opposed to that of 'mainland Japanese' (*yamatunchu*, or derogatively also termed *naicha*). As an effect thereof, Ryukyuan languages remained the default language choice for private domains across the Ryukyus (Heinrich 2015a).

Language and identity after 1945

After 1945, issues of language and identity in the Ryukyus took a dramatic and unexpected turn. The occupying US forces stressed the differences between mainland Japan and the Ryukyus and drew attention to the discrimination that Ryukyuans had suffered at the hands of mainland Japanese (see e.g. OCNO 1944). The aim by the US in promoting a 'Ryukyuan policy' was, however, very much in its own strategic interests in the region. Deprived of a choice for Ryukyuan autonomy, Ryukyuans had to chose either between continued occupation by the US or a return to the Japanese state (Taira 1997).

It is of utmost importance to be conversant with Ryukyuan history in order to understand the radical shift away from Ryukyuan languages to Japanese in the postwar years. The Battle of Okinawa, in which almost one quarter of Okinawa's population was killed, had devastating effects on daily life. Many Okinawans had to live in camps build by the US military for years, suffered from malaria, and, once these camps were dissolved, they found that more than 20 percent of their land had been confiscated in order to build US military infrastructure there. Okinawa had turned into the 'Pacific Cornerstone' of the US, serving as its main military hub during the Korean War (1950–1953) and the Vietnam War (1955–1975). From 1945 to 1972, Okinawa was de facto governed by the US military, first under the United States Military Government of the Ryukyus (until 1950) and then under the United States Civil Administration of the Ryukyu Islands. Control of the US military over the Archipelago was confirmed by the Treaty of San Francisco, signed in 1951 between Japan and the Allied Powers. Article 3 of the treaty stated that (United Nations Treaties Services 1999–2005):

> "Japan will concur in any proposal of the United States to the United Nations to place under its trusteeship system, with the United States as the sole administering authority, Nansei Shoto [Ryukyu Islands, P.H.] south of 29 degrees north latitude [···]. [T]he United States will have the right to exercise all and any powers of administration, legislation and jurisdiction over the territory and inhabitants of these islands, including their territorial waters."

As a reaction to this situation, a strong irredentist movement emerged in Okinawa, and in mainland Japan, calling for an end of 'alien rule' (*i-minzoku shihai*) over the territory after the Treaty of San Francisco. A popular Reversion Movement (*fukki undō*) emerged, which also marked the end of the idea of Ryukyuan independence (Higa 2004).

In a situation where all infrastructure was destroyed, and where children studied in 'open sky classrooms' (*aozora kyōshitsu*), as school buildings had been destroyed, and where children learned to write with their fingers in the sand, language policy was not high on the agenda. This not withstanding, considerations were made to ban the Japanese language and to shift back to Ryukyuan languages in all domains in the immediate postwar years (Nakamatsu 1996: 62–63). Douglas McArthur, the Supreme Commander of Allied Forces, personally supported this initiative, as it would further distance Ryukyuans from the mainland Japanese, facilitating thereby US control over the Ryukyu Islands (Motonaga 1994: 184).

Just like the initial plan to spread English across the Ryukyus (Ishihara 2004), however, the US soon lost all interest in language planning activities in this region. This left all initiatives to Ryukyuans. 1946 saw the establishment of a Textbook Compilation Division within the Department of Culture and Education. There, the idea of developing textbooks in Ryukyuan languages was discussed. No minutes were made of these meetings, but it is known that this idea was quickly refuted. Ogawa (2015: 578) states that "in all likelihood, deciding which variety of Ryukyuan was to serve as the basis for a written language must have been seen to constitute the biggest problem preventing the compilation of Ryukyuan textbooks." As an effect, school education in the occupied Ryukyu Islands followed from 1950 onwards the model of mainland Japan, and from 1951 onwards mainland Japanese textbooks were imported and used (Heinrich 2012: 103). The chance to restore use of Ryukyuan languages in higher domains had been missed.

Studying Japanese in school and using Japanese textbooks is one thing, abandoning the Ryukyuan languages in the families and neighborhoods quite another. From the 1950s onwards, the Ryukyuan languages stopped being passed on to younger generations, because under US occupation Japanese became the tool for social advancement. More concretely, Japanese was employed in order to rid Okinawa of 'alien rule' and, so it was popularly imagined, to pave the way towards a better future. Ryukyuans insistence on being Japanese, in the face of US claims that they were not, was underlined by claims that Japanese was indeed 'their language'. In other words, in order to stress their Japaneseness, they shifted to Japanese in the families. As an effect thereof, no generation was raised speaking Ryukyuan languages after the 1950s. They were raised in Japanese as an effort to instill them with a Japanese identity. In the occupied Ryukyus, the Japanese language and other symbols of Japaneseness such as the national flag (*hinomaru*) and the national anthem (*kimi ga yo*) enjoyed a popularity unmatched in post-war mainland Japan at that time (Oguma 1998: 564). The efforts by Ryukyuans to self-assimilate into the Japanese nation grew more intense the longer the occupation lasted and the more discrimination they suffered from the US military.

The occupation years made it abundantly clear to Ryukyuans that, at that time, there was no room for hybrid identities. If Ryukyuans wanted to become Japanese, they had to become just like mainland Japanese, that is, abandon all markers of Ryukyuan identity. The fight for reversion to Japan included, crucially, sharing the same history, culture and language as the mainland. Hence, everything Ryukyuan was seen to stand in the way. It was pushed aside, if not actively disposed of. The modernist dream of ordering the world started to realize its objective of bringing homogeneity and clarity to the population within the confines of state territory.

4. Language and identity in the Ryukyus: The ecological position

The movement for return to the fatherland had been a movement, which sought to improve the economic wellbeing of Ryukyuans by freeing themselves from US occupation. The current language and culture revitalization movements in the Ryukyus are different in that they mainly promote a more meaningful life. These efforts, therefore, seek to transform conceptions about Ryukyuan people, their local languages and identities. It's not about money, but who they want to be.

Efforts at cultural revitalization preceded language revitalization. The former started around the time of the Tokyo Olympics in 1964, while attention placed on language grew only more organized from the Heisei Period (1989~) onwards. An 'Okinawa boom' in mainland Japan in the 1990s also brought more appreciation for Ryukyuan language and culture from the outside, and this crucially fanned these revitalization efforts (Hara & Heinrich 2015). Still, due to the complexities of revitalizing Ryukyuan languages, new speakers of Ryukyuan languages have not yet been raised.

Language activists are struggling with a number of problems. One is that no Ryukyuan language is standardized, modernized or has ever served as a popular medium of written communication. While there exists an awareness about the existence of local languages in the minds of Ryukyuan language speakers, who distinguish between *yamatuguchi* (Japanese) and *shimakutuba* or (Ryukyuan) *hōgen* (dialects), there exists no pan-Ryukyuan language and identity. Rather, identity is located on the immediate community and language variety. In particular, the Amami Islands in Kagoshima Prefecture and Okinawa Prefecture do not easily align (Maeda 2014). Furthermore, dialect leveling is rampant, as an effect of language shift and the emergence of larger communities caused by higher mobility, enhanced infrastructure, a changing economy and the spread of mass-media. Furthermore, Okinawan substrate Japanese (*uchinaa yamatoguchi*), a new dialect of Japanese which emerged with the spread of Japanese in 1880, serves those born after 1970 as a new symbol of Ryukyuan identity, or as a new 'we-code' (Sugita 2014).

In view of the current sociolinguistic situation, language revitalization requires adding new functions and new registers to the Ryukyuan languages in a number of contexts. In a word, Ryukyuan language ecology needs to be restored. For ecologists, abandoning a language implies abandoning the benefits this language brings about. There are fields in which the benefits of Ryukyuan languages never ceased to be valued, i.e. literature, poetry, music and local religion. Hence, these are domains where the languages are mainly maintained today. Okinawan poet Baku Yamanoguchi (1903–1963), for example, described how he and his friends decided from early on that Okinawan poetry would not be possible without the use of Okinawan language, or elements of Okinawan (see Clarke 2015: 636).

On a more theoretical plane, restoring an endangered language requires the co-existence of three elements (Hara & Heinrich 2015: 661): "(1) efforts towards language revitalization, (2) an active desire for emancipation from the majority, and (3) envisioning of an improved society." In particular the last two points, underline the centrality of identity in language revitalization activities. It is from the last two elements that new functions for the endangered language need to be developed. Clarke (2015: 646) has a point in writing that "the revitalization of Ryukyuan will succeed only if it reflects an attractive, vibrant and relevant cultural identity." The Ryukyuan languages can only survive if the Ryukyuan society has any real benefit in using Ryukyuan, but such benefits first need to be restored. Language revitalization is therefore not simply about language, but rather much more concerned with "'envisioning a new society' liberated from the ills associated with socio-cultural and political domination" (Hara & Heinrich 2015: 650). Note in this context, that modernists are not aware of the fact that modernity can also be oppressive. They view modernity solely from the center of power, and in so doing fail to identify 'dark sides of modernity' such as language endangerment.

Language ecologists in the Ryukyus, and everywhere else, understand that the revitalization of endangered languages requires a need for cultural renewal, and that this also includes a critical reconsideration of the assimilist ideologies, practices and institutions. Folklorization, that is to say, the narrowing of an endangered language to those functions the majority sees as harmless in their quest to dominate minorities, is insufficient for the maintenance of any language. Functions serving their speakers in real daily life must be added. Speaking the endangered language must contribute to the wellbeing of their speakers. We can witness such discussions in the present-day Ryukyus. For example, at its 6th annual meeting in March 2014, the Ryukyuan Heritage Language Society identified 12 important functions where the Ryukyuan languages contribute to Ryukyuan well-being (Heinrich, field notes).

(1) Transmit and promote a deeper reflection of the Ryukyus in Ryukyuan;
(2) Restore Ryukyuan self-esteem and confidence;
(3) Promote in education Ryukyuan perspectives on language, history and culture;
(4) Restore cohesion between older and younger generations;
(5) Familiarize the younger generations with Ryukyuan heritage culture;
(6) Maintain, strengthen and apply Ryukyuan cultural heritage;
(7) Contemporize Ryukyuan languages and make them relevant for the future;
(8) Regain control over Ryukyuan self-image and education;
(9) Maintain choices for choices for language, identity and culture;
(10) Stop conformism in Ryukyuan identities and behaviors to models from the Japanese mainland;
(11) Contribute to communal happiness and wellbeing;
(12) Recognize Japan's cultural diversity and promote intercultural tolerance.

These are important societal functions where Ryukyuan languages have an edge over Japanese. International scholars are in agreement with the efforts of the Ryukyuan Heritage Language Society. In October 2014, on the occasion of an international symposium by the Foundation for Endangered Languages (FEL) in Okinawa, a revised and shortened list was submitted as 'FEL XVIII Declaration' in the name of all participants to Okinawa Prefecture, Kagoshima Prefecture and the Agency for Cultural Affairs (*Bunkachō*). The declaration reads as follows:

Whereas:
1. UNESCO recognizes six Ryukyuan languages spoken in Okinawa Prefecture and Kagoshima Prefecture
2. UNESCO promotes the teaching of indigenous languages in school in order to maintain the many benefits of social bilingualism
3. At present the Ryukyuan languages enjoy no official status and still await their introduction to school
4. All Ryukyuan languages are set to become extinct by 2050 if no counteraction is taken.

It was the resolution of the Foundation for Endangered Languages convened in Okinawa for their XVIII conference from 17–20 September 2014, to recommend, in conscious agreement with members of the Ryukyuan Heritage Language Society:

A. the appointment of Ryukyuan languages as second official languages and
B. their introduction into the school system in Okinawa Prefecture and Kagoshima Prefecture in the belief that they would richly benefit the local communities. Specifically, they believe that these policies would:
(1) transmit and promote a deeper and more adequate reflection on Ryukyuan language, history and culture in education
(2) contribute to communal welfare and self-esteem
(3) strengthen control over Ryukyuan self-image and education
(4) maintain choices for language, knowledge, identity, culture for future generations
(5) recognize Japan's historical and present cultural diversity and promote intercultural tolerance.

Bath, 7 October 2014
Nicholas D.M. Ostler
(Chairman, Foundation for Endangered Languages)

The ecologist perspective on language manifests also in the opinions and attitudes of language revitalists across the Ryukyus. Consider some examples. Iriomote Takao (2007, interview) from the Ishigaki Islands in the south of the Ryukyus, stated regrets about language choices once made and wished that the Ryukyuan language would not have been abandoned in the past.

Question: Did you perceive it to be unsatisfactory to not speak your local language when you went to school in Kuroshima?
Iriomote: Not at all! [laughs]
Question: How is that today?
Iriomote: Today? Today, I think it would be better if I could speak it well. I'd like to be able to speak the language from where I was born. You know in the case of Kuroshima, there was not a single teacher from Kuroshima itself, so the teachers could not speak *hōgen* (Ryukyuan dialect). What is more, in that period, when you spoke *hōgen*, then your grades went down.

Photographer Higa Toyomitsu, who has interviewed hundreds of survivors of the Battle of Okinawa in Okinawan, states that interviewing them in Japanese was never an option for him (Higa 2005, interview):

Higa: Well translation is one thing, but a translation never captures everything. I always regard the facial expression of my interviewees as part of their language. You cannot translate that. Their Okinawan identity is mirrored therein. This is lost if you write it down or if you translate it.
Question: I see, there exists no such thing as a translation then?
Higa: Yes, when changing language, it becomes something different. A facial expression is more than a means of communication. It reflects their identity and their soul. All of that is *shimakutuba* [community language, P.H.].

As a last example, consider the opinion of Chie Inamine, an Okinawan language teacher at the University of the Ryukyus, who gave the following account why Okinawan matters in her view (Inamine 2006, interview):

"One has to think of the Okinawan language in its interrelation with Okinawan culture. […] Okinawans breathe the air of Okinawa, they drink the water of Okinawa, they step on the soil of Okinawa and all of this exists only in Okinawa and so there are things that Okinawans communicate to fellow Okinawans."

The picture which emerges here is thus one where Ryukyuan languages play important roles in the lives of these people, and where diversity is not seen as 'disorder' or 'a problem' to be 'solved' but as an asset and a resource for getting things done. These ideas are spreading in the Ryukyus today, and they are becoming increasingly powerful as well. In other words, the process of ideological clarification, which is necessary for language revitalization, is currently unfolding in the Ryukyu Islands.

5. Outlook

It is not possible to save endangered languages on the basis of modernist attitudes — a shift to ecological positions is inevitable for maintaining diversity. Stressing homogeneity where there is none has two major shortcomings. It plays a role in alienating indigenous minorities from their language and culture by ignoring it, and it presents Japan as being non-diverse to migrants, enlarging the barrier towards their inclusion as new members of Japanese society. And this is why the issue of Ryukyuan language endangerment is about much more than the Ryukyuan languages and their spakers. It is a problem of building sociocultural environments where diverse people can co-exist while being truly and genuinely equal. Restoring the language ecology in a way that the Ryukyuan languages can survive is an important step to contributing to the well-being of the diverse people living in the place called Japan. It is important to adjust Japanese policies to the postmodern realities of Japan. Doing so contributes to the interests of everyone living in Japan. These policies can build upon the ecological attitudes existing and spreading across the Ryukyu Islands of Japan.

Interviews

Higa, Toyomitsu, 2005-10-05, Nishihara-Town, Okinawa.
Inamine, Chie, 2006-07-19, Nishihara Town, Okinawa.
Iriomote, Takao, 2007-07-21, Ishigaki City. Okinawa

References

Anderson, Mark (2015) "Substrate-influenced Japanese and Code-Switching" in: Patrick Heinrich, Shinsho Miyara & Michinori Shimoji (eds): *Handbook of the Ryukyuan Languages*. Berlin/Boston: Mouton de Gruyter: 481–509.

Bauman, Zygmunt (1992) *Intimations of Postmodernity*. London: Routledge.

Bellevaire, Patrick (2001) "Les noms d'Okinawa. Une japonité singulière" in *Mots: Les langages du politique* 66: 71–89.

Cerulo, Karen A. (1997) "Identity Construction. New Issues, New Directions" in: *Annual Review of Sociology* 23: 385–409.

Christy, Alan S. (1993) "The Making of Imperial Subjects in Okinawa" in: *Positions* 1.3: 607–639.

Clarke, Hugh (2015) "Language and Identity in Okinawa and Amami: Past, Present and Future" in: Patrick Heinrich, Shinsho Miyara & Michinori Shimoji (eds): *Handbook of the Ryukyuan Languages*. Berlin/Boston: Mouton de Gruyter: 631–647.

Craig, Albert M. (1968) "Fukuzawa Yukichi. The Phiosophical Foundation of Meiji Nationalism" in: Robert Ward (ed.): *Political Development in Modern Japan*. Princeton: Princeton University Press: 99–148.

Fishman, Joshua A. (1973) "Language Modernization and Planning in Comparison with other Types of National Modernization" in: *Language in Society* 2: 23–43.

Fishman, Joshua A. (2001) *Reversing Language Shift*. Clevedon: Multilingual Matters.

Giddens, Anthony (1990) *The Consequences of Modernity*. Stanford: Stanford University Press.

Gluck, Carol (1985) *Japan's Modern Myths*. Princeton: Princeton University Press.

Hara, Kiyoshi & Patrick Heinrich (2015) "Linguistic and Cultural Revitalization" in: Patrick Heinrich, Shinsho Miyara & Michinori Shimoji (eds): *Handbook of the Ryukyuan Languages*. Berlin/Boston: Mouton de Gruyter: 649–665.

Heinrich, Patrick (2015a) "Language Shift" in: Patrick Heinrich, Shinsho Miyara & Michinori Shimoji (eds): *Handbook of the Ryukyuan Languages*. Berlin/Boston: Mouton de

Gruyter: 613–630.

Heinrich, Patrick (2015b) "Japanese Language Spread" in: Patrick Heinrich, Shinsho Miyara & Michinori Shimoji (eds): *Handbook of the Ryukyuan Languages*. Berlin/Boston: Mouton de Gruyter: 593–611.

Heinrich, Patrick (2012) *The Making of Monolingual Japan. Language Ideology and Japanese Modernity*. Bristol: Multilingual Matters.

Higa, Kōbun (2004) *Okinawa dokuritsu no keifu – Ryūkyū-koku o yumemita rokunin* [Genealogy of Okinawan Independence. Six Persons who dreamt about the Ryukyu State]. Naha: Ryūkyū Shinpō-sha.

Higa, Shunchō (1963) "Okinawa no kotoba wa doko e iku" [Where is Okinawan heading to?] *Gengo seikatsu* [Language Life] 142: 2–12.

Ishihara, Masahide (2004) "SCAR's Language Policy and English Language Education in Okinawa" in: *Okinawan Journal of American Studies* 1: 19–27.

Katsukata, Keiko & Mazuma Maetakenishi (eds.) (2010) *Okinawa nyūmon – kūfuku no sahō* [Introduction to Okinawan Studies – Manners of Hungriness]. Tokyo: Shōwadō.

Kerr, George H. ([1958]2000) *Okinawa. The History of an Island People*. Rutland. Tuttle Publishing.

Kondō, Kenichirō (1995) "Kokutei kyōkasho no Okinawazō" [Portraits of Okinawa in Imperial Textbooks] in: *Hokkaidō daigaku kyōiku gakubu kiyō* [Bulletin of the Educational Department at Hokkaidō University] 68: 161–175.

Kondō, Kenichirō (2006) *Kindai Okinawa ni okeru kyōiku to kokumin tōgō* [Educational and National Mobilization in Modern Japan]. Sapporo: Hokkaido University Press.

Kondo, Kenichiro (2014) "Japanese Language Education in Modern Okinawa until 1945" in: Mark Anderson & Patrick Heinrich (eds): *Language Crisis in the Ryukyus*. Newcastle upon Tyne: Cambridge Scholars Publishing: 54–81.

Lee, Yeonsuk (2000) *The Ideology of Kokugo. Nationalizing Language in Modern Japan* (translated by Maki Hirano Hubbard). Honolulu: University of Hawai'i Press.

Lemke, Jay L. (2000) "Across the Scales of Time. Artifacts, Activities, and Meanings in Ecosocial Systems" in: *Mind, Culture, and Activity* 7.4: 273–290.

Maeda, Tatsurō (2012) "Hanshi kotoba o tettei ni kansuru ken" [On thoroughly Teaching Spoken Language] in: *Nihongo nihongaku kenkyū* [Journal for Japanese Studies] 2: 131–140.

Maeda, Tatsurō (2013) "Kagoshima-ken no kokugo kyōiku ni okeru hyōjungo / hōgen ideorogii" [National Languages / Dialect Ideology in National Language Education in Kagoshima Prefecture] in: *Nihongo nihongaku kenkyū* [Journal of Japanese Studies] 3: 24–43.

Maeda, Tatsurō (2014) "Amamian Language Life: Experiences of Migration and 'Dialect Correction'" in: Mark Anderson & Patrick Heinrich (eds.) *Language Crisis in the Ryukyus*. Newcastle upon Tyne: Cambridge Scholars Publishing: 236–254.

Motonaga, Moriyasu (1994) *Ryūkyū-ken seikatsugo no kenkyū* [Studies on Everyday Language in the Ryukyus]. Tōkyō: Shunjūsha.

Nakamatsu, Takeo (1996) *Ryūkyū gogaku* [Ryukyuan Language Studies]. Naha: Okinawa Gengo Bunka Kenkyūjo.

OCNO = Office of the Chief Naval Operations (1944) *Ryukyu (Loochoo) Islands*. Washington D.C.: Office of the Chief Naval Operations.

ODJKJ = Okinawa dai-hyakka jiten kankō jimukyoku (ed.) (1983) *Okinawa dai-hyakka jiten* [Encyclopaedia of Okinawa]. Naha: Okinawa Times.

Ogawa, Shinji (2015) "Orthography Development" Patrick Heinrich, Shinsho Miyara & Michinori Shimoji (eds): *Handbook of the Ryukyuan Languages*. Berlin/Boston: Mouton de Gruyter: 576–589.

Oguma, Eiji (1998) *'Nihonjin' no kyōkai* [The Boundaries of 'the Japanese']. Tōkyō: Shinyōsha.

Rabson, Steve (2012) *The Okinawan Diaspora in Japan*. Honolulu: University of Hawai'i Press.

Said, Edward (1978) *Orientalism*. London: Rutledge and Kegan Paul.

Shinzato, Keiji (2001) "Okinawa ni okeru hyōjungo seisaku no kōzai" [Merits and Demerits of Standard Language Planning in Okinawa] in: Fumio Inoue et al. (eds): *Ryūkyū hōgen-kō* [Considerations of Ryukyuan Dialects] (vol. III). Tōkyō: Yumani Shobō: 238–244.

Sugita, Yuko (2014) "The Discovery of Okinawa-substrate Japanese as a 'We-code':" in: Mark Anderson & Patrick Heinrich (eds): *Language Crisis in the Ryukyus*. Newcastle upon Tyne: Cambridge Scholars Publishing: 169–205.

Taira, Koji (1997) "Troubled National Identity. The Ryukyuans/Okinawas" in: Michael Weiner (ed.): *Japan's Minorities. The Illusion of Homogeneity*. London: Routledge: 140–177.

Taniguchi, Kenichi (2008[1970]) *Waga Okinawa* [Our Okinawa] (2 vol.). Tōkyō: Nihon Tosho Sentā.

United Nations Treaties Services (1999–2005) Treaty of Peace with Japan. Online available at: http://www.taiwandocuments.org/sanfrancisco01.htm (accessed 23/06/2015).

Yasuda, Toshiaki (1999) *'Kokugo' to 'hōgen' no aida* [Between 'National Language' and 'Dialect']. Tōkyō: Jibun Shoin.

Yoshimura, Sayaka (2014) "Japanese Language Education in the Meiji Period" in: Mark Anderson & Patrick Heinrich (eds.) *Language Crisis in the Ryukyus*. Newcastle upon Tyne: Cambridge Scholars Publishing: 31–53.

第 10 章　要約

モダニストとエコロジストの言語と
アイデンティティへのアプローチ
琉球諸島の事例

パトリック・ハインリヒ（ヴェネツィア大学）　　　　　　　（松井真之介訳）

　本章では言語およびアイデンティティに対する、モダニストとエコロジストの立場からという、大きくかけ離れた2つのアプローチについて議論する。この2つの立場の違いは日本列島の最南西部で話される琉球諸語の事例をもって説明される。

　言語計画というものは単に顕在化した言語的問題の解決を目的とするものではない。言語政策は所属の概念やアイデンティティについての思想を変えようと模索するものである。人々がどのように自己規定するかに関しては政治的な含みがあるため、国家は国民的アイデンティティを創出するのに積極的な役割を果たしてきたのである。その結果、言語政策は集団的アイデンティティを導くプロセスが実行される一つの主要な場となったのである。モダニストのイデオロギー方針に従うと、これは通常国民全体にとってある1つの言語だけを押し付けることを意味してきた。「成功」を経験したそのような政策があるところでは、言語計画は決定的に他の言語の消滅危機に一役買っているのである。一国一言語はただの観念でしかないということは、世界には7000言語以上存在するのに国はわずか200しかないという事実からも明らかである。

　どの国家も実際に単一言語ということはなく、またそんな国はこれまで存在していない。しかし単一言語政策は政策や観念以上のものである——それは多言語の人々の生活に決定的な影響を及ぼすからである。国が単一言語の姿勢とイデオロギーをとった結果、「作り物としての国民」と「国家に実際に住む人々」との間隙に落ち込んだ人々はみな、そのイメージされる国民像に合わなければ、国民的連帯の結束から排除される危険がある。また土着の

マイノリティに関していえば、これは同化主義者の言語政策ということになる（そして移民マイノリティに関していえば、「統合的な」政策ということになる）。したがってマイノリティの視点からみると、モダニストの言語政策へのアプローチは、彼らの言語や文化、アイデンティティが考慮されず、評価されず、支援されないうえ、マジョリティに合わせよというイデオロギー的に圧力をかけられもするので、不平等の性質を持つのである。またモダニストの意識で異なる人々を「等しく」扱うことは、マジョリティとは異なる人々に「同質性」を押し付けることに他ならないのである。それは結局不平等に行き着くと言い換えることもできよう。多様に異なる人々が別々の扱いを求めること、それだけがマジョリティとマイノリティの間の「平等性」に行き着くのである。これが要するにエコロジカルな立場なのである。

　モダニストとエコロジストの言語イデオロギーや態度がぶつかる根底には、ひとつには何が秩序を構成し、何がそれを乱すのかに対する見方の違いがある。エコロジストは多様性の根底にある機能性を理解し、維持しようと模索するが、モダニストは秩序を整えることの衝動を感じるのである。モダニストにとっての秩序は「同質性」や「明快さ」となって現れるが、エコロジストはその対極、つまり「多様性」や「あいまいさ」を評価するのである。影響としては、モダニストは秩序を強制しようと努力するのに対し、エコロジストは多元主義の機能性を維持しようと望む。モダニストは権力の中心から世界を眺め、そこからその景色が「自然」か「普通」であるかを認識するが、エコロジストは周縁やすき間に興味を持ち、どうやって中心とは違う機能を果たすかに関心を抱く。結果、モダニストはあらゆる人や物事を自分たちが中心で見つけたパターンに当てはめようとし、エコロジストたちは出くわした多様性を維持することに力を注ぐ。アイデンティティ・ポリティクスに関して保証する結果は、モダニストはあらゆる人に対して共有する単一言語主義を課すことであり、エコロジストは共有する価値や態度にまつわるアイデンティティの構築を目的にすることである。

　モダニティが広まる以前、言語多様性は問題とは見られていなかった。それはモダニストの態度が一般的になる19世紀末、琉球諸島が日本国の「辺

境地域」になって以降のことである。当時あらゆる日本人は平等だと想定され、またモダニストは平等性について言語的文化的同質性の秩序を強制することによって達成される至高の目標だと見なしていたので、多様性は当初、「問題」を構成するものだと思われていた。言語計画はモダニストの原則方針に従うと、この問題を「解決する」ことを指していた。したがって、ないはずの言語的同質性を表明するために琉球諸語は日本語の「大方言」であると定義され、しかもそれらは「日本語の方言」から最もそれたものであるため、中央の言語、すなわち東京の日本語とそれらを置き換えさせられる努力がなされたのである。しかし方言学者のイデオロギーとは対照的に、琉球諸語は日本語のある種の副産物的現象ではない。言い換えると日本語の方言ではないのである。それどころか、琉球諸語は日本語の姉妹言語、それはすなわち例えばフランス語とイタリア語のような関係性なのである。事実日本語は琉球王国時代には外国語であり、武士階級のごく一部が学習し話すものでしかなかった。日本語は1880年以降、外国語として教育システムを通じて一般的に広がり始めたにすぎなかったのである。琉球における日本の言語教育は本土とは異なる教科書やカリキュラム、教授法を必要とした。何より決定的だったのは、日本語が学校教育システムによって普及した後であっても、現地の人々は日本語を自らの言語とはみなさなかったことである。それはヤマトゥグチ、つまり日本本土の言語と呼ばれるか、あるいはナイチゴ、つまり日本内地の言語と呼ばれたのである。

　しかし、琉球各地における日本語普及政策は、本土民と琉球人との間のコミュニケーションギャップをうめる必要性を大きく超えてやってきた。日本語は琉球人を本土の文化や習俗に適応させるためにも普及されたのである。つまり、それは琉球人に本土の日本人のアイデンティティを与える明確な目的を持って普及されたのである。そしてそのような日本化運動の成功を確実なものにするために、日本語の普及は当初から琉球諸語および文化の根絶への取り組みを伴っていたのである。琉球諸語抑圧の焦点は、日本語使用のレベルアップを重要視するというより、むしろそれによって琉球の教師自身が日本語と戦ったという事実に依拠するというところにもあるだろう。

1945年以降、琉球における言語およびアイデンティティの問題は劇的で予期せぬ展開を迎えた。1950年代からは、アメリカ占領のもと、日本語が沖縄を「外国の支配」から開放するための主要ツールとなり、また日本語がよりよい未来への道を切り開くための手段だと一般的にイメージされていたため、琉球諸語は若い世代へ伝えられなくなった。琉球諸語が日本語であるという主張は、アメリカがそうでないと主張しているのを尻目に、日本語こそ「我々の言語」であるという主張によって強調された。言い換えると、彼らは自分の日本性を重視するがために、家族内では日本語に切り替えたのである。琉球人による日本民族への自己同化の取り組みは、アメリカの占領が続けば続くほど、また米軍から受ける差別が大きくなるほど、より強いものへとなっていった。

　その状況は、1972年沖縄の日本復帰後にようやく変わり始めた。琉球文化の諸相を維持する最初の取り組みが行われ、そのような取り組みは平成時代以降、言語維持および言語再生の努力も含んでいた。これらの取り組みに通底する視点はエコロジストのものである。琉球列島においても、また他のどこでも言語エコロジストは、消滅危機言語の再生が文化的刷新を必要とすることを理解し、またこれが同化主義者のイデオロギーおよび実践、制度の批判的再考をも含んでいることも理解している。民俗化、すなわちマジョリティがマイノリティ支配を模索するとき、マイノリティの消滅危機言語をマジョリティが無害とみなす機能にまで縮小することはどんな言語維持にとっても不十分である。毎日の実生活において、それらの話者の必要を満たす機能が回復されなければならないのだ。消滅危機言語を話すことは、その話者たちの幸福に資さなければならない。

　モダニストの姿勢に基づいて消滅危機言語を保護することは不可能であり、そこではエコロジストの視点への転換は多様性の維持のために避けられている。存在しない同質性の強調は2つの大きな欠点を持つ。それは、彼ら固有の言語や文化を無視することによってそれらから土着のマイノリティを引き離す役割を果たしてしまうことと、そうすることによって彼らを日本社会の一員として包摂することに対する障壁を高め、日本が移民に対して多様では

ないことを見せつけてしまうことである。だからこそ琉球諸語の消滅危機問題は琉球諸語とその話者の問題にとどまらないのである。そのことは、多様な人々が真に純粋に平等でありつつ共存できる社会文化環境を構築する必要性を示唆するものである。琉球諸語が生き延びられる方法で言語エコロジーを再興することは、日本と呼ばれる場所に住む多様な人々の幸福に対して重要な貢献をするであろう。また日本の政策を、日本に存在するポストモダン的現実に合わせることも重要である。そうすることは現在の日本に住むあらゆる人々の利益に与するだろう。そしてこのような政策は、日本における琉球諸島を含む世界の大部分に存在しかつ広がっているエコロジストの姿勢によって構築されなければならないのである。

Chapter 11
Songs, Language and Culture: Ryukyuan Languages in the Okinawan uta-sanshin tradition

Matt Gillan (International Christian University)

Okinawa is home to one of modern Japan's most prominent and successful traditional music scenes. Since the early 20th century, Ryukyuan language songs accompanied by the sanshin (a 3-stringed plucked lute) have been a popular pastime for Okinawans of all ages and backgrounds. Both the classical (*koten*) repertory that developed in the old Ryukyu court, and the folk songs (*min'yō*) of Okinawa's villages, have become so popular that there are probably more amateur and professional performers of *sanshin*-accompanied songs in Ryukyuan languages today than at any time in the past. The two largest Okinawan broadcasters have actively promoted traditional music and the performing arts since the 1950s, and Okinawan record companies continue to release traditional and new songs in the Ryukyuan languages. Since 1972, the Japanese government has made a series of cultural heritage designations of Okinawan music and dance, meaning that Okinawa has more living national treasures in traditional performing arts than any other Japanese prefecture. Partly in recognition of the cultural importance of the traditional Okinawan performing arts, the Japanese government funded the construction of a National Theatre in Okinawa in 2004, one of only five such national theatres in the country, encouraging a resurgence of Okinawa's classical musical drama kumiudui[1].

The success of traditional song and drama has been in stark contrast to the continuing decline of the Ryukyuan languages in everyday life. For many Okinawans who are predominantly monolingual in Japanese, at least during the non-musical parts of their lives, songs are one of the most immediate and important contexts for interacting with Ryukyuan languages, either because they themselves sing, or through a more passive relationship with radio, television, recordings, or live performance. Clearly, music and the performing arts are highly relevant when considering issues of language survival and maintenance in modern Okinawa. At the same time, the cultural position of minority languages in song and in everyday speech are quite different, and have developed under quite distinct rules and expectations.

In this chapter I examine the use of Ryukyuan languages in song, in particular those accompanied by the sanshin[2], and consider some of the issues that arise when music becomes a context for preserving or promoting endangered languages. How is music useful for language maintenance? How is language constructed and controlled within the context of song? What problems arise when music becomes one of the most important contexts for language preservation? I argue that, in many cases, language choices made in song are quite different from those made in everyday speech, and are often bound by quite specific rules and expectations. At the same time, songs are not merely vehicles into which spoken languages are inserted and performed, but are sites in which languages are actively constructed and negotiated.

1. Minority languages and song

The relationship between music and endangered languages has been noted in many parts of the world, and several studies have shown how music serves as a way of preserving and promoting minority languages even when their use in everyday speech is in crisis. Heather Sparling's (2007) study of the Canadian Gaelic singer Mary Jane Lamond demonstrates how the use of Gaelic in her music can create a validity for this language even when the majority of listeners do not understand its literal meaning. Leanne Hinton's 1984 study of Havasupai songs in North America notes that, in the context of a rapid decline in all the verbal arts, singing was the context in which this endangered language survived most strongly (1984: 27). In extreme cases, as with the African languages still used in several Cuban ritual traditions, music has the potential to preserve languages that have entirely fallen out of use in everyday speech in particular communities (Christopher

2013). Catherine Grant (2010, 2011) has likewise described how the approaches of documentation and revitalization that have been applied to threatened languages may also hold significant relevance for safeguarding musical heritage. Despite the symbiotic relationship enjoyed by music and language in many minority cultures, Grant notes that there has been relatively little research to date on the parallels between language and music specifically in relation to their vitality and viability (2011: 96).

The development of the Ryukyuan languages has long been intricately connected with song and the performing arts, and it would be almost impossible to consider either in isolation from the other before the 20th century. Most of the extensive written body of what is known as 'Ryukyuan literature' (*Ryūkyū bungaku*) consists primarily of song lyrics and kumiudui dramas that were (and continue to be) performed in semi-melodic heightened speech (*tonae*). While there are relatively long traditions in Okinawa of literary writing in Chinese or Japanese that was meant to be read silently (for example the 18th century Japanese language stories by Heshikiya Chōbin), there are few examples of literary material in Ryukyuan languages that are not connected to singing or drama in some way. The Okinawan linguist Miyara Tōsō's (1893-1964) 1960 definition of (pre-20th century) Ryukyuan literature, for example, contains 8 categories: ritual chants (誦詠), 'old' songs (古謡), omoro, Ryukyuan songs (琉球歌謡), kumiudui, kyōgen (狂言), puppet plays (人形芝居), and 'others' — including legends and folk tales (Miyara Tōsō 1980 vol. 12: 271). With the exception of the last of these, all were originally sung or chanted, and incorporate musicality to some degree.

Traditional song and drama texts continued to play an important role in the formation of Okinawan linguistic identities after Okinawa was incorporated into the Japanese state in 1879. The early-20th century Okinawan linguist and folklorist Iha Fuyū drew heavily on Ryukyuan song and drama texts in his analyses of Ryukyuan languages. His *Kōchū Ryūkyū Gikokushū* (Annotated collection of Ryukyuan plays), based on an extant manuscript detailing the performances given for the Chinese *Sappōshi* envoy to Ryukyu in 1838, remains a primary text for the study and performance of kumiudui plays. Iha also published a dictionary of kumiudui vocabulary (*Ryūkyū gikyoku jiten*) in 1928, and a large number of articles on Okinawan folk song lyrics (Iha 1974, 1975).

Miyara Tōsō likewise made frequent use of song lyrics as source material for his research on Okinawan languages. His *Yaeyama Koyō*, published in 2 volumes in 1928 and 1930, contained a selection of Yaeyaman work songs in local languages, with Japanese translations and musical staff transcriptions. Interestingly, as Miyara states in the introduction to this work, his inclusion of melody transcriptions (by the Yaeyaman composer and educator Miyara Chōhō) was an attempt to promote these songs as material for actual performance, rather than simply as linguistic relics of a disappearing language (Miyara 1980 vol.11: 3). Miyara's publications were intended primarily for a non-Yaeyaman (non-Okinawan) audience, and his suggestion that the songs should continue to be performed as music shows that Miyara was well aware of the potential of song in helping to promote disappearing Ryukyuan languages.

Miyara continued to publish on Okinawan song lyrics for most of his life. A 1944 article states the importance of traditional songs for the study of historical forms of Okinawan languages that were already changing and disappearing:

> By studying these songs, we thus have a source of material for the study of language in old [Yaeyama]. Up until the middle of the Meiji period, it was difficult to travel to and from Yaeyama, and there was relatively little interchange with the outside. This, combined with the lack of formal education, means that the old [language] is preserved relatively well [in Yaeyaman songs].
>
> (Miyara Tōsō Zenshū 1980 vol.11: 439)

The close connection of Ryukuan languages with song lyrics continued to be a theme for later linguists. Hokama Shuzen's many works continued a tradition of song lyric collection and annotation (Hokama 1979). A more recent collection of *Okinawan Literature* (*Okinawa bungaku*), overseen by the literary scholar and folklorist Hateruma Eikichi, follows a similar pattern, covering folk and art song texts, folk tales, drama, as well as written literature in Japanese and Chinese (Okinawa-ken kyōiku bunka shiryō sentā 2003).

2. Ryukyuan languages in the classical *uta-sanshin* tradition

Among the pre-20th century items of performed Ryukyuan literature, the most popular genres today, by far, are the classical (*koten*) songs and the related folk-song (*min'yō*[3]) tradition that became prominent from the early 20th century. Both of these are accompanied by the sanshin, a 3-stringed plucked lute with a resonating membrane of python skin that was almost certainly introduced to the Okinawan mainland from the Fujian province of China some time after the late 14th century[4]. By the late 18th century, a large repertoire of court songs had developed to be sung to sanshin accompaniment, and this repertoire forms the basis of the modern *uta-sanshin* tradition. The importance of the sanshin to Okinawan songs cannot be overstated. A well-known verse from the late-18th century *Ryūka Hyakkō* attributes the origins of both to a legendary musician Aka Inku as the founder of the *uta-sanshin* (*sanshin*-accompanied song) tradition:

Uta tu sanshin nu (8) *mukashi hajimari ya* (8)
Inku niagari nu (8) *kami nu misaku* (6)
The ancient origins of song and *sanshin* are the work of the legendary Inku
(Source: Shimabukuro 1964: 49)

As this verse suggests, the introduction of the sanshin was important not only because it began to be used to accompany pre-existing songs (although this may have also been the case), but because it was the impetus for the creation of a completely new form of lyrical composition, one that has come to be known as *ryūka* 琉歌. In its narrowest meaning, *ryūka* refers to lyrics consisting of a fixed 8-8-8-6 mora structure (known as the '*ryūka* structure'). The creation of the word itself probably dates to the 17th century as a way of distinguishing this newly constructed Ryukyuan poetry form from the *waka* of Japan that were increasingly studied by members of the Ryukyu court at the time. The origins of the form can be found in the later volumes of the *Omoro Sōshi* published in the early 17th century, and the majority of the subsequent Okinawan mainland classical uta-sanshin repertory is also in 8-8-8-6 structure. A 'long-form' version of the *ryūka* structure is also found, especially in the kumiudui drama repertoire, consisting of an extended series of lines of 8-syllable length concluded by a 6-syllable concluding line. In a broader sense, '*ryūka*' is also used to describe other lyrical forms sung to *sanshin* accompaniment, the most common of which are the *rakafū* form (7-5-8-6 or 5-5-8-6 mora), and the *kuduchi* form (a combination of 7-5 mora)[5].

The overwhelming majority of Ryukyuan classical songs comprise the performance of a single ryūka over a fixed melody. Most *uta-sanshin* melody titles take the suffix '*fushi*' — literally melody — to which an identifying phrase is attached. Place names are common, as in the songs *Chin bushi* ('Song from Kin village'), *Shui bushi* ('Song from Shuri'), or *Nyufa bushi*. Alternatively, the title may reflect the content of the song's 'original' lyrics, as in *Fishi ni wuru tui bushi* ('song about the birds on the reef', often abbreviated to *Fishi bushi* – 'song about the reef'), *Guin bushi* ('song about auspicious meetings'), or *Kuwadīsa bushi* ('song about the *kuwadīsa* tree'). Despite the connection between the title of a melody and the lyrical content, most melodies are commonly not confined to a particular lyric, and can be performed with a variety of verses of the same mora-structure (usually the 8-8-8-6 ryūka form). Conversely, the same lyric may often be performed to a large variety of melodies. The following verse is one of many examples and is commonly performed to melodies including Aha bushi, Yunabaru bushi, and many others:

Kariyushi nu ashibi (8)	嘉例吉の遊び	This auspicious gathering
Uchi hariti kara ya (8)	打ちはりてぃからや	with our hearts as one
Yu nu akiti tīda nu (8)	夜の明けてぃ太陽の	let it continue until
Agaru madin (6)	上がるまでぃん[6]	the sun comes up

(source: Shimabukuro 1964:217))

While the language of most *ryūka* is ostensibly a form of the spoken dialect of the Shuri village of the Okinawan mainland, the uta-sanshin repertory was also a context in which Ryukyuan languages were heavily influenced by Japanese vocabulary, grammar and ideas. The Okinawan writer Ōshiro Tatsuhiro has attributed the profound shift between the language used in the older omoro tradition and that of the *ryūka* of the 17th century and later to a rapid Japanization of the Ryukyu court culture following the Satsuma invasion of Ryukyu in 1609 (Ōshiro 2002 vol.12: 299-300). Most Ryukyu court musicians from the 16th century onwards underwent extensive training both in Japanese poetry, and the performance of Japanese singing traditions, in particular noh chanting. This training was a huge influence on the development of Ryukyuan court music, and in particular on the language used in *ryūka*.

A substantial number of *ryūka* show the influence of Japanese waka. A well-known example can be seen in a comparison of the standard verse for the Ryukyuan song *Kuti bushi* with a 10th century verse from the Japanese *Kokin wakashū*:

Kuti bushi

Tuchiwa naru matsi nu (8)	The everlasting pine
kawaru kutu neesami (8)	that could surely never change
itsin haru kuriba (8)	always deepens its colour
iru du masaru (6)	with the coming of spring

(Source: Shimabukuro 1964:27)

from Kokin Wakashū volume 1

Tokiwa naru (5)	Even the green
matsu no midori mo (7)	of the everlasting pine
haru kureba (5)	deepens its colour
ima hito shio no (7)	with the coming
iro masarikeri (7)	of spring

(Source: Katagiri Youichi 1998 (vol.1):24

An important point about these two verses is that, rather than simply adding a mora to the original 7 or 5 mora lines of *waka* to produce lines of 8 or 6 mora, the recomposition into ryūka form has been achieved largely by dismantling the structure of the original waka and redistributing the same vocabulary across the 30 mora of the ryūka — the 5 mora in the first phrase of the waka have been combined with the first 3 mora of phrase two to produce the initial 8 mora of the ryūka, for example.

The kuduchi lyrical form, which, after ryuka, is the second most-common form in the uta-sanshin repertory, exhibits even stronger influence from the Japanese language, both due to its 7-5 mora structure and to linguistic elements such as vocabulary and grammar. Take the first verse of the well-known song *Nubui kuduchi*:

Tabi nu njitachi (7)	Setting off on our journey
Kwannundu (5)	Kannon temple
Shinti Kwannun (7)	We bow down before the
Fushi ugadi	Kannon statue with 1000 hands
Kugani shaku tuti (7)	Take the golden cup
Tachi wakaru (5)	and bid farewell

The majority of the vocabulary of this, and most other *kuduchi*, are far closer to the Japanese language, albeit in Ryukyuanized pronunciation, than would have been found in the spoken language of Shuri.

One of the most important contexts for the development of the ryūka form was the musical drama genre kumiudui, first performed in front of the Chinese Sappōshi envoy of 1719. Kumiudui incorporates dialogue in melodic speech patterns, the majority of which is composed in the 8-8-8-6 *ryūka* structure, together with songs from the *uta-sanshin* repertory and classical Ryukyuan dances. Like the *uta-sanshin* tradition, the language of kumiudui deviates considerably from the historical spoken language of Shuri and other parts of Ryukyu, both in vocabulary and syntax. In the introduction to Iha's 1928 *Ryūkyū gikyoku jiten*, Hashimoto Shinkichi described the language of kumiudui as:

> An artificially constructed language that incorporates the extinct vocabulary of *omoro* and even words from Japanese. It cannot therefore be considered from a linguistic perspective in the same way as a normal language that has been transmitted naturally.
>
> (Iha 1974 vol. 8: 4).

As with *uta-sanshin*, kumiudui plays employ many Ryukyuan adaptatations of Japanese language vocabulary, or newly coined phrases that are not found in everyday speech. For example, the phrase '*diyō charu munu ya*' used as a self-introduction (*nanori*) of the upper class Aji characters in plays such as *Nidō Tichiuchi* and *Mekarushi*, is believed to have been invented by the Kumiudui pioneer Tamagusuku Chōkun (1684-1734) as a replacement for, and translation of, the *nanori* used by characters in Japanese noh plays (Iha 1974: 353)

In some cases, Japanese imported words in *kumiudui* have been reused in subsequent folk song lyrics. One example is the term *ichiya* 一夜 (a 'single night' c.f. standard Shuri '*chuyuru*' 一夜. The term appears in Tamagusuku Chōkun's play *Shūshin kaneiri*, after the young male character Wakamatsi has stayed the night in a woman's house:

Ichiya karisumi nu	一夜かりそめの	A woman who
Yadu nu wunna	宿の女	accommodated me for a single night
Aku-yin nu tsina nu	悪縁の縄の	Will not release me
Hanachi hanasaran	はなちはなさらぬ	from her evil grasp
		(Source: Iha 1974:59)

Tamagusuku's adoption of the term *ichiya* here seems to be the first use of the term in Ryukyuan languages. (The term *wunna* (woman), rather than the usual Okinawan *winagu*, is also an import from the Japanese language). Perhaps because of Tamagusuku's precedent, *ichiya* continues to appear in subsequent Ryukyuan language song lyrics, for example Uehara Naohiko's late 1970s composition *Ichiya-bana* (The flowers of a single night).

From the 1920s a new genre of commercially recorded songs emerged that has come to be known as *min'yō* (folk song)[7]. The first specialist Okinawan record label was Marufuku records founded in Osaka in 1927 by the Okinawan emigrant musician Fukuhara Chōki (1903-81). As well as recording traditional material and songs from the kageki repertoire, Fukuhara began composing new melodies and lyrics. Many of the new Okinawan compositions, such as Fukuhara's *Imin kouta* (1927) were in the Japanese language, but many also used predominantly the Okinawan language and traditional *ryūka* structure, like Higa Ryōjun's *Nan'yō kouta* (1939):

Kuishi furusatu nu (8)	Saying a sad goodbye to
Uya-chōdē tu wakari (8)	my parents in my hometown
Akugari nu nan'yō (8)	I came across to
Watati chashiga (6)	the Southern Islands

(Bise and Matsuda 2010:80)

As with many earlier examples, this 20th century verse maintains the traditional 8-8-8-6 structure, and the pronunciation is consistent with that of the Okinawan mainland, yet vocabulary such as *furusatu* (home-town), an Okinawanised form of the Japanese *furusato*, show the continued influence of the Japanese language.

The *min'yō* tradition continues to play an extremely important part of the modern Okinawan music world, with many new songs in Ryukyuan languages appearing every year. The majority of these continue to be composed in the traditional ryūka structure, as well as in the Japanese-influenced 7-5 mora structure. One of the best-known songs of the 20th century was Kadekaru Rinshō's *Jidai no Nagare* (the passing of time):

Tū nu yū kara (5)	唐ぬ世から	From dominance by China
Yamatu nu yū (5)	大和ぬ世	To dominance by Japan
Yamatu nu yū kara (7)	大和ぬ世から	From dominance by Japan
Amerika yū (5)	アメリカ世	To dominance by America
Hirumasa kawataru (8)	ひるまさかわたる	It has changed so strangely
Kunu uchinaa (5)	くぬ沖縄	Our Okinawa

This song, predominantly in a combination of 5 and 7 mora (the melody is an adaptation of the traditional *Hana kuduchi*), is well-known for its expression of Okinawa's unstable political relationship with its larger neighbours, and the lyrics continue to be re-used in more recent compositions. They appear almost verbatim (except for an extra line emphasizing the subsequent 'return' of Okinawa in 1972) in Sadoyama Yutaka's 1972 song *Duchui muni* (Talking to myself). More recently, the lyrics have been appropriated in the Okinawan reggae singer I-Van's 2014 song *Final Ryukyu Soldier*, in which he changes the '*hirumasa kawataru…*' to the standard Japanese '*kaishite kure orera no ryūkyū*' (Give us back our Ryukyu).

3. Ryukyuan languages in the performing arts under Japan

Whether acting as a context for the introduction of Japanese vocabulary and lyrical ideas into Ryukyu, or providing a platform for expressing dissatisfaction with Okinawa's subjugation by larger countries, *uta-sanshin* songs have always been created with an eye on the outside. With the dissolution of the Ryukyu court and incorporation of Okinawa into the Japanese state in 1879, the situation of performing arts in the islands underwent rapid change. In particular, court performers who had previously operated under royal patronage were faced with making a living through paid performances to the general public. One result was the establishment of new theatres at which songs, dances, and new dramatic forms were performed alongside the classical kumiudui, music and dance of the old court culture. Most importantly for the Ryukyuan languages, new dramas such as the *kageki* (歌劇 song-drama) and later *Uchinā shibai* (沖縄芝居, Okinawan language dramas that incorporated song and spoken word) began to be composed in large numbers. Examples such as Ganeko Yaei's *Tumai Ākā* (1910), Majikina Yūkō's *Ījima Handōgwā* (1924), and more recent plays such as Ōgimi Kotarō's *Oka no ippon matsu*, continue to be popular today.

Uchinā shibai seems to have been vastly influential in the early to mid-20th century in keeping interest in the dialect of Naha[8]. Many Okinawans born in outlying islands such as in Yaeyama have told me that they understand the Okinawan mainland language mainly through what they learned listening to these *shibai*. Partly due to its early popularity among ordinary Okinawan people, the early 20th century *shibai* and *kageki* dramas also came under attack from the ruling Okinawan elite and the police force (which contained large numbers of mainland Japanese in senior positions). The main problem with these new dramatic forms seems to have been their perceived power to corrupt the morals of the Okinawan population through their representations of emotional romantic relationships between men and women. As early as 1899, there were efforts to control the staging of commercial dance and drama performances (Ōno 2003: 88-94), and these efforts continued and intensified in the years leading up to WWII. In 1917 steps were taken to abolish the existing theatres, due to their overwhelming influence. The *Ryukyu Shinpō* newspaper reported in 1917 how:

...even elementary school children are singing the songs of the *kageki*, showing how its bad influence is still something to be feared. These dramas always appeal to the lower classes, and never attempt to develop their dramatic potential. The classical Ryukyuan kumiodori and dance genres demand a high level of technique, but the level is falling down to appeal to factory workers and prostitutes.

(*Ryukyu Shinpō* 12 April 1917)

While the theatres quickly reformed, and continued to be hugely popular among many Okinawans for much of the 20th century, the controversy continued. In particular, *Shibai* and *kageki* genres were increasingly seen as a threat to the effort by the ruling classes in pre-war Okinawa to assimilate into Japanese linguistic society. The actor Majikina Yūkō (1889-1982) remembered how, in the pre-WWII years:

The police would usually show up at the theatre at around 6:00 or 7:00 in the evening. They didn't understand much of the language we were using on stage, or the lyrics of the songs used in *kageki* musicals, so they gave notice that it was difficult to regulate. They used to hate the *kageki* and the Okinawan language too. Even with *kumiodori*, they asked us to translate the whole plot into Japanese.

(Okinawa Bunka Kyōkai 1975: 59)

In the early 20th century the government seems to have given some leeway to songs in the Okinawan language, as opposed to spoken dialogue. The Okinawan dance scholar Nishihira Shumo (1898-?) remembered how "They allowed dialogue [on stage] to be carried out [in Okinawan] if it was sung, but spoken dialogue in Okinawan was banned completely" (Okinawa bunka kyōkai 1975: 58). Nevertheless, in 1942, the Naha police announced that all dramas must be performed in the Japanese language, while *kageki* musicals were to be banned entirely (Ōno 2003: 213).

4. Ryukuan languages and music in the post-WWII broadcast media

Following WWII, the American military administration, partly in an effort to emphasize Okinawa's difference from Japan, were relatively active in promoting traditional performing arts in Ryukyuan languages. Around this time, the new medium of radio also began to be important for the dissemination of traditional music and drama. The use of Ryukyuan languages in public broadcasting has been sporadic, and, in contrast to many minority language cultures around the world, Okinawa has been relatively slow in implementing broadcasts in the spoken Ryukyuan languages. The most prominent examples of Ryukyuan language use in broadcasting have made at least some use of traditional music. The language choices made in public broadcasting sheds light both on the cultural position of Ryukyuan languages in Okinawa, and on the ways that traditional music acts as a facilitator for the use of these languages.

An Okinawan branch of the Japanese NHK radio station was briefly operational during WWII, but the first fully operational radio station was not established until the Ryukyu Broadcasting Corporation (RBC) was founded in 1954. In these early years, radio reception had still not reached many parts of Okinawa, and a broadcasting system known as *Oyako Rajio* (parent-child radio) was influential in allowing people access to traditional song in Ryukyuan languages. Programs were broadcast from a central station to a number of regional 'receivers' (the 'parent'), from where they were relayed through a local public address system to people's homes (the 'children')[9]. This system continued up to the 1960s, when television began to reach the majority of Okinawan houses, and was influential in promoting a boom in new compositions in a traditional Okinawan style. A CD of archive recordings from these early radio shows has recently been released on the Campus Record label (2014). As can be heard from these recordings, the presentation of these shows was delivered in the Japanese language, in a standard (for the time) 'NHK' accent with no discernible trace of Okinawan speech patterns. In contrast, the language of almost all of the songs, most of which were newly composed folk songs and *shibai* numbers, was that of the southern Okinawan mainland. Thus, we can see that the standards and expectations for language use in broadcasting of the time were very different for sung and spoken languages. While it was acceptable to broadcast songs sung entirely in Okinawan, a language with which the majority of the Okinawan population were still comfortable in the 1950s, the spoken introduction to these songs was only permissible in the standard broadcasting language – Tokyo (NHK) Japanese.

The Ryūkyū Broadcasting Corporation (RBC) has been active in presenting traditional music in Okinawan languages. From the year of its establishment as a radio station in 1954, the station was broadcasting a regular program, *Furusato no koten* (Hometown classics) playing the Ryukyu classical music repertory, initially presented by the educator and musician Yonaha Seigyū (1895-1972). One of the most influential and successful broadcasters has been Uehara Naohiko (b. 1938), who has presented the weekday radio show *Min'yō de chū uganabira* (Saying hello with folksong) on the RBC station since 1961, as well as subsequently taking over the *Furusato no koten* program. Both of these shows are delivered in a mixture of Japanese and Ryukyuan languages, although Uehara currently makes little attempt to use a standard 'NHK' pronunciation as in the earlier Oyako rajio broadcasts. Both programs also give analyses and explanation of song lyrics, *ryūka* and other aspects of Ryukyuan language and culture.

Okinawa's other major radio station, Rajio Okinawa (ROK), established in 1960, has likewise been influential in promoting the use of Okinawan languages in a musical context. One of this station's best-known initiatives has been the annual *Mīuta taishō* (New song award) competition for new compositions in a traditional style. Regarding use of language, the entrance form for the competition in 2011 (written in Japanese) states that "entries should be predominantly in the Okinawan language (the document uses the word *hōgen* (dialect), although states that "exceptions will be made if the content makes it unavoidable")[10]. In an interview in March 2015, the head of the judging panel for this competition told me that many of the judges in recent years had marked down entries that used Japanese words or phrases (Shinjō, personal communication 15th March 2015). The requirements also stipulate the use of traditional instruments – *sanshin*[11], *taiko*, *fue* (flute) or *kūchō*, and specifically ban the use of 'Western' instruments such as mandolin, guitar and electric instruments such as synthesizers. This condition is somewhat surprising, given these instruments' widespread use and acceptance in much new Okinawan traditional music since the 1920s.

An encouraging recent development has been the establishment in September 2014 of an internet radio station, *Shimakutuba Hōsōkyoku*[12], that broadcasts 24 hours a day in Okinawan languages, and also transmits recorded music, most of which in a traditional style. The station is partially funded through commercials and, while it is too early to assess its impact on the preservation of Ryukyuan languages, represents an exciting development in Okinawan broadcasting culture.

The use of Ryukyuan languages in local television broadcasts has, like radio, relied very heavily on the use of music, dance and *shibai* dramas. The oldest example (and one of a very small number) is the program *Kyōdo Gekijō* on OTV (Okinawa Television), a twice-monthly program that has run since 1960, the year after the station's launch[13]. The program has been an important way of promoting Okinawan *shibai*, as well as folksong and dance performances. As with most radio programs, there is quite a stark division between the spoken language used by the program's presenters — nearly always standard Japanese — and that of the songs and *shibai* that the program features — Ryukyuan. Once again, the unwritten rules for language choice in this broadcast medium are quite different for ordinary spoken language, and that which is performed or sung.

Ryukyuan languages have been featured fairly often in recent years in Okinawan tv commercials and, as with other broadcast formats, music has been an important way to make the Ryukyuan language 'acceptable' to viewers. An analysis of these commercials reveals much about the position that Okinawan language holds in Okinawan cultural life. Where Ryukyuan has been used, the product has usually been either ostensibly 'Okinawan', or targeted towards an older audience that retains Okinawan as a first language. An example of the first kind can be found in the long-running series of commercials for the Okihamu company, a producer of ham and pork products (a large number of these commercials are posted on YouTube). An example from 1989 features an Okinawan language song lyric, onto which a Japanese language sales pitch is overlaid:

Chū ya uyuwē ayakari du	Let us celebrate this auspicious day
Okihamu kwacchī…	by eating Oki ham

As in the Oyako rajio example, language use in this example is split very clearly between the Okinawan lyrics of the sung section, and the Japanese of the spoken message introducing the product.

A more recent example from 2012 parodies the female *tonae* (heightened speech) pattern of kumiudui plays, using a predominantly Shuri pronunciation and the traditional ryūka 8886 mora structure:

Wan'ya Oki hamu nu (8)	I am the princess of
Uminai du yayuru (8)	Oki ham

This is followed by a sung section to the melody of the song *Sensuru bushi*, used in several kumiudui plays and the folksong repertory.

Sōgachi hamu ya kwacchī do	Eat ham at New Year
Okihamu kadōti chāganjū	Eat Okihamu and be healthy

As in the previous example, the spoken section of the commercial is delivered in Japanese:

Oseibo wa yappari Okihamu	For a New Year's present it has to be Okihamu

The Okihamu commercials are only one example of Okinawan songs being used to promote 'Okinawan' products, and other examples include the Orion beer company, and several awamori liquor companies who have used Okinawan musicians singing in Okinawan languages.

In recent years there have also been a number of television and radio commercials for cemetery spaces and household Buddhist shrines delivered in Okinawan language and music (including one featuring the singer Noborikawa Seijin). A striking aspect of all of these commercials is that they are all appealing to images of tradition in Okinawan life. The 1989 commercial refers to an unspecified celebration at which ham might be eaten. The second two refer to the gift-giving traditions of *oseibo* and *ochūgen* (at New Year and Summer respectively). Striking, also, is the use of music (and musicians) in these commercials to make the use of

Okinawan language approachable in a way that it would not be simply as spoken language.

An interesting recent initiative towards Okinawan language maintenance through music that seems to have taken root to some extent in Okinawan life has been the creation of Okinawan language versions of the so-called 'radio calisthenics' (*rajio taisō*) songs that have been broadcast daily on major Japanese radio stations since the 1920s (Kuroda 1999). The (Japanese language) broadcast is still often used, as it is in the Japanese mainland, in Okinawan sports meetings (*undōkai*) and for ordinary Okinawans to congregate for communal exercise in the early mornings. The first Okinawan language version was locally-produced in the Okinawan main island by the singer Kyan Hitoshi. This version spawned a number of similar initiatives, such as that in the Shika-aza dialect of Ishigaki in 2009, when Onaga Chijun, a member of the Arakawa village community group, approached other group members with the idea of making a version of the song that could be 'enjoyed by the older residents of the village'[14]. The original Japanese text of the song was translated into Shika-aza dialect, and passed the project on to a local radio presenter, Teruya Kanbun, to perform. This version became the first to obtain copyright permissions to use the original (Japanese) *rajio-taisō* melody, and has gone on to sell several thousand copies in Okinawa and Japan. The recording was subsequently taken up by local school sport and community events, and continues to be used in local festivals 2014 (although not in the daily *rajio-taisō* practices of Arakawa villagers). There have also been Okinawan language versions of the song using the speech of the Okinawan mainland, Miyako, and Amami Ōshima (for which several regional variations have been recorded). All of these use the standard NHK song with piano accompaniment, to which sanshin has been added in some cases (in Ishigaki and Amami for example).

These Okinawan examples also seem to have been the impetus for a much wider movement throughout Japan to simultaneously promote local language use and community spirit through the *rajio-taisō* phenomenon. In recent years, there have been versions using the Japanese dialects of Tōhoku, Akita, Osaka, and many others, as well as those in English, Italian and Susu. 2 Major Japanese record labels have released compilation cds of the NHK *rajio taisō* song with a variety of regional dialect lyrics, including *Rajio taisō daiichi — gotōji songu* [Radio

Calisthenics no.1 — 'regional songs'] on the Nippon Columbia label, and Rajio taisō daiichi – okunikotoba-hen [Radio Calisthenics no.1 — 'local songs'] on the Teichiku label, which also contains the original Arakawa version.

The spawning of this Japan-wide movement arguably leads to a dilemma — by grouping itself with what are overtly seen as dialects of Japanese (in contrast to the Okinawan language, there has been almost no movement to promote the speech of Tōhoku, for example, as a distinct language), what implications are there for the status of Ryukyuan as an independent language? In the course of my interviews, it is obvious that the issue of dialect vs. language is still one that does not hold much urgency for most Okinawans. In response to my direct question over whether there was any problem with the Ishigaki version appearing on a compilation cd together with other Japanese 'dialect' versions, Teruya Kanbun (the singer of the Ishigaki version) told me:

> I don't really think too much about it, I think of it [the Ishigaki version] as a 'dialect' (*hōgen*) version. Even within Ryukyu, the Yaeyaman dialect is quite different. When we [Yaeyamans] go to 'Okinawa', we would need a dictionary to speak in the Okinawan mainland dialect.
>
> (Interview, August 2014)

Teruya was also very specific about his version representing only one particular village in Ishigaki:

> Within Yaeyama, there are differences between each village, so we deliberately gave our version the title 'Arakawa', rather than simply 'local language' (*sïma muni*). For example, from the perspective of someone from Kohama, our version uses many words that they don't use in Kohama. So we deliberately limited ourselves to 'Arakawa'.

While there has been an encouraging shift from the use of 'dialect' (*hōgen*) to 'language' (*gengo*) among some Okinawans, and an attempt to sidestep the issue through terms such as *shimakutuba*, *sïma muni* (both translate as 'island' speech or 'local' speech) or *uchināguchi* (Okinawan 'speech'), the use of the term *hōgen* is still widespread. (I noted its use above in the *mīuta* competition, and both RBC and ROK use this term predominantly.) Another example can be seen in a local speech contest sponsored by the Yaeyama Cultural Association (Yaeyama Bunka Kyōkai) in Ishigaki in 2014, which described itself as *Suma muni hōgen o hanasu kai* (Competition to speak local speech dialect)[15].

A more recent development in the use of technology and media to promote Ryukyuan languages can be seen through the use of the internet. Examples range from personal blogs and home pages to Facebook communities and online databases. As with earlier radio and television broadcasts, one of the main focuses for the study of Ryukyuan languages on the internet has been songs and music. One of the oldest song-related blogs is *Taru no shimauta majime kenkyū* (Taru's serious study of Okinawan songs)[16], established in 2005 by the Miyazaki-born Hiroshima resident Seki Hiroshi, and with more than 2 million page views to date. Seki is an accomplished performer of the Okinawan folk song repertory, and the blog was established through his own studies of the Okinawan language in songs, giving Okinawan lyrics and Japanese translations for upwards of 400 songs, together with analyses of Okinawan vocabulary and grammar. Seki is also an administrator of an active Facebook group for Okinawan language learners and speakers, *Uchināguchi kōza*. The group currently has well over 5,000 members (June 2014) and attracts daily posts from beginners to competent users of the language.

A more recent blog is *Sumamuni Hirome-tai* スマムニ広め隊[17], established in April 2014 by the Yaeyaman educator Higashiōhama Tsuyoshi. The blog focuses exclusively on the languages of Yaeyama, particularly that of the main Shikaaza settlement where Higashiōhama is from. Like Seki's blog, *Simamuni Hirome-tai* consists of translations to Japanese and analyses of vocabulary and grammar of song lyrics, as well as traditional Yaeyaman sayings. One of Higashiōhama's innovations has been an attempt to translate lyrics to the Yaeyaman song *Tubarāma* into English, and our initial introduction came through working together on this project.

5. Pronunciation

I turn finally to one example of the way in which Ryukyuan languages are negotiated by performers at a micro level in the performance of the utasanshin tradition. Since the year 2000 I have participated in the Okinawan music world as non-native-speaking learner and performer of both classical and folk uta-sanshin traditions. During that time I have encountered a very large number of other non-native-speaking learners, including mainland Japanese, learners from outside Japan, and younger Okinawans who have almost no facility with spoken Ryukyuan languages. While most outsiders learn to negotiate the musical aspects of these traditions fairly accurately, and in many cases attain a good degree of language comprehension through studying song lyrics, an issue that arises frequently, and for most non-native-speaking performers, is that of pronunciation.

The issue of pronunciation in song can be found in many song traditions around the world, both traditional and comtemporary. The folk singer Ewan Mac-Coll famously insisted that singers at his British folk clubs should only sing in the language or dialect they spoke or had grown up with as a first language (Brocken 2003: 35). Trudgill (1983: 141-144) has described the sometimes laughable attempts of British rock and pop singers to imitate the pronunciation and vocalizations of the American south from which they drew their models. There is perhaps more flexibility regarding pronunciation where issues of race or cultural identity are less prevalent — it is relatively common to hear lied or opera singers singing in languages in which they have a noticeable non-standard accent, for example. Yet, as Roland Barthes (1977:184) described in his praise of the French classical singer Panzera, the 'truth' of language as performed in song lies not in "its functionality (clarity, expressivity, communication)" but in the "enunciation" of its vowels and consonants.

While issues of pronunciation have become particularly pertinent with the large-scale loss of Ryukyuan language use from everyday life, debates surrounding pronunciation in Okinawa go back to at least the early 20th century, and probably before. The uta-sanshin world that developed within the Ryukyu court has always had a strong preference for the upper-class sociolect of Shuri, and many Okinawan performers from outside Shuri, even those who were fluent and monolingual in a different Ryukyuan dialect, encountered problems being accepted into this world. The early 20th century dancer, actor and musician Iraha Inkichi (1886-1951), who grew up in Yonabaru, only 5km from Shuri, had to fight to overcome the linguistic 'handicap' of being born outside the elite Shuri linguistic zone (Yano 1993: 360). The Yaeyaman musician Ōhama Anpan largely abandoned the public performance of the Ryukyu classical tradition as he felt he could not fully master the Shuri pronunciation and vocal techniques (Ōsoko, personal communication 2002). Much of the debate has focused not only on language loss in relation to Japanese, but rather what is seen as a dilution of the 'correct' upper-class dialect of Shuri in relation to the language used in the commercial theatres of Naha and elsewhere, and that used in the folk song repertory. The Shuri-born kumiodori actor Kin Ryōshō (1908-1993) was known to be particularly critical of other actors, even those born in Shuri, for what he saw as their incorrect pronunciation. In the programme for a 1978 recital, the Okinawan scholar Arasaki Seibin praised the Shuri-born actor Majikina Yūkō not for his dramatic abilities (for which he was also renowned), but for the 'correctness' of his pronunciation of the Shuri dialect (Majikina Yūkō Seitan 100 nen kinen jigyōkai 1989: 23).

Part of the problem, as we have already seen, is that the language of song and *kumiudui* is not simply the spoken language of Shuri, but a combination of historical vocabulary, Japanese words, and specialist literary vocabulary. The literary language of kumiudui has undergone a process of standardization and canonization since at least the early 20th century. Iha Fuyū's 1928 dictionary of kumiudui vocabulary was an early example of this process. The Okinawan scholar Higashionna Kanjun wrote in 1955 how Majikina Yūkō, a first-language speaker of the Shuri dialect, had asked him the 'correct' pronunciation of the words *haru/faru* — 'spring' or 'cloudless', a matter Higashionna resolved by referring both to historical Ryukyuan pronunciation, and the pronunciation of Japanese noh plays (Higashionna 1980: 477).

For this reason, it is not enough simply to be a native-speaker of a Ryukyuan language (even of the Shuri dialect), but most performers must undergo a period of learning to perform the very specific language of uta-sanshin and other performing arts. Correct pronunciation continues to be a hugely important issue in the preservation and teaching of Ryukyuan language in song, and one that arises frequently in the context of teaching. Higa Yasuharu, a prominent *uta-sanshin* performer who is a proficient speaker of the southern-Okinawan-mainland language, told me how he often criticized one of his best-known students, who despite enjoying a prominent professional career as a performer, is less proficient in the spoken language:

> I still correct him even now. If I think he doesn't sound like me (*boku no nioi ga shinai* – lit. 'doesn't smell like me'), I let him know. I mean, if his vocal production is not like mine. For example, he might sing "sā hana~" [from the song *nakafū bushi*], but it's not right. I tell him his throat is too open, or that it's too nasal, that he should make a more focused sound…but the main problem is that his pronunciation doesn't sound like Uchināguchi. He is simply pronouncing the sounds, but not the nuance (*nyuansu*) of [Uchināguchi]. If you don't manage to get that feeling into it, then it may sound technically good to outsiders, but the authentic 'smell' (*nioi*) of Ryukyu classical music becomes diluted.
>
> (interview, April 2014)

The Yaeyaman musician Daiku Tetsuhiro also told me that there was a fundamental difference between performers such as himself, who have ability in speaking Ryukyuan languages (the Shika-aza dialect of Yaeyama in Daiku's case), and those younger performers who learn traditional songs without speaking the language in everyday life:

> Pronunciation is becoming a big issue at the moment. If you can't carry out a conversation [in the Yaeyaman language], then however hard you try to copy the song lyrics phonetically, even though you may be able to produce an accurate imitation, it doesn't come across properly [*futsū ni haitte konai*]. I think pronunciation is really important.
>
> (interview, March 2015).

The importance of pronunciation in some ways represents the importance of Ryukyuan languages as living traditions. Most native-Ryukyuan language speakers quite rightly pride themselves on their facility with the sung language, a facility that, despite requiring special training, is almost unattainable for non-native speakers. It is also worth noting that, whereas pronunciation in spoken languages may change fairly rapidly, the high level of attention to minute details of pronunciation that is found in performed song traditions in Okinawa and many other places around the world is one way in which distinctions begin to form between sung and spoken language. It remains to be seen how the performed use of language in uta-sanshin changes as the spoken language of Okinawa continues to move further from the language of traditional song.

6. Beyond tradition

In this chapter, I looked at some of the ways that song and drama have intersected with the development Ryukyuan languages. As many examples from around the world have shown, music and performing arts would seem to be very useful in promoting minority languages and sidestepping more political considerations — music allows a degree of playfulness with language that is forgiving of grammar, vocabulary and, often, literal meaning. This certainly seems to have been true in allowing Okinawan languages to be broadcast relatively unproblematically on radio and television programs and commercials even when the language of the spoken presentation is Japanese.

One of the most striking aspects of Ryukyuan language use in music has been the presence of the sanshin. While Ryukyuan languages are still used widely in very localized ritual song traditions without sanshin accompaniment, it is notable that the majority of musical examples to break out of a very confined geographical and social context have depended on use of the sanshin. Newer Okinawan songs that do not employ the sanshin have, in contrast, not used Okinawan languages. There are several notable exceptions, such as Sadoyama Yutaka's *Duchui munī*, the songs of the Miyako singer Shimoji Isamu or, more recently, the songs of the Ishigaki band Kīyama Shōten, yet such examples are still quite unusual.

Part of the attraction of Okinawan music for many non-Okinawan speakers is undoubtedly the exoticism of the Okinawan language, at once both related to and yet very different from the Japanese language. But at the same time, for many listeners, the language, and even the singing style, are peripheral to the sound of the sanshin itself. One of the top selling Okinawan music cds in recent years has been the 2005 release *Sanshin Plays Okinawan Songs*. Takara Masahiro, the owner of the Takara Record store in Naha that produced the release, told me that the impetus for the cd came from a large number of requests from Japanese tourists for a recording of Okinawan music 'with the sanshin, but without singing'[18]. With the exception of a very small number of exceptions, the traditional Okinawan musical repertory contains almost no instrumental pieces, and this cd of 'songs without voices', although it focuses on traditional and modern Okinawan song melodies, is an unusual experiment. This example shows how, for many outsiders and maybe Okinawans too, while the sanshin may be accessible and 'soothing'[19], the Okinawan language and voice production is either too incomprehensible or too old-fashioned to make for easy listening.

There is no doubt that the sanshin is an important emblem of Okinawan identity and pride, and has been invaluable in supporting the use of Okinawan languages. Without wishing to criticize the rich musical tradition of Okinawa, I also argue that there is perhaps a danger, in the very close relationship of the sanshin and Okinawan language, of a kind of self-folklorization of Okinawan, where the language is not given the freedom to express issues outside 'Okinawan-ness'. The Okinawan novelist and playwright Ōshiro Tatsuhiro, whose huge output has included works in both Japanese and Okinawan languages, wrote in 1955 of the difficulty of creating a sense of 'modernity' and 'realism' in plays using the Okinawa language of the Uchinā shibai (Ōshiro 1990: 142-147). Partly because of their strong relationship with tradition and with the past, a relationship that is promoted by the connection with traditional music, Ōshiro (and other Okinawans) have had difficulty in reimagining Ryukyuan as a living, modern language.

To give another (only slightly musical) example, in a recent television program featuring the popular Okinawan comedian Jun senshu, a proficient speaker of the Ryukyuan dialect of the Okinawan mainland, created humour by attempting to order a meal at a drive-through restaurant entirely in the Okinawan language. Part of the humour came from the fact that the young female assistant was unable to understand most of what was being said, but the main joke came from the fact that, rather than using imported terms for French fries or hamburgers, as is done in Japanese, Jun translated these terms using only existing Okinawan words. The joke was further emphasized by his performance of an Okinawan language parody of the Japanese band Golden Bomber's 2010 hit song *Memeshikute* (Like a woman), emphasizing the 'unnatural' sound of the Okinawan language in a pop song context. This 'unnaturalness' comes, of course, because listeners are not used to hearing Okinawan used in this way.

One of the challenges for the maintenance of any minority language is how to move beyond very local constructions of identity based on the past, to deal with modern-day issues. While the uta-sanshin tradition has been hugely influential in providing a focus for Okinawan cultural identity, as well as providing a link to the language patterns of past generations, it remains to be seen how both Ryukyuan language and musical traditions continue to adapt to the modern world.

Note

1   組踊 The Japanese pronunciation 'kumiodori' is also commonly used.
2   My focus on sanshin-accompanied songs here is partly due to space considerations, but mainly because these songs (both from the classical repertory and more modern compositions) are by far the most culturally prominent musical genre to use the Ryukyuan languages. The largely unaccompanied ritual song repertoire that continues to be performed in villages throughout Okinawa, while an important context for language preservation, has a relatively low presence in Okinawan cultural life outside the village level. There have also been surprisingly few attempts to use Okinawan languages in non-traditional musical genres. I deal with some of these later in the chapter.
3   *Min'yō* 民謡, a late 19th century Japanese translation of the German word *volkslied*, is the term most commonly used in modern Okinawa to describe the non-classical songs accompanied by sanshin. Other terms, such as *shimauta* (island songs) are also sometimes used.
4   The sanshin doesn't begin to make a regular appearance in documents until around the mid-16th century A Chinese envoy to the Okinawan mainland in 1534 reports the playing of a 'stringed instrument' in Ryūkyū, probably a version of the *sanshin*. The first use of a name for the instrument comes in the diary of an official of the Shimazu clan in southern Kyushu, who describes members of a Ryūkyū envoy in 1575 playing an instrument called the *shahisen*.

5. There are also a number of other regional traditions, such as the rich sanshin-accompanied folk song tradition of Yaeyama, which has a large number of sanshin adaptations of what were originally work songs using a combination of 5 and 4 mora phrases (for example the song *Basï nu turï*), and which are not usually classified as *ryūka*.
6. Ryukyuan song lyrics are traditionally written in Japanese/Chinese script, although often have different pronunciation from the modern Japanese norm.
7. Strictly speaking, the term *min'yō* is also used to refer to all non-classical song genres in Okinawa. I use the term here to refer to the sanshin-accompanied songs that are not part of the classical Ryukyu court tradition.
8. Like kumiudui, the language of Uchinā shibai shows many differences from everyday speech (Maeda 1981: 52), but is based on the language of Naha. Early *kageki* plays while performed in an adapted version of the Naha dialect, were often based on scenarios written in the Japanese language, with dialogue improvised in Okinawan by the actors while onstage. For this reason, there are usually no original scripts for these early plays, and scripts that do exist were usually transcriptions of particular performances rather than blueprints created before the play was performed. In the latter 20th century, as *kageki* and *shibai* became progressively canonized, so productions increasingly began to follow fixed versions of these plays. Even in modern times, Okinawan language plays are often written in Japanese for subsequent translation into Okinawan.
9. Bise Katsu, interview April 2014.
10. http://www.rokinawa.co.jp/event/images/niuta22moushikomi.pdf accessed 13th June 2014.
11. Written 三味線 rather than the more common 三線
12. http://www.crest-ryukyu.co.jp/uchina/ accessed 27th April 2015.
13. http://www.otv.jp/kyougeki/ accessed 30th June 2014.
14. http://ryukyushimpo.jp/news/storyid-150967-storytopic-5.html accessed 25th June 2014.
15. http://sumamuni.ti-da.net/ accessed 29th June 2014.
16. http://taru.ti-da.net/ accessed 16th June 2014.
17. http://sumamuni.ti-da.net/ accessed 16th June 2014.
18. Facebook post, and subsequent e-mail correspondence with the author, 25th June 2014. Takara also told me that a separate instrumental cd (Cao Xuejing 2002) of Okinawan song melodies played on the Chinese erhu (fiddle) had sold over 100,000 copies.
19. One of the buzzwords of the recent Okinawan music boom in Japan has been '*iyashi*' — healing.

References

Barthes, Roland (1977) *Image, music, text*. New York: Noonday Press.
Brocken, Michael (2003) *The British folk revival* 1944-2002. Aldershot: Ashgate.
Christopher, Emma (2013) "Josefa Diago and the Origins of Cuba's Gangá Traditions." *Transition*

111, no. 1: 132–44.

Grant, Catherine (2010) "The Links between Safeguarding Language and Safeguarding Musical Heritage." *International Journal of Intangible Heritage* 5: 45–59.

Grant, Catherine (July 2011) "Key Factors in the Sustainability of Languages and Music: A Comparative Study." *Musicology Australia* 33, no. 1: 95–113.

Hinton, Leanne (1984) *Havasupai Songs : A Linguistic Perspective*. Tübingen: Gunter Narr Verlag.

Majikina, Ankō (1974, 1929) "*Kumiodori to Nōgaku to no kōsatsu* [Thoughts on the relationship between Kumiudui and Noh]", in F. Iha *Iha Fuyū Zenshū* vol. 3, 323-356, Tokyo: Heibon-sha.

Majikina Yūkō Seitan 100 nen kinen jigyōkai (eds.) (1989) *Majikina Yūkō Seitan 100 nen kinen geinō kōen* [performance program].

Sparling, Heather (2007) "One foot on either side of the chasm" *Shima: The International Journal of Research into Island Cultures* 1, no. 1.

Trudgill, Peter (1983) *On Dialect: Social and Geographical Perspectives*. Oxford: Basil Blackwell.

大城 立裕（1990）『沖縄演劇の魅力』那覇：沖縄タイムス社,『大城立裕全集』東京：勉誠出版、2002。

沖縄県教育文化資料センター（編）（2003）『新編沖縄の文学』沖縄時事出版．
沖縄文化協会（編）（1975）『沖縄の伝統文化』那覇：沖縄タイムス社．
伊波 普猷（1974）『伊波普猷全集 Vol. 3』東京：平凡社．
伊波 普猷（1975）『伊波普猷全集 Vol. 8』東京：平凡社．
大野 道雄（2003）『沖縄芝居とその周辺』名古屋：みずほ出版．
片桐 洋一（1998）『古今和歌集全評釈〈上〉』Tōkyō: 講談社．
島袋 盛敏（1964）『琉歌大観』NP: 博栄社．
外間 守善（1971）『南島古謡』東京：三一書房．
備瀬 喜勝、松田 一利（編）（2010）『沖縄民謡　歌詞集』沖縄：キャンパス．
宮良 当壮（1980）『宮良当壮全集』第一書房．
半田 一郎（1999）『琉球語辞典──那覇・首里を中心とする沖縄広域語準拠』東京：大学書林．
真栄田 勝朗（1981）『琉球芝居物語』青磁社．
矢野 輝雄（1993）『沖縄芸能史話．新訂増補版』榕樹社．
黒田 勇（1999）『ラジオ体操の誕生』東京：青弓社．

Recordings

『親子ラジオは島うたラジオ』キャンパス BYC-13、2013
『Sanshin Plays Okinawan Songs』CHIKUTEN, 2005
『ラジオ体操第1 お国言葉編』テイチクエンタテインメント、2013

『ラジオ体操第1 ご当地版』日本コロムビア、2013

This work was supported by JSPS Kakenhi Grant Number 26370108.

第 11 章　要約

唄、言語、文化
沖縄の「唄三線」伝統における琉球諸語

マット・ギラン（国際基督教大学）　　　　　　　　　　　（松井真之介訳）

　沖縄は、現代日本で最も重要かつ成功した伝統音楽シーンの本拠地の一つである。三線（三つの弦を張るリュート型の撥弦楽器）の伴奏で歌われる琉球語による唄は、あらゆる年代やさまざまな背景を持つ沖縄人にとって一般的な娯楽であった。古の琉球王朝の宮廷で発展した古典的なレパートリー（「古典」）も、沖縄の村落の民俗歌謡（民謡）のどちらも非常に人気となったので、今ではおそらくアマチュア、プロフェッショナル問わず、琉球諸語による三線伴奏の歌い手は過去のどんな時期よりも存在していることだろう。沖縄の二大放送局では1950年代以降、伝統音楽と伝統的舞台芸能の紹介を活発に行ってきており、沖縄のレコード会社は琉球諸語による伝統歌謡および新曲をリリースし続けている。1972年以降、日本政府は沖縄音楽と沖縄舞踊の文化財指定を継続して行っているが、それは沖縄が伝統芸能において他の都道府県より多くの生きた民俗遺産を持っているということを意味する。伝統的な沖縄芸能の文化的重要性を評価する一端として、日本政府は2004年に国立劇場おきなわの建設資金を提供している。これは日本に5つしかない国立劇場の1つであり、沖縄の古典的な音楽劇であるクミウドゥイ（くみおどり、組踊）の復活を促進している。

　伝統歌謡と伝統演劇の成功は、日常生活における琉球諸語の継続的な衰退と際立った対照をなしてきた。少なくとも彼らの生活の音楽に関わりない部分においてはもっぱら日本語のモノリンガルである多くの沖縄人にとって、唄というものは彼ら自身が歌うか、あるいはラジオやテレビや録音、ライヴを聞くなどより受動的な関係を通じてかいずれかにおいて、琉球諸語にふれあう最も直接的で重要な手段の一つである。今日の沖縄において言語の生き

残りと保存の問題を考える際、音楽と舞台芸能は明らかに重要な価値をもつのである。同時に、歌における少数言語の文化的地位と、日常の話し言葉における文化的地位はかなり異なっており、それらはかなり異なった別個のルールと想定のもとで発展してきたのである。

　本章において、発表者は唄、特に三線の伴奏による唄における琉球諸語の使用について検討し、音楽が危機言語の保存や使用奨励の手段になる際に生じる諸問題を考察する。どのようにして音楽は言語保持に有用であるのか？どのようにして言語は唄という文脈の中において構築され、扱われるのか？音楽が言語保全のもっとも重要な手段の一つとなる際にはどのような問題が生じるのか？　多くの場合、唄でなされる言語選択は日常の話し言葉においてなされるそれとはかなり異なっており、その選択はしばしばかなり特別なルールと想定によって結び付けられていることを発表者は議論する。同時に、唄は話し言葉が入れられ演じられる単なる手段というだけではなく、言語が活発に構築され行き交わされる場であるのだ。

　琉球諸語の発展は長い間、唄と舞台芸能が複雑に絡み合っており、20世紀以前はそれらを切り離して存立させることはほぼ考えられないことであっただろう。沖縄には黙読を想定している中国語もしくは日本語の文学作品（例えば平敷屋朝敏の、18世紀の日本語による物語など）の比較的長い伝統がある一方で、歌謡もしくは演劇と結びつかない琉球諸語の文学作品はほとんど見当たらない。伊波普猷、宮良當壯、外間守善のような20世紀沖縄の言語学者たちは、琉球諸語についての画期的な研究の中で、琉球の唄と演劇のテクストについて多く描いている。

　20世紀以前の舞台用の琉球文学の演目の中で、現在最も人気のあるジャンルは断然古典的歌謡（古典）と、20世紀初頭から重要になった古典に関連する民俗歌謡（民謡）である。このどちらも三線を伴って奏される。三線とは、蛇皮の共鳴膜をつけた三絃のリュート型撥弦楽器であり、14世紀末以降の時期に中国の福建地方から沖縄本島にもたらされたことがほぼ確実となっている。三線の導入は、8-8-8-6拍の韻文で構成される全く新しい形式による詩作の創出を生み出すくらい重要なことであった。「琉歌」として知られる

形式である。ほとんどの琉歌で使われる言葉は、表向きには沖縄本島の首里村の方言である一方で、唄三線のレパートリーは、そこで使われている琉球諸語が日本語の語彙や文法、考え方から著しく影響を受けたものでもある。

琉球処分および日本国への沖縄編入にともない、それまで宮廷の庇護のもと管理されていた宮廷芸師たちは一般大衆への有料興行でもって生計を立てなければいけない事態に直面した。その一つの結実が「歌劇」（歌劇、唄芝居）や後の「ウチナーシバイ」（沖縄芝居）のような、唄と琉球語による問答が合体した新しい演劇の創出であった。ある程度、芝居と歌劇は早くに一般の沖縄人の人気を獲得したため、20世紀初頭には沖縄の支配エリートおよび警察権力からの攻撃を受けることになり、1940年代までには琉球諸語によるあらゆる演劇上演が禁止されることとなった。

第二次大戦以降、日本と沖縄の差異を強調するため、米国軍政府は琉球諸語による伝統芸能の普及に比較的力を注いだ。この時期にラジオという新しいメディアも伝統音楽や伝統演劇の普及にとって重要となり始める。しかし公共放送における琉球諸語の使用は散発的であり、世界の多くの少数言語文化と比べると、沖縄は琉球諸語の話し言葉による放送の提供に関しては相対的に緩やかであった。放送における琉球諸語の使用で最も顕著なことは、少なくともいくつかの伝統音楽を使用する機会を作ったことである。沖縄の主要な二つの放送局には、ROKラジオ沖縄が毎年行う「ミィウタ大賞」（新唄大賞）コンテストのような、新しい音楽素材での創作を積極的に促す長時間の番組を持つと同時に、どちらも琉球諸語による古典歌謡と民謡を流す長時間の番組がある。

ローカルTV放送局における琉球諸語の使用は、ラジオ同様著しく音楽、舞踊、芝居における使用によるところが大きい。そしてそこにはほとんどのラジオ番組でと同じように、番組DJが使う話し言葉——ほぼ通常の日本語共通語——と番組が力を入れる歌や芝居の言語——琉球語——の著しい隔たりがあるのだ。

琉球諸語は近年かなり頻繁に沖縄のTVコマーシャルでも使われており、他の放送形式でも同様に、音楽は琉球言語を視聴者の「好みにあうものに」

する重要な手段である。この文脈において琉球語の使用というものは、沖縄人の生活における言語の地位についてよく示してもいる。琉球語が使われる場合、その製品は通常表向きは「沖縄製」のものか、琉球語を第一言語として使い続けている高齢の視聴者向けのものであるか、ということである。

音楽を通じた琉球語の維持保存に向けた最近の動きとして、「ラジオ体操」の歌と呼ばれるものの琉球語ヴァージョンの創出がある。ラジオ体操とは1920年代以来、日本の主要なラジオ局で毎日放送されているラジオ発の柔軟体操である。これら琉球語の「ラジオ体操」の歌は、日本全国にわたってローカル言語の使用とコミュニティ精神を同時に促進させるより大きな動きへのきっかけにもなったのである。これは近年の、日本語の方言ヴァージョンによるコンピレーションCDからも明らかだろう。発表者は、このような日本語方言の文脈内における琉球言語の売り出し方が、琉球語の政治的地位に何か影響を与えているかどうか考察する。

琉球諸語の普及のため使われるテクノロジーやメディアにおけるより近年の発展形態としては、インターネットの使用を通じたものが見受けられるだろう。個人ブログや個人ホームページからフェイスブックのコミュニティやオンラインのデータベースにいたるまで、その使用例は多岐にわたっている。初期のラジオやテレビ放送と同じように、インターネット上での琉球諸語学習の主な目的の一つは歌と音楽である。発表者はこのような例についてもここで考察する。

最後に、発表者は、唄三線上演時の発音の問題を考察する。発音は現代沖縄の音楽世界に関する発表者の調査において特に重要なものであり、それは階級および地域のアイデンティティ両方の問題と密接につながっている。話し言葉における発音がかなり急速に変化しうる一方、沖縄および世界中の多くの場所で上演される唄の伝統において見受けられる発音の細かい違いへの高度な注意は、言語の固定性というものが言語に課される過程であり、それゆえ唄の言葉と話し言葉の間に生じる差異の原因でもある。沖縄の話し言葉が伝統歌謡の言語から隔たり続けたように、唄三線において言語の実際の使用法がどのように変化したかは今後の課題である。

音楽における琉球語使用の最も際立った面は、三線の存在であった。琉球諸語が非常にローカルな儀礼歌唱の伝統において三線の伴奏なしで未だに広く使われている一方、非常に狭い地理的社会的文脈から飛び出した大部分の音楽は、三線の使用に依ってきたことは注目すべきである。このように、三線は琉球諸語の生存にとって有益である一方で、発表者は言語にとって、発展し現代化される余地を与えられることが重要であることも議論したい。

　本研究はJSPS科研費JP26370108の助成を受けたものです。

Chapter 12
Identification and Practical Situation of Endangered Languages in China

Huang Xing (Chinese Academy of Social Sciences) Bao Lianqun (Oita University)

With modernization and globalization, some ethnic languages and Chinese dialects are showing different levels of endangerment on the mainland of China. To save and maintain those languages in danger, Chinese government bureaus, such as the Ministry of Education and the State Ethnic Affairs Commission, have formulated a series of language policies and language planning. However, language maintenance involves a systematic process, including how do identify a language as endangered, which minority language should be defined as endangered, how to implement the language policies, how to make a language survey, and how to develop endangered languages' multimedia database.

1. The Problem of Language Identification

When we talk about endangered languages, we should firstly solve the problem of 'language identification'. If a language that has only one variety is endangered, it means that the language is endangered. However, if the endangered variety is merely one of the dialects of the language and the other dialects (especially lingua franca) still have functions such as social interaction or cultural heritage, it means the language is not endangered.

Currently, there is no recognized criteria for language identification. International academia usually follows the criteria of intelligibility and identity, which declares that varieties do not belong to one language only if they can mutually communicate and native speakers of the varieties have common language identity.

However, pertaining to criteria for language identification, Chinese academia focus on the ethnic properties of languages and historical relationships among them, which means that an ethnic group had better share a common language. If modern varieties cannot communicate, they can be identified as a language by their cognates and common literary language. For example, though there are many obvious differences among modern dialects of Chinese, Tibetan and Mongolian, these dialects are identified as languages because of their common characters and literary languages. On account of the different criteria for language identification adopted by international organizations and Chinese academia based on the same language facts, their results are very different regarding the quantity of languages. That is to say, the 130 languages in China (including China mainland, Hong Kong, Macau and Taiwan) identified by Chinese academia are recognized as more than 300 distinct languages by international organizations such as UNESCO, ISO and SIL international.

The disagreement between Chinese academia and international society on the identification of languages leads to the disagreement on the practical situation of endangered languages in China. For example, in the language code formulated by ISO, Mandarin (ISO code: [cmn]), Gan [gan], Huizhou [czh], Jinyu [cjy], Hakka [hak], Min Bei [mnp], Min Dong [cdo], Min Nan [nan], Min Zhong [czo], Pu-Xian [cpx], Wu [wuu], Xiang [hsn], Yue [yue] and Waxianghua [wxa] each have their own code and are identified as different languages. Except for Mandarin, all the Chinese varieties are endangered to varying degrees. However, in China, they are merely different dialects of Chinese. Therefore, Chinese, which is represented by Mandarin, is not endangered. Moreover, Buriat [bxu] and Kalmyk-Oirat [xal] are regarded as endangered languages. But in China they are merely dialects of Mongolian and Mongolian as a whole is not identified as an endangered language. Similarly, three dialects of Tibetan in China—Khams, Amdo and Central—are also identified as three languages and have their own ISO codes.

2. The Problem of Endangered Language Identification

UNESCO (2003) proposed a index containing 9 factors to evaluate the degree of language vitality and endangerment:

(1) intergenerational language transmission
(2) absolute number of speakers
(3) proportion of speakers within the total population
(4) shifts in domains of language use
(5) response to new domains and media
(6) materials for language education and literacy
(7) governmental and institutional language attitudes and policies, including official status and use
(8) community members' attitudes towards their own language
(9) type and quality of documentation

Based on the index, Huang (2013) introduced the assessment result of the language vitality and endangerment in Chinese ethnic languages. We restate his opinion here.

The traits found in Chinese ethnic languages below the definitively endangered level (3 level) include:

1. The absolute number of speakers is very few (factor 2).
2. There is a larger proportion of speakers in other languages (especially, Chinese) around (factor 3).
3. There is no character or literary language (factor 4, 5, 6, 9).
4. They are not the main languages of ethnic groups speaking them, or speakers still do not have official ethnic identity. As a result, those languages are not incorporated into the government's language plan. (factor 7)

In modern society, the language planning and policies formulated by the government are a crucial factor which effects the language use. It plays an important role in official language use, adaptation for new media, formation of characters and literary language and application to publications. Especially concerning language planning, since the government usually plays an leading role in various social activities including language projects, whether ethnic languages are planned by local governments or protected and improved through practical language projects is particularly important.

3. Protection Measures for Endangered Languages

UNESCO (2003) argues that five measures need to be taken to protect endangered languages. How these measures are carried out in China is briefly introduced below.

Basic linguistic and pedagogical training

According to *the National Common Language Law of China (2001)*, in all Chinese schools, the medium of instruction must be Mandarin. Ethnic language education is generally limited. Generally speaking, in residences of Chinese ethnic minorities where traditional ethnic writing systems are used, such as Tibetan, Mongolian, Uyghur, Kazakh and Korean, there are both primary and secondary schools which offer ethnic language courses and schools which merely teach Chinese. As for other Chinese ethnic minorities, the medium of instruction is basically Chinese. So-called bilingual teaching generally means that ethnic languages are used as supportive languages to teach and explain the content in Chinese textbooks. There are no teaching programs, textbooks and teaching methods for ethnic languages.

In modern society, if a language does not come into the mother tongue education system, it cannot last for a long time. Therefore, mother tongue education is a basic condition to protect endangered languages. But conditions of mother tongue education are very strict. At least, the language needs to be standardized and has its own writing system. Yet there are only a few ethnic languages that meet these conditions.

Sustainable development in literacy and local documentation skills

This measure means formulation of characters for unwritten ethnic languages in order to compile and publish materials for language education and literacy. Except for traditional ethnic writing systems such as Tibetan, Mongolian, Uyghur,

Kazakh, Korean, Sibo and Tai, learning from the Soviet Model, the government has formulated characters for more than ten ethnic groups such as Zhuang and Miao since 1950s. But these characters are rarely used or basically out of use. Most Chinese ethnic languages (about 100) do not have their own writing system and official and folk documents can only be written in Chinese or other dominant ethnic languages.

In the *National Intangible Cultural Heritage Law of China* issued in 2011, the first type of intangible cultural heritage is "the traditional oral literature and the language as its carrier". The other types of intangible cultural heritages are also documented and inherited in local ethnic languages or dialects. Therefore, the lack of ethnic writing symbols poses a serious barrier to recording and protecting "local documentation" of ethnic intangible cultural heritages. For this reason, some ethnic groups record and inherit their local documentation either in alphabets created by folk societies or individual scholars which have no official or legal status or in writing systems of the same ethnic languages used in foreign countries.

Supporting and developing national language policy

Systematic ethnic language policies and management systems have been established from the central government to local ethnic autonomous governments in China. They are explicitly shown in laws such as the Constitution, the Law on Regional Ethnic Autonomy and autonomous regulations in autonomous regions. However, China's economic system has become increasingly market-oriented during the recent 20 years. An obvious trait or defect of the market economy is that the market tends to pursue efficiency but ignore fairness. Undoubtedly, the language with the highest social communicative efficiency is the national common language. Thus, in China, a country where the popularity of the national common language is relatively low, the promotion of the use of the national common language in Chinese dialect areas and ethnic language areas occupies an important position. At the same time, the policy that the government consistently guarantees and protects the language right of ethnic minorities continues to be carried out.

The latest ethnic language policy of the Chinese government is shown in the National Outline for Medium- and Long-Term for Language Development and Reform (2012-2020) issued by the Chinese Ministry of Education in 2011. This document plans that the focus of the Chinese ethnic language planning by 2020 includes: (1) speeding up the promotion and popularity of the national common language in ethnic minority areas. (2) scientific protection of ethnic languages and characters. (3) standardization and informatization of ethnic languages and characters. (4) national census of ethnic languages. (5) scientifically recording and protecting ethnic languages.

Supporting and developing educational policy

The educational policy of ethnic languages is an important part of educational policy in China. Meanwhile, it faces the same problem as the ethnic language policy aforementioned, that is, the relation between mother tongue education and the promotion of the national common language in school. The way to address the problem is bilingual education. The solution put forward in the National Medium- and Long-Term Plan for Education Reform and Development (2010-2020) issued by the Chinese Ministry of Education in 2011 is promoting bilingual education. It includes: (1) offering Chinese courses and promoting the national common language. (2) respecting and protecting the right that ethnic minorities receive education in their native languages. The means by which bilingual education is carried out include teacher training, teaching research and developing and publishing textbooks.

However, it should be acknowledged that mother tongue education under the bilingual system in China is rather different from the bilingual education recommended by UNESCO. Namely, in China, "So-called mother-tongue education, however, often does not refer to education in the ancestral languages of ethnolinguistic minorities (that is, endangered languages), but rather to the teaching of these languages as school subjects. The most common educational model of teaching ethnolinguistic minority children in schools still uses locally or nationally dominant languages as the medium of instruction.".

Improving living conditions and respect for the rights of speaker communities

There is no doubt that the mother tongue right is a basic human right. Generally speaking, vulnerable groups concerning mother tongue use are also vulnerable groups on other human rights.

In the Progress in China's Human Rights Cause in 2013—the latest white paper on human rights issued by the Chinese government—20% of the entire document refers to the various rights of ethnic minorities, which declares "the government continues to carry out favorable policies for ethnic minorities and ethnic minorities are entitled to various legitimate rights". The use of the mother tongue is one of these "various legitimate rights". The mother tongue right of ethnic minorities refers in particular to the legitimate application of ethnic languages to areas such as administration, judiciary, news, publication, radio, television and education. For example, in the area of education, the bilingual education in Chinese and ethnic languages is promoted and ethnic languages can be used in the college entrance examination.

However, in China's general opinion on human rights, the most important is the survival and development right which people equally have. The survival and development right means people's access to good income, education, employment, social security, health, housing conditions and cultural services. From the perspective of the language tool which is indispensable to have this access, citizens who speak the national common language have more advantage than those who speak their uncommon mother tongue. That is, if citizens of ethnic minorities cannot fluently speak the national common language, the equal civil right that they ought to have will be effected. Therefore, creating conditions for the application and development of ethnic languages and improving the ability of ethnic minorities to speak the national common language are two requirements for ethnic minorities to have full human rights.

4. Case Study of Endangered Languages in China

According to Huang Xing (2013:154-156), authorized by UNESCO, experts of the Institute of Ethnology and Anthropology of the Chinese Academy of Social Sciences made a questionnaire survey concerning the vitality and diversity of almost all ethnic languages (105). These languages are divided into 6 levels (0-5) according to their vitality index. From the Chinese traditional viewpoint, languages above level 4 are not endangered. The survey results show that most Chinese ethnic languages belong to level 2-4 and there are only a few languages belonging to level 0 (extinct), 1 (extremely endangered) and 5 (safe). Here we will introduce two cases of endangered languages—Mongolian and Manchu in the Altaic Language Family distributed in northern China. This case study is limited to the Mongolian and Manchu used in the Heilongjiang Province. According to the criteria of language identification, Mongolian and Manchu each have their separate ISO codes and are considered as separate languages in China. Then we can measure these languages according to the protection measures aforementioned (UNESCO 2003).

If we employ the vitality level defined by Huang Xing (2013), we can find that Mongolian belongs to the level 5 (safe) while Manchu belongs to the level 0 (extinct). What should be noted is the area where the case is studied. Though Mongolians are mainly distributed in the Inner-Mongolia, there are Mongolians outside the Inner-Mongolia. Therefore, the organization that coordinates the Mongolian education in 8 provinces is set up in the Inner Mongolia.

Before we measure these languages in the light of the criteria aforementioned, we will firstly introduce the social environment, the educational situation and the language application of these languages.

Mongolians and the Mongolian Language in the Heilongjiang Province

There are 150, 000 Mongolians in the Heilongjiang Province according to the census in 2010 (Bao 2011, 2013), which account for 0.4 percent of the total population in this province. The Mongolians separately dwell in the Dorbed county (40,000), the Zhaoyuan county (17,000), the Tailai county (16,000), the Fuyu county (5,000), the suburbs of Qiqihar and the downtown of Harbin. And they are also scattered in other areas.

The Mongolians are scattered and there is no school or class teaching in Mongolian outside the Dorbed county. Therefore, as mentioned in the section 3, "In modern society, if a language does not come into the mother tongue education system, it cannot last for a long time. Therefore, mother tongue education is a basic condition to protect endangered languages." Although the Chinese government persists in protecting ethnic languages, because of the practical situation of ethnic languages and the socio-economic development, protective policies cannot be adequately implemented. Nowadays, many preschool children and Mongolian students receiving compulsory education have lost their mother tongue. They merely learn a few simple vocabulary and grammar in class through the bilingual education. In this case, it is very difficult for Mongolian as a mother tongue to be inherited. Except for some areas in the Dorbed county, the Mongolians under the age of 50 hardly use Mongolian as their family language and most people have turned to Chinese which is the national common language in China. Bao (2011, 2013) has reported the language application, attitude and linguistic traits in this area in details.

Since 2000, Bao has surveyed Mongolians and the Mongolian language in the Heilongjiang province several times and concludes that Mongolian is endangered there (2011). He wished that the Chinese government could continue to take protective measures and he also made some propositions to promote the school education (2013). Bao, Mongolian teachers of the Heilongjiang College of Education and local government officials made active efforts to promote Mongolian education in schools and to protect and inherit the Mongolian language (2013). Though ethnic languages are impacted by the current market economic system in China, the National Outline for Medium- and Long-Term for Language Development and Reform (2012-2020) issued by the Chinese Ministry of Education in 2011 still underlined the importance to scientifically record and keep ethnic languages and characters while popularizing the national common language.

The Mongolian population who speak Mongolian in the Heilongjiang province is far fewer than the standard of a 5 level language. The Mongolians speaking Mongolian account for less than 1/3 Mongolian population in the Heilongjiang province. The application of this language is increasingly narrow and it is basically not applied to the new media. Despite the fact that the Mongolians in the Heilongjiang province use *the Mongolian textbook* which is co edited by the three northeast provinces, it aims at teaching Mongolian as a second language. Though Mongolian is identified as the official language in the ethnic autonomous regulation of the Dorbed county, it merely exists in the official document and is never practically implemented. The members of the ethno-linguistic group have different attitudes to their mother tongue. However, the general attitude is that they have little option but to learn Chinese for a better job. This conforms to the human rights of ethnic minorities put forward by the Chinese central government and the survival and development right in China's human right concept mentioned in the section 3. As mentioned in the section 3, "creating conditions for the application and development of ethnic languages and improving the ability by which ethnic minorities speak the national common language are two requirements for ethnic minorities to have complete human rights."

Manchus and the Manchu language in the Heilongjiang Province

It is well-known that Manchus have a long history and rich culture. The Heilongjiang province is the place from where the ancestors of Manchus originated. The Sushen people, the ancestor of Manchu, lived there as early as 4,000 B.C (Bo Shaobu 2008). In the early 17th century, Nurhaci, the ancestor of Manchus, united all Jurchen tribes and established a regime named Jin, known to history as post Jin. In 1626, Hong Taiji,the Nurhaci's son, was enthroned. He named his ethnic group Manchu in replace of Jin or post Jin. Hong Taiji declared that the name of the regime was Qing on April 11th, 1636. The Qing dynasty held the power of the whole country for 276 years before the Republic of China was established in 1911. Hitherto, the Manchu as a national community has gone through 4 regimes including the Ming dynasty, the Qing dynasty, the ROC and the PRC for 379 years.

Manchu belongs to the Tunguska group in the Altaic Language Family. It has a genetic relationship with many languages in China such as Hezhen, Sibo, Oroqen and Evenki. Manchu originates from Jurchen and 70% vocabularies of Manchu is in common with Jurchen and the other vocabularies are also related (Bo Shao Bu 2008: 147). In the Qing dynasty, Manchu is called "nation language" or "Qing language". Manchu is an agglutinative language and its characters were created in 1599 when Nurhaci asked for Erdene Gagai and other scholars to create it modeled after the Mongolian character and refered to the phonetic traits of Manchu. In 1632, Hong taiji asked for Dahai to improve the old Manchu character and added markers to characters in order to distinguish phonemes which could not have been distinguished before. Afterwards, this improved character was called the marked Manchu character or the new Manchu character in order to distinguish it from the old Manchu character.

Shortly after Manchus controlled the whole country, the Manchu language began to fall into decline during the period of Qianlong. After the People's Republic of China was established, the new China government encouraged to learn and protect ethnic languages. In the Article 13 of the Certain Provisions of the Law on Regional Ethnic Autonomy issued by the General Office of the State Council in 2005, it is clearly defined that "the state guarantees the freedom of ethnic minorities to use and develop their languages and characters…encourages people of all nationalities to mutually learn languages in national autonomous areas." However, the situation of Manchu has not improved and the anticipated goal mentioned has not been achieved. Nowadays, Manchu is classified as a "dying" language without any vitality (Huang 2013: 12). With the globalization speeding up, more and more ethnic minorities citizens have learned and grasped Chinese. Thus the Manchu-speaking population increasingly declines and the function of Manchu is increasingly weaker. The Manchu language has become an endangered language. With the initiation of the research project to protect endangered languages in China, local government, residents and researchers have made efforts to protect the language and culture of Manchu.

According to the census in 2010, the population of Manchu is 10,410,585. Manchu is the third largest ethnic minority in China. There are 5,336,895 Manchus in the Liaoning province which account for 51.26% of the Manchu population in China. Six Manchu autonomous counties are set up there. According to the fifth census in 2000, there are 1,037,080 Manchus in the Heilongjiang province (Bo Shaobu 2008: 92). That is to say, nearly 1/10 Manchus live in the Heilongjiang province. There are 206 Manchu villages in the Heilongjiang province and five villages of them are set up with other ethnic groups. Though there are so many Manchu villages, even nationally, the largest concentration of Manchu native speakers is the Sanjiazi village in the Fuyu county of the Heilongjiang province. There are few or no Manchu speakers in the other villages. Huang (2013) classifies Manchu as a "dying" language. Manchu is rarely or not used in daily communication. Nevertheless, nearly ten old people can speak Manchu in the Sanjiazi village. Recently, many Manchus have voluntarily begun to learn Manchu in China. Manchu classes are also set up in some areas such as Beijing and the Liaoning province. The government of the Fuyu county of the Heilongjiang province led an activity to protect and save the language and culture of Manchus in the Sanjiazi village. We surveyed Manchu speakers in the Sanjiazi village in March 2012, March and September 2013.

In the 17th century, three military families attached to the Qiqihar navy—Ji, Meng and Fu—settled in the Sanjiazi village (literally, three families). Hence the village get its name. There are 300 households and 1000 residents now. 60 percent of the residents are Manchus. The Sanjiazi village (ilan boo) is the only Manchu village (tokso) where Manchu speakers concentrate. Therefore, the Manchu langauge in the Sanjiazi village is called "the living fossil of the Manchu langauge" by the Chinese government. Though there are 10 people speaking Manchu there, their language competences are different.

The Chinese government has made efforts to protect Manchu. For example, the Sanjiazi village was designated as "the ethnic custom habits tourist area". In order to protect and inherit the language and culture, the local government has taken the measures described below.

The government of the Fuyu county invested money in repairing old houses in the Sanjiazi village. In 2006, the government built a new school building and improved the educational condition. The Manchu staff room is set up and Manchu teachers themselves edit a Manchu Reader. A simple museum was also established in the school of the villlage. Historical stories about Manchu people was put up with pictures everywhere. At the same time, a Manchu teacher's salary was also increased. All students begin to learn Manchu from grade 3. Manchu courses are also set up in the middle school of the Youyi town in the Fuyu county. The government of the Fuyu county in Qiqihar sent 6 Manchu teachers to the Heilongjiang University for further education in order to improve their teaching standards. They also designated 16 Manchu as "Manchu language and culture bearers" and gave them 200 yuan in order to encourage them to inherit the language and culture of Manchu.

Except for the Manchu primary school in the Sanjiazi village, Bao Lianqun also surveyed the practical situation of the Manchu education in the Zhalong central primary school in Qiqihar. This school runs Manchu language or cultural courses once a week (Bao 2015).

On August 3-5, 2010, the "National Symposium on Manchu language and culture in Sanjiazi village" was held by the minority language and culture college of the Minzu University of China, research center of Manchu language and culture of the Heilongjiang University and the local government of the Fuyu county. Promotional DVDs for propaganda purposes were also produced. By this means, they set the foundations for inheriting Manchu language and culture. There were 49 students in the Sanjiazi Manchu school and 31 of them are ethnic minority students. Though they learn Manchu in the primary school, they stop learning in the middle school. Therefore, as things stand, the goal to transmit the Manchu language and culture is still not achieved.

5. Conclusion

In this paper, we introduced the language identification criteria in China and foreign countries, the language endangerment criteria and protection measures for endangered languages. We also introduced case studies of endangered languages. As mentioned in section 3, "so-called mother-tongue education, however, often does not refer to education in the ancestral languages of ethnolinguistic minorities (that is, endangered languages), but rather to the teaching of these languages as school subjects." Obviously, this is usually not conducive to protecting ethnic languages. By analyzing the practical situation of Mongolian and Manchu, we can recognize the difficulty in protecting and inheriting endangered languages. Meanwhile, it is necessary for us to summarize our work so that we can implement and support ethnic minorites' legitimate rights issued by the Chinese government and improve the human rights of ethnic groups whose language is endangered. By these means, the situation of endangered ethnic languages will be improved and the human rights of ethnic minorities will be safeguarded. Only in this way, can the harmonious society where all nationalities in China develop and prosper be established.

References
M. Paul Lewis et al. (2009, 2013) Ethnologue: Languages of the World, Dallas.
UNESCO (2003) UNESCO Survey: Linguistic Vitality and Diversity, Paris.

包聯群（2011）『言語接触と言語変異──中国黒龍江省ドルブットモンゴル族コミュニティ言語を事例として』、現代図書。
包聯群（2013）「モンゴル人コミュニティの言語維持、言語継承と言語復興」、『現代中国における言語政策と言語継承』（第1巻）、包聯群編著、三元社、47-94頁。
包聯群（2015）「消滅の危機に瀕する満州語の社会言語学的研究──中国黒龍江省を事例として」、『現代中国における言語政策と言語継承』（第2巻）、包聯群編著、三元社、127-176頁。
波・少布（2008）『黑龙江满族』、哈尔滨出版社。
黄行（2013）"中国少数民族语言传承状况因素分析"，『現代中国言語政策と言語継承』、（包聯群編著）、三元社、153-164頁。
黄行（2009）"语言识别与语言群体认同"，『民族翻译』第2期。
中国国务院新闻办（2014年5月）『2013年中国人权事业的进展』、白皮书。
中国教育部（2010年7月）『国家中长期教育改革和发展规划纲要（2010-2020年)』。
中国教育部国家语委（2012年12月）《国家中长期语言文字事业改革和发展规划纲要（2012-2020年)》（教语用[2012] 1号文件）。
中国全国人大（2000年10月）『中华人民共和国通用语言文字法』。
中国全国人大（2001年2月）『中华人民共和国民族区域自治法』(修订)。

第 12 章　要約

中国における危機言語の認定基準及び使用状況

黄行（中国社会科学院）、包聯群（大分大学）

　近代化やグローバル化により、中国において少数民族言語と中国語方言の一部はすでにそれぞれ異なる程度の危機的傾向にある。そのため、中国教育部、国家民族委員会などの言語文字を主管する中国政府関連部局は、危機言語を救助し保護する一連の政策と計画を制定した。危機言語を救助し保護するというのが一つの系統的なプロジェクトであり、具体的には、危機言語の認定基準、少数民族危機言語の選出認定、危機言語保護の執行基準、危機言語の調査と保護の操作規範、危機言語のマルチメディアコーパスの開発などの重要な内容に及ぶものである。

　現在、危機言語を認定する国際基準（例えば、UNESCO & SIL Internationalが提案した基準）を参考にしたうえで、中国の国内事情を勘案し、中国における危機言語の基準に関する調査研究と論証及び制定作業を行う必要がある。

　本稿の初頭部分では、中国と国際社会における言語の系統分類の認定基準の差異について論じた。同様な言語事実に対して、言語の系統分類の認定基準が異なることによって、中国学界と国際組織は中国の言語識別と区分の結果においてその類別と数で非常にかけ離れている。即ち、中国学界は中国の言語を約130種類と認証したが、UNESCO、ISOとSIL Internationalなどの国際組織は、その言語及びその下位にある多数の方言も含めて300種類ぐらいの独立言語と認証している。このような中国の言語の系統分類認証の不一致は、中国の危機言語の状況に対する両者の認識に、大きな差が存在することを反映している。

　第二節では、ユネスコの危機言語専門家が2003年に発表した「言語活力と言語危機」の文書を参照にし、「言語活力」の危機レベルを評価する9項

目の主要指標を提案した。中国少数民族の「言語活力と言語危機」をこうして評価したことは、著しく危機レベル及びそれ以下にある中国少数民族言語のすべてが以下のような特徴を持つことを証明できる。

（1）使用言語の絶対的人口が少ないこと。（2）周辺にはさらなる大きな言語群が分布し、特に周囲に漢語しかないこと。（3）文字と書き言葉を持たないこと。(4)すべてが所属民族の主体言語ではなく、コミュニティの民族アイデンティティがまだ定められていない言語を使用していること。その理由で政府の言語発展管理の計画などに盛り込まれていないなどの共同の特徴がある。

第三節では、ユネスコの危機言語専門家が「言語活力と言語危機」で提案した危機言語を保護するために取るべき5項目の措置が中国でどのように実施されているかについて検討した。

（1）「基本的な言語学と教育訓練」。中国の法律では、あらゆる学校の教育言語は標準中国語で行わなければならないと定めている。ただしモンゴル語、チベット語、ウイグル語、ハサク語、朝鮮語などの地方少数民族中学校において民族言語のカリキュラムを開設できるが、他の少数民族地域の学校では、基本的に中国語のみで授業を行うことになる。

（2）「読み書き能力の育成と地元言語の記録技能の面においての持続発展の実現」、中国において、モンゴル語、チベット語、ウイグル語、ハサク語、キルギス語、朝鮮語、シベ語、タイ語などの伝統的な民族文字以外、多くの少数民族言語（おおよそ100種類）は当民族の伝統文字や文学などがなく、当地域の政府と民間の書き言葉による活動や文献記録などは中国語を使用しなければならない。

（3）「国家の言語政策への支持と改善」。中国において、中央政府から民族自治地方まで少数民族の言語政策と管理体制は系統的に形成されたが、ここ20年ほどで、中国の経済体制は日増しに市場化へ転向し、社会コミュニケーションの効率が最も高い国家共通の標準中国語（「普通話」）は市場効率が低い民族言語を徐々に取って代わることにいたった。このため、国家共通語（普通話）を普及させることが最も重要な位置に置かれることになった。

(4)「教育政策への支持と改善」。中国の少数民族の児童は、学校で受ける最も一般的な教育パターンは依然として当地域あるいは国の強勢言語を用いて教育の媒介語としている。

　(5)「生活条件を改善し、危機言語を持つ人々の人権を尊重する」。政府が公表した「中国人権報告」では、公民平等の「生存権と発展権」は最も重要な「人権」であると見なされている。中国政府は、公民は国家共通語（標準中国語）を学ぶ行為を、「人権」を得るもので、これらの「人権」を獲得するのは非共用の母語のそれよりもさらに将来性があり、明らかに優勢であると見なしている。一方、少数民族のために母語を使用し発展する条件をつくることと少数民族が国家共通語の運用能力を向上することは少数民族が公民の「人権」を十分に享有するものであり、この二つを必須的な基本保障と見なしている。

　第四節では、中国の言語活力において、最高レベル（活力がある）と最低レベル（活力がない）にある二つの少数言語（モンゴル語と満洲語）を事例として、その使用状況、言語教育、家庭での使用状況及びその言語継承の実態などについて紹介する。モンゴル語は内モンゴルにおいて、政府用言語とされているが、内モンゴル以外の地域でこのような規定がない。黒龍江省ドルブットモンゴル族自治県において、モンゴル人の母語流失状況が非常に厳しく、明らかに危機傾向にある。また、中国において、満洲人は1000万人を超えており、その数は漢民族とチワン族の次である。清代において、満洲語はかつて中国の国語であったが、現代満洲語はすでに「死亡」に近い危機言語になってしまった。そのため、黒龍江省富裕県、遼寧省など満洲人が集中的に居住する地域の政府は残されている満洲言語と文化の保護や救助活動を展開している。しかし、効果があまり見られず、満洲語を継承する目的に達していないのが実情である。

Chapter 13
Endangered Language Speakers Networking: Thailand's Mahidol Model for Language Revitalization and Maintenance

Suwilai Premsrirat (Mahidol University, Thailand)

1. Introduction

Language is humankind's principle tool for interacting and for expressing ideas, emotions, knowledge, memories and values. Languages are also primary vehicles for expressions of intangible cultural heritage, essential to the identity of individuals and groups. However, because of globalization, modern economic development, mass media and urban culture have played a large role in the destruction of indigenous languages and cultures in various parts of the world. Nationalism, as seen in the language policy of countries which promote only one official language at all levels of education and in the mass media, has speeded up the decline in the use and existence of local vernacular languages. It is, therefore, an unavoidable fact that the world's linguistic and culture diversity is currently under siege. Languages — and the individual cultures they represent — are disappearing at an alarming rate. The numbers may be as drastic as the catastrophic loss of 90% predicted by linguist Michael Krauss, Director of the Alaska National Language Center, or closer to some of the more 'optimistic' projections that see only half of the world's languages dead or dying by the end of this century - the majority of them minority languages.

However, there are increasing responses at the global level to seek better ways of supporting the speakers of endangered languages whose strong commitment to their mother tongue is the most crucial factor for language maintenance and ensuring sustainable result. There are also reports of effective community involvement and experience in safeguarding and revitalizing endangered languages and a number of national language policy initiatives that support such efforts. In Thailand, at least 15 out of the 70 languages in the nation are classified as seriously endangered (Suwilai 2007). Other languages are not safe and show signs of contraction whereas the large language groups in the border regions are facing language identity issues, cultural conflict, and political unrest, especially in Thailand's deep south.

This paper discusses the community-based language revitalization model generally known as the "Mahidol Model" for working on language revitalization and maintenance. It is the result of a 10-year cooperative effort between 23 ethnolinguistic communities, Mahidol linguists and their partners in related fields such as education, botany and public health. A special focus is the networking among speakers of endangered languages themselves and the stakeholders from private and government agencies, as well as international organizations.

2. The Language Situation in Thailand[1]

Thailand is situated at the heart of Southeast Asia and is one of the most complex areas of languages and ethnicities in the subregion.

The 70+ languages of Thailand belong to five language families: Austroasiatic (22), Austronesian (3), Tai (24), Sino-Tibetan (19), and Hmong-Mian (2) (Premsrirat, 2004). These languages are hierarchically interrelated within Thai society, with standard Thai, the official and national language, occupying the highest position. Immediately below Thai in the hierarchy are its major regional variants: Kammuang (Northern Thai), Lao Isan (Northeastern Thai), Paktay (Southern Thai), and Thai Klang (Central Thai), each acting as the lingua franca of local communities. Lower still are a number of ethnic minority languages, several of which are at risk of extinction (on which more below). Ethnic minority speakers are therefore bilingual or multilingual and live in a diaglossic environment. They speak their ethnic language at home with family, neighbors, and members of their ethnic group. They speak the regional variant of the national language or the national language itself in social domains where the situation demands or when the people they are speaking to do not understand their ethnic language. In schools and government offices, on formal occasions, and in the mass media, only standard Thai is used.

At present, at least 15 ethnic languages in Thailand are considered severely endangered. They are small-enclave languages surrounded by larger language groups and are scattered over various parts of the country. Nine of these languages belong to the Austroasiatic family and are indigenous to mainland Southeast Asia. These are: Chong, Kasong, Samre, Chung, So (Thavung), Nyah Kur, Lavua, Maniq, and Mlabri. Three belong to the Sino-Tibetan family: Gong, Mpi, and Bisu. Two are Austronesian: Urak Lawoi and Moken/Moklen, and one is Tai: Saek. Among these, Kasong, Samre, and Chung have no realistic hope of surviving the death of the last few elderly speakers, and they are being documented as extensively as possible. Meanwhile, languages with more speakers, including Thailand (or Northern) Khmer, Mon, and Patani Malay, are declining, and even regional variants of Thai such as Kammuang (Northern Thai), Paktai (Southern Thai), or Lao Isan (Northeastern Thai) are not safe and are showing signs of contraction, especially in the areas of vocabulary and grammar. Only standard Thai is safe (cf. Suwilai Premsrirat 2007).

Large language groups in border regions are not only facing the problem of language decline among the younger generation, but most cannot access government services such as education, health or justice. In general, ethnic minority peoples are considered, by outsiders, as slow or underachieving and not likely to succeed in the modern development process. In some areas such as in Thailand's Deep South where the majority of the population are Muslim Melayu-Thai speakers, there is resistance to many government services. The language identity issue and cultural conflict are amongst underlying factors contributing to violence and political unrest.

Using the eight stages of Fishman's Graded Intergenerational Disruption Scales (GIDs) (Figure 4), the degree of language endangerment in Thailand can be identified. We have found that all languages in Thailand, large and small, with the exception of Standard Thai (official language) are classified as being on the weak side for reversing language shift. However, there are attempt to use the Mother Tongue - Based Bi/Multilingual Education in pre-primary and primary school in larger language groups at the border such as Patani Malay in the south, Mon in the west, Thailand Khmer in the northeast, and some hill tribes in the north such as Hmong and Karen. Pilot projects are conducted as action research based projects in government schools. If this bi/multilingual approach is sustained, the status of these languages could move down to stage 4 on the strong side, while languages that are taught as a subject in school could move down to stage 5 on the weak side. Chong, Nyah Kur, So (Kusuman), So (Thavung), and Lavua. Other languages are on stage 6 if still used in the home, such Lavua (Papae), or stage 7 if only elderly people can still speak it such as Chong, Nyah Kur, Thavung, and Gong and stage 8 if there only a few living speakers as with Samre, Chung and Kasong.

Weak side	Stage 8	So few fluent speakers that community needs to re-establish language norms; often requires outside experts (e.g., linguists). *[Kasong, Samre and Chung (Sa-oc)]*
	Stage 7	Older generation uses language enthusiastically but children are not learning it. *[Chong, Lawa (Gong), S o(Thavung), Nyahkur]*
	Stage 6	Language and identity socialization of children takes place in home and community. *[Maniq (Sakai), Lua (Lavua), UrakLawoc, Moklen, Mlabri, Saek, Mpi and Bisu]*
	Stage 5	Language socialization involves extensive literacy, usually including non-formal L1 schooling or teaching L1 as a subject "Local Studies" in school. *[Chong, Mon, So (Kusuman), Thailand Khmer]*
Strong side	Stage 4	L1 used in children's formal education in conjunction with national or official language. *[Patani Malay, Thailand Khmer, Lavua, and Mon]*
	Stage 3	L1 used in workplaces of larger society, beyond normal L1 boundaries.
	Stage 2	Lower governmental services and local mass media are open to L1.
	Stage 1	L1 used at upper governmental level.

Figure 1. Scale of degree of language endangerment (adapted from Fishman 1991)

3. What is being done to slow down the death of languages?

First, academics and language speakers are being encouraged to document as much as possible the language, culture and oral traditions of languages at risk before they are lost forever. Second, the language speakers/ethnolinguistic communities are being encouraged to conduct language revitalization programs with academic support from academics (linguists, anthropologists, education experts and so on) and with initial financial support from the Thailand Research Fund (TRF) and other funding agencies. Last, the Thai government is restructuring the national language policy to facilitate and support the use of ethnic minority languages along with the national language (Thai) and international languages.

Language Revival Efforts from Grassroots Communities

Language endangerment and language decline or language loss is often most clearly felt by elderly language speakers. They also often feel the need for language revitalization as shown in the excerpt below.

Figure 2: Linguists documenting language and oral traditions

A Mon lady uses a vivid metaphor to describe the Mon language endangerment situation comparing it to a fruit which *"is breaking off from the stem"* and the language revitalization activity as *"the last breath" of the speakers"*.

4. Mahidol Model for Language Revitalization and Maintenance of Endangered Languages and Cultures

Language revitalization is an attempt to provide a new domain of language use in order to increase the use of the language and the number of users. According to Crystal's (2000) six postulates to guide attempts of revitalization, an endangered language will positively progress if its speakers 1) increase their prestige within the dominant community; 2) increase their wealth relative to the dominant community; 3) increase their legitimate power in the eyes of the dominant community; 4) have a strong presence in the educational system; 5) can write their language; and 6) can make use of electronic technology. Since many ethnic minority languages (large and small in Thailand) have been classified as being potentially endangered at various stages, a group of linguists at Mahidol University have pioneered a cooperative program to preserve these languages. Endangered language speakers and communities work alongside the academics, participating in language documentation and description as well as in the language revitalization and maintenance program. The focus is to put community members at the heart of revitalization efforts through involvement in almost all steps of the revitalization process, including orthography development, creation of local vernacular literature, collection of local knowledge,

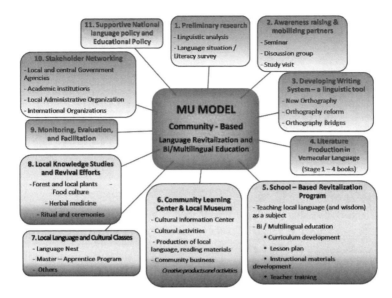

Figure 3: Mahidol Language Revitalization Model

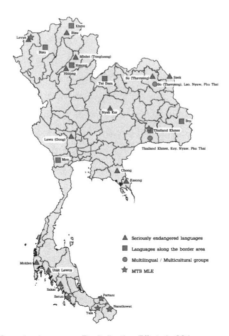

Figure 4: On-going Language Revitalization Efforts in 23 language groups

and instruction of the language to the next generation of speakers. The Mahidol Revitalization Model has been implemented with the cooperation of 23 language groups and the academic and psychological support of the Mahidol research team. The community - based language revitalization and maintenance model that has emerged from these efforts incorporates the basic principles of reversing language shift (Fishman 1991), yet is sensitive to the distinct needs of each individual community.

The Mahidol Model (figure 3) consists of 11 component activities which are adapted to utilize the best fit to the unique contextual needs of individual communities. 1) The first step in the model is preliminary research, which consists of assessing the morbidity of a language in an area, surveying the literacy of the people, and performing a linguistic analysis. 2) Once the linguistic situation is understood, awareness raising activities such as seminars, discussion groups, and study visits are arranged to mobilize partners. 3) After partnerships have been established, a writing system is developed for the language. 4) With a writing system that has been deemed acceptable by the community, literature production commences; local authors create stories for big books, small books of different stages, and dictionaries that the language speakers compile themselves. 5) The next step is to introduce the language into the formal school system. For small, seriously endangered languages such as Chong, Nyahkur and So (Thavung), the language is taught as a subject in local schools. This involves developing a curriculum and instructional materials, lesson planning, and teacher training. For the bigger language groups (especially the languages at the border areas around the country) or languages that the children still actively speak such as Patani Malay, Thailand Khmer and Lavua, a mother tongue-based bilingual education is conducted in order to address the language identity crisis or cultural conflict and to raise students' levels of achievement in school. This form of language revitalization commences when the child first starts school. 6) One way to strengthen the presence of the language is through the establishment of a community learning center and local museum for the community at large. It serves as an information center for the public where cultural information can be provided, cultural activities and language classes can take place, production of new literature can occur, and community business can be conducted. 7) Language Nests may be set up for small children prior to kindergarten, as has been done among the Bisu and the Kasong (both severely endangered). 8) Of fundamental importance is using the language to document local knowledge of forest plants for use in herbal medicine, rituals and ceremonies, and for food culture. 9) All of these activities undergo continuous monitoring and evaluation, with facilitation as necessary. 10) Networking within the community, at the national level and international level to promote the revitalization efforts and the maintenance of the local language is essentials. 11) The eventual goal is to influence national language and educational policies so as to guarantee that ethnic minority languages are protected and promoted alongside the national and international languages. This aims to ensure full government support for children's rights "to an education in their own culture and provided in their own language" (United Nations Declaration on the Rights of Indigenous Peoples, Article 14 Section 3).

5. Endangered Language Speakers Networking

Networking is an essential component of the Mahidol Model. This involves creating connections, between speakers of the same language and other endangered languages, as well as stakeholders from government and non-governmental agencies at the local and national level, as well as international organization and overseas institutions. Networking plays an important role in language revitalization from the beginning of a project.

Language revitalization often begins as cooperation between academic institutions and community members. However, other forms of support are needed to create a sustainable project. These include academic support, financial support, psychological support, and institutional support, on both the policy making and administrative levels. Figure 5 displays two related networks, the language revitalization stakeholder web and the local community participation web.

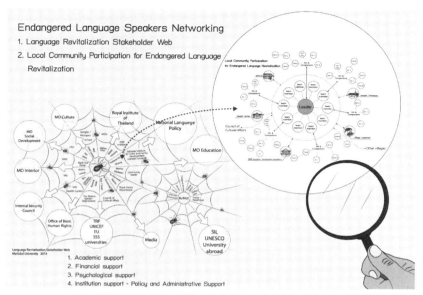

Figure 5: Endangered Language Speakers Networking

Language Revitalization Stakeholder Web

Along the steps of the MU Model Revitalization, various networking is needed. The networking for each of the revitalization program of various language groups has gradually been formed, as follows,

1) *Academic support:*. The first connection is the Mahidol University Resource Center for Language Documentation, Revitalization and Maintenance of Endangered Languages and Cultures and their networks such as the Royal Society of Thailand, local universities, SIL International, the Forestry Department, etc. Individual specialists can include linguists, educators, anthropologists, ethno-botanists, health personnel, nutritionists, experts in herbal medicine, etc.

2) *Financial support:* Funding is important for organizing language revitalization meetings and activities. The Thailand Research Fund (TRF) understands the language revitalization ideology and has supported several

ethnolinguistic communities to work on their own language revitalization programs as community-based research projects conducted by the language speakers themselves as the owners of the project. With the help of Mahidol research facilitators who visit them on a regular basis, the community members organize activities, write progress reports, and submit financial reports.. Other funding agencies which have supported language revitalization in Thailand include UNICEF, the Delegation of the European Union to Thailand, the Foundation for Revitalization of Local Languages and Wisdom and Mahidol University.

3) *Psychological support:* Language revitalization is an idealistic act of the active members of an endangered ethnolinguistic community who have the dream of keeping their language and culture alive by transmitting them to their younger generation. It is a cause for which they must be willing to sacrifice time and, for daily wage earners, money to write stories, compile a dictionary or teach the ethnic language at school. When financial compensation is available, it is never of an amount higher than what they would be earning through other activities. Encouragement, admiration and support from people inside and outside their community are essential to sustaining the program. Some have achieved the goal of having their language and culture registered as a "Cultural Treasure of the Nation" by the Ministry of Culture, giving them a sense of pride.

4) *Institutional support:* Support on both the policy making and local administrative levels are very important. This would include such things as a government school agreeing to teach the ethnic language as a subject, the faculty of education of a local university agreeing to cooperate in teacher training, or the Ministry of Education designating funds for the expansion of bi/multilingual programs.

Local Community Participation in Endangered Language Revitalization

Language speaker networking within their communities is an essential part of language revitalization because the language speakers are the implementers. Networking plays an important role from the very first step of revitalization. Normally the elderly speakers initiate the idea of language preservation. They feel the loss and the need for local language and cultural wisdom preservation and talk about it to friends who understand their situation. The Mahidol Resource Center for Language Documentation, Revitalization and Maintenance of Endangered Languages and Cultures is one place where they can get help. Several language groups have already had some connections with Mahidol linguists from their past linguistic fieldwork. Some have learnt about Mahidol research work on language revitalization programs by other means. Once they join a Mahidol Revitalization project, the community members are required to form a team of about 10 people headed by a leader who is well known or well respected in the community.

To work with Mahidol research team under the MU model, the community team members are designated community researchers, as their language revitalization project will be supported by Thailand Research Fund. The community research team is the hub of all activities in diagram 3 (above). The research project leader may not always be a formal leader such as the village headman but is usually an informal or "natural" leader who is an elderly or middle-aged person and who has been actively involved in the community. He or she may have a team co-leader. The project activities normally follow the Mahidol Model steps of language revitalization especially the first few steps such as the language situation survey and orthography development followed by literature production or reading materials development, before going on to school-based language revitalization or community learning center establishment or local knowledge studies and revival efforts (such as botany, herbal medicine, handicraft, food culture and food security).

Once the language revitalization project has officially started, workshops for various topics/activities are organized and the networking is expanded. Each activity requires the assistance of community members who are knowledgeable in certain areas. It is obvious from our experience that recruiting more members to the join the team is normally based on pre-existing kinship and friendship networks. As time passes, younger community members are often brought into the network, and they in turn involve more friends and relatives. Often those who work in the local institutions such as a health center, local school or district cultural council will also join in some relevant activities. Mahidol facilitators provide academic support or serve as resource persons for the community team when needed.

> ***Orthography development*** requires cooperation between 1) people who are literate in Thai (the national language) and who have a good knowledge of their local language 2) elderly people who have a very good knowledge of their language though may not know how to read and write 3) the younger generation who are literate in Thai but may not be able to speak the local language well. a linguist who knows the structure of the target language.
>
> ***Literature production (reading materials in local language)*** is usually done through a writer's workshop. Ideal workshops will involve 1) community scholars who are local artists or who know about the group's history, rituals, folklore, poetry, handicrafts, or other forms of local culture 2) story tellers 3) aspiring authors 4) young people who can read, write and, sometimes, draw.
>
> ***Teaching a local language in school*** requires 1) interested teachers and school directors who can help with developing the curriculum, teaching techniques, and instructional materials. 2) peoples of various specialties in the community who can give ideas about cultural values and other appropriate topics for the children to study, and are able to participate in developing various kinds of instructional materials that based on local culture and knowledge 3) persons who are accepted by the community as being qualified to teach language and culture classes (even if they lack formal teaching credentials).

The core community research team keeps contact with the Mahidol Revitalization Center through Mahidol research facilitators who visit the community once every two months. The community researchers also participate in seminars and workshops with other language groups at least once a year, in addition to coming to celebrate UNESCO's International Mother Language Day on 21 February of every year.

6. Case Studies

The following sections will present case studies of specific language revitalization activities among various ethnic groups.

Orthography development

The development of a writing system helps to ensure the survival of a language. In our experience, the local speakers normally prefer to use practical Thai-based writing systems because they were forced to learn Thai in school and thus know the letters and their use. By learning their mother tongue using a Thai based script, minority children find it relatively easy to transition to reading and writing Thai—something which also pleases officials concerned with national security and unity.

Native speakers and linguists work together to develop a writing system that is accepted and standardized. For those with a traditional writing system, an orthography bridge may be needed. For example. among the Mon (Mae Klong) people, a practical Thai-based orthography was developed as a tool for helping people study the Mon traditional writing system (which is considerably more complex, reflecting an ancient form of the language).

Once people have practiced using and improving the writing system, they can write whatever they have in mind, including stories, songs, poetry, personal experiences, and folklore. The authors are proud of their work. A dictionary can be compiled and literature in local languages can be produced. The writing tools can also be used for recording oral literature and local knowledge about herbal medicine. For those ready to offer an ethnic language class in school, teaching and learning materials will be produced in the local language.

However, to some languages groups, the script or traditional writing system is an important part of their ethnic identity. The choice of script can thus be controversial. For example, Patani Malay can be written in any of three scripts: an Arabic based script (Jawi), a Romanized script (Rumi), and a Thai based script. All three have different advantages and disadvantages. but due to the identity issue all three have been included in a multilingual school curriculum that will be discussed later in this paper.

School-based language revitalization

The importance of the role of the school in revitalization efforts cannot be over-estimated. Spolsky (2009: 253) points out that "The school domain is critical in the development of the language policy of a speech community. Left to the internal participants — teachers and students — language management should be straightforward: teachers (able to speak also the language of their students) should start with this and move them towards proficiency in this and whatever other variety or varieties the school considers a necessary part of the plurilingualism of an educated citizen". School-based language revitalization is highly prestigious and often the dream of minority language speakers. Language groups that still have enthusiastic speakers often prefer to have their language taught in school as part of their language revitalization program. There are two types of programs currently underway in Thailand.

Mother Tongue (MT) as a Subject (Chong, NyahKur, Thailand Khmer, Mon (Ratchaburi) languages)

Mother Tongue-Based Multilingual Education (MTB MLE) (Patani Malay-Thai, Thailand Khmer-Thai, Mon-Thai, Lavua-Thai, Hmong-Thai)

Chong and Patani Malay have been selected as case studies to present two kinds of school-based language revitalization programs that involve the strong participation of the language community.

Mother Tongue (MT) as a Subject: Chong Language Revitalization Project (CLRP)

Chong is an indigenous language spoken in Chantaburi Province, Thailand. At present, there are about 2,000-4,000 speakers. Chong belongs to the Austroasiatic language family (Pearic branch) and is known for its four registers. There has been a rapid decrease in the number of speakers over the last 30 years. Few Chong people under 30 speak Chong; Thai has become their first language. Only the older people use Chong in certain situations.

The CLRP began with minor cooperation between Chong elders and Mahidol University linguists with whom they had formed good relationships following earlier linguistic field work in the Chong area, when Chong people were invited to help with Field Methods classes for graduate linguistics students. The Chong people were aware that their language was declining. They also realized that their language could be written down and could be taught to other people as well as to the younger generation. They then joined hands with their Mahidol University linguist friends for language revitalization.

The pilot project began with community motivation and commitment. They then received financial support from the Thailand Research Fund (TRF) to conduct community-based research to solve the problem of language shift and to work on a language revitalization program. Apart from that, they received academic support (as well as psychological support) from an academic institution (Mahidol University, with its network of linguists and education experts) and other people in the region.

Since most ethnic minorities, like the Chong, want to have their language taught to their children at school, language development is needed so that ethnic minority languages can be used in education as a tool for language revitalization. As part of the school-based-language revitalization project, a writing system for Chong was developed, and reading materials were produced. The Chong language is taught as a subject (in the "Local Studies" section of the curriculum) to students in primary schools in the area. The CLRP thus included orthography development, literature production, curriculum development, and teaching Chong as a subject in school. Other ethnolinguistic groups in similar situations, such as the NyahKur and the Northern Khmer, have used the Chong project as a model, adapting it for their own purposes.

Mother Tongue-Based Multilingual Education (MTB MLE): Patani Malay–Thai Bi/multilingual Education in Southern Thailand

The Patani Malay (PM) language is spoken by more than 1 million Muslim people living along the Thai-Malaysian border. Language identity is a volatile issue in this area, and is one of the main underlying causes of recent political unrest and violence. The PM language is not officially accepted or used in education. It is also declining in urban areas of Narathiwat, Pattani and Yala, where a Thai-PM mixed language or Creole is being developed, and in Satun, where language death is obvious. Another related problem is chronic under-achievement in schools. Children attend schools where Thai, the official/national language (but a language which is not their mother tongue), is the only medium of instruction and the content is not relevant to the children's local context. Because of this, Patani Malay speaking children score the lowest in the annual national examinations given by the Ministry of Education. These exams have found that 35% - 40% of Patani Malay grade 3 students are still illiterate.

To address the problems of these learners, Mahidol University started a Mother Tongue-Based Bi/multilingual Education Project in 3 schools in Patani Malay communities in Southern Thailand in 2008, on the basis of a 2007 language situation survey. The goals are to facilitate Patani Malay speaking children to speak, read and write well in both Patani Malay and Thai, to retain their Patani Malay identity at the local level and their Thai identity at the national level, and to be able to live with dignity in the wider Thai society in order to foster true and lasting national reconciliation. The project was designed to develop the cognitive skills of the learners as well as their ability to use Thai as a language of learning in the later years of their primary education. The project adheres to the following principles of curriculum design: 1) Academic development based on Ministry of Education standards coupled with the community's values and goals; 2) Language development in a step-by-step process, starting with their mother tongue (Patani Malay) and gradually bridging to the official language (Thai), developing the four skills of listening, speaking, reading, and writing in both languages; and 3) Socio-cultural development that helps the students preserve their local cultural identity as well as develop a national Thai identity.

The Patani Malay-Thai bilingual project is being piloted in 33 primary schools in the 4 southernmost provinces of Thailand. Kindergarten 1 and 2 classes are taught mostly in Patani Malay, while oral Thai language is introduced gradually. After the children have mastered basic literacy skills using the Thai based PM script, they begin learning Thai literacy. followed by English (see Figure 6). This approach will continue through to primary grade 6. The Southern Border Province Administrative Center expanded the project into 15 schools in academic year 2012, and additional expansion is expected in the future.

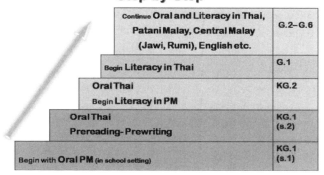

Figure 6: Language learning and literacy process

Reconsideration of National Language Policy

Despite an attempt to guarantee the freedom of expression and non-discrimination on the basis of fundamental human rights, and an implicit recognition of the intimate connection between language and forms of cultural expression, the current national language policy is radically out of step with the realities of multilingualism. A national language policy that promotes a multicultural society and supports the use of ethnic languages in public life, education, and local mass media is crucial in order to meet the demands and needs of the various marginalized minority groups in Thailand. Such a policy will open up opportunities to positively exploit the variety of accumulated wealth and wisdom embodied within such unique cultures and linguistic histories and will provide sustainable public benefits in terms of both economic and security gains.

Current draft of National Language Policy of Thailand

In 2006, a group of linguists began drafting the National Language Policy of Thailand. This was done in response to complex issues related to language use languages in Thai society in the face of globalization and ASEAN integration. The draft National Language Policy, which was signed by two prime ministers, addresses six core issues: 1) Thai for Thai students and Thai nationals 2) Regional languages (including ethnic languages) Ethnic 3) International languages (including languages of commerce and 4) Teaching Thai to migrants seeking employment in Thailand 5) Language needs of the visually and hearing Impaired and 6) Translation, interpretation, and localization Standards.

The draft recommendations relating to regional/ethnic languages are actually quite strong, asserting the right of ethnic communities to maintain their languages and cultures as national treasures, and to have their languages taught as subjects in school In addition, provision is made for the type of bi/multilingual education program currently being used in Thailand's Deep South. Full implementation of the policy will thus be beneficial to the endangered languages of Thailand.

7. Conclusion

Networking is a very important component of language revitalization and maintenance. It gets the revitalization process going and helps sustain it. It provides the type of support that the language speakers need to advance their language preservation goals. This support comes from kin and companion networking within the community and also from various stakeholders and institutions at the provincial, national, and international levels. The very fact that community members discuss these issues in their mother tongues helps expand the use of the language, something which becomes even more important as the speakers write stories and poems, and document their local wisdom by themselves. The experience of the Mahidol researchers and community researchers who work together on various revitalization projects show the inherent value in preserving and promoting minority languages and cultures as a source of diversity, knowledge, pride and inspiration that can serve national as well as local goals. This encourages more active involvement in all spheres of a society by minority citizens and boosts their contribution to national development.

Language revitalization programs as those mentioned here represent a bottom-up reaction by ethnic minority people struggling for the survival and preservation of their language, culture, and identity. These grassroots efforts are in turn supported by top-down actions, as outside academics work with local speakers to document their language, while also working with the government to develop national policies that are supportive to ethnic languages. In Thailand, the experience Mahidol staff have gained from working with ethnic communities has helped shape the Royal Society of Thailand's National Language Policy, which supports the use of ethnic minority languages in public, in school, and in the local media or mass media alongside the national language and international languages. All of this has been made possible by networking on multiple levels.

Note

1   For full details, see Premsrirat (2006a, 2007a, 2007b) and Premsrirat, Choosri, & Suwankasses (2001).

References

Crystal, D. (2000) *Language Death*. Cambridge, Cambridge University Press.
Fishman, J. (1991) *Reversing language shift*. Clevedon, England: Multilingual Matters.
Krauss, M. (1992) The world's languages in crisis. *Language* 68 (1), 4-10.
Suwilai Premsrirat. (Forthcoming) "Mahidol Model for the Preservation of Language Diversity: Thailand Experience". In Suwilai Premsrirat and David Hirsh (Eds.). *Indigenous Language Revitalization: Insights from Thailand*. Peter Lang. International Academic Publisher.
Suwilai Premsrirat (2014) "Redefining "Thainess": Embracing Diversity, Preserving Unity". In Pranee Liamputtong (Ed.), Contemporary Socio-Cultural and Political Perspectives in Thailand. London: Springer.
Suwilai Premsrirat (2010) The role of MTB MLE in ECD and education: Experiences and challenges in Southern Thailand. Paper presented at *MDGs Conference*, November 2010. Accessed from 20 May 2016.http://www.seameo org/LanguageMDGConference2010/presentations.html), UNESCO.
Suwilai Premsrirat (2008) Language for national reconciliation: Southern Thailand. *EENET* (Enabling Education Network).Issue 12 August 2008. Accessed from 20 May 2016. www.eenet.org.uk.
Suwilai Premsrirat (2007) Endangered languages of Thailand. *International Journal of Sociology of Language*, 186, 75-93.
Suwilai Premsrirat (2006) Thailand: Language situation. *Encyclopedia of Language and Linguistics 2nd Edition*, edited by Keith Brown. Oxford: Elsevier.
Suwilai Premsrirat (2001) The future of NyahKur. In R.S. Bauer (ed.), Collected papers on *Southeast Asian and Pacific Linguistics* (pp. 155-165). Canberra: The Australian National

University.

Suwilai Premsrirat (1998) Language maintenance and language shift in minority languages of Thailand. In *Studies in Endangered Languages*. Papers from the International Symposium on Endangered Languages, Tokyo, November 18-20 1995, edited by Kazuto Matsumura, Tokyo, Japan.

Suwilai Premsrirat & Malone, D. (2006) Language development and language revitalization in Asia. *Mon – Khmer Studies* 35,101-120.

Suwilai Premsrirat and Uniansasmitah Samoh (2012) "Planning and Implementing Patani Malay in Bilingual Education in Southern Thailand". JSEALS. Paul Sidwell (Ed.).

第 13 章　要約

消滅危機言語話者のネットワーク
言語復興と維持に関するタイの「マヒドン・モデル」について

スウィライ・プレムスリラット（マヒドン大学）　　　　　（松井真之介訳）

　タイにおいては、国内の70言語のうち少なくとも15言語が深刻な消滅危機言語に分類されている（Suwilai 2007）。特にタイ最南部において国境地域の大きな言語グループが、言語アイデンティティ問題や文化的衝突、政治不安に直面している一方で、それ以外の言語も安定しておらず、縮小傾向を見せている。本発表では言語復興とその維持について調査研究するために、一般的に「マヒドン・モデル」として知られるコミュニティベースの言語復興モデルについて議論する。これは23の民族言語コミュニティとマヒドン大学の言語学者たち、それから教育や植物学、公衆衛生のような、関連する分野のパートナーたちの間で行われた10年にわたる共同作業の結実である。発表では特に、消滅危機言語の話者自身および個人から政府機関、国際組織にわたるステークホルダー間のネットワーク化について焦点を当てている。

　現在、タイにおける少なくとも15の民族言語が深刻な消滅危機にさらされていると考えられている。これらは大きな言語グループに囲まれた飛び地分布する弱小言語であったり、国内の色々な場所に散在する言語であったりする。この15言語のうち9言語すなわち、Chong語、Kasong語、Samre語、Chung語、So語（Thavung語）、Nyah Kur語、Lavua語、Maniq語、Mlabri語はオーストロアジア語族に属しており、東南アジア本土に土着の言語である。またGong語、Mpi語、Bise語の3言語はシナ・チベット語族に属している。Urak Lawoi語とMoken語もしくはMoklen語の2言語はオーストロネシア語族に属し、残るTai語（Saek語）は上記の分類の外にある。これらのうち、Kasong語とSamre語、Chung語はわずかに残る最後の高齢話者の死後、生き延びることは現実的に望めない状態であり、可能な限り多く記録

されている最中である。その一方で、タイ北部のクメール語、モン語、パタニ・マレー語を含む、より多くの話者を持つ言語も衰退中であり、カムアン語（北タイ語）、パクタイ語（南タイ語）あるいはラオ・イサーン語（北東タイ語）のようなタイ語の地域変種でさえ安心できず、特に語彙や文法の面で縮小傾向をみせている。安定しているのは標準タイ語のみである（cf. Suwilai Premsrirat 2007）。

　国境地域の大きな言語グループは若者世代における言語衰退の問題に直面しているだけでなく、そのほとんどが教育や保健、あるいは司法のような政府の公共サービスへのアクセスもできないという問題も抱えている。一般的に、エスニック・マイノリティは遅れていて成績が悪く、現代の発展プロセスにおいては成功が難しそうであると外部者からは思われている。人口の大部分がムスリムのタイ・マレー語話者というタイ最南部のようないくつかの地域では、数々の政府公共サービスへの抵抗がみられる。言語アイデンティティ問題と文化的衝突は、暴力や政治不安の一因となる隠れたファクターの一つである。

　言語の死を遅くするために何がなされているのであろうか？　第一に、学者や言語の話者たちは、消滅危機にさらされた言語や文化、口承伝統が永遠に失われる前にそれらをできるだけ多く記録するよう促されている。第二に、その言語の話者や民族言語コミュニティは、学者たち（言語学者、人類学者、教育の専門家など）による学術的支援や、タイ研究財団（TRF）やその他の財務機関による最初の経済的支援をもとに、言語復興プログラムを実行することを求められている。最後に、タイ政府は国家言語（タイ語）および国際言語に加えて、エスニック・マイノリティの言語使用を促進し支援する国家言語政策を再編成中である。

　タイの消滅危機言語は、フィッシュマンの段階別世代間崩壊尺度（1991）の8つの段階を使ってそのステイタスを確認している。そこでは、（公用語の）タイ語を除いて、大小問わずタイのあらゆる言語が、虚弱で言語交替される側にあると分類されていることがわかる。多くのエスニック・マイノリティの言語が様々な段階で消滅危機言語であると分類されてきたため、マヒドン

大学の言語学者たちはこれらの言語保存のために率先して協同プログラムを実行した。このマヒドン復興モデルは23の言語グループと、マヒドン大学の研究チームによる学術的および心理的サポートによって実行された。それはコミュニティベースの言語再生および維持モデルである。

「消滅危機言語・文化の復興および維持のためのマヒドン・モデル」とはどのようなものなのだろうか？　マヒドン大学のファシリテーターたちは、正書法発展のために以下のような人々を人的リソースとして学術的サポートを提供している：①タイ語（国語）に精通している人々、②読み書きは知らないと思われるが、自言語の知識が豊富な高齢者、③タイ語に精通しているが、ローカル言語はよく話せないと思われる若者。(ローカル言語の文献を読む)文学的な成果は通常、作家のワークショップを通じてなされる。理想的なワークショップは以下のような人々が参加するであろう：①その地域のアーティストであったり、そこのグループの歴史や儀礼、民間伝承、詩、工芸、あるいはその他の文化に精通するコミュニティの学識者、②語り部、③意欲のある著述家、④読み書きでき、時には描画もできる若者。そして学校におけるローカル言語の教授には以下のことが求められる：①カリキュラムを発展させ、テクニックや教材を教えるサポートができる、関心の高い教師や校長、②子どもたちに対して学ぶべき文化的価値や他の適切な話題についてアイデアを出すことができ、また地域の文化や知識に基づいた様々な教材の開発に参加できる、様々な専門をもつコミュニティの人々、③（たとえその人が公的な教員資格を持たなくても）言葉や文化のクラスを教えるに値すると認められてコミュニティに受け入れられている人。

　言語復興は、言語使用および使用者数を増加させるために言語使用に関する新しい領域を提供する一つの試みである。クリスタルの、言語復興に関する試みを指導する6つの基本条件（2000）によると、もし消滅危機言語の話者が、①支配コミュニティの中で自尊心を高める場合、②支配コミュニティと関連する自らの資源を増やす場合、③支配コミュニティの視点から正当な力を伸ばす場合、④教育システムにおいて強いプレゼンスを持つ場合、⑤自言語を記述できる場合、それから⑥エレクトコニクス技術を駆使できる場合、

消滅危機言語はいい方向に進むだろうという。(タイにおける大小の) エスニック・マイノリティ言語の多くが潜在的に様々な段階の消滅危機言語として分類されているため、マヒドン大学の言語学者グループはこれらの言語を保存するための共同プログラムを先導して実行してきた。消滅危機言語の話者とコミュニティは、言語復興および維持プログラムへの参加と同様に言語資料の収集と記述にも参加しながら、学者たちと共同で活動している。重要なのは、正書法の発展、ローカルな土着文学の創生、ローカルな知識の収集、次世代の話者への言語教育を行いつつ、コミュニティメンバーがこの復興プロセスにほぼ全段階で参加することを通じて、再生計画の中心にコミュニティメンバーを据えることである。

　マヒドン大学の復興モデルのステップには、多様なネットワーク化が必要である。このネットワーク化はマヒドン大学モデルの重要な構成要素である。これは、同じ言語の話者たちと地域レベル国家レベルの政府機関、非政府機関のステークホルダーとの間の関係創出、そして国際組織や海外の研究所との関係創出と同じように、別の消滅危機言語の話者たちとの間にも関係を創出することを必然的に意味する。

　様々な言語グループの再生プログラムそれぞれにとってのネットワーク化が徐々に形成されてきた。それは以下のとおりである。①学術的サポート：最初の連携は、消滅危機言語および文化の記録・再生・維持のためのマヒドン大学リソースセンターと、タイ王立研究所、地方大学、国際SIL (SILインターナショナル)、森林管理局など。専門家個人としては言語学者、教育者、人類学者、民族植物学者、医療関係者、栄養学者、生薬専門家などが含まれる。②経済的サポート：言語復興の会議や活動を組織するためには、基金が重要である。タイ研究財団 (TRF) はこの言語復興の考えを理解し、その言語話者自身がプロジェクトの主体として動いている言語復興プログラムをコミュニティベースの研究プロジェクトとして実行できるように、いくつかの民族言語コミュニティを支援している。タイにおける言語復興を支援する他の基金としては、UNICEFや駐タイ欧州連合代表部、ペスタロッチ財団、応用言語学財団、駐タイ・スイス大使館、マヒドン大学が挙げられる。③心

理的サポート：消滅の危機にある自分たちの言語や文化を若い世代に伝えることでそれらを生きたものとして続かせたい、と願う危機言語コミュニティの活動的なメンバーにとって、言語復興は理想の行為である。このような動機があるから、彼らは物語を書き、辞書を編集し、民族言語を学校で教えるために時間や、日給労働者にとっては金銭を犠牲にすることを厭わない。自尊心をもって、母語や自文化を文化省の「国定文化遺産」として登録するという目標を達成したメンバーもいる。④制度的サポート：政策の策定支援および地域行政レベルの支援ともに非常に重要である。これは、公立学校が教科として民族言語教授に賛成するとか、地方大学の教育学部が教員養成の協力に賛意を示すとか、あるいは教育省が二言語／多言語プログラムの拡大資金を認定するとか、があげられるだろう。

　ここで挙げた言語復興プログラムは、言語や文化、アイデンティティの生存や保存のために奮闘するエスニック・マイノリティの人々によるボトムアップ的反応の結果である。これらの草の根的な努力は、民族言語に協力的な国家政策を推進する政府とも連携しつつ、外部の学者が地域の話者と共同しその言語を記録するような感じで、今度はトップダウン的な活動によって支援されるのである。

| 編著訳者紹介 | List of contributors |

編者／Editors

桂木 隆夫［かつらぎ たかお］

学習院大学法学部政治学科教授。東京大学法学政治学研究科博士課程修了、法学博士。研究テーマは、公共哲学、民主主義と市場研究、言語政策と言語権。主要著作：『公共哲学とはなんだろう』（勁草書房、2005年）、『ことばと共生』（共編著、三元社、2003年）。

Takao Katsuragi is Professor of the School of Political Science in the Faculty of Law, Gakushuin University, Tokyo. He holds a PhD from the Graduate School of Law and Political Science at Tokyo University. His work focuses on public philosophy, theories of democracy and the market, language policy and language rights on which he has written several books including *Kotoba to Kyōsei* (Language and Conviviality, Sangensha: 2003) and *Kōkyōtetsugaku towa nandarō* (What Actually is Public Philosophy? Keiso: 2005).

ジョン・C・マーハ［John C. Maher］

国際基督教大学、メディア・コミュニケーション・文化（専修分野）教授。リングアパックス・アジアプログラムディレクター。ロンドン大学、ミシガン大学、エジンバラ大学で哲学および言語学の学位取得。研究テーマは、多言語主義、言語の死と再生、地名学、記号論。主要著作：*Chomsky for Beginners* (Icon, 1996), *Multilingualism* (Oxford University Press, 2017).

John C. Maher is Professor of Linguistics in the Department of Media, Communication and Culture at International Christian University, Tokyo, and Programme Director of Linguapax Asia. He received degrees in philosophy and linguistics from the universities of London, Michigan and Edinburgh. His research interests include multilingualism, language death and revival, language and medical communication, toponymy, and semiotics. His books include *Chomsky for Beginners* (Icon, 1996) and *Multilingualism* (Oxford University Press, 2017).

* * *

数土 直紀［すど なおき］

学習院大学法学部政治学科教授。東京大学にて博士（社会学）取得。現在の研究テーマは、社会変動が階層意識、社会的不平等、社会関係資本に与える影響の解明。主要著作：『信頼にいたらない世界』（勁草書房、2013年）、『日本人の階層意識』（講談社、2010年）。

Naoki Sudo is Professor of Sociology in the Department of Political Studies, Gakushuin University. He holds a PhD from The University of Tokyo. His work focuses on the effects of social changes on social class identity, social inequality, and social capital. He has written several books on these issues, including *Shinrai ni Itaranai Sekai* (The Untrustworthy World, Keiso: 2013) and *Nihonjin no Kaisoishiki* (Social Class Identity of the Japanese, Kodan-sha: 2010).

藤田ラウンド 幸世［ふじたらうんど さちよ］

立教大学、独立大学院異文化コミュニケーション研究科特任准教授。研究テーマは、社会言語学と応用言語学の学問領域から日本社会のマルティリンガリズム、バイリンガル教育。主要著

作：Fujita-Round, S. & Maher, J. C. (2017 in press) 'Language Policy and Political Issues in Education', in T. McCarty & S. May (eds.) *Encyclopedia of Language and Education* (3rd edition), Volume 1, NY: Springer、藤田ラウンド幸世（2013）「国際結婚家族で母語を身につけるバイリンガル」、加賀美常美代編著『多文化共生論』明石書店がある。

Sachiyo Fujita-Round is a specially appointed Associate Professor in the Graduate School of Intercultural Communication at Rikkyo University. She received her PhD at International Christian University, Tokyo. Her research focuses on the micro and macro levels of bilingualism and multilingualism in sociolinguistics, as well as linguistic ethnography describing bilingual language identity and education. She is the co-author, with J. C. Maher of 'Language Policy and Political Issues in Education' in T. McCarty & S. May (eds.) *Encyclopedia of Language and Education* (3rd edition), Volume 1, (Springer: 2017 in press). Her publications also include the paper, *Kokusaikekkon de bogo wo minitsukeru bairingal* (A Bilingual Acquiring the Mother Tongue/s in An Intermarriage Family, Akashishoten: 2013).

原 聖 [はら きよし]

女子美術大学芸術学部教授。一橋大学大学院社会学研究科博士後期課程単位修得退学。研究テーマは、西欧少数言語、とりわけケルト諸語圏の言語復興運動、ならびに書きことばの社会史的研究。西欧の民衆版画などの民衆文化史研究。東アジアとの比較研究。主要著作：『周縁的文化の変貌』（三元社、1990年）、『〈民族起源〉の精神史』（岩波書店、2003年）、『ケルトの水脈』（講談社、2006年）、編著『書記伝統のなかの標準規範に関する歴史的東西比較研究』（女子美術大学、2016年）。

HARA Kiyoshi is Professor of Cultural Anthropology in the Department of Arts, Joshibi University of Art and Design. His research interests include linguistic revitalization movements of minority languages in Western Europe, especially Celtic languages, and the social history of written languages; cultural history of popular images of Western Europe, and their comparative history with East Asian countries.

His publications include: Regional dialect and cultural development in Japan and Europe, *International Journal of the Sociology of Language*, 175/176(2005), pp. 193-211. Effects of globalization on minority languages in Europe – focusing on Celtic languages, in: Coulmas, Florian (ed.) *Language Regimes in Tranformation*. Berlin, Mouton de Gruyter, 2007, pp. 191-205. Languages of long literary tradition and standard language theory – focusing on Celtic languages, in: HARA Kiyoshi, HEINRICH Patrick (eds.), *Standard Norms in Written Languages – Historical and Comparative Studies between East and West*, Joshibi University of Art and Design, 2016, pp. 121-140.

オレンカ・ビラッシュ [Olenka Bilash]

アルバータ大学第二言語教育学教授。研究テーマは、継承言語、危機言語、第二言語教授法、教育および学習開発方法論。ウクライナの民主化の研究。主要業績：上記の分野に関する論説の他、1999年に言語教育に関するすぐれた論考に対するACTFL Stephen A. Freeman Awardを受賞。

Olenka Bilash is Professor of second language education at the University of Alberta. Her research interests include heritage languages, endangered languages, second language pedagogy, teacher education and learning resource development, and qualitative research methodology. She has written articles in all of these areas, including that which won ACTFL's Stephen A. Freeman Award for the best published article on language education in 1999. Her recent research grant focuses on the democratic reform of Ukraine.

アランナ・ワシルク [Alanna Wasylkiw]

トロントのGVEのオンライン・教育、教育工学専攻新入生の教育主任、またエドモントンのウクライナ・バイリンガル学校教師。2014年にアルバータ大学において教育工学をテーマとして教育

学（修士）を取得。主要業績：Web 2.0 上に複数の共著論文を発表。

Alanna Wasylkiw completed her Masters in Education (University of Alberta) in 2014 with a specialization in Educational Technology and currently works as an Academic Operations Manager at GVE Online Education, an EdTech startup in Toronto, Ontario. Prior to this position, Alanna worked as an elementary classroom teacher and technology learning facilitator at a Ukrainian bilingual school in Edmonton, Alberta. She has co-authored several publications on Web 2.0 tools.

イェリサバ・セスナ [Jelisava Sethna]

学習院大学外国語教育研究センター講師、東京外国語大学講師、リングアパックス・アジア所長。研究テーマは、多言語教育、言語教育方法論、terminology transfer。主要著作：*Miska* vs. *Mausu: Secondary Inter-lingual Term Formation in the Slovenian and Japanese Languages. Language, Culture and Communication*, Vol.7. p.127-141. Rikkyo University (2015) and *Linguapax Asia: A Retrospective Edition of Language and Human Rights Issues, Collected Proceedings of Linguapax Asia Symposia 2004 – 2009*. Tokyo: Linguapax Asia (as co-editor)(2010) Also available in electronic form at www.linguapax-asia.org。

Jelisava Sethna is a lecturer at the Foreign Language Teaching and Research Centre at Gakushuin University, and Tokyo University of Foreign Studies (TUFS). Her research interests include bilingual and multilingual education, language teaching methodology and terminology transfer. She is a founding member of Linguapax Asia and has been its Director since 2011.
Her publications include: *Miška* vs. Mausu: Secondary Inter-lingual Term Formation in the Slovenian and Japanese Languages. *Language, Culture and Communication*, Vol.7. p.127-141. Rikkyo University (2015) and *Linguapax Asia: A Retrospective Edition of Language and Human Rights Issues, Collected Proceedings of Linguapax Asia Symposia 2004 – 2009*. Tokyo: *Linguapax Asia* (co-editor)(2010) Also available in electronic form at www.linguapax-asia.org

比嘉 光龍 [ふぃじゃ ばいろん]

うちなーぐち（おきなわ語）講師。沖縄キリスト教学院大学、沖縄国際大学にて非常勤講師。沖縄大学地域研究所特別研究員。主要著作：『沖縄語リアルフレーズBook』（研究社）2015年に刊行。琉球新報と並び沖縄県を代表する沖縄タイムス「ワラビー（毎日曜刊）」紙一部の日本語をうちなーぐち訳し5年。現在も継続中。高1英語教科書 *Power On*（東京書籍、2017〜2021まで）の全10章中の第8章は［Mr. Fija and Uchinaaguchi］と筆者の活動掲載予定。

Byron Fija is an Okinawan language teacher at Okinawa Christian University and Okinawa International University, and special research associate at the Regional Research Institute, Okinawa University. He is the author of an Okinawan language textbook titled *Okinawan Real Phrase Book* published by Kenkyūsha in 2015. He has been translating articles from Japanese into Okinawan for five years for the Okinawa Times' Sunday special local language section *Warabii* on behalf of the newspaper and of Okinawa Prefecture. He will write on his various activities for the support of the Okinawan language for the new high school English textbook *Power On* from 2017 to 2021 under the title "Mr. Fija and Uchinaaguchi".

片山 和美 [かたやま かずみ]

現在、東京でソフトウェア開発を行う会社に勤務。2010年頃からアイヌ語の学習を始め、東京で開催されているアイヌ語講座や、インターネットを利用した勉強会等に参加する。2016年4月から親子のアイヌ語講座のアシスタントを勤め、ニュージーランドの先住民族マオリの言語学習法であるテ・アタランギ法や、歌やゲームを使った教育を行っている。

Kazumi Katayama is currently working for a company developing software in Tokyo. She started studying the Ainu language from around 2010 onward, participating in Ainu language courses held in Tokyo and in Internet-based Ainu study circles. Since April 2016, she has served as an assistant for parents-and-children Ainu language courses. In this course, Ainu is taught through songs and games, along the lines of language learning methods of the indigenous Maori of New Zealand..

パトリック・ハインリヒ［Patrick Heinrich］
ヴェネツィア大学アジア・北アフリカ学部の准教授。現在の研究テーマは、社会言語学、危機に瀕する言語と言語教育。言語に関する研究によりしっかりと社会学の理論と方法論を組み込もうとしている。地域の焦点は日本、特に琉球諸島。主要著作：*The Sociolinguistics of Urban Language Life* (Dick Smakmanと共編、Routledge 2017)、*Handbook of the Ryukyuan Languages*（宮良信詳、下地理則と共編、Mouton de Gruyter 2015)、等々。最新の著書は *The Making of Monolingual Japan*（Multilingual Matters 2012)。

Patrick Heinrich is Associate Professor in the Department of Asian and Mediterranean African Studies, Ca' Foscari University in Venice. His present research interests focus on sociolinguistics, language endangerment and language education. His research endeavors to incorporate sociological theory and methodology more firmly into the study of language. His regional focus is Japan, in particular the Ryukyu Islands. Edited books include *The Sociolinguistics of Urban Language Life* (with Dick Smakman, Routledge 2017), *Handbook of the Ryukyuan Languages* (with Shinsho Miyara and Michinori Shimoji, Mouton de Gruyter 2015). His latest monograph is *The Making of Monolingual Japan* (Multilingual Matters 2012).

マット・ギラン［Matt Gillan］
国際基督教大学シニア准教授。八重山地方の民族音楽と文化をテーマとして、ロンドン大学東洋アフリカ研究学院より音楽民族学の博士号を取得。研究テーマは、民族音楽と言語（沖縄の民族音楽の実践を通して）。主要著作：*Songs from the Edge of Japan - Music-making in Yaeyama and Okinawa* (Ashgate 2012), as well as articles in *Ethnomusicology, Asian Music* and other journals. He is also active as a performer and teacher of Okinawan traditional music.

Matt Gillan is Senior Associate Professor of music at International Christian University, Tokyo. He received his PhD in ethnomusicology from SOAS, University of London, with a thesis exploring the connections of music and cultural identity in Yaeyama in the south of Okinawa. His research continues to focus on the music of Okinawa, with a particular interest in the intersections of song, language, and embodied understandings of music. He is the author of *Songs from the Edge of Japan - Music-making in Yaeyama and Okinawa* (Ashgate 2012), as well as articles in *Ethnomusicology, Asian Music* and other journals. He is also active as a performer and teacher of Okinawan traditional music.

黄行［Huang Xing］
中国社会科学院・民族学人類学研究所の教授。専門は言語学、研究テーマは、中国の少数民族の研究である。主要著作：「現代中国における少数民族の言語政策についての分析」(『中国社会言語学』2014年第1期）と「中国における民族言語アイデンティティについて」(『語言戦略研究』2016年第1期）など。

Huang Xing is Professor at the Institute of Ethnology and Anthropology of CASS. He research focuses on the ethnic linguistics. His publications include The Understanding of Minority Language Policies of China (*The Journal of Chinese Sociolinguistics*, Volume 1, 2014) , and On the Ethnologue Identity of China (*Chinese Journal of Language Policy and Planning*, Volume 1, 2016).

包聯群 [Bao Lianqun]

国立大学法人・大分大学経済学部／経済学研究科の准教授。研究テーマは、言語学（社会言語学）、中国語学である。主要著作：『言語接触と言語変異——中国黒龍江省ドルブットモンゴル族コミュニティ言語を事例として』（現代図書、2011年）と「民族語言でのバイリンガル動詞——北方少数民族コミュニティ言語におけるモンゴル語／満洲語と中国語とのバイリンガル動詞を事例として」（『民族語言』2013年第4期、75-81頁、中国社会科学院）など。

Lianqun Bao is an Associate professor in the Faculty of Economics at Oita University. Her research focuses on sociolinguistics and minority languages. Her publications include *Language Contact and Language Change: A case study of the Dorbed Mongolian community in Heilongjiang Province, China* (Gendai Tosho:2011), Bilingual verbs in Languages spoken in Minority Communities of Northern China (*The Journal of Minority languages of China*, Volum 4, 2013. pp.75-81.)

スウィライ・プレムスリラット [Suwilai Premsrirat]

タイ、マヒドル大学教授、同大学「危機言語と文化の記録と復興のための情報センター」所長、「アジアの言語と文化研究所」所長。モナシュ大学より言語学の博士号を取得。研究テーマは、タイおよび周辺国の少数民族言語の研究。主要業績：2006年に National Research Council of Thailand Outstanding Researcher Award 受賞、2016年に UNESCO King Sejong Literacy Prize 受賞。*Thesaurus and Dictionaries of Khmu Dialects of Southeast Asia* (5vols, 2002), *Patani Malay in Thai Education* (2015).

Suwilai Premsrirat has a PhD in Linguistics from Monash University, Australia. She is the Founding Director of the Resource Center for Documentation, Revitalization and Maintenance of Endangered Languages and Cultures, Research Institute for Languages and Cultures of Asia (RILCA), Mahidol University, Thailand. She has researched ethnic minority languages in Thailand and its neighbors since 1975. Under her direction, Mahidol University staff have facilitated language revitalization in 25 minority languages. She is a recipient of the National Research Council of Thailand Outstanding Researcher Award (2006), the Comité International Permanent des Linguistes Award for Endangered Language Research (2008) and UNESCO King Sejong Literacy Prize 2016. Since 2006, she is a member of the Royal Society of Thailand's National Language Policy Committee. She is the author of five volume of *Thesaurus and Dictionaries of Khmu Dialects of Southeast Asia* (2002) and *the Patani Malay in Thai Education* (2015).

翻訳者／*Japanese Translation*

﨑山 拓郎 [さきやま たくろう]

宮崎公立大卒業。神戸大学大学院総合人間科学研究科修了。神戸大学大学院人文学研究科退学。専門は英文学、言語教育学。主要著作：「ウォルター・ペイターの道徳性について——テリー・イーグルトンとの比較を通じて」（『神戸英米論叢』2010）「リチャード・ローティとウォルター・ペイター」（『神戸英米論叢』2011）など。

Takuro Sakiyama completed the master's program in English literature at the graduate school of international studies, Kobe University. His works focus on English literature in 19th and 20th, critical theory, and language pedagogy. He has written several papers on these issues, including "A Study of Pater's Morality through Comparison of Walter Pater with Terry Eagleton." (2010), "Ricard Rorty and Walter Pater: Marius as Liberal Ironist" (2011).

松井 真之介 [まつい しんのすけ]

神戸大学大学院総合人間科学研究科・博士（学術）。専門はフランスを中心としたマイノリティ

研究、ディアスポラ学、アルメニア学。主要著作:「フランスの教育行政管理を回避する地域語学校の取り組み──バスク語、カタルーニャ語を中心に」『フランス教育学会紀要』第26号、2014年、藤野一夫編『公共文化施設の公共性』(共著、水曜社、2011年)。

Shinnosuke Matsui is Research Fellow at the Research Center for Promoting Intercultural Studies, Kobe University. He holds a PhD from Kobe University. His research focuses on minority studies mainly in France, diaspora studies and Armenology. He has written several papers and a book on these issues, including "The efforts by Regional Language Bilingual Schools which avoid the French educational administration: examples of Basque and Catalonia Language Schools" (2014) and *Civic virtue of public cultural facilities* (coauthor, ed. by Kazuo Fujino, Suiyosha: 2011).

学習院大学東洋文化研究叢書

言語復興の未来と価値
理論的考察と事例研究

Minority Language Revitalization : Contemporary Approaches

発行日
2016年12月28日　初版第1刷

編者
桂木隆夫＋ジョン・C・マーハ

発行所
株式会社 三元社
〒113-0033　東京都文京区本郷1-28-36 鳳明ビル
電話 03-5803-4155　ファックス 03-5803-4156

装丁
臼井新太郎

印刷・製本
モリモト印刷株式会社

Minority Language Revitalization : Contemporary Approaches
2016 © Takao Katsuragi, John C. Maher
ISBN978-4-88303-415-4
http://www.sangensha.co.jp